Application of Big Data for National Security

T0383304

Application of Big Data for National Security

A Practitioner's Guide to Emerging Technologies

Edited by

Babak Akhgar

Gregory B. Saathoff

Hamid R. Arabnia

Richard Hill

Andrew Staniforth

Petra Saskia Bayerl

AMSTERDAM • BOSTON • HEIDELBERG • LONDON
NEW YORK • OXFORD • PARIS • SAN DIEGO
SAN FRANCISCO • SINGAPORE • SYDNEY • TOKYO

Butterworth-Heinemann is an imprint of Elsevier

Acquiring Editor: Sara Scott
Editorial Project Manager: Marisa LaFleur
Project Manager: Punithavathy Govindaradjane
Designer: Greg Harris

Butterworth-Heinemann is an imprint of Elsevier
The Boulevard, Langford Lane, Kidlington, Oxford OX5 1GB, UK
225 Wyman Street, Waltham, MA 02451, USA

ISBN: 978-0-12-801967-2

British Library Cataloguing-in-Publication Data
A catalogue record for this book is available from the British Library

Library of Congress Cataloging-in-Publication Data
A catalog record for this book is available from the Library of Congress

For information on all Butterworth-Heinemann publications
visit our website at http://store.elsevier.com/

Contents

SECTION 1 INTRODUCTION TO BIG DATA

SECTION 3 METHODS AND TECHNOLOGICAL SOLUTIONS

List of Contributors

Vida Abedi
Virginia Polytechnic Institute and State University, USA

Babak Akhgar
CENTRIC, Sheffield Hallam University, UK

Petra Saskia Bayerl
CESAM/RSM, Erasmus University Rotterdam, Netherlands

Ben Brewster
CENTRIC, Sheffield Hallam University, Sheffield, UK

John N.A. Brown
Universidade Lusófona de Humanidades e Tecnologia, Portugal

Jean Brunet
Capgemini, France

John N. Carbone
Raytheon Intelligence, Information and Services, USA

Nicolas Claudon
Capgemini, France

Pietro Costanzo
FORMIT Foundation, Italy

James A. Crowder
Raytheon Intelligence, Information and Services, USA

Francesca D'Onofrio
FORMIT Foundation, Italy

Julia Friedl
FORMIT Foundation, Italy

Sara Galehbakhtiari
CENTRIC, Sheffield Hallam University, UK

Kimberly Glasgow
John Hopkins University, USA

Richard Hill
University of Derby, UK

Rupert Hollin
SAS, EMEA/AP, USA

Gabriele Jacobs
CESAM/RSM, Erasmus University Rotterdam, Netherlands

Benn Kemp
Office of the Police & Crime Commissioner for West Yorkshire, UK

Lu Liu
University of Derby, UK

Laurence Marzell
SERCO, UK

Bethany Nowviskie
University of Virginia, USA

John Panneerselvam
University of Derby, UK

Kellyn Rein
Fraunhofer FKIE, Germany

Gregory B. Saathoff
University of Virginia, USA

Fraser Sampson
West Yorkshire PCC, UK

Richard J. Self
University of Derby, UK

Andrew Staniforth
Office of the Police & Crime Commissioner for West Yorkshire, UK

Marcello Trovati
University of Derby, UK

Dave Voorhis
University of Derby, UK

Mohammed Yeasin
Memphis University, USA

Ramin Zand
Memphis University, USA

About the Editors

Babak Akhgar is professor of informatics and director of the Centre of Excellence in Terrorism, Resilience, Intelligence and Organised Crime Research (CENTRIC) at Sheffield Hallam University, UK, and fellow of the British Computer Society. He has more than 100 refereed publications in international journals and conferences on information systems with a specific focus on knowledge management (KM). He is a member of editorial boards for several international journals and has acted as chair and program committee member for numerous international conferences. He has extensive and hands-on experience in the development, management, and execution of KM projects and large international security initiatives (e.g., the application of social media in crisis management, intelligence-based combating of terrorism and organized crime, gun crime, cybercrime and cyberterrorism, and cross-cultural ideology polarization). In addition to this, he is the technical lead of two EU Security projects: "Courage" on cybercrime and cyberterrorism and "Athena" on the application of social media and mobile devices in crisis management. He has coedited several books on intelligence management. His recent books are titled *Strategic Intelligence Management*, *Knowledge Driven Frameworks for Combating Terrorism and Organised Crime*, and *Emerging Trends in ICT Security*. Professor Akhgar is a member of the academic advisory board of SAS, UK.

Gregory Saathoff is a forensic psychiatrist who serves as a professor within the University of Virginia's School of Medicine and is executive director of the University of Virginia's Critical Incident Analysis Group (CIAG). CIAG serves as a "ThinkNet" that provides multidisciplinary expertise in developing strategies that can prevent or mitigate the effects of critical incidents, focusing on building relationships among leadership in government, academia, and the private sector for the enhancement of national security. He currently serves in the elected role of chairman of the General Faculty Council within the University of Virginia. Formerly a Major in the US Army, Dr Saathoff was appointed in 1996 to a U.S. Department of Justice commission charged with developing a methodology to enable the FBI to better access nongovernmental expertise during times of crisis, and has served as the FBI's conflict resolution specialist since that time. From 2009–2011, he chaired the Expert Behavioral Analysis Panel on the Amerithrax Case, the largest investigation in FBI history. A consultant to the U.S. Department of Justice, Department of Defense, and Department of Homeland Security, he brings behavioral science subject matter expertise and leverages CIAG's network of relationships to strengthen CENTRIC's US-European connections among government and law enforcement entities. In addition to his faculty role at the University of Virginia, Dr Saathoff also holds the position of visiting professor in the Faculty of Arts, Computing, Engineering and Sciences at Sheffield Hallam University.

Hamid R. Arabnia is currently a full professor of computer science at University of Georgia (Georgia, USA). Dr Arabnia received a PhD degree in Computer Science from the University of Kent (Canterbury, England) in 1987. His research interests include parallel and distributed processing techniques and algorithms, supercomputing, big data analytics, and applications in medical imaging, knowledge engineering, security and surveillance systems, and other computational intensive problems. Dr Arabnia is editor-in-chief of *The Journal of Supercomputing* (Springer); *Transactions of Computational Science and Computational Intelligence* (Springer); and *Emerging Trends in Computer Science and Applied Computing* (Elsevier). He is also on the editorial and advisory boards of 28 other journals. Dr Arabnia is an elected fellow of International Society of Intelligent Biological Medicine (ISIBM).

He has been a PI/Co-PI on $8M funded initiatives. During his tenure as graduate coordinator of computer science (2002–2009), he secured the largest level of funding in the history of the department for supporting the research and education of graduate students (PhD, MS). Most recently, he has been studying ways to promote legislation that would prevent cyberstalking, cyber harassment, and cyberbullying. Prof Arabnia is a member of CENTRIC advisory board.

Richard Hill is professor of intelligent systems and head of department in the School of Computing and Mathematics at the University of Derby, UK. Professor Hill has published over 150 peer-reviewed articles in the areas of multiagent systems, computational intelligence, intelligent cloud computing, and emerging technologies for distributed systems, and has organized a number of international conferences. Latterly, Professor Hill has edited and coauthored several book collections and textbooks, including *Guide to Cloud Computing: Principles and Practice*, published by Springer, UK.

Andrew Staniforth is a serving police detective inspector and former special branch detective. He has extensive operational experience across multiple counterterrorism disciplines, now specializing in security-themed research leading an innovative police research team at the Office of the Police and Crime Commissioner for West Yorkshire. As a professionally qualified teacher, Andrew has designed national counterterrorism exercise programs and supports the missions of the United Nations Terrorism Prevention Branch. Andrew is the author of *Blackstone's Counter-Terrorism Handbook* (Oxford University Press, 2009, 2010, 2013), and *Blackstone's Handbook of Ports & Borders Security* (Oxford University Press, 2013). Andrew is also the author of the *Routledge Companion to UK Counter-Terrorism* (Routledge, 2012) and coeditor of the *Cyber Crime and Cyber Terrorism Investigators Handbook* (Elsevier, 2014). Andrew is a senior research fellow at CENTRIC, and research fellow in Criminal Justice Studies at the University of Leeds School of Law.

Petra Saskia Bayerl is assistant professor of technology and organizational behavior at Rotterdam School of Management, Erasmus University, Netherlands and program director of technology at the Centre of Excellence in Public Safety Management (CESAM, Erasmus). Her current research lies at the intersection of human–computer interaction, organizational communication, and organizational change with a special focus on the impact of technological innovations and public safety. Over the past four years, she has been involved in two EU-funded security-related projects: COMPOSITE (comparative police studies in the EU) and CRISADMIN (critical infrastructures simulation of advanced models on interconnected networks resilience). She is also a visiting research fellow at CENTRIC, Sheffield Hallam University, UK.

Foreword by Lord Carlile of Berriew

I am delighted to provide the foreword for the *Application of Big Data for National Security*. The publication of this new and important volume provides a valuable contribution to the still sparse literature to which the professional, policy-maker, practitioner, and serious student of security and information technology can turn. Its publication serves as a timely reminder that many countries across the world remain at risk from all manner of threats to their national security.

In a world of startling change, the first duty of government remains the security of its country. The range of threats to national security is becoming increasingly complex and diverse. Terrorism, cyber-attack, unconventional attacks using chemical, nuclear, or biological weapons, as well as large-scale accidents or natural hazards—anyone could put citizens' safety in danger while inflicting grave damage to a nation's interests and economic well-being.

In an age of economic uncertainty and political instability, governments must be able to act quickly and effectively to address new and evolving threats to their security. Robust security measures are needed to keep citizens, communities, and commerce safe from serious security hazards. Harnessing the power of Big Data presents an essential opportunity for governments to address these security challenges, but the handling of such large data sets raises acute concerns for existing storage capacity, together with the ability to share and analyze large volumes of data. The introduction of Big Data capabilities will no doubt require the rigorous review and overhaul of existing intelligence models and associated processes to ensure all in authority are ready to exploit Big Data.

While Big Data presents many opportunities for national security, any developments in this arena will have to be guided by the state's relationship with its citizenry and the law. Citizens and their elected representatives remain cautious and suspicious of the access to, and sharing of, their online data. As citizens put more of their lives online voluntarily as part of contemporary lifestyle, the safety and security of their information matters more and more. Any damage to public trust is counter-productive to national security practices; just because the state may have developed the technology and techniques to harness Big Data does not necessarily mean that it should. The legal, moral, and ethical approach to Big Data must be fully explored alongside civil liberties and human rights, yet balanced with the essential requirement to protect the public from security threats.

This authoritative volume provides all security practitioners with a trusted reference and resource to guide them through the complexities of applying Big Data to national security. Authored and edited by a multidisciplinary team of international experts from academia, law enforcement, and private industry, this unique volume is a welcome introduction to tackling contemporary threats to national security.

Lord Carlile of Berriew CBE QC

Preface by Edwin Meese III

What is often called the "information age," which has come to dominate the twenty-first century, is having at least as great an impact on current society as did the "industrial age" in its time, more than a century ago. The benefits and constructive uses of Big Data—a big product of the information age—are matched by the dangers and potential opportunities for misuse which this growing subject portends. This book addresses an important aspect of the topic as it examines the notion of Big Data in the context of national security.

Modern threats to the major nations of the world, both in their homelands and to their vital interests around the globe, have increased the national security requirements of virtually every country. Terrorism, cyber-attacks, homegrown violent extremism, drug trafficking, and organized crime present an imminent danger to public safety and homeland defense. In these critical areas, the emergence of new resources in the form of information technology can provide a welcome addition to the capabilities of those government and private institutes involved in public protection.

The impressive collection of authors provides a careful assessment of how the expanding universe of information constitutes both a potential threat and potential protection for the safety and security of individuals and institutions, particularly in the industrialized world.

Because of the broad application of this topic, this book provides valuable knowledge and thought-provoking ideas for a wide variety of readers, whether they are decision-makers and direct participants in the field of Big Data or concerned citizens who are affected in their own lives and businesses by how well this resource is utilized by those in government, academia, and the private sector.

The book begins with an introduction into the concept and key applications of Big Data. This overview provides an introduction to the subject that establishes a common understanding of the Big Data field, with its particular complexities and challenges. It sets forth the capabilities of this valuable resource for national security purposes, as well as the policy implications of its use. A critical aspect of its beneficial potential is the necessary interface between government and the private sector, based on a common understanding of the subject.

One of the book's strengths is its emphasis on the practical application of Big Data as a resource for public safety. Chapters are devoted to detailed examples of its utilization in a wide range of contexts, such as cyberterrorism, violent extremist threats, active shooters, and possible integration into the battlefield. Contemporary challenges faced by government agencies and law enforcement organizations are described, with explanations of how Big Data resources can be adapted to effect their solutions. For this resource to fulfill its maximum potential, policies, guidelines, and best practices must be developed for use at national and local levels, which can continuously be revised as the data world changes.

To complement its policy and operational knowledge, the book also provides the technological underpinning of Big Data solutions. It features discussions of the important tools and techniques to handle Big Data, as well as commentary on the organizational, architectural, and resource issues that must be considered when developing data-oriented solutions. This material helps the user of Big Data to have a basic appreciation of the information system as well as the hazards and limitations of the programs involved.

To complete its comprehensive view of Big Data in its uses to support national security in its broader sense—including the protection of the public at all levels of government and private activity—the book examines an essential consideration: the public response and the political environment in which difficult decisions must be made. The ability to utilize the advantages of Big Data for the purposes of national security involves important legal, social, and psychological considerations. The book explains in detail the dilemmas and challenges confronting the use of Big Data by leaders of government agencies, law enforcement organizations, and private sector entities. Decisions in this field require an understanding of the context of national and international legal frameworks as well as the nature of the public opinion climate and the various media and political forces that can influence it.

The continuing advances in information technology make Big Data a valuable asset in the ability of government and the private sector to carry out their increasing responsibilities to ensure effective national security. But to be usable and fulfill its potential as a valuable asset, this resource must be managed with great care in both its technical and its public acceptance aspects. This unique book provides the knowledge and processes to accomplish that task.

Edwin Meese III is the 75th Attorney General of the United States (1985–1988).

Acknowledgments

The editors wish to thank the multidisciplinary team of experts who have contributed to this book, sharing their knowledge, experience, and latest research. Our gratitude is also extended to Mr Edwin Meese III, the 75th Attorney General of the United States, and Lord Carlile of Berriew CBE QC for their kind support of this book. We would also like to take this opportunity to acknowledge the contributions of the following organizations:

CENTRIC (Centre of Excellence in Terrorism, Resilience, Intelligence and Organised Crime Research), UK

CIAG (Critical Incident Analysis Group), USA

CESAM (Center of Excellence in Public Safety Management), NL

INTRODUCTION TO BIG DATA

AN INTRODUCTION TO BIG DATA

1

John Panneerselvam, Lu Liu, Richard Hill

WHAT IS BIG DATA?

Today, roughly half of the world population interacts with online services. Data are generated at an unprecedented scale from a wide range of sources. The way we view and manipulate the data is also changing, as we discover new ways of discovering insights from unstructured data sources. Managing data volume has changed considerably over recent years (Malik, 2013), because we need to cope with demands to deal with terabytes, petabytes, and now even zettabytes. Now we need to have a vision that includes what the data might be used for in the future so that we can begin to plan and budget for likely resources. A few terabytes of data are quickly generated by a commercial business organization, and individuals are starting to accumulate this amount of personal data. Storage capacity has roughly doubled every 14 months over the past 3 decades. Concurrently, the price of data storage has reduced, which has affected the storage strategies that enterprises employ (Kumar et al., 2012) as they buy more storage rather than determine what to delete. Because enterprises have started to discover new value in data, they are treating it like a tangible asset (Laney, 2001). This enormous generation of data, along with the adoption of new strategies to deal with the data, has caused the emergence of a new era of data management, commonly referred to as Big Data.

Big Data has a multitude of definitions, with some research suggesting that the term itself is a misnomer (Eaton et al., 2012). Big Data challenges the huge gap between analytical techniques used historically for data management, as opposed to what we require now (Barlow, 2013). The size of datasets has always grown over the years, but we are currently adopting improved practices for large-scale processing and storage. Big Data is not only huge in terms of volume, it is also dynamic and has various forms. On the whole, we have never seen these kinds of data in the history of technology.

Broadly speaking, Big Data can be defined as the emergence of new datasets with massive volume that change at a rapid pace, are very complex, and exceed the reach of the analytical capabilities of commonly used hardware environments and software tools for data management. In short, the volume of data has become too large to handle with conventional tools and methods.

With advances in science, medicine, and business, the sources that generate data increase every day, especially from electronic communications as a result of human activities. Such data are generated from e-mail, radiofrequency identification, mobile communication, social media, health care systems and records, enterprise data such as retail, transport, and utilities, and operational data from sensors and satellites. The data generated from these sources are usually unprocessed (raw) and require various stages of processing for analytics. Generally, some processing converts unstructured data into semi-structured data; if they are processed further, the data are regarded as structured. About 80% of the world's data are semi-structured or unstructured. Some enterprises largely dealing with Big Data are

Facebook, Twitter, Google, and Yahoo, because the bulk of their data are regarded as unstructured. As a consequence, these enterprises were early adopters of Big Data technology.

The Internet of Things (IoT) has increased data generation dramatically, because patterns of usage of IoT devices have changed recently. A simple snapshot event has turned out to be a data generation activity. Along with image recognition, today's technology allows users to take and name a photograph, identify the individuals in the picture, and include the geographical location, time and date, before uploading the photo over the Internet within an instance. This is a quick data generation activity with considerable volume, velocity, and variety.

HOW DIFFERENT IS BIG DATA?

The concept of Big Data is not new to the technological community. It can be seen as the logical extension of already existing technology such as storage and access strategies and processing techniques. Storing data is not new, but doing something meaningful (Hofstee et al., 2013) (and quickly) with the stored data is the challenge with Big Data (Gartner, 2011). Big Data analytics has something more to do with information technology management than simply dealing with databases. Enterprises used to retrieve historical data for processing to produce a result. Now, Big Data deals with real-time processing of the data and producing quick results (Biem et al., 2013). As a result, months, weeks, and days of processing have been reduced to minutes, seconds, and even fractions of seconds. In reality, the concept of Big Data is making things possible that would have been considered impossible not long ago.

Most existing storage strategies followed a knowledge management–based storage approach, using data warehouses (DW). This approach follows a hierarchy flowing from data to information, knowledge, and wisdom, known as the DIKW hierarchy. Elements in every level constitute elements for building the succeeding level. This architecture makes the accessing policies more complex and most of the existing databases are no longer able to support Big Data. Big Data storage models need more accuracy, and the semi-structured and the unstructured nature of Big Data is driving the adoption of storage models that use cross-linked data. Even though the data relate to each other and are physically located in different parts of the DW, logical connection remains between the data. Typically we use algorithms to process data in standalone machines and over the Internet. Most or all of these algorithms are bounded by space and time constraints, and they might lose logical functioning if an attempt is made to exceed their bound limitations. Big Data is processed with algorithms (Gualtieri, 2013) that possess the ability to function on a logically connected cluster of machines without limited time and space constraints.

Big Data processing is expected to produce results in real time or near–real time, and it is not meaningful to produce results after a prolonged period of processing. For instance, as users search for information using a search engine, the results that are displayed may be interspersed with advertisements. The advertisements will be for products or services that are related to the user's query. This is an example of the real-time response upon which Big Data solutions are focused.

MORE ON BIG DATA: TYPES AND SOURCES

Big Data arises from a wide variety of sources and is categorized based on the nature of the data, their complexity in processing, and the intended analysis to extract a value for a meaningful execution. As a consequence, Big Data is classified as structured data, unstructured data, and semi-structured data.

STRUCTURED DATA

Most of the data contained in traditional database systems are regarded as structured. These data are particularly suited to further analysis because they are less complex with defined length, semantics, and format. Records have well-defined fields with a high degree of organization (rows and columns), and the data usually possess meaningful codes in a standard form that computers can easily read. Often, data are organized into semantic chunks, and similar chunks with common description are usually grouped together. Structured data can be easily stored in databases and show reduced analytical complexity in searching, retrieving, categorizing, sorting, and analyzing with defined criteria.

Structured data come from both machine- and human-generated sources. Without the intervention of humans for data generation, some machine-generated datasets include sensor data, Web log data, call center detail records, data from smart meters, and trading systems. Humans interact with computers to generate data such as input data, XML data, click stream data, traditional enterprise data such as customer information from customer relationship management systems, and enterprise resource planning data, general ledger data, financial data, and so on.

UNSTRUCTURED DATA

Conversely, unstructured data lack a predefined data format and do not fit well into the traditional relational database systems. Such data do not follow any rules or recognizable patterns and can be unpredictable. These data are more complex to explore, and their analytical complexity is high in terms of capture, storage, processing, and resolving meaningful queries from them. More than 80% of data generated today are unstructured as a result of recording event data from daily activities.

Unstructured data are also generated by both machine and human sources. Some machine-generated data include image and video files generated from satellite and traffic sensors, geographical data from radars and sonar, and surveillance and security data from closed-circuit television (CCTV) sources. Human-generated data include social media data (e.g., Facebook and Twitter updates) (Murtagh, 2013; Wigan and Clarke, 2012), data from mobile communications, Web sources such as YouTube and Flickr, e-mails, documents, and spreadsheets.

SEMI-STRUCTURED DATA

Semi-structured data are a combination of both structured and unstructured data. They still have the data organized in chunks, with similar chunks grouped together. However, the description of the chunks in the same group may not necessarily be the same. Some of the attributes of the data may be defined, and there is often a self-describing data model, but it is not as rigid as structured data. In this sense, semi-structured data can be viewed as a kind of structured data with no rigid relational integration among datasets. The data generated by electronic data interchange sources, e-mail, and XML data can be categorized as semi-structured data.

THE FIVE V'S OF BIG DATA

As discussed before, the conversation of Big Data often starts with its *volume*, *velocity*, and *variety*. The characteristics of Big Data—too big, too fast, and too hard—increase the complexity for existing tools and techniques to process them (Courtney, 2012a; Dong and Srivatsava, 2013). The core concept of Big

Data theory is to extract the significant *value* out of the raw datasets to drive meaningful decision making. Because we see more and more data generated every day and the data pile is increasing, it has become essential to introduce the *veracity* nature of the data in Big Data processing, which determines the dependability level of the processed *value*.

VOLUME

Among the five V's, volume is the most dominant character of Big Data, pushing new strategies in storing, accessing, and processing Big Data. We live in a society in which almost all of our activities are turning out to be a data generation event. This means that enterprises tend to swim in an enormous pool of data. The data are ever-growing at a rate governed by Moore's law, which states that *the rate at which the data are generated is doubling approximately in a period of just less than every 2 years*. The more devices generate data, the more the data pile up in databases. The data volume is measured more in terms of bandwidth than its scale. A quick revolution of data generation has driven data management to deal with terabytes instead of petabytes, and inevitably to move to zettabytes in no time. This exponential generation of data reflects the fact that *the volume of tomorrow's data will always be higher than what we are facing today*.

Social media sites such as Facebook and Twitter generate text and image data through uploads in the range of terabytes every day. A survey report of the *Guardian* (Murdoch, Monday May 20, 2013) says that Facebook and Yahoo carry out analysis on individual pieces of data that would not fit on a laptop or a desktop machine. Research studies of IBM (Pimentel, 2014) have projected a mammoth volume of data generation up to 35 zettabytes in 2020.

VELOCITY

Velocity represents the generation and processing of in-flight transitory data within the elapsed time limit. Most data sources generate high-flux streaming data that travel at a very high speed, making the analytics more complex. The speed at which the data are being generated demands more and more acceleration in processing and analyzing. Storing high-velocity data and then later processing them is not in the interest of Big Data. Real-time processing defines the rate at which the data arrive at the database and the time scale within which the data must be processed. Big Data likes low latency (i.e., shorter queuing delays) to reduce the lag time between capturing the data and making them accessible. With applications such as fraud detection, even a single minute is too late. Big Data analytics are targeted at responding to the applications in real time or near–real time by parallel processing of the data as they arrive in the database. The dynamic nature of Big Data leads the decisions on currently arriving data to influence the decisions on succeeding data. Again, the data generated by social media sites are proving to be very quick in velocity. For instance, Twitter closes more than 250 million tweets per day at a flying velocity (O'Leary, 2013) and tweets always escalate the velocity of data, considerably influencing the following tweets.

VARIETY

Variety of Big Data reveals heterogeneity of the data with respect to its type (structured, semi-structured, and unstructured), representation, and semantic interpretation. Because the community using IoT is increasing every day, it also constitutes a vast variety of sources generating data such as images, audio and video files, texts, and logs. Data generated by these various sources are ever-changing in nature, leaving most of the world's data in unstructured and semi-structured formats. The data treated as most significant now may turn out not to be significant later, and vice versa.

VERACITY

Veracity relates to the uncertainty of data within a data set. As more data are collected, there is a considerable increase in the probability that the data are potentially inaccurate or of poor quality. The trust level of the data is more significant in the processed value, which in turn drives decision making. This veracity determines the accuracy of the processed data in terms of their social or business value and indicates whether Big Data analytics has actually made sense of the processed data. Achieving the desired level of veracity requires robust optimization techniques and fuzzy logic approaches. (For additional challenges to Big Data veracity, see Chapters 17 and 18.)

VALUE

Value is of vital importance to Big Data analytics, because data will lose their meaning without contributing significant value (Mitchell et al., 2012; Schroeck et al., 2012). There is no point in a Big Data solution unless it is aimed at creating social or business value. In fact, the volume, velocity, and variety nature of Big Data are processed to extract a meaningful value out of the raw data. Of the data generated, not necessarily all has to be meaningful or significant for decision making. Relevant data might just be a little sample against a huge pile of data. It is evident that the non-significant data are growing at a tremendous rate in relation to significant ones. Big Data analytics must act on the whole data pile to extract significant data value. The process is similar to mining for scarce resources; huge volumes of raw ore are usually processed to extract the quantity of gold that has the most significant value.

BIG DATA IN THE BIG WORLD
IMPORTANCE

There is clear motivation to embrace the adoption of Big Data solutions, because traditional database systems are no longer able to handle the enormous data being generated today (Madden, 2012). There is a need for frameworks and platforms that can effectively handle such massive data volumes, particularly to keep up with innovations in data collection mechanisms via portable digital devices. What we have dealt with so far are still its beginnings; much more is to come. The growing importance of Big Data has pushed enterprises and leading companies to adapt Big Data solutions for progressing towards innovation and insights. HP reported in 2013 that nearly 60% of all companies would spend at least 10% of their innovation budget on Big Data that business year (HP, 2013). It also found that more than one in three enterprises had actually failed with a Big Data initiative. Cisco estimates that the global IP traffic flowing over the Internet will reach 131.6 exabytes per month by 2015, which was standing at 51.2 exabytes per month in 2013 (Cisco, 2014).

ADVANTAGES AND APPLICATIONS

Big Data analytics reduces the processing time of a query and in turn reduces the time to wait for the solutions. Combining and analyzing the data allows data-driven (directed) decision making, which helps enterprises to grow their business. Big Data facilitates enterprises to take correct, meaningful actions at the right time and in the right place. Handelsbanken, a large bank in northern Europe, has experienced on average a sevenfold reduction in query processing time. They used newly developed IBM software (Thomas, 2012) for data analytics to achieve this growth. Big Data analytics provides a fast, cheap, and rich understanding of problems facing enterprises.

Real-time data streaming increasingly has a lead role in assisting human living. The KTH Royal Institute of Technology in Sweden analyzed real-time data streams to identity traffic patterns using the IBM components of Big Data solutions (Thomas, 2012). Real-time traffic data are collected by using global positioning systems (GPS) from a variety of sources such as radars in vehicles, motorways, and weather sensors. Using IBM InfoSphere stream software, large volumes of real-time streaming data in both structured and unstructured formats are analyzed (Hirzel et al., 2013). The value extracted from the data is effectively used to estimate the traveling time between source and destination points. Advice is then offered regarding alternative traveling routes, which serves to control and maintain city traffic.

As discussed earlier, processing of massive sets of data is becoming more effective and feasible, in just fractions of seconds. The level of trustworthiness of the data is an important consideration when processing data. Enterprises are concerned about risk and compliance management with respect to data assets, particularly because most information is transmitted over a network connection. With these applications, we are enjoying significant benefits such as better delivery of quality, service satisfaction, and increased productivity. The more the data are integrated and the more complex they are, the greater the significance is of the risk it poses to an organization if the data are lost or misused. The need to safeguard data is directly reflected in continuity planning and the growth of the organization. With this in mind, about 61% of managers reported that they have plans to secure data with Big Data solutions (Bdaily, 2013). Big Data is big business. Research studies indicate that the companies investing more in Big Data are generating greater returns and gaining more advantages than companies without such an investment. Companies leaning toward Big Data solutions are proving to be tough and strong competitors in the industry. People are attracted by the policies of online shopping providers such as eBay because they provide a wide access and availability zone, offers such as free shipping, tax reductions, and so on. A huge community might concurrently be using the same site over the Internet, and Big Data allows the service providers to manage such a heavy load without issues including network congestion, bandwidth and server issues, and traffic over the Internet affecting users' experience.

Big Data applications have important roles in national security activities such as defense management, disaster recovery management, and financial interventions (Gammerman et al., 2014). Generally, governments consider securing financial interventions to be one of their primary tasks for fighting against international crimes. Financial transactions across countries involve various levels of processing and every level may include different languages and currencies and different methods of processing and different economic policies. Such a process also includes information exchange through various sources including voice calls, e-mail communication, and written communication. As discussed, most of these sources generate data in unstructured formats lacking inherent knowledge. Big Data solutions facilitate effective processing of such diverse datasets and provide better understanding of inter- and intra-dependency factors such as customs, human behavior and attitudes, values and beliefs, influence and institutions, social and economic policies, and political ideologies, and thus enable the right decisions at the right time to benefit the right entities. Big Data solutions also allow potential risk calculation, gross domestic product management, and terrorism modeling by delving into historical records along with current data despite the huge pile of datasets.

Big Data is used in health care applications to improve quality and efficiency in the delivery of health care and reduce health care maintenance expenditure. With real-time streaming capability, Big Data applications are also used to continuously monitor patient records, helping in the early detection and diagnosis of medical conditions. Big Data solutions benefit local education authorities, which involve various levels of digital data processing under several layers of local governments in the United Kingdom. Local education authorities function as a collective organization, and Big Data solutions offer easy provisions in funding management, progress monitoring, human resource management, coordination of admissions, etc. Similarly, we see Big Data applications in a variety of domains such as online education, cyber security, and weather tracking.

ANALYTICAL CAPABILITIES OF BIG DATA
DATA VISUALIZATION

Visualization of large volumes of data can enable data exploration to be performed more efficiently. Such exploration helps identifying valuable data patterns and anomalies. Analytic capabilities provide a variety of data visualization types including bubble charts, bar-column representations, heat grids, scatter charts, and geospatial maps such as three-dimensional building models, digital terrain models, and road/rail networks. Modern software interfaces allow the construction of more complicated and sophisticated reports for the user's consumption.

GREATER RISK INTELLIGENCE

Big Data allows greater visibility and transparency of the organization's risk profile. Reactive discovery of current incidents and proactive analysis of emerging issues help enterprises to reduce the risks of being susceptible to fraud and internal hackers. To this end, Big Data analysis benefits governments to strengthen their security policies and law enforcements by the way of instantly identifying suspicious behaviors. The sophisticated machines and environmental sensors in enterprises often generate data related to their operating and health conditions. Such data are referred to as Machine-to-Machine (M2M) data and are usually ignored because of their massive volume. Big Data analytics provides the analysis capability to help maintain equipment components in a timely, preventive manner, thus avoiding costly industrial downtime and increasing operational efficiency.

SATISFYING BUSINESS NEEDS

The three major requirements of enterprises are operations, risk, and value management. In the beginning, it is difficult for enterprises to identify which data sources have significant value and which data are worth keeping. Keeping abundant data that are low in value is of little use. Big Data analytics enhances the organization's capability of making quick decisions by providing a rapid estimation of the significant value of the data, thus supporting time and value management. With the aid of Big Data solutions, simultaneous management of operations, risk, and data value is now within the reach of more enterprises. Thus, uncovering the hidden values of under-rated data highly benefits organizations and governments with deeper data mining and helps them to identify the motivation of activities involving digital transactions and to prevent frauds and international crimes.

PREDICTIVE MODELING AND OPTIMIZATION

Predictive insights refers to the ability of organizations to better understand the risks involved in their actions, driving the process towards the intended outcome and guiding the adoption of design modifications in the processing architecture. Big Data platforms allow the extraction of these predictive insights by running multiple iterations of the relevant data. Massively parallel processing of Big Data allows organizations to develop and run predictive modeling to optimize results. Predictive models are run in an environment that hosts the relevant data, avoiding the complex process of moving massive data across networks. Such a strategy is referred to as database analytics. The architecture is optimized by reducing risks involved with the applications, avoiding any infrastructure failure, and designing an appropriate processing model based on the requirements of the data and the required outcome.

STREAMING ANALYTICS

The efficiency of the operating nodes is usually configured in such a way that they can be reused to handle streaming data. Real-time analysis of streamed data is made possible without much data loss and at minimum cost. The architecture is now capable of processing data streaming from various data sources to integrate the necessary data in an instant and generate outputs with the lowest possible processing time. Queries can be executed in a continuous fashion enabled by a high degree of parallelism and automatic optimization.

IDENTIFYING BUSINESS USE CASES

Often, data gain value in novel situations. Once a useful pattern emerges by means of data exploration, the value sources can be identified and further refined to gain quality benefits. These quality benefits are visualized by the analytics and should be in line with the objectives set forth by the organization.

VIDEO AND VOICE ANALYTICS

Voice and video data are generated mostly in an unstructured format. In addition, the streaming of such data results in velocity issues as well as high analytics complexity. Big Data platforms can perform effective capturing of such data with the aid of NoSQL databases. In some cases, the image file of the video may be uninteresting because of its massive volume. However, the value in the image data is significant for forming the metadata. Big Data analytics is capable of extracting individual frames of videos and important transcripts of audio files. Voice and video analytics have a vital role in enterprises such as call centers, telecommunication networks, CCTV surveillance, and so on.

GEOSPATIAL ANALYTICS

Geospatial data sources include land drilling, offshore drilling, abandoned wells, and mobile data. Poor governance of such data often has a profound impact on a business's goals and may cause considerable economic loss. Big Data analytics aids the effective maintenance of geospatial data and contributes towards more effective productivity management. Big Data processing allows intelligent exploitation of hidden information, which in turn facilitates high-resolution image exploitation and advanced geo-spatial data fusion for effective interpretation. Such advancements in data interpretation also highly benefit antiterrorism activities facilitated by accurate GPS tracking, unmanned aerial vehicles and remotely piloted aircraft videos, and so on.

AN OVERVIEW OF BIG DATA SOLUTIONS
GOOGLE BIGQUERY

Google BigQuery (Google) is a cloud-based SQL platform that offers real-time business insights with an analysis capability up to several terabytes of data in seconds. Iterative analysis of massive sets of data organized into billions of rows is available through a user interface. BigQuery can be accessed by making calls to the BigQuery Rest API supported by a variety of client libraries such as PHP, Java, and Python.

IBM INFOSPHERE BIGINSIGHTS

This is a software framework from IBM that uses Hadoop to manage large volumes of data of all formats. BigInsights increases operational efficiency by augmenting the data warehouse environments, thereby allowing storage and analysis of the data without affecting the data warehouse (Harriott, 2013). Operational features of the framework include administration, discovery, deployment, provision, and security.

BIG DATA ON AMAZON WEB SERVICES

Amazon Elastic MapReduce, built around the Hadoop framework, provides an interface to Big Data analytics tools. Its DynamoDB is a NOSQL-based database that allows the storage of massive data in the cloud. Amazon Web Services Big Data solutions are targeted at reducing the up-front costs for enterprises and may thus be more cost-effective for smaller enterprises.

CLOUDS FOR BIG DATA

With the adoption of cloud services to increase business agility, Big Data applications will drive enterprises even more quickly toward clouds. Clouds are offering services instantly, and rapid provisioning (Ji et al., 2012) is available at a moment's notice. Experiments performed by Big Data applications are much easier in clouds than hosting them internally in the enterprise. With its wide availability, clouds permit elastic provisioning of the resource requirements for Big Data processing (Talia, 2013). The "try before you commit" feature of clouds is particularly attractive to enterprises that are constantly trying to gain a competitive advantage in the marketplace. Some of the Big Data solutions such as Google BigQuery (see above) are only available as cloud services. Because the parallelization process involves a huge architecture, building such an environment with the required hardware and software tools is typically prohibitive for small-sized enterprises. In such a case, adopting cloud services proves to be a better option for enterprises, reducing implementation costs to levels that are viable and sustainable (Courtney, 2012b).

Apart from these advantages, there are, of course, drawbacks to processing Big Data in clouds. Pushing massive volumes of data over any network inevitably risks the overall performance of the infrastructure and also reduces availability and Quality of Service (QoS). Optimizing the bandwidth required to analyze the mammoth amount of Big Data is one of the remaining open challenges to cloud vendors (Liu, 2013). Often, enterprises want data to be processed in one physical location rather than a distributing processing across geographically remote clusters. Enterprises also need to front the migration costs involved in moving data to the cloud, because at times application deployment can cost three times as much as base software costs.

CONCLUSIONS

Developments in technology have started to uncover the concept of Big Data, and the understanding and reach of Big Data are becoming better than before. Big Data has applications in a wide range of technological implementations and will change the way that human activities are recorded and analyzed to produce new insights and innovations. Ultimately, this facilitates new capabilities by the way of faster responses to more complex data queries and more accurate prediction models. Big Data is particularly suited to applications in which the barriers to progress are fundamentally grounded in datasets that are large in volume, fast moving (velocity), wide ranging in variety, and difficult to trust (veracity), and have potential high value. Big Data is a potential solution to applications proving to be complex and time- and energy-consuming with current machine capabilities, leading us to a new and innovative way of dealing with business and science. Big Data allows us to do big business with big opportunities leading the way for big quality of life. Resolving the lesser relevance of Big Data and extending the deployment of Big Data solutions to every possible type of digital processing will uncover the value of underestimated and undervalued data and benefit humans to discover new innovations in technology.

REFERENCES

Barlow, M., 2013. Real-time Big Data Analytics: Emerging Architecture. O'Reilly.

Bdaily, 2013. Big Data: Realising Opportunities and Assessing Risk, Bdaily, Business News. Bdaily Ltd.

Biem, A., Feng, H., Riabov, A., Turaga, D., 2013. Real-time analysis and management of big time-series data. IBM Journal of Research and Development 57, 8:1–8:12.

Cisco, 2014. Cisco Visual Networking Index: Forecast and Methodology, 2013–2018. (Online). Available from: http://www.cisco.com/c/en/us/solutions/collateral/service-provider/ip-ngn-ip-next-generation-network/white_paper_c11-481360.html.

Courtney, M., 2012a. Big Data analytics: putting the puzzle together. Engineering and Technology Magazine 7, 56–57.

Courtney, M., 2012b. The larging-up of Big Data. IET Engineering and Technology 7, 72–75.

Dong, X., Srivatsava, D., 2013. Big Data integration. In: 29th International Conference on Data Engineering (ICDE). IEEE, Brisbane, pp. 1245–1248.

Eaton, C., Deroos, D., Deutsch, T., Lapis, G., Zikopoulos, P., 2012. Understanding Big Data. McGraw Hill.

Gammerman, A., Cole, J., Gollins, T., Lewis, H., Mandoli, G., Bennett, N., Lynch, M., Velasco, E., Tsai, 2014. Big Data for security and resilience. In: Cole, J. (Ed.), Pro. of Big Data for Security and Resilience: Challenges and Opportunities for the Next Generation of Policy-makers. RUSI and STFC, pp. 1–85.

Gartner, 2011. Gartner Says Solving 'Big Data' Challenge Involves More than Just Managing Volumes of Data. Gartner (Online). Available from: http://www.gartner.com/newsroom/id/1731916.

Google, Google BigQuery, What Is BigQuery? (Online). Available from: https://cloud.google.com/bigquery/what-is-bigquery.

Gualtieri, M., 2013. The Forrester Wave: Big Data Predictive Analytics Solutions, Q1 2013 Forrester Research. Available from: http://www.sas.com/resources/asset/Forrester85601-LR8KBD.pdf.

Harriott, J., 2013. InfoSphere BigInsights, Bringing the Power of Hadoop to the Enterprise (Online). Available from: http://www-01.ibm.com/software/data/infosphere/biginsights/.

Hirzel, M., Andrade, H., Gedik, B., Jacques-Silva, G., Khandekar, R., Kumar, V., Mendell, M., Nasgaard, H., Schneider, S., Soule, R., Wu, R., 2013. IBM streams processing language: analyzing Big Data in motion. IBM Journal of Research and Development 57, 7:1–7:11.

Hofstee, H., Chen, C., Gebara, F., Hall, K., Herring, J., Jamsek, D., Li, J., Li, Y., Shi, J., Wong, P., 2013. Understanding system design for Big Data workloads. IBM Journal of Research and Development 57, 3:1–3:10.

HP, 2013. HP Unleashes the Power of Big Data, Expanded Portfolio Accelerates Adoption, Monetization of Information (Online) HP, Las Vegas. Available from: http://www8.hp.com/us/en/hp-news/press-release.html?id=1416090#.Ud7rcPnI3Qg.

Ji, C., Li, Y., Qiu, W., Awada, U., Li, K., 2012. Big Data processing in cloud computing environments. In: 12th International Symposium on Pervasive Systems, Algorithms and Networks (ISPAN). IEEE, San Marcos, pp. 17–23.

Kumar, A., Lee, H., Singh, R., 2012. Efficient and secure cloud storage for handling big data. In: 6th International Conference on New Trends in Information Science and Service Science and Data Mining (ISSDM). IEEE, Taipei, pp. 162–166.

Laney, D., 2001. 3D Data Management: Controlling Data Volume, Velocity, and Variety META Group. Available from: http://blogs.gartner.com/doug-laney/files/2012/01/ad949-3D-Data-Management-Controlling-Data-Volume-Velocity-and-Variety.pdf.

Liu, H., 2013. Big Data drives cloud adoption in Enterprise. Internet Computing 17, 68–71.

Madden, S., 2012. From databases to Big Data. IEEE Internet Computing 16, 4–6.

Malik, P., 2013. Governing big data: Principles and practices. IBM Journal of Research and Develpoment 57, 1:1–1:13.

Mitchell, I., Loke, M., Wilson, M., Fuller, A., 2012. The White Book Big Data. Fujitsu Services Ltd.

Murdoch, J., Monday May 20, 2013. Critics of Big Data have overlooked the speed factor. The Guardian (Online). Available from: http://www.theguardian.com/news/datablog/2013/may/20/big-data-critics-overlooked-speed-not-size.

Murtagh, R., 2013. Seize the Data: 5 Ways to Leverage Big Data for Social Media & Search. Incisive Interactive Marketing LLC, New York.

O'Leary, D., 2013. Artificial Intelligence and Big Data. IEEE Intelligent Systems 28, 96–99.

Pimentel, F., 2014. Big Data + Mainframe. Smarter Computing. IBM.

Schroeck, M., Shockley, R., Smart, J., Romero-Morales, D., Tufano, P., 2012. Analytics: The Real-world Use of Big Data (Online) IBM Institute for Business Value. Available from: http://www-935.ibm.com/services/us/gbs/thoughtleadership/ibv-big-data-at-work.html.

Talia, D., 2013. Clouds for scalable Big Data analytics. Computer 46, 98–101.

Thomas, R., 2012. IBM Big Data Success Stories. IBM. pp. 1–70.

Wigan, M., Clarke, R., 2012. Big Data's big unintended consequences. IEEE Computer 46, 46–53.

DRILLING INTO THE BIG DATA GOLD MINE: DATA FUSION AND HIGH-PERFORMANCE ANALYTICS FOR INTELLIGENCE PROFESSIONALS

2

Rupert Hollin

INTRODUCTION

We are living in the age of Big Data. The volume, velocity, and variety of data to which agencies have access can often exceed their ability to store, process, and analyze that data to support accurate and timely decision making.

Across the world, law enforcement and intelligence agencies are facing an increasingly complex range of threats from a myriad of different sources; Nation States, groups and individuals with completely different motivations and a growing arsenal of modus operandi. Whether tackling cross-border organized crime or lone wolf terrorist threats, the need to continually adapt countermeasures continues. Agencies have invested heavily in collection platforms and technologies to capture and analyze information, the volume of which is increasing exponentially. When faced with the many types of data now available, the potential for information overload is high. This is especially true for intelligence professionals charged with turning this data into actionable intelligence to help counter these threats, increasing the risk of missing key pieces of information leading to reputational damage at the least, and at the worst failure to prevent a real and credible threat.

Since the attacks on New York and Washington in September 2001, we have seen growing urgency across the Western world and beyond to tackle the ever-present threat of terrorism, a need that has been underlined in the intervening years by high-profile incidents such as the London suicide attacks of July 7, 2005, Anders Breivik's twin attacks in Norway in 2011, and the Boston Marathon bombings in the United States in April 2013. Developments in Syria and Iraq indicate that this trend is likely to continue. Add to this the increase in organized criminal activities such as arms trading, human trafficking, and drug smuggling, coupled with tough financial constraints, and it is clear that agencies need to improve their effectiveness whilst driving economic efficiencies.

THE AGE OF BIG DATA AND HIGH-PERFORMANCE ANALYTICS

Terrorism, crime, and other threats to national security can be properly addressed only through the availability of timely reliable intelligence. Successful operations need to be able to use information from a range of sources including human intelligence, signals intelligence, and open-source intelligence. The

FIGURE 2.1

Anticipated growth of data, 2009–2020.

growing volume and unstructured nature of available data requires committed investments in data exploitation (see Figure 2.1). Gaining value from these data is critical to ongoing success.

In the past, most agencies worked with data that they held internally within their organization and the intelligence they were generating themselves in the form of intelligence reports or information gathered from the investigations they were carrying out. In this tightly controlled environment, data growth was largely manageable.

The situation today has changed radically because data volumes have increased in all elements of our lives. The same applies to agencies that now have data available to them that increasingly originate from or are held outside their own organization. In the Internet age, to gain a truly holistic view of activities, new and emerging technology solutions such as social media, automatic number plate recognition, telecommunications, and financial and other sensor data have an increasingly important role in agency life.

Analysts need to call on all of the information available to them and assess it to obtain a clear picture of how a situation is evolving over time. This is increasingly difficult in an environment where adversaries are exploiting the Internet, social media networks and other digital channels to great effect. Analysts often have to review huge volumes of information, looking for that golden nugget of relevant information that could bring an investigation to a positive conclusion.

At the same time, much of the data being generated no longer take the form of easy-to-manage structured data saved in a tabular format within relational databases. Instead, a significant proportion of data are unstructured in the form of word documents, transcripts, witness statements, or Internet content, which presents another key Big Data challenge. These data can be extremely valuable—especially given the latest advances in text analytics to automatically generate keywords and topics, categorize content, manage semantic terms, unearth sentiment, and put all of that into context (see Chapters 11–13).

TECHNOLOGY CHALLENGES

The downside to all this is that, given the vast type, quantity, and formats of available data, it is unlikely that users know what is relevant or what should be searched for. What about all the important information hidden in the data that has not been questioned because it appears unrelated—the "unknown unknowns"?

Overwhelmed by the scale and complexity of the data being generated, most agencies' legacy databases simply cannot cope. There is a growing acceptance that siloed systems are a thing of the past and that such silos prevent users from seeing the bigger picture that their data could potentially reveal. To help address this challenge, agencies must consider using the latest data storage and processing technology, such as Hadoop, which uses lower-cost commodity hardware to reliably store large quantities of data (see also Chapters 9–11) and supports the power of parallel processing enabling rapid access to the data. The inability of an organisation to access the entire Big data store in a timely manner and identify useful and relevant data inevitably leads to missed opportunities and potentially poor intelligence.

Once the data is available in your 'data lake' the ability to carry out comprehensive searches across data sources is a critical part of an analysts Big Data arsenal, but also assumes that there is a starting point. This might be a known organization or individuals who can lead the analyst to further valuable sources of intelligence. When faced with organized threats, national security agencies are frequently in a position to ask such targeted questions about an organization, its methods of operation, who its members are and with whom they interact. Exploring the data available and gathering new data is the key to success. However, in these examples, that success is achieved through asking specific questions about the vast quantities of data available to build the intelligence picture, identifying the known unknowns and then gathering further data to fill in the gaps.

The next step to truly unlocking the Big Data gold mine requires the adoption of high-performance analytics (HPA) solutions, creating the ability to process vast volumes of data quickly and efficiently, to uncover hidden patterns, anomalies, and other useful information that can be used to make better decisions. High-performance analytics has the potential to enable law enforcement or national security agencies to integrate and analyze huge volumes and varieties of data, structured and unstructured, to review and anticipate changes in criminal and terrorist activity. For example, Figure 2.2 shows an analysis that was performed on casualties inflicted by different types of explosive attack. The figure indicates a gradual reduction in numbers of wounded or killed people in all types of attack owing to better preventative measures, but also that improvised devices were still responsible for several hundreds of wounded people. These data can be graphically presented to users in a matter of seconds and manipulated to predict future possibilities.

High-performance analytics delivers the potential to help agencies quickly access and analyze every bit of relevant data and thereby move from a pay and chase approach, in which agencies put in place technology to react to events that have already happened, to a more proactive predict and prevent environment.

The real benefit of applying HPA to Big Data is that agencies do not need to know what they are looking for before they start. Instead, analytical techniques will model the data and push information of interest back to them, drawing attention to relevant content, effectively pushing the needle out from inside the haystack. This information can then be processed through standard analysis and investigation processes to determine whether it is viable intelligence, effectively converting Big Data into actionable intelligence.

BUILDING THE COMPLETE INTELLIGENCE PICTURE

Although human intervention is always needed to provide the necessary element of domain knowledge and expertise, advances in text analytics capabilities help analysts by pre-sifting data.

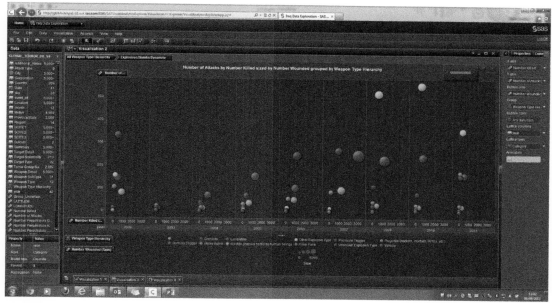

FIGURE 2.2

SAS visual analytics illustrating preferred attack types deployed by a terrorist cell and related casualties/deaths (2008–2011).

Sophisticated linguistic rules and statistical methods can evaluate text, minimizing inconsistency and ambiguity. The latest text analytics technology can automatically determine keywords and topics, categorize content, manage semantic terms, unearth sentiment, and put things into context. By applying text analytics, agencies can start to extract intelligence from unstructured data and turn it into a more structured format that can then be analyzed in conjunction with existing structured data.

This is a critical element of the Big Data processing cycle for agencies, because they can exploit all of the data they have, not just the structured content. As all investigators will highlight, often it is the text, such as witness descriptions, that contains the most valuable intelligence. It is all about approaching Big Data holistically with a full suite of capabilities to achieve the best results.

Advanced analytics extracts insights from Big Data, supporting the analyst beyond the ability just to ask specific questions or run specific queries. Multiple analytical techniques can be applied to large data volumes to uncover the key nuggets of intelligence (see Chapters 8 and 10–13).

Front end, operational technology also has a key role in addressing all of these issues and challenges. Investigators assigned to specific cases need to be working from a single integrated information technology (IT) platform that provides excellent visibility into all the critical information, eliminates double-entry, and provides a streamlined process workflow, helping save time and drive faster responses to threats.

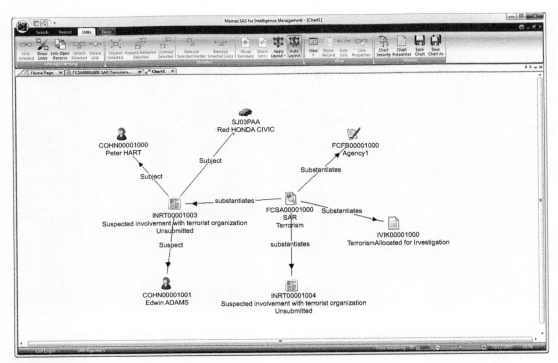

FIGURE 2.3

SAS for fusion centers: using link charts to visualize relationships between persons, vehicles, and information reports.

Agencies sharing information in a fusion center environment, for example, need to be able to search and exploit data effectively using analytic techniques and also to leverage technology to reveal patterns, anomalies, key variables, and relationships in the data, such as those shown in Figure 2.3, ultimately leading to new insights and better answers, faster.

They urgently require systems that present teams with the relevant information in one place and then allow them to use analytics to effectively pinpoint and evaluate the information that is critical to the case.

This is where providers such as SAS (SAS, 2014) can help deliver solutions that allow investigators to identify and share intelligence more effectively, analyze data, uncover hidden patterns and networks, and ultimately reduce threats.

It is critical that any system that is implemented be flexible enough to be tailored to fit an agency's operational processes, and not the other way around. One of the biggest risks and greatest hidden costs involved in the purchasing of any IT solution is the need to change existing processes to fit around a new system.

It is vital that the chosen system be able to be tailored on an ongoing basis to meet the changing and future needs of a particular organization. This ensures that the agency can mitigate risk by evolving and adapting to address new or emerging legislation, ultimately improving the overall return on investment.

EXAMPLES
SCENARIO 1: FUSION AND MICHIGAN STATE POLICE

The Michigan State Police (MSP) use SAS in support of statewide information sharing and to support the operations of the Michigan Intelligence Operations Center (MIOC).

The Michigan State Police Department is working closely with the Department of Homeland Security to establish the MIOC for Homeland Security in East Lansing, Michigan, with an operational node in the Detroit area. It is required that all MIOC personnel, regardless of physical location, have full access to MIOC software solutions.

The MIOC for Homeland Security provides information to patrol officers, detectives, management, and other participating personnel and agencies on specific criminals, crime groups, and criminal activity. The MIOC for Homeland Security supports antiterrorism and other crime-specific objectives by collecting, analyzing, and disseminating information to a number of communities of interest. The success of the MIOC for Homeland Security is based on the secure collection and sharing of criminal intelligence information among concerned partners within the state regardless of the type of threat.

Using the SAS solution for fusion centers, MIOC serves as the primary criminal intelligence processing system in the state of Michigan and provides access to over 600 law enforcement agencies as well as 21,300 certified police officers and numerous state and federal departments as they identify and prevent criminal acts directed toward citizens from both domestic and international threats.

Information can be provided on specific criminals, crime groups, and criminal activities, and criminal intelligence information can be shared among concerned partners within the state, regardless of the type of threat.

SCENARIO 2: NATIONAL SECURITY AND INTELLIGENCE SOLUTION IN THE MIDDLE EAST

Digital information was stored in databases on different unlinked systems with limited search capabilities, which meant that finding information was labor-intensive and time-consuming.

SAS provided an intelligence solution that migrated several national systems into one centralized security information warehouse. This provided a single unified view of information from different agencies including:

* Immigration data: 25 million records per year
* Policing: 9 million records per year
* Traffic, driver, and vehicle details: 20 million records per year
* Hotel reservations: 3 million records per year

This system proved particularly successful in identifying and tracking down suspects based on their hotel booking history. This National Security Agency now has a unified view of information from all participating agencies, reduced time needed to find information, improved response rate to threats, reduced training costs, and the ability to take in more information from further agencies in the future.

CONCLUSION

Faced with vast amounts of data in a variety of formats, agencies struggle to transform them into usable, consistent intelligence. They struggle to see the bigger picture because of information silos and a lack of analytical and visualization tools at their disposal.

However, agencies have become increasingly clear about the value of Big Data in preventing and solving crime and threats to national security. We have seen an ongoing shift in mindsets, in which data are increasingly seen as an opportunity rather than a problem, and the latest technologies are available now to enable agencies to start taking advantage of that opportunity.

Without the right tools, pinpointing relevant data in Big Data that might potentially be useful can be resource-intensive and unaffordable. With the right solutions, irrelevant information can be sifted out and areas of interest highlighted.

Today's latest analytics technologies enable faster, better decision making by improving analysis of the huge and ever-growing volume of data. The ability to scour Big Data using High Performance analytics and data management will become increasingly crucial in enabling intelligence professionals to reveal hidden insights and produce better decisions. A prerequisite for processing and analyzing all available information is the ability to extract it, preferably automatically, from many different sources and formats and to apply suitable data quality processes. The final step is then to use the insight gained in support of operational effectiveness.

REFERENCE

SAS, 2014. SAS the Power to Know. SAS, Cary, NC (Online). Available from: http://www.sas.com/en_us/home.html.

CORE CONCEPTS AND APPLICATION SCENARIOS

HARNESSING THE POWER OF BIG DATA TO COUNTER INTERNATIONAL TERRORISM

3

Andrew Staniforth, Babak Akhgar

INTRODUCTION

The United Kingdom (UK) has long been an island under siege from extremists who believe they can advance their aims through acts of violence. For over a century the British security apparatus of the state has prevented terrorist atrocities and has pursued those who wish to destroy its free and democratic way of life. Yet, although the UK has developed one of the world's most sophisticated counterterrorism architectures, successful terrorist attacks have occurred with alarming regularity.

The rapid developments that have been made to counterterrorism since the catastrophic events of September 11, 2001 in the United States (US) are unprecedented in the UK's long history of protecting the nation's security. As 9/11 marked the dawn of a new era of global terrorism, technological advancements in communications through the creation of the Internet, social media, and the volume of open source information changed—and continue to change—the very nature of terrorism. To respond to the immediacy of the terrorist threat, major cultural shifts in counterterrorism have taken place alongside societal views and attitudes toward national security. As a result, counterterrorism is no longer the hidden dimension of statecraft and has moved out of the shadows in recent years. While the British government has rightly made strides toward an increasingly open and public facing domestic security apparatus, the nature of counterterrorism remains enshrined in a preventative ethos.

To prevent terrorism and render visible what others do not want authorities to know, counterterrorism must be intelligence-led and so necessitates a covert approach. That being said, not all countermeasures need to be cloaked in secrecy for them to be effective, and the contemporary phase of counterterrorism has evolved important new trends alongside palpable moves toward expansion and localism. Countering terrorism today is a collaborative approach. No one single government agency or department can protect the nation from the diverse range of threats required to be tackled at home and overseas. Collaboration in counterterrorism was amplified after the discovery of the home-grown terrorist threat of embedded citizens living in UK communities, which served to challenge the traditional pursuit of terrorists and raised concerns as to whether the police and their intelligence agency partners had the capacity and capability to protect the public they serve. The severity of the post-9/11 terrorist threat prompted a relentless pursuit of information by intelligence and law enforcement agencies, who developed an increasing appetite for capturing unprecedented volumes of data—much of which was thrust upon them during the investigation of major counterterrorism operations. This chapter first examines the unique operational challenges faced by intelligence and law enforcement agencies during the early phases of tackling the post-9/11 terrorist threat. Exploring specific counterterrorism operations and the difficulties of progressing in multiple investigations while capturing increasingly large volumes of data highlights how the use of Big Data can support contemporary counterterrorism investigations.

A NEW TERROR

In 2003, Omar Khyam, a 24-year-old man from Crawley, West Sussex, began planning an ambitious terrorist attack in the UK. The scale and scope of his deadly and determined attack were unprecedented at the time and would stretch the UK's security apparatus to near the breaking point. Recruited and radicalized by the ideological rhetoric of Islamist extremists, Khyam led a small group of British citizens who sympathized with the Al Qaeda cause. The terrorist cell included his younger brother, 18-year-old Shujah Mahmood, as well as Jawad Akbar, aged 22, and Waheed Mahmood, aged 33. The four men, all from Crawley, shared Pakistani backgrounds; meetings in Britain over the conflict in Kashmir led them to become interested in the mujahedeen fighters in the disputed region (Summers and Casciani, 2007). Each man traveled to Pakistan to support jihadi groups and their armed campaigns, but the jihad was no longer just in Kashmir—it was in Afghanistan, too—and the Crawley terrorist cell, fuelled by the ideology promoted by Osama bin Laden, developed a deep antipathy toward the War on Terror. Frustrated with being unable to join the insurgency in Afghanistan and angry over the 2003 invasion of Iraq, Khyam and his cell members decided they should bring extreme jihadist violence to the streets of Britain (Summers and Casciani, 2007). To carry out a successful terrorist attack, Khyam knew that they would require military experience. In July 2003, to enhance the skills of the terrorist cell, Khyam helped organize a special secret training camp in which some of the group learned weapons and explosives skills (Cowan, 2006). The cell members mulled over several ideas for a terrorist attack in the UK, one of which was to poison the beer at a football stadium (Summers and Casciani, 2007). Another suggestion proposed targeting trains, pubs, and nightclubs in Britain. They discussed attacking the Bluewater shopping center in Kent, the Ministry of Sound nightclub in south London, and even National Grid to maximize economic damage. The terrorist cell's ambitions were limited only by their individual and collective macabre creativity, but in November 2003 they settled on delivering indiscriminate mass murder by detonating a huge bomb.

FERTILIZER PLOT

The Khyam-led terror cell conducted successful early experiments with a small explosive device composed of 1.5 kg of ammonium nitrate fertilizer. This experiment convinced the group that a much larger device could be used (Summers and Casciani, 2007). The cell then purchased 600 kg of ammonium nitrate (Summers and Casciani, 2007). Fertilizer has long been a constituent part of homemade explosives used by paramilitary militant groups around the world with devastating results. More important, ammonium nitrate–based fertilizer bombs had been used by the Irish Republican Army in the UK; as an essential component part of the device, it was openly available in large quantities. The terrorist conspirators stored the industrial-sized bag of agricultural fertilizer at a self-storage unit in Hanwell, West London (Sampson and Staniforth, 2012). Unbeknownst to the plotters, diligent staff at the depot had become suspicious and alerted the police. A major covert terrorist investigation was launched under the code name Operation CREVICE.

The Security Service (MI5) had already developed a keen interest in the activities of Khyam because of his suspected links to an Al Qaeda sympathizer working in both Britain and Pakistan (news.bbc.co, 1538). However, it was the call from a member of the public at the storage facility that provided the evidence to UK authorities that a significant terrorist plot was being planned. As part of the major covert terrorist investigation, the police and Security Service decided to replace the ammonium nitrate with an identical but harmless substance. This action successfully served to remove the imminent threat to the public. So long as it only contained an inert substance, no explosive device could be detonated, but investigators knew that it was only a matter of time before the terrorist cell would uncover the result of their covert actions. The removal of the key component part of the bomb provided valuable time to gather intelligence on the terrorist cells links with Al Qaeda, the extent of their network, and the exact location of the intended bombing. To support the operation, listening devices were placed in several of the defendants' homes and a vehicle, which provided detailed surveillance coverage of the terrorists' activities. The Security Service and the police then watched and waited for the plot to unfold, gathering both intelligence and evidence to secure the terrorists' conviction at court.

INTERNATIONAL DIMENSION

Investigations soon revealed that a larger terrorist cell network existed beyond the core group from Crawley. New plotters had been identified, including Anthony Garcia, age 27, from Ilford, Essex, Nabeel Hussain, aged 20, from Horley, Surrey, and Salahuddin Amin, aged 30, from Luton, Bedfordshire. In addition, on the other side of the Atlantic, Mohammed Junaid Babar, a 31-year-old Pakistani-born US citizen, was identified as part of the CREVICE cell conspirators (Cowan, 2006). With a melancholy irony that is all too familiar to terrorist investigators, it would later be revealed that Babar had flown to Afghanistan to fight against the Americans several days after 9/11, even though his mother had been caught up in the 9/11 World Trade Center attack (Cowan, 2006). She had escaped from the first of the Twin Towers where she worked, when it was hit by Al Qaeda suicide bombers. Operation CREVICE revealed that Babar had traveled first to London, where he stayed for three or four days before traveling to Pakistan, where he met members of the Crawley-based terrorist cell. Another terrorist plotter, Canadian Mohammed Momin Khawaja, aged 29, from Ottawa, was also identified. Khawaja was assisting the terrorist plot by designing a remote-control detonator for the fertilizer-based device (News, 2008). The discovery of Khawaja and Babar added a new trans-Atlantic dimension for the operatives investigating Operation CREVICE. New information was discovered from the intrusive surveillance of Jawad Akbar's home in Uxbridge, West London, on February 22, 2004 (Laville, 2006). During a conversation with cell leader Khyam, Babar appeared to suspect that they were under surveillance, saying, "Bruv, you do not think this place is bugged, do you?" "No, I do not think this place is bugged, bruv," replied Khyam (Laville, 2006). During the recording Akbar suggested that the Ministry of Sound nightclub in London would be a soft target, saying, "What about easy stuff where you do not need no experience and nothing, and you could get a job, yeah, like for example the biggest nightclub in central London where no one can even turn round and say 'Oh they were innocent,' those slags dancing around?" (Laville, 2006). Akbar later suggested that the UK nightclubs and bars were "really, really big," asking his fellow conspirators, "Trust me, then you will get the public talking yeah, yeah … if you went for the social structure where every Tom, Dick, and Harry goes on a Saturday night, yeah, that would be crazy, crazy thing, man" (Laville, 2006). Khyam stated, "The explosion in the clubs, yeah, that's fine, bro, that's not a problem. The training for that is available … to get them into the Ministry of Sound really isn't difficult" (Laville, 2006). During the recorded conversation the men also discussed the use of terror in the jihad. Akbar stated, "I still agree with you on the point that terror is the best way and even the *Qur'an* says it, isn't it?" (Laville, 2006).

As the plotters advanced their preparations, the police and Security Service operatives monitored their activities as part of a long game, waiting for the moment to move to executive action and arrest the cell members. Significant amounts of data were now being collected by MI5 and police investigative teams. The rich mix of open source information and covert intelligence data, all of which needed to be recorded, assessed, prioritized, and acted upon, was unprecedented in its volume for a single counterterrorism operation that now had international dimensions.

EXECUTIVE ACTION

During late March 2004, the Security Service and police were forced to bring Operation CREVICE into its final phase. Information had been gained by staff at the storage facility, who reported that Khyam had mentioned he would not require storage after the end of March. This piece of information led authorities to the natural conclusion that the ammonium nitrate was to be moved either to another location for longer-term storage or as part of the final construction of the bomb (Summers and Casciani, 2007). In either case, the risks presented to the public and the ongoing covert investigation outweighed whatever gains could be made through further extending the operation. On March 29, the members of the terrorist cell were arrested. A further terrorist plotter, Khawaja was arrested in Ottawa, Canada, and Amin was later detained in Pakistan.

The executive action phase of Operation CREVICE provided compelling evidence of the reach of contemporary terrorist investigations: A new era had dawned. What had started in the town of Crawley had quickly spread across several continents. In total, approximately 700 police officers from five separate police forces were engaged in a series of raids, again showing the extensive resources required to bring modern terrorist suspects to justice. At the commencement of the CREVICE plotters' trial at the Old Bailey in London in March 2006, Khyam, Mahmood, Akbar, Waheed Mahmood, Garcia, Hussain, and Amin all denied conspiracy to cause explosions in the UK. Khyam, Garcia, and Hussain denied possessing 600 kg of ammonium nitrate fertilizer for terrorist purposes, whereas Khyam and Shujah Mahmood denied having aluminum powder, a key component part in the development of a fertilizer-based bomb. Although the attack planned by Khyam would not have realized the mass casualties of the Al Qaeda Planes Operation of 9/11, the British plot to build a massive bomb from fertilizer nevertheless could have resulted in hundreds of deaths. Expert analysis of the kind of weapon that the convicted conspirators were making revealed that it could have led to a repeat of previous large-scale terrorist attacks. Professor Alan Hatcher, a former military bomb disposal expert, revealed that "If they had got it right, it would have been catastrophic" (Summers, 2007). According to Professor Hatcher, the CREVICE cell had all the ingredients for a crude but effective bomb. Mixed with other ingredients including aluminum powder and sugar, 600 kg of ammonium nitrate fertilizer, purchased from an agricultural merchant in Sussex, would have made a deadly device with devastating power if used in a crowded area (Summers, 2007). The Central Criminal Court also heard from Gary Smart, the general manager of the Ministry of Sound night club in London. He told the court that if the packed club were attacked, "It is clear that the consequences could be devastating. With such a large number of people in such a confined space, the impact could result in loss of life, injury, or structural damage" (Laville, 2006).

VULNERABILITIES EMERGE

Despite the operational challenges and complexities of a yearlong trial, Omar Khyam was found guilty of conspiring to cause explosions likely to endanger life between January 1, 2003 and March 31, 2004. Also convicted were Waheed Mahmood, Jawad Akbar, Salahuddin Amin, and Anthony Garcia. In passing sentence, the judge, Sir Michael Astill, told the five convicted men, "You have betrayed this country that has given you every opportunity. All of you may never be released. It's not a foregone conclusion" (Summers and Casciani, 2007). Two other men, Nabeel Hussain and Shujah Mahmood, were found not guilty. The jury deliberated for 27 days, a record in British criminal history. Outside the Old Bailey, the solicitor for Nabeel Hussain read a statement on his client's behalf, which said, "I have always maintained my innocence of the allegations against me. I have never been an extremist or believed in extremism. I am so glad this ordeal is over" (Summers and Casciani, 2007). In October 2008, in a packed Ottawa courtroom in Canada, Mohammed Momin Khawaja was found guilty on five charges of financing and facilitating terrorism related to building a remote-control device to trigger the CREVICE bombers' fertilizer explosive. The terrorism charges against Khawaja were the first laid under Canada's Anti-Terrorism Act introduced in the wake of 9/11. At the time of his arrest for his part of the CREVICE plot, Khawaja was a software developer for Canada's Foreign Affairs Department. He pleaded not guilty but Ontario Supreme Court Justice Douglas Rutherford concluded that proof that he was working actively with the Crawley-based group could be found in the evidence, which included intercepted e-mails, a trip for training in Pakistan, and money transfers. Justice Rutherford wrote in his judgment that "Momin Khawaja was aware of the group's purposes and whether he considered them terrorism or not, he assisted the group in many ways in the pursuit of its terrorist objective. It matters not whether any terrorist activity was actually carried out" (News, 2008).

Operation CREVICE was truly a landmark case in the development of counterterrorism investigation and prosecution in the UK. At that time, it was the largest and most complex counterterrorism investigation ever conducted by UK authorities. Operation CREVICE had achieved its strategic aim of protecting the public from harm, putting terrorists in prison after due legal process. Despite a successful outcome, the sheer mass of information obtained during the investigation presented its own challenges to authorities. Unbeknownst to intelligence and law enforcement agencies at the time, if subjected to rigorous review and follow-up, the volume of information captured during Operation CREVICE would have revealed early signs and indicators of future threats to public safety. They were threats—with the benefit of hindsight—that were not assessed, prioritized, or followed on the radar of UK security forces, and as a result, they were not fed into the broader national threat assessment picture. While understanding the demands placed on authorities to protect the public from a new and severe form of terror with finite resources, the collection of increased amounts of information began to expose vulnerabilities in the capacity and capability of the counterterrorism apparatus to effectively exploit large volumes of existing data recorded on their systems.

ASSESSING THE THREAT

Once the UK's intelligence machinery of government had positively identified the domestic terrorist threat in 2003, it quickly responded to it. Operation CREVICE in particular had forestalled an attack that was intended to cause mass casualties (News, 2008). For the first time in the history of the Security Service, the Director General was invited to a meeting of the full cabinet in April 2004 to be personally congratulated by Prime Minister Tony Blair (News, 2008). Much work needed to be done to better understand the potency and potential longevity of the Islamist terrorist threat in the UK, but investigations of several Islamist groups in May 2005 had concluded that none were actively planning an attack (Andrew, 2009). The Joint Terrorism Analysis Centre (JTAC), established in 2003 to assess the threat from international terrorism, had reported that "We judge at present there is no group with both the current intent and the capability to attack the UK" (Intelligence and Security Committee, 2006). In addition, a JTAC report on the terrorist threat to UK rail and underground networks, which was issued to the transport sector in May 2005, summarized the threat on its front page as follows: "Rail and underground networks have been attractive targets to terrorists worldwide; Madrid attacks offer inspiration for further attacks against rail networks; attacks on UK rail networks feature highly in terrorists' menu of options; but there is no suggestion of a current threat to UK rail or underground" (Intelligence and Security Committee, 2006). Given the information available at the time, JTAC decided to reduce the UK threat level from Severe General to Substantial, although the accompanying report that outlined the reasons for the reduction in the threat level suggested that Substantial continued to "represent a high level of threat" and that it was possible "that there was current UK attack planning of which it was unaware" (Intelligence and Security Committee, 2006). The JTAC report also explicitly warned that an attack "might well be mounted" without warning (Intelligence and Security Committee, 2006). Despite the cautionary assessment from JTAC about unknown attacks, it appeared that the combined efforts of the UK security forces, at home and overseas, had managed to curb the vaulting ambitions of British citizens inspired by the ideology of Al Qaeda.

While the imminence of a threat from homegrown terrorists appeared faintly, if at all, on the radar of intelligence agencies after the national threat level was downgraded, 2005 was already proving to be a busy period for those engaged in policing and protecting national security. In the beginning of July, the G8 Summit at Gleneagles in Scotland was well under way. One of the largest police operations the UK had ever undertaken was proving successful as a direct result of many months of planning and preparing to meet the challenges of potential terrorist and extremist threats. The world's most powerful and influential heads of state had gathered to discuss a variety of world issues, including poverty in Africa and rising debt among Third World countries. This latter issue became center stage for the summit, resulting in a massive demonstration of 250,000 people on the streets of Edinburgh in support of the Make Poverty History campaign. Despite the operational challenges and potential for extremist or terrorist attacks, the new Deputy Director General of the Security Service, Jonathan Evans, who had been appointed in February 2005, recalled how by that stage it had so far "been a quiet week" (Andrew, 2009). On the July 6, the International Olympic Committee announced that the 2012 Olympics Games would be staged in London. Members of the public and supporters of the London Olympic bid, who had gathered at Trafalgar Square, cheered as the news was broadcast live on large screens across the capitol. Celebrations continued well into the nigh, and Prime Minister Tony Blair expressed his gratitude for the work and dedication of the team engaged in bringing the Olympics to London.

This was the celebratory backdrop when many Britons (and Londoners in particular) awoke the following morning, Thursday, July 7. The newspapers and other news media carried stories and photographs of the previous day's celebrations. Early morning rush hour in London had started as normal. There were some delays to the Underground, including on the Northern line, but nothing unusual to report (House of Commons, 2005). Later that morning news would reach the emergency services of an unfolding national critical incident, a crisis of such profound magnitude that it would shape the way in which the actions of government would protect its citizens from future terrorist attacks. It would also prove to be the worst atrocity in the nation's capital since the Blitzkrieg of the Third Reich during World War II.

SUICIDE TERROR

On the morning of July 7, 2005, four young men, described by others as looking as if they were going on a camping holiday, boarded a train form Luton to London (Sampson and Staniforth, 2012). This tight-knit group was in fact British Al Qaeda-inspired suicide bombers, making their final preparations to deliver a deadly attack that had been secretly planned beneath the radar of the sprawling UK counterterrorism intelligence machinery. The train from Luton arrived at London King's Cross station at 8:23 AM, slightly late owing to a delay ahead of them on the rail network. At 8:36 AM, the four young men, Mohammed Siddique Khan (aged 30), Shehzad Tanweer (aged 22), Jermaine Lindsay (aged 19), and Hasib Hussain (aged 18) departed the train and were captured on closed-circuit television cameras on the concourse close to the Thameslink platform, heading in the direction of the London Underground system (Staniforth, 2009). A few moments later, at around 8:30 AM, they were seen hugging each other. They appeared happy, even euphoric (Sampson and Staniforth, 2012). They then split up, each carrying an estimated 2–5 kg of homemade explosives in their rucksacks (House of Commons, 2005). The time had come to break the fraternal bond of their terrorist cell and execute their individual contributions to a deadly coordinated attack.

From their movements at this time, it appears that north, south, east, and west coordinated strikes were planned. This calculated attack seems to have been clearly designed to maximize destruction and chaos amid the 3.4 million passenger journeys made on the London Underground every day (tfl.gov. uk). At 8:50 AM, the Eastbound Circle Line train boarded by Tanweer and packed with commuters exploded (House of Commons, 2005). Forensic evidence suggested that Tanweer was sitting toward the back of the second carriage with the rucksack next to him on the floor (House of Commons, 2005). When he detonated the device, the blast killed eight people including Tanweer himself and injured a further 171 innocent members of the public. At Edgware Road, Khan was also in the second carriage from the front, most likely near the standing area by the first set of double doors (House of Commons, 2005). He was probably also seated with the bomb next to him on the floor. Shortly before the explosion, Khan was seen fiddling with the top of the rucksack. The explosion from the homemade explosives killed seven people including Khan and injured a further 163. On the Piccadilly Line, Lindsay was in the first carriage as it traveled between King's Cross and Russell Square. It is unlikely that he was seated on the crowded train, which had 127 people in the first carriage alone (HM Government, 2012). Forensic evidence suggested that the explosion from the rucksack device occurred on or close to the floor of the standing area between the second and third set of seats (Staniforth, 2009). The most devastating of the blasts on the morning of July 7, this killed 27 people including Lindsay, leaving a further 340 people injured. On the Northern line the explosive device of Hussain failed to detonate. He left the London Underground at King's Cross station and soon boarded a number 30 bus traveling eastward from Marble Arch. This bus was crowded after the closures on the Underground caused by the other attacks. Hussain sat on the upper deck, toward the back. Forensic evidence suggested that the bomb was next to him in the aisle or between his feet on the floor (Staniforth, 2009). A man fitting Hussain's description was seen on the lower deck earlier, fiddling repeatedly with his rucksack (Staniforth, 2009). At 9:47 AM, the bus was diverted down Tavistock Square, when Hussain detonated the rucksack device, killing 14 people. Within just 57 minutes, 52 innocent lives were lost and 784 people were injured. Four otherwise unremarkable British citizens, inspired by Al Qaeda, had managed to deliver an attack of military proportions in the middle of the nation's capital. The attack was undetected by all of the state's security apparatus in operation at that time, leaving the public and those in authority asking what more could have been done to prevent the attack.

JOINING THE DOTS

The Security Service mounted their response to the 7/7 bombings under Operation STEPFORD, which soon discovered that it had previously encountered two of the suicide bombers, Mohammed Siddique Khan and Shezhad Tawneer, on the periphery of its investigation into Operation CREVICE (Sampson and Staniforth, 2012). MI5 also discovered that it had on record a telephone number that, it was able to identify after (but not before) the attacks as that of a third suicide bomber, Lindsay (Andrew, 2009). There were no Security Service traces for Hussain. According to MI5, the first evidence of Khan's involvement was discovered on Saturday July 9, when credit cards in his name were found at the sites of the two attacks (Andrew, 2009). Subsequent investigations by MI5 revealed that Khan and Tanweer had visited Pakistan in 2003 and spent several months there with Tanweer in the winter of 2004–5, probably in contact with Al Qaeda, planning and training for the 7/7 attacks (Andrew, 2009).

At midday on Friday, July 8, Home Secretary Charles Clarke visited MI5 headquarters at Thames House and seemed impressed by the early stages of Operation STEPFORD (Andrew, 2009). After meetings with ministers, Director General Manningham-Buller told her senior MI5 colleagues that evening that Tony Blair and Charles Clarke were "onside, not keen on knee-jerk responses, not witch-hunting and keen to let the police and MI5 get on with the job" (Andrew, 2009). She had also told Security Service personnel in the Thames House restaurant earlier that day that, "What happened on Thursday is what we've feared, been warning about, and have worked so hard to prevent. We were shocked by the horror but, while we had no intelligence that could have prevented it, not surprised" (Sampson and Staniforth, 2012).

The events of 7/7 and the post-incident investigation conducted by the police and MI5 had a profound impact on contemporary counterterrorism practice. Yet, more than five years after the attacks, the British public had yet to learn how their fellow citizens had died and whether departments of the state and the emergency response could have prevented their deaths.

HELD TO ACCOUNT

In the capacity of Assistant Deputy Coroner for Inner West London, from October 11, 2010 to March 3, 2011, Right Honorable Lady Justice Hallet heard the evidence in the inquest touching the deaths of the 52 members of the public who were killed as a result of four suicide bombs. In the coroner's report published on May 6, 2011, Hallet LJ stated that "I sat without a jury and have given verdicts of unlawful killing, with the medical cause of deaths recorded as 'injuries caused by an explosion' in respect of each deceased" (HM Government, 2012). On March 11, 2011, Hallet LJ announced in public that her report would be submitted under Rule 43 of the Coroner's Act 1984. She was satisfied that the evidence she had heard gave rise to a concern that circumstances creating a risk of other deaths would occur or continue to exist in the future, and she was of the opinion that action should be taken to prevent its re-occurrence or continuation. In the light of her conclusion, Hallet LJ made nine recommendations to the authorities that had the power to take action. The nine recommendations provided lessons to be learned from the events of that morning in July. No crisis should be wasted in terms of organizational learning and development to improve responses to terrorist events of such magnitude. It was not until the close of the 7/7 inquest that a full and accurate picture emerged, which served to highlight the full scale of the challenges that emergency first responders and the states national security apparatus confronted in what is now recognized as a new era of public accountability and professional responsibility. The coroner found that none of the victims died because of the delays in the emergency response, but improvements in communication were needed between transport executives and the emergency services during a crisis (Dodd, 2011).

The 7/7 inquest also focused on UK law enforcement and intelligence agencies efforts to prevent coordinated suicide attacks. Although the coroner found that MI5 could not have prevented the attacks, she used her statutory powers to recommend that they must learn from and act on the lessons arising from the inquest. The first of two recommendations for the Security Service concerned undercover photographs taken before the 7/7 attacks of the Al Qaeda cell ringleader from Leeds, Mohammad Sidique Khan. The Security Service had denied that it had in its possession sufficient intelligence to assess Khan as a serious threat or danger to the public before he martyred himself on July 7. Surveillance images of Khan and one of his suicide cell members, Shehzad Tanweer, were obtained by MI5 in February 2004 as part of the investigation under Operation CREVICE. In April 2004, copies of the images were sent to the US. The second recommendation for MI5 that resulted from the inquest concerned how the Security Service prioritized the level of threat posed by terrorist suspects and the records it kept and how it reached those decisions. Hallet LJ found confusion about the level of priority given by MI5 to investigate Khan, but crucially refrained from criticizing the Security Service for not treating him as more of a threat. She did, however, find that inadequate recording of decisions risked "dire consequences" if potential errors could not be picked up by supervisors at MI5 (HM Government, 2012).

The 7/7 inquest had called the Security Service to account in a way that reflected a new era of public scrutiny of the state's security forces. As the main domestic partner of MI5 in pursuing terrorists, the police service was also called on to provide details of its knowledge, awareness, and actions in preventing terrorism before the tragic events of 7/7. The high volume of counterterrorism operations being conducted in the post-9/11 era brought pressure upon state security forces to prioritize their efforts against the resources they had available. As a result, many new dots were found but they were never joined. Associates would drift in and out of major operations and many would be acquaintances remaining on the periphery of investigations, whereas many more would in fact have nothing to do with terrorism and would not be the primary subjects of the operations being conducted at the time. The links between Khan and the key conspirators of Operation CREVICE more than a year before 7/7 presented new challenges. In 2008, Lord Carlile of Berriew Q.C., then Independent Reviewer of Terrorism Legislation, stated, "The reality that violent Jihadists all over the world are working together against the established order, and that with rare exceptions there are links of some kind to weave all the terrorist cells into an international destructive tapestry, is well argued" (Staniforth, 2009). In January 2009, Security Service Director General Jonathan Evans publicly acknowledged that "if another attack took place, the Security Service would probably discover, as after 7/7, that some of the terrorists responsible were already on its books. But the fact that we know of an individual and the fact that they have had some association with extremists doesn't mean we are going to be indefinitely in a position to be confident about everything that they are doing, because we have to prioritize" (Andrew, 2009).

The lessons of 7/7 and the recommendations arising from the coroner's report remain vital for the continued development of public safety and accountability. The security apparatus of the state had done everything in its power to protect its citizens from terrorist attack, but it was clear that it held information in its systems that could have supported the early identification of and possible further investigation into the 7/7 terrorist cell.

STRATEGIC APPROACH

At the time of the catastrophic terrorist attack in the US on September 11, 2001, the UK government, like the US and many other countries in the developed world, had no sophisticated or coherent cross-departmental strategy to counter international terrorism. In short, the UK had no plan to institute of any rigor that would have been able to effectively respond to a major Al Qaeda indiscriminate attack. Of course, the UK security apparatus had memories of the long counterterrorist campaign in Northern Ireland to draw upon and the foundations that had been laid down in terms of a corpus of emergency terrorism legislation on the statute book. Throughout the history of counterterrorism practice in the UK, collaboration between government departments had been key to the success of many operations, and the intelligence community had learned the value of close cooperation with the police service. Nevertheless, the characteristics of violent jihadist terrorism, with its vaulting ambitions, strident ideology, and disregard for civilian casualties—indeed for all human life, with adherents prepared to give their lives in their attacks— represented new challenges for Parliament and public, government and law enforcement alike.

In the immediate aftermath of 9/11, the Cabinet Office in London initiated work on developing a comprehensive national counterterrorism strategy called CouNter-TErrorism STratgy (CONTEST). Mapped within CONTEST were four pillars, which became known as the 4Ps: Pursue, to stop terrorists attacks; *Prevent*, to stop people becoming terrorists, or supporting violent extremists; *Protect*, to strengthen protection against terrorist attack; and *Prepare*, to mitigate an attack's impact when it cannot be stopped. The strategy that emerged from this work had a clear strategic aim: "to make it possible for society to maintain conditions of normality so that people could go about their normal business, freely and with confidence, even in the face of suicidal terrorist attacks" (Omand, 2010). The conditions "freely, and with confidence" were an important reminder to seek security in ways that uphold British values, such as liberty and freedom under the law. The strategy was later presented to the Cabinet and adopted in 2003, but the details remained confidential and were not published by the government until 2006. An updated version, CONTEST 2, was published in 2009, and a third generation, CONTEST 3, was published in 2011 by the coalition government.

In developing the four-pillar structure of CONTEST, the Cabinet Office believed that the strategy was easily understood as a logical narrative, translated into specific programs of action across government, the private sector, and the voluntary sector, and as has been shown, capable of being updated and extended in response to developments in the threats and in our technologies for countering them. It was important that the complexities of such a wide-ranging strategy were simplified and focused because successful delivery would depend on a joint approach and the strength of partnerships. The creation of CONTEST as an overarching public strategy has given clarity and direction to all agencies and provided the framework with which separate organizations can allocate resources and assets for a combined effect. As CONTEST developed, additional focus was on the principles of the 4P's. The structure of CONTEST enables Prevent and Pursue to focus on the actual human threat from terrorists, designed to reduce the risk by stopping them, whereas Protect and Prepare focus on the capacity and capability of the UK to reduce vulnerability to attacks when they occur. By simultaneously tackling areas to reduce te risk and minimize vulnerability, this approach collectively serves to reduce the threat.

The development of Prevent reveals an important element of counterterrorism practice in the UK: that the public, often the victim of terrorist attacks, can help prevent them, but to do so it need to be informed and kept updated so that all can work together toward shared values of freedom, tolerance, democracy, and human rights. The immediacy and the diversity of the post-9/11 threats brought about a series of fresh challenges. At the core of many of the changes required to tackle Al Qaeda-inspired terrorism was the problematic shift to the preemption or interception of terrorism. This was a shift necessitated by the suicidal component of terrorist tactics demonstrated during 7/7, a shift that had far-reaching implications for national security, and in particular for the police service. The policing of political violence—traditionally categorized as intelligence-led and politically sensitive—had historically generated structures that had been remote, secretive, and specialist. Yet the contemporary evolution of terrorism had spawned important new trends and demanded a new policing response. Contemporary terrorism now involved embedded citizens as much as foreign extremists. Although that phenomenon may not have been new to other parts of the world, it certainly represented a significant change in Britain. As a direct result, concepts such as community involvement, multi-agency working and public assurance—now widely accepted and practiced in local policing—were to migrate into the policing of political violence. All police officers, not just specialist counterterrorism officers, therefore had to share in the tasks. Counterterrorism policing thus became a matter for all in the police, for all of their strategic partners, and for all of the public. Empowering partners, stakeholders, and communities themselves to assist in the fight against terrorism significantly increased the amount of information being gathered by authorities. Combined with increasing use of the Internet and social media and the development of smart mobile communications, the impact on terrorism and the measures deployed to counter it were profound.

CHANGING THREAT LANDSCAPE

The Internet has changed, and continues to change, the very nature of terrorism. The Internet is well-suited to the nature of terrorism and the psyche of the terrorist. In particular, the ability to remain anonymous makes the Internet attractive to the terrorist plotter. Terrorists use the Internet to propagate their ideologies, motives, and grievances. The most powerful and alarming change for modern terrorism, however, has been its effectiveness for attracting new terrorist recruits, often the young and most vulnerable and impressionable in our societies. Modern terrorism has rapidly evolved, becoming increasingly nonphysical, with vulnerable homegrown citizens being recruited, radicalized, trained, and tasked online in the virtual and ungoverned domain of cyberspace. With the increasing number of citizens putting more of their lives online, the interconnected and globalized world in which we live provides an extremely large pool of potential candidates to draw into the clutches of disparate terrorists groups and networks.

The openness and freedom of the Internet unfortunately supports self-radicalization: the radicalization of individuals without direct input or encouragement from others. The role of the internet in both radicalization and recruitment into terrorist organizations remains a growing source of concern for security authorities. This concern was amplified as a new global threat from the Islamic State (IS) emerged in 2014. The violent progress of IS through towns and villages in Iraq had been swift, aided by foreign fighters from Britain. During the summer of 2014, IS gained control of large swathes of Iraq, leading Prime

Minister David Cameron to warn his Cabinet that violent IS jihadists were planning attacks on British soil (Staniforth, 2014a). The warning came amid growing concerns among senior security officials that the number of Britons leaving the UK to fight alongside extremist groups abroad was rising.

The export of British-born violent jihadists is nothing new, but the call to arms in Iraq this time had been amplified by a slick online recruitment campaign urging Muslims from across the world to join the fight and to post messages of support for IS. The rise in the UK threat level from Substantial to Severe in September 2014 was supported by figures published from the Channel program of the Association of Chief Police Officers, which seeks to support individuals who may be vulnerable to violent extremism. The Channel program had seen a 58% rise in referrals during 2013, dealing with 1,281 people in 2013–14, up from 748 the previous year (Staniforth, 2014a).

In a chilling online recruitment video designed to lure jihadists to Iraq, 20-year-old Nasser Muthana, a medical student from Cardiff, and his 17-year-old brother Aseel, declared their support for IS. In the video, Nasser states, "We understand no borders. We have participated in battles in Syria, and in a few days we will go to Iraq and will fight with them" (Staniforth, 2014a). Nasser attained 12 General Certificates of Secondary Education at grade A, studied for his A levels, and was offered places to enroll for medicine degrees at four UK universities the previous September, but instead he volunteered to swell the ranks of the Al Qaeda-inspired IS. Unbeknownst to his parents or the authorities, the former school council member and his younger brother, who was studying A levels at the time, traveled to Syria via Turkey to fight the Assad regime. Recognizing the early signs and potential indicators of radicalization development remains a challenge for the police, partners, the public, and parents. The father of the brothers-in-arms fighting for IS, Mr Muthana, declared no knowledge of their intended travel plans to Syria and had reported them missing to the police in November 2013 (Staniforth, 2014a). Mr Muthana was devastated that his sons had turned to violent extremism, stating that "Both my sons have been influenced by outsiders, I do not know by whom. Nasser is a calm boy, very bright and a high achiever." He went on to say that "He loved rugby, playing football, and going camping with friends. But he has been got at and has left his home and everyone who loves him" (Staniforth, 2014b).

The Internet allows individuals to find people with shared views and values and to access information to support their radical beliefs and ideas. The unregulated and ungoverned expanse of the Internet knows no geographical boundaries, thus creating a space for radical activists to connect across the globe. This is especially problematic because easy access to like-minded people helps to normalize radical ideas such as the use of violence to solve grievances. Yet, it is impossible and well beyond the scope of any single government to solve the issue of radicalization by simple processes, such as the suggestion to clean up the Internet. Whereas the Internet provides a vital communication tool for terrorists, it has equally provided intelligence and law enforcement agencies with prime sources of evidence and intelligence about what terrorists are thinking and planning; but the full potential of the Internet, social media, and smart mobile communications has yet to be harnessed by those engaged in preventing terrorism and violent extremism.

EMBRACING BIG DATA

Recent developments in UK counterterrorism practices provide evidence of the operational reality in responding to the full range of contemporary terrorist threats. Modern counterterrorism is complex and investigators require all the help and support they can muster to keep communities safe from violent extremists. Although major steps have been taken to strengthen counterterrorism responses, the exploitation of open source information and the prioritization of intelligence already captured remain real operational challenges. With the addition of a new era of public responsibility and accountability, security officials would be well advised to put current counterterrorism practices under the microscope to examine how, moving forward, the counterterrorism machinery of the state can effectively harness the power of the Internet, social media, and associated smart mobile communications. The challenges for UK counterterrorism authorities identified thus far specifically relate to increasing volumes of data. This has presented practical difficulties in appropriately resourcing analytical capacity and capability, but the volume of data it represents fades into insignificance compared with what is termed "Big Data."

"Big Data" is the term applied to large and complex datasets that come from many sources such as financial transactions, social media, and Internet searches, and has many applications especially within intelligence management and analytics for law enforcement agencies (CENTRIC, 2014). Big Data represents the greatest opportunity to increase the effective delivery of counterterrorism. Big Data analytics can help identify terrorist networks and their associations using open source intelligence (OSINT) combined with traditional intelligence sources (see Chapter 1). It can also rapidly support the identification of radical roots within online communities using capabilities such as social media analysis to identify informal networks, emerging topics, influencers, links between individuals, groups, or concepts, and sentiment analysis (see Chapters 10, 11, and 13). In essence, Big Data analytics can concurrently channel the intelligence and knowledge requirements for the Prevent, Pursue, Protect, and Prepare pillars of the CONTEST counterterrorism strategy in a coherent and holistic manner.

Using the strategic intelligence model of Akhgar et al. (Akhgar et al., 2013) for national security (i.e., assessment of threats in a proactive manner through knowledge-based decision making processes and holistic risk assessment) allows the creation of a high-level canonical set of requirements toe realize and implement Big Data analytics. The potentials for law enforcement agencies and security services in the context of CONTEST strategy can be summarized as:

1. Development of a unified Big Data vision across the national security apparatus
2. Definition of Big Data analytics capabilities for the concurrent realization of CONTEST pillars' objectives. This includes a national Big Data strategy and a technology agnostic deployment methodology.
3. Scoping the integration between OSINT and traditional data sources (e.g., imagery intelligence and human intelligence)
4. Implementation of a knowledge architecture and data models for proactive monitoring and reactive response capabilities (e.g., gaining intelligence to prevent radicalization and disrupt terrorist attacks)
5. Building holistic deployment processes and infrastructure (e.g., legal and ethical procedures, return on investment on Big Data in terms of operational effectiveness and cost saving, key performance indicators, training, software and hardware capabilities)

The set of high-level requirements to realize and implement Big Data analytics for law enforcement ensures that the use of Big Data is fully embraced throughout the apparatus, architecture, and operational activities for tackling terrorism. The requirements serve to augment all efforts across the national security landscape to maximize the potential of Big Data analytics by providing an agreed-upon, shared, and coherent program that will rapidly increase the effectiveness of counterterrorism operations.

CONCLUSION

Throughout the history of UK counterterrorism practice, shocking and dramatic incidents at home and abroad have only served to deepen the resolve of the government to develop and strengthen its response. The tragic events of 9/11 and 7/7 provided the genesis for developing a stronger and more sophisticated approach to counterterrorism designed to meet the future challenges of an unpredictable world. Yet beyond resolute determination, such events must instill a re-dedication to preparedness so that new ways of working can be identified; practitioners push the boundaries of counterterrorism practice beyond the current state of the art; and most important, all in authority can embed progressive developments to ensure that the primary driver for change in counterterrorism practice is not simply the next successful attack.

The discovery of the homegrown terrorist threat has challenged the traditional pursuit of terrorists. The British government now seeks to ensure that mechanisms are in place to be able to draw on the valuable information and goodwill of communities from which aberrant extremists are recruited and radicalized. A major shift toward harnessing the capacity of the public and open source information to support the broader counterterrorism effort has been an important development in recent years. Such developments need to continue apace, and the full impact of Big Data on counterterrorism practices, focusing on the ability to better deliver safety and security to the public, must be further explored. In times of financial recession and austerity, the financial efficiency savings of Big Data opportunities must also be considered.

Harnessing the power of Big Data presents a unique opportunity to keep one step ahead of terrorist adversaries, but seamless integration and application to current counterterrorism practices also present numerous challenges. The handling of such large datasets raises acute concerns regarding existing storage capacity, together with the ability to share and analyze large volumes of data. The introduction of Big Data capabilities will require the rigorous review of existing intelligence models and associated processes to ensure counterterrorism practitioners have the tools to tackle terrorists using the power of Big Data analytics.

Although Big Data presents many opportunities, any developments to tackle terrorism in this arena will have to be guided by the state's relationship with its citizenry and the law. In the post-Snowden era, which has revealed the extent of state surveillance, citizens remain cautious and suspicious of access to their online data. Any damage to public trust is counterproductive to contemporary counterterrorism practices, and just because the state may have developed the technologically and techniques to harness Big Data does not necessarily mean that it should. The legal, moral, and ethical challenges to Big Data must be fully explored alongside civil liberties and human rights, yet balanced with protecting the public from terrorist threats. Those in authority must also avoid at all costs the increased use of Big Data as a knee-jerk reaction to placate the public and the press after a terrorist attack. Experience over recent years shows that in the aftermath of terrorist events political stakes are high: politicians and legislators fear being seen as lenient or indifferent and often grant executive broader authorities without thorough debate.

New special provisions intended to be temporary turn out to be permanent. Although the government may frame its new provisions in terms of a choice between security and liberty, sometimes the loss of liberty is not necessarily balanced by a gain in safety, and the measures introduced become counterproductive. The application of Big Data should be carefully considered and not quickly introduced, because any misuse of its power may result in long-term damage of relations with citizens and communities as a result of the overextended and inappropriate use of Big Data capabilities. Big Data analytics must not be introduced by stealth, either, but through informed dialogue, passing though the due democratic process of government. Citizens are more likely to support robust measures against terrorists that are necessary, appropriate, and proportionate, but many citizens, and politicians for that matter, will need to be convinced that harnessing the power of Big Data is an essential part of keeping communities safe from terrorism and violent extremism.

It is important never to forget that compared with other types of serious crime, terrorism remains a relatively rare occurrence; but the cost is high when attacks succeed. Terrorism therefore continues to demand a determined response. The history of terrorism in the UK reveals with alarming regularity that terrorist plotters achieve their intended objectives, defeating all of the state's security measures put in place at the time. Unfortunately, this pattern is not set to change. The police and intelligence agencies will prevent further terrorist atrocities, but there is a strong likelihood that they will not stop them all. In the light of that conclusion, all in authority must dedicate themselves to increasing counterterrorism capabilities and developing new approaches to better protect the public. To ignore or dismiss the positive benefits of Big Data would be misplaced and unwise. Harnessing the power of Big Data would be a game-changer for counterterrorism policy makers, professionals, and practitioners.

REFERENCES

Andrew, C., 2009. The Defence of the Realm: The Authorised History of MI5. Penguin Books, London.

Akhgar, B., Yates, S., Lockley, E., 2013. Chapter 1 introduction: strategy formulation in globalized and networked age–a review of the concept and its definition. In: Akhgar, B., Yates, S. (Eds.), Strategic Intelligence Management. Butterworth-Heincemann Publication, Waltham, MA, pp. 1–8.

Cowan, R., Friday, March 24, 2006. FBI Informer 'met Britons on Afghan Jihad'. The Guardian. [Online]. Available from: http://www.guardian.co.uk/uk/2006/mar/24/terrorism.world1.

CENTRIC, 2014. Big Data, Intelligence Management and Analytics Workshop. [Online]. Available from: http://research.shu.ac.uk/centric/index.php/news/8-news/114-big-data-intelligence-management-and-analytics-workshop.

Dodd, V., Friday, May 6, 2011. July 7 Inquest: Coroner's Recommendations. The Guardian. [Online]. Available from: http://www.guardian.co.uk/uk/2011/may/06/77-inquest-coroners-recommendations.

House of Commons. Report of the Official Account of the Bombings in London on 7th July 2005. House of Commons. Available from: https://www.gov.uk/government/uploads/system/uploads/attachment_data/file/228837/1087.pdf.

HM Government, 2012. Coroner's Inquests into the London Bombings of 7 July 2005: Review of Progress. HM Government. Available from: https://www.gov.uk/government/uploads/system/uploads/attachment_data/file/97988/inquest-7-7-progress-report.pdf.

Intelligence and Security Committee, 2006. Report into the London Terrorist Attacks on 7 July 2005. Intelligence and Security Committee. Available from http://fas.org/irp/world/uk/isc_7july_report.pdf.

Laville, S., Friday, May 26, 2006. Terror Trial Hears tapes of Plot to Blow up Club. The Guardian. [Online]. Available from: http://www.guardian.co.uk/uk/2006/may/26/topstories3.terrorism.

Newsbbcco. http://news.bbc.co.uk/1/hi/uk/6153884.stm.

C.B.C. News, Wednesday, October 29, 2008. Khawaja Found Guilty in Terrorism Trial. CBC News. [Online]. Available from: http://www.cbc.ca/news/canada/ottawa/story/2008/10/29/khawaja-verdict.html.

Omand, D., 2010. Securing the State. C Hurst & Co., London.

Summers, C., Casciani, D., Monday, April 30, 2007. Fertiliser Bomb Plot: The Story. BBC News. [Online]. Available from: http://news.bbc.co.uk/1/hi/uk/6153884.stm.

Sampson, F., 2012. In: Staniforth, A. (Ed.), The Routledge Companion to UK Counter Terrorism. Routledge, Oxford.

Summers, C., Monday, April 30, 2007. Bomb Was Potentially 'catastrophic'. BBC News. [Online]. Available from: http://news.bbc.co.uk/1/hi/uk/6149806.stm.

Staniforth, A., 2009. PNLD Blackstone's Counter-terrorism Handbook. Oxford University Press, Oxford.

Staniforth, A., Tuesday, September 16, 2014a. Islamic State, Terror and the Impact on UK Policing. Police Oracle. [Online]. Available from: http://www.policeoracle.com/news/Terrorism+and+Allied+Matters/2014/Sep/15/Islamic-State,-terror-and-the-impact-on-UK-policing_85467.html/specialist.

Staniforth, A., Tuesday, July 1, 2014b. Gap year terrorist: higher education and foreign fighters. Police Oracle. [Online]. Available from: http://www.policeoracle.com/news/Terrorism+and+Allied+Matters/2014/Jul/01/Gap-year-terrorist-Higher-education-and-foreign-fighters–_84035.html/specialist.

tflgovuk. http://www.tfl.gov.uk/static/corporate/media/newscentre/archive/7103.html.

BIG DATA AND LAW ENFORCEMENT: ADVANCES, IMPLICATIONS, AND LESSONS FROM AN ACTIVE SHOOTER CASE STUDY

4

Kimberly Glasgow

THE INTERSECTION OF BIG DATA AND LAW ENFORCEMENT

We live in an age in which the challenge of protecting the public from crimes, disasters, and other dangers remains ever-present. Whereas violent crime rates in the United States (US) have dropped in the past decade (Federal Bureau of Investigation, 2012), active shooter and mass casualty incidents appear to be trending upward (Blair et al., 2014). Law enforcement agencies have regularly pursued new methods, data sources, and technologies that hold promise to improve public safety, such as public surveillance cameras (La Vigne et al., 2011).

More recently, Big Data sources and analytics are beginning to be explored in the public safety arena. Computer science, physics, bio-informatics, economics, and political science are among fields that have already seen progress through adopting Big Data, but have encountered pitfalls as well (Boyd and Crawford, 2012; Lazer et al., 2009), particularly if the data they are engaged with are "digital traces" of online activity. Many businesses have embraced Big Data as critical to gaining market advantage, yet still struggle with developing analytics that provide actionable insights (LaValle et al., 2011). Law enforcement can learn from these experiences as it seeks to adapt the use of Big Data to its unique challenges and constraints.

What do we mean by "Big Data" in a law enforcement or public safety context? The sheer size of the data in question—gigabytes, terabytes, even petabytes of data—could be sufficient to deem it "big". However, a more nuanced and useful definition might be "data whose size forces us to look beyond the tried-and-true methods that are prevalent at that time" (Jacobs, 2009). Furthermore, data that are complex, heterogeneous, or ambiguous in nature may demand moving beyond tried-and-true methods sooner than a larger but well-understood, well-structured, and predictable dataset. The velocity at which data arrive can pose another problem.

Potential sources of Big Data for law enforcement and public safety are varied. Some are familiar sensor-based feeds, such as public surveillance cameras or traffic cameras that can produce huge amounts of video data. Technological innovations such as computer-aided dispatch and other electronic record management efforts produce volumes of data that can be mined in hopes of reducing crime

(Byrne and Marx, 2011), perhaps in conjunction with relevant data from the U.S. Census, the Federal Bureau of Investigation, the National Institute of Justice, or comparable sources. Such data sources have well-understood structures and properties and may have been intentionally built to support law enforcement needs. Both the sensors and the databases in question are likely to be law enforcement assets. This greatly simplifies the challenges of working with this type of Big Data. Forensic analyses of computer hard drives or cloud data stores as part of criminal investigations can also involve extremely large quantities of data (Garfinkel, 2010). In this case, the focus is on gathering evidence pertinent to a specific investigation of a known suspect from systems used by that suspect.

Another potential source of Big Data for law enforcement is social media (see Chapter 11). Social media has been widely adopted in the US, with nearly three-quarters of online adults reporting they use one or more types of social media regularly (Duggan and Smith, 2013). Through social media, people can freely and easily create, post, and share online content in many forms, including text, images, audio, and video. They can converse with others, build and maintain social networks, plan, organize and execute events, exchange knowledge and commentary, rate and recommend, interact in educational or scientific endeavors, and engage in a host of other social activities. Although thousands of social media platforms exist, a far smaller number have been widely adopted and are likely to be broadly relevant as information sources in a public safety context.

Social media can be an unparalleled real-time source of information about the thoughts, feelings, behaviors, perceptions, and responses to events for large numbers of individuals. In particular, the microblogging platform Twitter has been observed to provide a timely source of direct observations and immediate reactions to events such as natural disasters (Starbird et al., 2010), human-caused disasters such as the London riots (Glasgow and Fink, 2013), as well as campus shootings and other violent crises (Heverin and Zach, 2012) with strong public safety implications.

Social media have been recognized as a potential tool for local governments during crisis events both as a way of keeping the public accurately informed and as a source of situational awareness. Some law enforcement agencies have begun employing social media actively. One notable example is the Boston Police Department. Shortly after the initial explosions near the finish line of the Boston Marathon in April 2013, during the early stages of the investigation of the bombing and the manhunt and throughout the following weeks, the Boston Police Department used Twitter to communicate with the public. They provided updates on police activities and the status of the investigation, announced road closures, requested public assistance with the investigation, and expressed sympathy for the victims (Davis et al., 2014). In general, police departments that use Twitter have been observed to predominantly tweet information on recent crimes or incidents, department-related activities, traffic problems, and crime prevention tips (Heverin and Zach, 2011).

Law enforcement has significant experience and familiarity with sensors such as cameras. Social media, the output of humans as social sensors in their communities, may seem arcane and unfamiliar in comparison. The scale of publicly shared social media and the inherent technical complexities of acquiring, processing, and interpreting it can seem daunting. A social media post containing a keyword of interest such as "shooting" could be an accurate eyewitness text description of a crime accompanied by a photograph of the event, global positioning system coordinates, and a precise timestamp. Alternately, it could be a sarcastic comment, a joke, song lyrics, an uninformed opinion, a different meaning of the term ("shooting hoops"), a falsehood, hearsay, or some other form of self-expression unrelated to a crime. Billions of social media messages are posted each day, which further complicates the challenge of finding the right information for law enforcement.

Beyond searching for specific relevant posts in a sea of data, it may also be important to uncover trends or patterns in large collections of social media data, to detect anomalies or understand connections between individuals or groups.

CASE EXAMPLE AND WORKSHOP OVERVIEW

These examples clearly indicate the use of social media for law enforcement but do not tap into the broader Big Data analytic potentials of social media. To examine the issues of using Big Data to support law enforcement and public safety, this chapter describes a focused case example. The case was an active shooter event in an enclosed public space, a suburban shopping mall, during business hours.

On January 25, 2014, authorities received reports of shots fired at a shopping mall in Columbia, Maryland. A young man had entered the mall, shot and killed two employees of a skate shop, and fired on additional patrons of the mall before taking his own life. He clearly met the Federal Emergency Management Agency definition of active shooter, "one or more suspects who participate in an ongoing, random or systematic shooting spree, demonstrating the intent to harm others with the objective of mass murder" (FEMA, 2013).

Law enforcement personnel arrived at the mall within 2 min. In all, hundreds of officers from Howard County, Maryland and allied agencies, special weapons and tactics teams from throughout the region, and explosives experts from several agencies responded to the event. They effectively secured the large and complex scene of roughly 1.6 million square feet, over 200 stores, multiple floors, and numerous entry and exit points. They searched the facility, evacuated thousands of mall patrons safely, ensured medical attention was provided to the injured, confirmed there was only one perpetrator, and identified and removed an improvised explosive device left by the perpetrator at the scene. During and after the incident, the Howard County Police Department (HCPD) actively used social media, particularly Twitter, to communicate directly with the public, providing informational updates and guidance and correcting misinformation (Police Executive Research Forum, 2014). Law enforcement handling of the incident was viewed positively, a sentiment reflected in this Twitter message:

> Again. I cannot reiterate this enough. If you are a police department follow @HCPDNews to learn how to manage a crisis. #ColumbiaMall

A few months later, Johns Hopkins Applied Physics Laboratory (JHU/APL) sponsored a workshop on social media as a data source during emergencies and disasters. The event was a collaboration among 17 expert participants from HCPD, the Division of Fire and Rescue Services, the Office of Emergency Management, the Public Information Office, and the National Institute of Justice and a team of JHU/APL researchers, data scientists, engineers, and computer scientists. It explored how social media Big Data could provide insights during a crisis and how these insights could be applied in incident response and other law enforcement and public safety contexts. In addition, methods for measuring the effectiveness of official messaging in incident response were examined. Based on gaps and needs identified by experts in the course of response to the mall shooting or developed through professional experience in policing and public safety, JHU/APL staff developed prototype analytics and tools to illustrate potential approaches to resolving these gaps. This exercise advanced the art of the possible and illuminated potential challenges.

Initial sessions of the workshop focused on information sharing. A panel discussion on the mall shooting incident and response was conducted and a timeline was presented. Brainstorming sessions explored high-level topics regarding response to the mall shooting:

- What would you want to do that you could not?
- What would you want to know that you did not?
- What would you want to convey/communicate that you did not?
- Were the tools you used limiting in any way?

These discussions brought forth both incident-specific observations and broader needs of the law enforcement and public safety community. To help spur creativity for how social media and Big Data approaches could contribute to these challenges, JHU/APL demonstrated a small set of social media tools and technologies that helped illustrate the art of the possible.

The output of the brainstorming and discussion sessions was synthesized and used to prioritize goals for quick-turnaround prototyping of potential analytics and tools. These approaches were applied to large-scale social media data gathered for the incident and demonstrated to law enforcement and public safety participants at the end of the workshop. Feedback was collected after the initial information sharing and brainstorming sessions and at the end of the workshop. We worked through the active shooter case guided by the experience of law enforcement and other public safety officials who responded to the incident. We examined actual social media data from that local area during the time frame of the incident. This combination generated unique and powerful insights into key issues, promising strategies and potential pitfalls in using Big Data to help meet law enforcement and public safety needs.

At a high level, desirable features of a system to support the use of social media for law enforcement included:

Usability and accessibility-oriented features:

- Easily tailored, flexible, or customizable
  - Searching, filtering
  - User roles
- Available when and where needed
- Easy to use
  - Consistent with existing concepts of operations
  - Support a variety of audiences
- Enable communication and outreach to the community
- Enable proactive monitoring of official social media communications and their effectiveness

Information-oriented features:

- Have mechanisms for assessing accuracy or validity of data
- Provide actionable information
  - Alerting
- Include both real-time and historical data
- Able to handle multiple media and data types
  - Video and images, as well as text
  - Maps and geographic information
- Support analyses of social information
  - Groups, networks, or organizations

Implicit in such a system are numerous technical challenges to be faced if hopes of making sense of Big Data or developing situational awareness are to be realized. These challenges go beyond coping with the scale and velocity of the data. They may require approaches drawn from machine learning or other fields to identify relevant signals in the noise of social media Big Data. Aggregations of large amounts of social media data may enable significantly different approaches or novel analytics that would not be part of the typical law enforcement repertoire.

Although crisis response to an active shooter incident was the motivation for the workshop, law enforcement and public safety experts quickly uncovered additional needs and opportunities for leveraging social media Big Data. The days after the incident were times of elevated risk. There was real potential for additional copycat attacks or other disturbing and potentially violent public incidents to be triggered or influenced in some way by the mall shooting. Two such incidents did occur at the mall during the following week. The need for timely, effective communications with the local populace spiked shortly after the first 911 call and continued long after the physical incident was resolved. Besides providing updates on the situation at the mall and the status of the investigation, public information officers had to monitor social media to manage and mitigate rumors and false information, such as persistent inaccurate claims of a romantic relationship between the victims and the shooter. Investigators digging into the background of the shooter found indicators of troubling online behavior more than a year before the shooting. Building and maintaining situational awareness in the present, monitoring and interacting with the public, examining past activities in investigative or intelligence contexts, and alerting or predictive capabilities can all contribute to crisis response and to a broader spectrum of law enforcement and public safety situations. Each of these thematic areas was explored in the workshop and will be described further. Other potential areas of interest, such as policy considerations for the use of social media by law enforcement, were outside the technical scope of this workshop, but have been addressed elsewhere (Global Justice Information Sharing Initiative, 2013). Budget and other resource constraints are also out of scope, but affordability and sustainability are practical considerations, particularly for smaller departments.

SITUATIONAL AWARENESS

I need to see the battlefield, not just the fight I'm in.

Law enforcement and other first responders need to ascertain critical factors in their environment to guide appropriate decision making and response to a dynamic situation. Failures to attain situational awareness during incident response can have catastrophic consequences (Endsley, 1995). Information overload and lack of awareness of key information are major impediments to attaining situational awareness. The scale of social media data is part of the problem. For example, the social media platform Twitter has tens of millions of new posts created every hour. The difficulties of finding the right data in this Big Data—data that are geographically relevant, topically relevant, temporally relevant, and associated with relevant individuals or groups—are even greater.

LOOKING INTO THE PAST

For homicides [in particular], we need to go back historically.

Investigations are conducted by law enforcement to establish the elements of an offense, identify the guilty party, and provide evidence of guilt (O'Hara and O'Hara, 1988). Determining what happened and who did it is different from maintaining situational awareness based on interpreting live information as it streams by. Analysis of Big Data from social media could identify potential witnesses, victims, and persons or locations of interest. It can surface leads or contribute to evidence collection or criminal network identification. Used appropriately as another tool in the toolbox for investigative and criminal intelligence work, social media data can contribute to public safety (Global Justice Information Sharing Initiative, 2013).

INTERACTING WITH THE PUBLIC

There was a tipping point, where we became the credible source of information, not the media.

Community policing has always recognized the importance of partnership and communication with the community. Members of the community are valuable sources of information and insight and can help solve problems of crime and social disorder (Community Policing Consortium, 1994). With the advent of social media, law enforcement communication with the public has moved from broadcast mode, typically mediated by the news media to interactive dialog and engagement. It requires listening, answering, and monitoring the public's understanding as well as sharing information. The luxury of having to prepare an official statement in time for the 5 pm news has been replaced by expectations of timely, even near-instantaneous social media updates. Events can quickly jump from local to regional, to national importance. Abilities to track and assess official social media communications and their effectiveness across large and varied audiences and to inform or correct inaccurate information in a focused fashion are important in times of emergency, as well as during day-to-day operations.

ALERTING AND PREDICTION

Can we identify threats before they become a reality?

The desire to predict criminal behavior is powerful in law enforcement and in the general public. Significant efforts have been made to predict those who are likely to commit crimes in the future: for example, to re-offend if granted parole (Berk and Bleich, 2013). Other work has focused on predicting where crime is likely to happen (geographic hot spots) or predicting identities of perpetrators (Perry et al., 2013). Crime data, demographic data, economic data, and geographic information are commonly used in these efforts, which have met with mixed success and tactical utility, with effectiveness varying depending on specific circumstances. Using social media data in a predictive or alerting capacity also poses challenges. However, detecting indicators in social media of threats or disturbances related to an upcoming public event or large gathering or more generally identifying relevant anomalies in baseline usage of social media could help law enforcement and public safety efforts to respond faster potentially intercede before an actual incident.

Tackling the Big Data generated by social media can contribute to each of these themes, but no single tool, technology, method, or algorithm is sufficient. Over the course of the workshop, a variety of methods and techniques were applied, individually or in concert with others, to build prototype capabilities. Such capabilities can help transform unwieldy quantities of information into manageable sources of information, insight, and opportunities for action. Multiple capabilities were integrated into a dashboard for ease of use and interaction with analytics. A selection of these capabilities will be described to illustrate how social media Big Data could be marshaled in support of public safety needs. First, background information on the social media data used in the workshop will be presented.

TWITTER AS A SOCIAL MEDIA SOURCE OF BIG DATA

Twitter is a popular and widely used social media platform for microblogging, or broadcasting short messages. Twitter has hundreds of millions of users worldwide, and they broadcast over 500 million messages, known as tweets, per day. Tweets may include text, images, and links. A public tweet can be seen by anyone with Internet access, not just followers of the sender or people with Twitter accounts.

Twitter users have developed the convention of hashtags, a type of marker included in a tweet. Hashtags are words, phrases, or abbreviations that are preceded by the hash symbol "#," such as #mallshooting. Users may choose to incorporate well-established hashtags in their tweets to provide a topical label, or they may spontaneously invent a new hashtag for a new event or idea. Use of a hashtag makes a tweet easily discoverable by anyone interested in that topic. Hashtags can be used to express emotion (#anguished) or evaluation (#ridiculous).

In addition, there are several distinct tweet-based social behaviors common in Twitter. "Retweeting" is directly quoting and rebroadcasting another user's tweet, often an indication that the message was considered noteworthy or important enough to share. Other behaviors include mentioning another user in one's tweet (that is, talking about that user) or directly addressing one's tweet to another user, as if talking to that person, albeit in a public forum. Thus, people can carry on conversations in Twitter involving two to many dozens of individuals. Twitter provides additional affordances, such as the ability to follow other users or "favorite" specific tweets.

Tweets are complex objects. In addition to the message content of the tweet, each tweet has many pieces of associated metadata, such as the username of the sender, the date and time the tweet was sent, the geographic coordinates the tweet was sent from (if available), and much more. Most metadata are readily interpretable by automated systems, whereas tweet message content may require text processing methods for any automated interpretation of meaning.

SOCIAL MEDIA DATA ANALYZED FOR THE WORKSHOP

Twitter was a clear choice for social media to analyze for the mall shooting. It was actively used by the local police and fire departments during the incident, as well as by those in the mall and surrounding areas. Twitter is widely used, and usage surges during crises and major events. Querying Twitter's Search Application Program Interface (API) for public tweets originating within a 5-mile radius around the location of the shooting from January 25 to February 25 returned 3.7 million tweets from 24,000 unique users, amounting to 4 terabytes of data. During just the hour of the shooting, over 10,000 tweets were sent from this small area. Clearly this scale of data is beyond law enforcement capability to monitor without assistance from tools and technology. Because Twitter's free API returns only a sample of the actual tweet activity, additional methods were employed to retrieve more tweets. Nonetheless, the data retrieved almost certainly are less than the actual amount. Over 300,000 of these tweets were tagged with geographic coordinates, allowing the location they were sent from within Howard County to be precisely pinpointed. Twitter data from this focused location-based search were complemented by data from the Twitter Decahose, a 10% feed of all tweets.

Like many social media platforms, Twitter allows users to share images, either by embedding the image in the tweet or by including a link to the image. From a sample of tweets that contained links to images, over 1000 images were retrieved. These images included photos taken by survivors sheltering in place within the mall. The images provide a basis for determining whether advanced methods could be applied to images themselves and not just to text. Automatic identification of photos containing objects such as firearms is one application.

TOOLS AND CAPABILITIES PROTOTYPES DURING THE WORKSHOP

Social media matters for law enforcement because it enables instantaneous, unmediated connection and communication with the public, serves as a source of information and leads for situational awareness or investigations, and can contribute to measures of effectiveness and outcomes relating to public safety. A number of capabilities to support law enforcement use of social media Big Data were prototyped during the workshop. Highlights of this work will be described.

WORD CLOUD VISUALIZATION

Our public safety experts advised that it was essential to have an easy way to attain a big picture or summary view of what was happening in social media, tailored to the specific situation faced by law enforcement. For the workshop, a word cloud visualization capability was developed that summarized the content of tweets. Word clouds are a simple, appealing way to show the most frequent words in a body of text (Feinberg, 2009). More popular words are larger, and layout and color can be used to provide more visual interest. Rather than generate a single, static display, we created a word cloud visualization which was updated on the fly based on the set of tweets that met the user's search query for the geographic region the user had zoomed in on. After applying standard natural language text processing techniques such as tokenization (rendering the content of the tweet into distinct words or symbols), stemming (reducing words to their more basic forms by removing suffixes, etc.), and stopword removal (eliminating common but uninformative words such as "and" and "the"), the resulting word cloud provided a simple snapshot of what people in that area were saying about a topic of interest. Because the most popular words could be far more frequent than the next few words, it is often necessary to scale the sizes of words in the visualization: for example, by computing a weighted average of the count and log value for the frequency of the word (see Figure 4.1 for an example).

DYNAMIC CLASSIFICATION OF TWEET CONTENT

Finding social media data about a topic of interest may seem as simple as typing a term into a search box, but experience shows that such an approach is riddled with false positives, hits that contain that term but are about something else. Given the scale of social media data, public safety officers could easily be swamped attempting to review search results full of irrelevant social media posts, and the output of analytics based on such inaccurate data would no longer be credible. For example, a sample of tweets in English from Howard County in the days preceding the mall shooting that contained forms

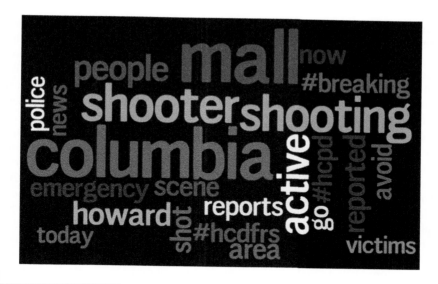

FIGURE 4.1

Word cloud visualization of social media from an active shooter event.

of the term "shoot" were more likely to be about other topics (basketball, photo shoots, drug use, etc.) rather than actual shootings. Roughly three-quarters of these tweets were false positives.

To address this problem, we applied a machine learning technique to automatically classify tweets that were genuinely about a shooting. Using machine learning, a classifier can be automatically built for a category, given a set of labeled training examples (for example, "shooting" and "not shooting" tweets). Presented with a new unseen text, the classifier will predict to which category the text belongs (Sebastiani, 2002). We created classifiers to identify shooting-related and fire-related tweets. These classifiers used a support vector machine implemented through LIBSVM (Chang and Lin, 2011). Based on results from testing data, both classifiers were accurate. For the workshop, we performed dynamic classification on tweets returned by a search, to improve the relevance of results. Such an approach helps separate wheat from chaff from a user's perspective and can improve the usefulness of any follow-on analytics or visualizations that use search results as their input, such as a word cloud. A classification approach can be particularly useful to support situational awareness, investigative, or alerting needs.

CONTENT-BASED IMAGE RETRIEVAL

We have kneejerk tendency to want a guy in blue to put eyes on.

Trained officers with a camera in hand might be the ideal source for photographs of crisis or natural disaster events to aid in developing situational awareness and to support mobilization and deployment of appropriate resources. However, they cannot be anywhere they might be needed at a moment's notice. Tapping into the social media image output of people who are in the vicinity of an event, whether they are eyewitnesses, bystanders, passers-by, or victims, multiplies the sensors available to public safety dramatically. The challenge lies in culling the relevant images. During the active shooter event, a tweet describing people "in the [store name] stockroom because the malls on lockdown" was posted accompanied by a photo. It is equally possible for a relevant image to be posted with ambiguous text ("oh my god") or with no text at all. Because social media users publicly share millions of images and videos each day, automated approaches to handing these data are needed. Content-based image retrieval methods analyze the image itself, commonly identifying features such as colors, shapes, and edges. They may be used to detect the presence of objects within the image, such as vehicles or people, discriminate between photos of indoor and outdoor scenes, or perform similar tasks.

Our case example involved an active shooter. To test the viability of identifying relevant images in social media for this case, we trained a classifier to detect social media images containing firearms. A convolutional neural network pretrained on images from ImageNet, a large image corpus (Deng et al., 2009), was used to extract features from the social media images (Sermanet et al., 2013). Many of these social media images are lower-resolution or poorer-quality photos than those typically used in image classification tasks. GentleBoost (Friedman et al., 2000), a type of machine learning algorithm, was then applied to predict the probability that an image contained a firearm, given its features. Trained on images labeled as containing AK47s, the classifier successfully identified previously unseen social media images with firearms. After sorting 1000 images based on the classifier score, those containing firearms were far more likely to rank highly, whereas low-scoring images were extremely unlikely to contain firearms. Eighteen of the top 20 highest-scoring images included firearms, whereas none of the bottom-ranking 450 images contained a firearm. Included among the top 30 images was a photo taken by the shooter of himself with his weapon, shortly before he began his attack. Although the photo did not actually appear in social media until after the attack was over (the shooter had set a delayed publication time for the post), and thus in no way could have helped predict or prevent the attack, the potential for image classification techniques to help law enforcement seems clear. Similar to text classification, image classification can support situational awareness, investigative, or alerting needs when dealing with Big Data.

This type of application differs considerably from the Next-Generation 911 system, which will modernize existing 911 capabilities to handle photos, videos, and other media types in addition to calls (Research and Innovative Technology Administration (RITA)—United States Department of Transportation, 2014). In the Next-Generation 911 context, images would be submitted to a public safety access point, much as phone calls are placed to 911 now.

MAXIMIZING GEOGRAPHIC INFORMATION

Knowing where a social media post was sent from, and thus where the sender was located, can be critical for interpreting the relevance and utility of the information and sender for crisis response. Knowing which tweets were coming from inside the mall during the active shooter event had obvious value. Although tweets containing latitude and longitude information can easily be placed on a map, most tweets do not contain this information. Leveraging other information in the tweet, whether that information appears in tweet content or other metadata associated with the tweet, such as user location information, can provide a way to approximate location when coordinates are not explicitly stated. Translating a location description, such as a street address or place name, into a position on a map is known as geocoding. We enriched tweets that lacked latitude and longitude information with the results of a geocoding service and used this information to plot and visualize tweet density, finding hot spots of social media activity during and after the shooting. Each of the four thematic areas can benefit from geographic information, although it may be particularly valuable for situational awareness and investigative applications.

DETECTING ANOMALIES

Anomalies are aberrations, exceptions, or unexpected surprises in data. Detecting anomalies translates to opportunities for action in a broad range of domains from credit card fraud to cyber intrusions, to malignant tumor diagnosis (Chandola et al., 2009). To detect anomalies in law enforcement and public safety contexts, we examined two types of anomalies: anomalous changes for specific topics of known relevance and for generic, nonspecific changes.

A number of established hashtags in the county are commonly used in public communications and public safety contexts. We created a visualization to summarize how many tweets contained relevant hashtags over time. In addition, we developed a capability to find contextual anomalies, large changes in frequency that are outside expected daily, weekly, monthly, or other patterns (see Figure 4.2). This method was also applied to the output of the "shooting" and "fire" text classifiers, in which it successfully detected actual shooting and fire events being discussed in social media. Applied to raw counts of tweets within the geographically bounded region, anomalous shifts in generic tweeting frequency can be detected. These could be indicators of events of an unspecified or unanticipated nature. In summary, basic monitoring and situational awareness can be enhanced with the potential to alert when anomalies are detected.

INFLUENCE AND REACH OF MESSAGING

The public is bypassing the media, and talking to us directly.

In the hours after the shooting, individual tweets from @HCPDNews, the police department's official Twitter account, were retweeted—shared or propagated by others—hundreds or even thousands of times.

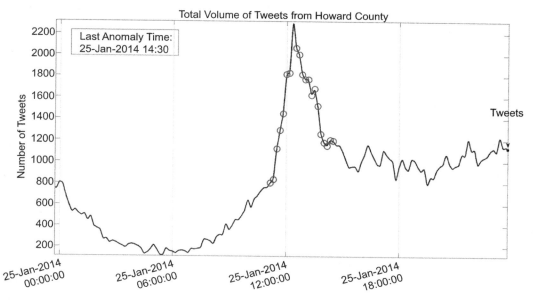

FIGURE 4.2

Detection of anomalies in social media activity.

These tweets spawned additional responses, such as mentions. Each of the retweets or mentions can trigger a cascade of further social media activity. Accurately detecting and measuring the influence, spread, or "contagion" of information or users who are sources of information in social media is complex (Romero et al., 2011). For incident management, it is essential to make sense of the flurry of activity surrounding their social media communications to the public, determine whether their messaging is effective, and shape future actions based on this knowledge. For the workshop, we explored two approaches to illuminate influence and spread of messaging. We used a dynamic graph visualization capability to show the network of activity that emerged in response to tweets from @HCPDNews. A heat map of these tweets was also plotted on Google Earth. This showed that the incident and @HCPDNews' messaging about it were not of purely local interest but had spread outside the region, attracting national and global attention. An important consideration in this work is determining the criteria for inclusion. Retweets are clearly relevant and relatively easy to identify, whereas tweets that paraphrase the originals have murkier provenance. We also prototyped mechanisms for focused interactions with sets of social media users. One example is the ability to send a tweet proactively to Twitter users known to be inside the mall, providing them with clear information on the actions of the police, what to expect, and how to respond.

TECHNOLOGY INTEGRATION

No single technology, technique, or approach is enough to meet these varied needs. We developed numerous methods and used them synergistically. A suite of open source technologies was leveraged to create the social media crisis response dashboard (see Figure 4.3). Used together, they could help

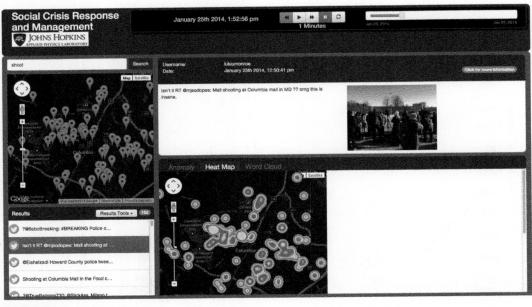

FIGURE 4.3

Prototype dashboard for social media in crisis response.

support public safety needs. For example, a graphical user interface used a set of REST[1] services to access a Lucene[2]-indexed SOLR[3] database of tweet data that could be queried geographically, via zooming in on a map, temporally, and through text. These results could be displayed as pins on a map (given geographic coordinates), as a word cloud, or in a heat map. Dynamic classification tags were used to improve query results. Anomaly detection time series information could also be displayed. We also explored using cloud data stores for social media data management.

LAW ENFORCEMENT FEEDBACK FOR THE SESSIONS

Law enforcement and public safety experts who participated in the workshop were uniformly positive in their evaluation of the effort and its results, particularly given the short time frame (less than a week). They found the workshop worthwhile, well organized, clear in its goals, a good use of their time, and a valuable learning experience. A number of them commented on how effectively social media information could be refined and presented to support their work, and on the desirability of future collaborations to help bring such capabilities into practice.

DISCUSSION

The potential for social media Big Data and affordances to reshape law enforcement and public safety, as it has been shaping business, politics, science, and basic human social interaction, has been explored in the context of crisis response to an active shooter event. We explored key issues and needs of law enforcement and public safety. Situational awareness, monitoring and interacting with the public, investigation and criminal intelligence, and alerting or predictive capabilities emerged as major themes.

The prototyped dashboard illustrated capabilities in all of these areas. Integrating open source technologies and libraries of algorithms, we parsed, enriched, classified, summarized, and visualized social media text and images. Through analytics tailored to law enforcement needs, we helped tame potential torrents of Big Data into focused, manageable, interpretable information to promote understanding and help guide action.

These efforts are best thought of as an initial foray into this space, not a turnkey solution. To meet public safety needs, Big Data must be tackled at many levels. Key concerns include:

- Access, storage, and management of large, heterogeneous datasets
- Development, use, and evaluation of analytics and metrics
- Exploration ability to query, sort, filter, select, drill down, and visualize social media information
- Linkage to action, including interaction with the public

We encountered a range of potential challenges. First is the challenge of geography. Knowing where someone was or where something happened can be essential in public safety; yet, most items in the social media Big Data source we used, Twitter, are not geotagged. Advances in methods are critical to

---

[1] http://en.wikipedia.org/wiki/Java_API_for_RESTful_Web_Services.
[2] http://en.wikipedia.org/wiki/Lucene.
[3] http://en.wikipedia.org/wiki/Apache_Solr.

associate or infer location information, potentially from mentions of landmarks or locations (geocoding) in the text (Fink et al., 2009), associated images, or past patterns of activity.

This ties into the challenge of relevance. To get the right information from Big Data, one must ensure the data not only come from the right location, but that they are about the right thing. Keyword-based methods must be augmented by more advanced language or image processing techniques to improve precision and recall, capturing more wheat while discarding the chaff. Both supervised and unsupervised machine learning methods can contribute to this challenge.

Law enforcement experts expressed the perspective that exhaustive data from their jurisdiction were more important than a larger dataset sampled over a broader area. This highlights another challenge: the challenge of completeness. Social media providers allow various degrees of access to the publicly shared information they host. They may limit the amount of data that can be accessed through their APIs or the types of queries that can be asked. It can be difficult to gauge how complete or representative a dataset is. It will be the case that for different types of law enforcement or public safety applications, those data do not need to be exhaustive to be informative. A sample may still successfully provide tips or leads or inform about trends.

Big Data derived from social media is leading to "a revolution in the measurement of collective human behavior" (Kleinberg, 2008), requiring advances in theory, computation, modeling, and analytics to cope. For law enforcement, this final challenge holds tremendous promise for improving our ability to serve and protect the populace. Further partnerships and collaborations among researchers, technologists, and public safety professionals will hold the key to meeting this challenge.

ACKNOWLEDGMENTS

The author would like to thank the dedicated members of the Howard County Police Department, Division of Fire and Rescue Services, the Office of Emergency Management, and the Public Information Office, who generously contributed their knowledge, insight, and experiences. Without them, none of this work would have been possible. The author would also like to acknowledge the tremendous efforts and contributions of the other members of the APL team: C.M. Gifford, C.R. Fink, J.M. Contestabile, M.B. Gabriele, S.C. Carr, B.W. Chee, D. Cornish, C. Cuellar, Z.H. Koterba, J.J. Markowitz, C.K. Pikas, P.A. Rodriguez, and A.C. Schmidt.

REFERENCES

Berk, R.A., Bleich, J., 2013. Statistical procedures for forecasting criminal behavior. Criminology & Public Policy 12 (3), 513–544.

Blair, J.P., Martaindale, M.H., Nichols, T., 2014. Active shooter events from 2000 to 2012. FBI Law Enforcement Bulletin. January 7, 2014.

Boyd, D., Crawford, K., 2012. Critical questions for big data: provocations for a cultural, technological, and scholarly phenomenon. Information, Communication & Society 15 (5), 662–679. http://dx.doi.org/10.1080/1369118X.2012.678878.

Byrne, J., Marx, G., 2011. Technological innovations in crime prevention and policing. A review of the research on implementation and impact. Journal of Police Studies 20 (3), 17–40.

Chandola, V., Banerjee, A., Kumar, V., 2009. Anomaly detection: a survey. ACM Computing Surveys 41 (3), 15:1–15:58. http://dx.doi.org/10.1145/1541880.1541882.

Chang, C.-C., Lin, C.-J., 2011. LIBSVM: a library for support vector machines. ACM Transactions on Intelligent Systems and Technology 2 (3), 27:1–27:27. http://dx.doi.org/10.1145/1961189.1961199.

Community Policing Consortium, 1994. Understanding Community Policing: A Framework for Action. Bureau of Justice Assistance, Washington, DC.

Davis III, E.F., Alves, A.A., Sklansky, D.A., March 2014. Social Media and Police Leadership: Lessons from Boston. New Perspectives in Policing. Available at: http://www.ncdsv.org/images/HKS_Social-media-and-police-leadership-lessons-learned-from-Boston_3–2014.pdf.

Deng, J., Dong, W., Socher, R., Li, L.-J., Li, K., Fei-Fei, L., 2009. ImageNet: a large-scale hierarchical image database. In: IEEE Conference on Computer Vision and Pattern Recognition, 2009. CVPR 2009, pp. 248–255. http://dx.doi.org/10.1109/CVPR.2009.5206848.

Duggan, M., Smith, A., 2013. Social Media Update 2013. Pew Research Center's Internet & American Life Project. Available at: http://www.pewinternet.org/2013/12/30/social-media-update-2013/.

Endsley, M.R., 1995. Toward a theory of situation awareness in dynamic systems. Human Factors: The Journal of the Human Factors and Ergonomics Society 37 (1), 32–64. http://dx.doi.org/10.1518/001872095779049543.

Federal Bureau of Investigation, 2012. Crime in the United States 2012: Violent Crime. Uniform Crime Report Crime in the United States, 2012 (Online). Retrieved: July 16, 2014. Available at: http://www.fbi.gov/about-us/cjis/ucr/crime-in-the-u.s/2012/crime-in-the-u.s.-2012/violent-crime/violent-crime.

Feinberg, J., 2009. Wordle-Beautiful Word Clouds (Online). Available at: http://www.wordle.net.

FEMA, 2013. Fire/Emergency Medial Services Department Operational Considerations and Guide for Active Shooter and Mass Casualty Incidents (Online). Available at: http://www.urmc.rochester.edu/MediaLibraries/URMCMedia/flrtc/documents/active_shooter_guide.pdf.

Fink, C., Piatko, C., Mayfield, J., Chou, D., Finin, T., Martineau, J., 2009. The geolocation of web logs from textual clues. International Conference on Computational Science and Engineering, 2009. CSE '09, vol. 4, pp. 1088–1092. http://dx.doi.org/10.1109/CSE.2009.584.

Friedman, J., Hastie, T., Tibshirani, R., 2000. Additive logistic regression: a statistical view of boosting (with discussion and a rejoinder by the authors). The Annals of Statistics 28 (2), 337–407.

Garfinkel, S.L., 2010. Digital forensics research: the next 10 years. Digital Investigation 7, S64–S73. http://dx.doi.org/10.1016/j.diin.2010.05.009.

Glasgow, K., Fink, C., 2013. Hashtag lifespan and social networks during the london riots. In: Social Computing, Behavioral-Cultural Modeling and Prediction, pp. 311–320. Springer, Berlin, Heidelberg.

Global Justice Information Sharing Initiative, 2013. Developing a Policy on the Use of Social Media in Intelligence and Investigative Activities: Guidance and Recommendations. Global Justice Information Sharing Initiative. Available at: https://www.iadlest.org/Portals/0/Files/Documents/DDACTS/Docs/DevelopSocMediaPolicy.pdf.

Heverin, T., Zach, L., 2011. Twitter for city police department information sharing. Proceedings of the American Society for Information Science and Technology 47 (1), 1–7. http://dx.doi.org/10.1002/meet.14504701277.

Heverin, T., Zach, L., 2012. Use of microblogging for collective sense–making during violent crises: A study of three campus shootings. Journal of the American Society for Information Science and Technology, 63 (1), 34–47.

Jacobs, A., 2009. The pathologies of big data. Communications of the ACM 52 (8), 36–44. http://dx.doi.org/10.1145/1536616.1536632.

Kleinberg, J., 2008. The convergence of social and technological networks. Communications of the ACM 51 (11), 66–72. http://dx.doi.org/10.1145/1400214.1400232.

LaValle, S., Lesser, E., Shockley, R., Hopkins, M.S., Kruschwitz, N., 2011. Big Data, analytics and the path from insights to value. MIT Sloan Management Review 52 (2), 21–32.

La Vigne, N.G.L., Lowry, S.S., Markman, J.A., Dwyer, A.M., 2011. Evaluating the Use of Public Surveillance Cameras for Crime Control and Prevention. Technical Report. Retrieved: July 16, 2014. Available at: http://www.urban.org/publications/412403.html.

Lazer, D., Pentland, A.(S.), Adamic, L., Aral, S., Barabasi, A.L., Brewer, D., Christakis, N., Contractor, N., Fowler, J., Gutmann, M., Jebara, T., King, G., Macy, M., Roy, D., Van Alstyne, M., 2009. Life in the network: the coming age of computational social science. Science (New York, N.Y.) 323 (5915), 721–723. http://dx.doi. org/10.1126/science.1167742.

O'Hara, C.E., O'Hara, G.L., 1988. Fundamentals of Criminal Investigation, fifth ed. Charles C Thomas, Spring-field, IL.

Police Executive Research Forum, 2014. Critical Incidents in Policing Series: The Police Response to Active Shooter Incidents. Police Executive Research Forum, Washington, DC. Available at: http://www.policeforum. org/assets/docs/Critical_Issues_Series/the%20police%20response%20to%20active%20shooter%20incidents% 202014.pdf.

Perry, W.L., McInnis, B., Price, C.C., Smith, S.C., Hollywood, J.S., 2013. Predictive Policing: The Role of Crime Forecasting in Law Enforcement Operations. Rand Corporation. Available at: https://www.ncjrs.gov/ pdffiles1/nij/grants/243830.pdf.

Research and Innovative Technology Administration (RITA)—United States Department of Transporta-tion, 2014. Next Generation 9-1-1 Research Overview (Online). Retrieved July 31, 2014. Available at: http://www.its.dot.gov/ng911/.

Romero, D.M., Meeder, B., Kleinberg, J., 2011. Differences in the mechanics of information diffusion across topics: idioms, political hashtags, and complex contagion on twitter. In: Proceedings of the 20th International Confer-ence on World Wide Web, pp. 695–704. http://dx.doi.org/10.1145/1963405.1963503 New York, United States.

Sebastiani, F., 2002. Machine learning in automated text categorization. ACM Computing Surveys 34 (1), 1–47. http://dx.doi.org/10.1145/505282.505283.

Sermanet, P., Eigen, D., Zhang, X., Mathieu, M., Fergus, R., LeCun, Y., 2013. Overfeat: Integrated Recognition, Localization and Detection Using Convolutional Networks. arXiv Preprint arXiv:1312.6229.

Starbird, K., Palen, L., Hughes, A.L., Vieweg, S., 2010. Chatter on the red: what hazards threat reveals about the social life of microblogged information. In: Proceedings of the 2010 ACM Conference on Computer Sup-ported Cooperative Work, pp. 241–250.

INTERPRETATION AND INSIDER THREAT: REREADING THE ANTHRAX MAILINGS OF 2001 THROUGH A "BIG DATA" LENS

Bethany Nowviskie, Gregory B. Saathoff

INTRODUCTION

In the wake of the notorious anthrax mailings of September and October 2001, investigators lacked computational tools and digitized information sources that have become more readily available today through modern bioinformatics[1] and in the form of comparative social, linguistic, and behavioral data-sets. Nor did the common fund of knowledge required to apply so-called "Big Data" analysis to behavioral science allow such techniques to be employed beyond a rudimentary fashion. The extensive and costly investigation into the identity of the mailer was led through the years that followed by the United States (US) Federal Bureau of Investigation (FBI) with the assistance of the US Postal Inspection Service. By 2007, the Department of Justice (DOJ) had determined that "the single spore-batch (of *Bacillus anthracis*) created and maintained by Dr. Bruce E. Ivins at the United States Army Medical Research Institute of Infectious Diseases ("USAMRIID") was the parent material for the letter spores" (DOJ, 2010). Dr. Ivins remained under investigation for these crimes both before and after his death by suicide in the summer of 2008.

Ivins worked in an extremely dangerous arena and—like other such researchers—as a condition of his employment, he assented to certain safeguards and active monitoring in the form of data collection. These safeguards were designed to protect the public from what has been called insider risk or insider threat (Shaw et al., 2009; Silowash et al., 2012). Therefore, Dr. Ivins did not retain the privacy protections held by civilian employees in most workplaces, either private or governmental. Because he worked in a top secret environment with biological select agents or toxins (BSATs) including anthrax, Ivins was also required to waive confidentiality of his medical and mental health records. Despite this waiver, Ivins' mental health records were never examined by federal investigators during his lifetime and do not appear to have been accessed before his hiring. Notably, they contained admission of crimes that would have precluded his employment and security clearance had this information come to light. Like the information collected on Ivins' communications and on his comings and goings in the

---

[1] One of the outcomes of this case was the development and advancement of modern bioinformatics by The Institute for Genomic Research.

workplace, his mental health records proved to be illuminating when a formal postmortem review was authorized by Chief Judge Royce Lamberth of the US District Court of Washington, DC.[2]

Although examination of the "Amerithrax" case could provide insight into the potential for *prediction* of bioterror incidents perpetrated by insiders, predictive uses of Big Data analysis (with all of their attendant concerns for privacy and civil liberties) are not a focus of this chapter. Nor is this a chapter on current best practices in deterring insider threat or a how-to in applying particular data analysis techniques. In fact, the Report of the Expert Behavioral Analysis Panel (EBAP), a nongovernmental independent panel of medical and systems experts, did not initiate or use data mining in its 2009–2010 review of relevant material. Rather, we will examine this historic case conceptually—particularly by tracing the retrospective inquiry into available records conducted by the Lamberth-authorized EBAP from July 2009 to August 2010. We do this in the context of current data mining techniques, available corpora for analysis, understandings of the relationship between algorithm and interpretation (Nowviskie, 2014a, 2014b), and ethical conversations surrounding Big Data.

Effective application of Big Data analysis could potentially augment the ability of investigators to solve difficult crimes involving insider threat. However, insider threat cases also pose an opportunity to reflect on important ethical and interpretive facets of computational text analysis and data mining. These range from judgments made during the selection, collection, and disclosure of data to the considered choice of algorithmic tools to aid in discovery, visualization, and expert interpretation by behavioral analysts.

It is important for law enforcement investigators to understand that Big Data analysis in crime-solving and behavioral analysis is rife with decision making and contingency (see also Chapters 15–18). Its conclusions can depend on the subjective standing points of those who assemble datasets, design the processes by which they are analyzed, and interpret the results. In other words, such techniques provide no push-button answers, only arrangements of information that must be interpreted in almost a literary sense and which, in fact, themselves depend on a chain of previous decision points, interdependencies, moments of expert intuition, and close interpretive readings (Chessick, 1990). It is little wonder, then, that many of our citations for this chapter come from the academic field of the digital humanities. For decades, scholars in the field have grappled with the relationship of algorithmic toolsets and data visualization techniques to the making of meaning and to deeply subjective, interpretive, and ethical questions in disciplines such as history, literature, and anthropology (Gold, 2012). Data mining is an aid to interpreting selected and processed (therefore, in some sense, pre-interpreted) datasets. It can be a crucial means of focusing investigators' attention, but is never a substitute for close and critical reading of sources or for psychological and behavioral analysis. That is the key lesson to be taken from this chapter.

---

[2] The review was commissioned in July 2009 and chaired by one of the current chapter's co-authors. It issued its report, *The Amerithrax Case: Report of the Expert Behavioral Analysis Panel*, in August 2010. Although initially sealed, a redacted version was released in March 2011 through the Federal Court order of Judge Lamberth. Any material cited in this chapter remains publicly available. No information provided in this chapter reflects Grand Jury material or still-undisclosed or privileged information that is protected through patient privacy law (*Health Insurance Portability and Accountability Act*).

IMPORTANCE OF THE CASE

This was the longest and most expensive investigation ever undertaken by the FBI. It began in 2001, in the wake of the September 11 jet airliner attacks on the World Trade Center in New York City and on the Pentagon in Washington, DC. Only 1 week after these dramatic and visually striking airliner attacks, a stealthy, unwitnessed attack was perpetrated in the form of anthrax-laden letters, postmarked after having been picked up from a mailbox in Princeton, New Jersey. The "ensuing criminal investigation," according to the DOJ Report (2010),

> was extraordinarily complex, given the possible breadth and scope of this bioterrorism attack. In the seven years following the attack, the Amerithrax Task Force expended over 600,000 investigator work hours, involving in excess of 10,000 witness interviews conducted on six continents, the execution of 80 searches, and the recovery of over 6000 items of potential evidence. The case involved the issuance of over 5750 federal grand jury subpoenas and the collection of 5730 environmental samples from 60 site locations. Several overseas site locations also were examined for relevant evidence with the cooperation of the respective host governments.

The human toll of the anthrax mailings included citizens in the private sector and government, resulting in five deaths as a result of inhalational anthrax and direct infections occurring in at least 17 others.

However, the impact on individual citizens included more victims than those who either died of anthrax or experienced bacterial infection. Thousands of possibly exposed but symptom-less individuals were treated with antibiotics as a public safeguard. Postal workers experienced a dramatic evolution and devolution of the US Postal Service. Policies and procedures relating to national security were modified, affecting scientists and laboratories in the academic, governmental, and private sectors. In the course of the investigation, one later-exonerated scientist, who had been named early on as a person of interest, ultimately received a $4.6 million settlement from the US government (Lichtblau, 2008). Because the anthrax used in the crime had originated at USAMRIID, scientists who worked there at Fort Dietrich experienced the stress of an ongoing federal investigation that occurred over the course of several years.

Finally, and perhaps most critically, concerns about the potential for bioterrorism raised by these incidents fed into the passage of the now-controversial USA PATRIOT Act and formed a key part of the justification for the US invasion of Iraq. The specter of the anthrax mailings was raised dramatically in a February 2003 speech to the United Nations Security Council, when former Secretary of State Colin Powell shared since-discredited intelligence as to Iraq's biological weapons capability. While suggesting that the Saddam Hussein regime may have produced up to 25,000 L of anthrax able to be distributed from spray tanks on unmanned drones, Powell brandished a prop vial to remind his audience that "less than a teaspoon full of dry anthrax in an envelope shut down the United States Senate in the fall of 2001" (CNN, 2003; Weisman, Friday September 9th, 2005).

Before this, the PATRIOT Act, signed into law by then-President George W. Bush in October 2001, and since repeatedly contested by civil liberties advocates, had dramatically expanded the ability of government agencies to collect and demand disclosure of information useful for Big Data pattern analysis of the activities of both private US citizens and foreign nationals. Researchers have noted a clear chilling effect on the day-to-day information-seeking behavior of average citizens—such as Google users apparently reluctant to conduct innocent searches for words like "anthrax"—in the months after the July 2013 revelations by Edward Snowden of improper government surveillance (Pasternack, 2014). Thus, the Ivins case sits squarely at a crucial nexus of personal, social, ethical, and historical consequences for both insider threat and bioterror prevention and for the use of Big Data in law enforcement.

THE ADVANCEMENT OF BIG DATA ANALYTICS AFTER 2001

Although the FBI's 2001 investigation involved, in part, the review of 26,000 e-mails, the analysis of 4 million megabytes of data in computer memory and information collected from 10,000 witness interviews and 5,750 grand jury subpoenas, the ready availability of truly astronomical amounts of digitized and born-digital information to law enforcement and academic research is a recent phenomenon (FBI, 2011). The legal landscape for surveillance and subpoena of digital data by the government expanded rapidly, although not without controversy and critique, under the USA PATRIOT Act of 2003. Commerce-driven analytic techniques that are commonplace now were not as regularly used at the turn of the past century, in part owing to the dearth of available consumer data. Mass digitization of the historical and contemporary print record under projects such as Google Books had just begun. Indeed, by some estimates, 90% of the world's actionable cultural data have been produced in the past 3 years (Nunan and Di Domenico, 2013). Finally, conversations about the ethical and interpretive dimension of Big Data analysis were not as sophisticated in 2001 as they are today (boyd and Crawford, 2012; Data and Society Research Institute, 2014; Lennon, 2014).

Increasingly generated from a rapidly expanding set of media technologies, Big Data now can be said to include five key categories: public data, private data, data exhaust, community data, and data generated through self-quantification (George et al., 2014). *Public data* are defined as those typically maintained and made available by a democratic government as a common good, whereas *private data* are held as a proprietary asset by corporations and private organizations. *Data exhaust* refers to passively collected, so-called "non-core" data that seemingly holds little interest on its own, but which can be recombined with other data sources to create new value. Examples include purchase transactions and Internet searches, which become valuable to advertisers, sociologists, and law enforcement when combined with other axes of information such as demographic, identity-based, and geospatial data. *Community data* incorporate generally unstructured or heterogeneous, volunteered data, primarily textual in nature, into informal, crowd-sourced networks that can be used to capture trends, such as consumer reviews or Twitter feeds. Finally, *data of self-quantification* are (mostly) deliberate recordings by individuals of their own personal actions and behaviors, tracked through devices such as health-monitoring wristbands and generally uploaded to proprietary cloud-computing databases by mobile applications (George et al., 2014).

In 2001, most of these types of data were not available for analysis using current powerful computational techniques able to reveal trends within and among gigantic socioeconomic and cultural datasets (George et al., 2014). Although contemporary text- and data-mining methods can help investigators draw a sharp outline of one individual's actions from his or her interactions at a group level (Nunan and Di Domenico, 2013) and can assist investigators in understanding changes in the behavior of a single individual and in the emotional tone or sentiment of his writings (Liu, 2010), access of investigators to born-digital information meeting the commonly accepted definition of "Big Data" (data both large in volume and high in variety and velocity) was much more limited at the time of the attacks.

RELEVANT EVIDENCE

A significant amount of circumstantial and scientific evidence implicating Dr. Ivins led the US DOJ to determine that he had been solely responsible for mailing the anthrax letters in September and October 2001. The DOJ further found that Ivins had the opportunity and ability to produce and mail the spores.

After this identification, Chief Judge Royce C. Lamberth of the US District Court for the District of Columbia authorized a report from the Expert Behavioral Analysis Panel (EBAP) cited above. The panel was charged with examining "the mental health issues of Dr. Bruce Ivins and what lessons can be learned from that analysis that may be useful in preventing future bioterrorism attacks" (Saathoff and DeFrancisco, 2010). Notably, the EBAP was not specifically authorized by Judge Lamberth to use algorithmic techniques to seek patterns or behavioral anomalies or to conduct sentiment analysis of Ivins' electronic communications, which represented only a small fraction of the available information on the case. Voluminous non-digitized records included interviews, application forms, security assessments, and health data. The resulting EBAP Report was therefore based on a review of Dr. Ivins' sealed psychiatric records and of the FBI and US Postal Service's extensive investigative file—not on a computer-assisted distant reading of the case.

Relying on the expertise of the Panel's nine members, the EBAP Report held that the investigative file and sealed psychiatric records supported the DOJ's determination that Ivins was responsible for the crimes, in that Ivins "was psychologically disposed to undertake the mailings; his behavioral history demonstrated his potential for carrying them out; and he had the motivation and the means." The Report further held that Ivins' psychiatric records "offer considerable additional circumstantial evidence in support of the DOJ's finding" (Saathoff and DeFrancisco, 2010).

Through its investigation, the panel found that Dr. Ivins had led a secretive, compartmentalized life with criminal behaviors dating back to his time in college four decades earlier. A meticulous scientist, Ivins was careful about divulging incriminating evidence, revealing his criminal behaviors mainly to select mental health professionals, who were bound by confidentiality rules preventing them from providing information to authorities. It was not until after Ivins' death on July 29, 2008 that the court order issued by Chief Judge Lamberth allowed access to all of his available mental health records. In addition, also after his death, FBI agents removed "two public-access computers from the Frederick County Public Libraries' C. Burr Artz Library in downtown Frederick, Maryland" (American Libraries Magazine, 2008). Information gleaned from digital forensic analysis of these machines was also made available to investigators.

Although the sophisticated toolsets and fund of knowledge possessed by bioinformatics researchers today did not exist at the time of the anthrax attacks, the first focus of investigation had to be on the spores themselves. Bacterial pathogenomics was in its infancy at the time of the mailings, which were in fact a major impetus to the growth and development of the field (Pallen and Wren, 2007). Although the scientific basis of the analysis of BSATs is beyond the scope of this chapter, it is worth noting that analysis of the mailed anthrax spores quickly proved them to be of the AMES strain. This was a highly lethal and identifiable form of anthrax then being used to develop an anthrax vaccine required on a large scale by the US military. What took much more time and effort, requiring the work of numerous independent laboratories and scientists, was the painstaking phylogenetic tracing of mutations, now known as microbial forensics. These specific signatures were ultimately found in only one original source: the strain maintained by Dr. Bruce Ivins at USAMRIID in Fort Dietrich, Maryland (DOJ, 2010).[3]

The double-blind scientific process of experimentation yielded a great amount of information over time, but it is important to understand that it was not available to law enforcement during and immediately after the attacks, only in the years that followed. Furthermore, Dr. Ivins' decision to insert himself into the investigation from an early stage, and without the authorization of superiors, served to impede the more traditional and circumstantial investigation. According to the final report issued by the DOJ, federal investigators learned in interviews that Ivins was "driven by obsessions" and that he had a long-standing practice of using false identities, "especially when mailing packages from distant post offices." When confronted with damning evidence, Ivins was unable to provide reasonable or consistent explanations for his behavior and "took a number of steps to stay ahead of the investigation." However, because a large number of independent scientists performed experiments yielding objective data that allowed investigators to trace the anthrax to Ivins' flask, he was not able to obstruct the scientific process so easily. The vector for the murder weapon, a flask identified as RMR-1029, was found to be in Ivins' sole possession.

In the course of their work, investigating scientists learned that Dr. Ivins possessed significant expertise in the type of equipment that had been used to prepare the spores for insertion into the mailed envelopes. His technical prowess in creating highly purified anthrax spores was unquestioned, given his significant role in leading the vaccine program.

The investigation then turned toward psychological predisposition, behavior, and motive, the area of the EBAP's expertise. An examination of Ivins' e-mail correspondence with supervisors regarding the future of his anthrax program revealed that the program was in jeopardy, in part because of questions from Senator Daschle and other lawmakers regarding the safety of the anthrax vaccine that he had developed. According to the DOJ's conclusion, Dr. Ivins' life's work appeared destined for failure, absent an unexpected event (DOJ, 2010). Examination of records dating back to his time as an undergraduate revealed Dr. Ivins' long history of vengeful behaviors directed toward others. The son of a Princeton graduate, he aspired to attend Princeton while in high school, but ultimately matriculated at the University of Cincinnati. From childhood, his family life was marked by significant emotional abuse as well as the repeated physical violence that his mother directed toward his father.

Preoccupied with fantasies of revenge, Ivins threatened college roommates with biological agents and shot pistols in occupied university buildings. He felt easily slighted. While an undergraduate, his romantic overtures toward a member of the Kappa Kappa Gamma sorority chapter at the University of Cincinnati were rebuffed. He then spent the rest of his life preoccupied with vengeance toward the national sorority and certain sorority members of his acquaintance. In the final year of his life, Ivins admitted that he had burglarized and vandalized a sorority house and made plans to kill Kappa Kappa

---

[3] Ongoing scientific inquiry and examination of the case has continued, most notably with a National Research Council review (2011), undertaken at the FBI's request. The Nuclear Regulatory Commission's finding is akin to the thesis we put forward here: that it is not possible to reach a definitive conclusion in this case on the basis of one type of evidence or method of analysis alone.

Gamma members. Through thorough investigation, it was determined that both sets of anthrax letters sent to the media in September and to the Senate in October 2001 were mailed from the same postal collection box in Princeton, New Jersey. Significantly, this mailbox was located across the street from the Princeton campus and next to the site of Princeton's Kappa Kappa Gamma administrative offices.

This kind of deep insight into Ivins' psychological state—specifically the likely association in his mind among Princeton University, Kappa Kappa Gamma, and the desire for revenge and validation—came only from a close reading of mental health records and relevant evidence held in small, sparse, and heterogeneous datasets. Insights such as these are difficult to glean from data analysis at scale, which typically requires large, dense, and relatively uniform (or uniformly encoded) sets of information. However, taken together with data gathered by the US Postal Inspection Service and the FBI, including information generated or discovered by biogenomic investigators, digital forensic analysts, and creators of psychological and other health records, some elements of the case, if examined today,–might lend themselves to sentiment analysis, authorship attribution, and forms of so-called "distant reading" or pattern analysis at scale (Moretti, 2005, 2013).

POTENTIAL FOR STYLOMETRIC AND SENTIMENT ANALYSIS

Bing Liu defines sentiment analysis simply as, "the computational study of opinions, sentiments and emotions expressed in text" (Liu, 2010). Sentiments mined from text corpora of any size may express attitudes or judgments, reveal affect or a psychological state, or contribute to the emotional and aesthetic effect an author wishes his or her words to have on an audience. Classification of utterances in sentiment analysis can occur either through supervised or unsupervised machine learning, but, like all natural language processing tasks, these techniques pose no simple solutions and rest on "no easy problems" (Liu, 2010). Similarly, stylometry, which is most often associated with authorship attribution, and which uses similarities in vocabulary and phrasing to suggest the originator of a disputed text, applies a constellation of computational linguistic techniques to complex problems in human language. Examples include the notable early case of the contested authorship of the Federalist Papers (Mosteller and Wallace, 1964) and the more recent attribution of a pseudonymous crime novel to *Harry Potter* author J.K. Rowling (Juola, 2014). Computational analyses of style have also been used to suggest the gender or personality attributes of a writer, but here, as with authorship determination, the standards of proof and of admissibility of evidence in forensic application are necessarily much higher than in literary or historical study (Juola, 2006). This is further complicated by the typically shorter and more fragmentary nature of texts relevant to forensic examination: a difficult problem, but not one that has proven insurmountable (Chaski, 2005).

The DOJ Final Report makes data-driven determinations: "Dr. Ivins made many statements, and took many actions, evidencing his guilty conscience." Many of these statements were made verbally and in interviews given to federal law enforcement. However, the bulk of the textual evidence in the case, often inconsistent and contradictory, was found in e-mails from Ivins' workplace, which contained words and phrases indicating his emotional state. Because Ivins was a civilian scientist who began his job at USAMRIID in Fort Dietrich in December 1980, he communicated through e-mail from the time it became available to his laboratory. As such, the extent of his e-mail correspondence is significant, especially because he addressed colleagues via e-mail with both professional and personal concerns and because it opens the possibility of a longitudinal study—of comparison over time. Although Ivins attempted to extensively delete potentially incriminating e-mails dating from the period leading up to the anthrax mailings, he was unsuccessful.[4] As federal agents focused on his laboratory, he remained unaware that his e-mails had been automatically saved within his computer system and were therefore available for review.

After the First Gulf War and claims by some that Ivins' anthrax vaccine may have been responsible for Gulf War syndrome, a constellation of symptoms arising in military personnel who were given the vaccine, Dr. Ivins was subjected to increasing public criticism for his work. He was also required to respond to Freedom of Information Act requests. Additional themes gleaned from a reading of his e-mails in this period include a sense of abandonment in his personal life. The DOJ Final Report notes that "Ivins's email messages revealed a man increasingly struggling with mental health problems." In addition to voicing frustration, Dr. Ivins expressed anger in his correspondence. As the investigation proceeded, Dr. Ivins shifted blame to others in interviews with law enforcement as well as in e-mails. In particular, he shifted blame to close colleagues who worked with him in the laboratory, including a former colleague whom, at one point, he planned to poison.

The voluminous e-mails Ivins sent from his government account are revealing in that they address his ongoing substance abuse as well as his feelings of frustration, anger, and rage. Any examination of these office e-mails as a digital data corpus would be incomplete, however. Dr. Ivins also used numerous pseudonyms in communicating on various Web sites, including the Wikipedia site for the Kappa Kappa Gamma sorority and in blog posts that revealed his homicidal plans toward an actress in a reality television series. Also, according to the DOJ findings, Dr. Ivins had long been fascinated with codes and secrecy. He referred repeatedly to a favorite book describing the steganographic use of DNA codons—three-letter sequences—that could be embedded within a seemingly normal communication to transmit secret messages. It is therefore possible that further textual evidence in this case has remained undiscovered, perhaps even hidden in plain sight. It is also possible that various sentiment analysis techniques could be applied retrospectively to the Ivins corpus, as a concrete experiment in determining their use in cases such as this. Do changes in tone correlate with evidence of criminal behavior? If so, does this imply that investigators, if properly authorized, might usefully scan for notable changes in sentiment across all the e-mail correspondence coming from a lab under investigation? Should they? What precedent would this set? What impact would the inevitable chilling effect of this monitoring have on scientific communication on a local and much larger scale?

Authorship attribution algorithms were likewise not applied to the problem of analyzing Ivins' writing style against that of the anthrax letters (and indeed, even if such approaches had been commonplace among investigators, it is not clear whether it would have been possible to obtain sufficient writing sample, given the brevity of the letters) (Chaski, 2005). Nonetheless, Dr. Ivins's use of written language in electronic messages was deemed by expert human readers to be similar to the language used in the anthrax mailings.[5] Similarly, this corpus of writing, taken alongside other real-world examples, could provide fodder for experiments in authorship attribution by law enforcement.

---

[4] Dr. Ivins also had a huge corpus of handwritten letters to aid in comparisons. He used both electronic and handwritten documents that helped facilitate effective compartmentalization, thus decreasing the potential for investigators to access all of his writings for analysis.

[5] To the extent possible at the time, the FBI attempted to compare the brief anthrax threat letters against its existing database of written threats. No prior authored threats of Dr. Ivins existed in the database. Therefore, the automated canvassing did not yield a match in content or style.

POTENTIAL FOR FURTHER PATTERN ANALYSIS AND VISUALIZATION

Beyond the insights that might be gained through sentiment and stylometric analysis of written language, the Amerithrax case illustrates potential for pattern analysis and visualization of midsize datasets. These data include biogenomic corpora as well as collected transactional information such as pharmaceutical prescription information, diagnostic codings, postal manufacturing, and financial data. Perhaps even more significant in this case are records of Dr. Ivins' behavior: specifically, of his comings and goings. Ivins' access to restricted anthrax spores was recorded with the help of a digitized entry log. This log detailed his vastly increased laboratory hours during the nights and weekends just before each mailing.

Although data relating to scientists' hours spent in the "hot suite" was available within the research facility's security system, it was not accessed until biogenomic evidence led investigators to USAMRIID and Ivins' laboratory. Although it may seem obvious now that this type of passively collected data would be of interest, Ivins had made statements that focused suspicion on other quarters and was therefore able to divert the investigation. Important in this case were changed patterns not only in the number of hours he spent in the highly restricted anthrax laboratory, but also in the timing of Ivins' presence there. A dramatic and atypical increase in hours during August, September, and early October, before the postmarking of the second group of letters, occurred at times when he was alone in that laboratory on weekends and at night. When questioned about this, Ivins was evasive and vague in his answers. He could point to no scientific endeavor that would have explained his long and unusually timed hours, other than to say that they occurred during a period of stress at home, which prompted him to prefer the laboratory to the presence of his wife and children.

In the days, weeks, and months following the attacks, Dr. Ivins behaved in ways that seemed helpful to investigators within the FBI and US Postal Inspection Service. In addition to privately identifying no less than seven colleagues as possible anthrax mailers, to divert attention from himself, he also engaged in behaviors that may have been designed to elicit positive attention, positioning himself as a researcher possessed of expertise that could benefit his colleagues during the investigation or which could provide a public service.

Notably, these positive behaviors (not of a type subject to self-quantification or passive collection of data exhaust) occurred just *after* the first group of letters had been postmarked, but *before* medical symptoms suggesting anthrax infection in any recipients could occur. Shortly after the postmarking of the initial mailings, Ivins reintroduced himself to a former colleague in the form of an e-mail. In it, he indicated that in the wake of the 9–11 attacks, he was prepared to assist the country in the event of bioterrorism. In the absence of any specific warning or sign of biological attack, this struck the former colleague as odd. Also within the narrow window between the postmarking of the first letter and publicized symptoms in recipients, Ivins joined his local chapter of the American Red Cross. His application specified that his occupation involved anthrax research. (In reviewing numerous other forms and applications that Ivins had filled out over the decades, the EBAP found it significant that this appeared to be the only moment at which he identified himself as someone versed in anthrax research.)

After the deaths of his victims, Ivins inserted himself into the official investigation by appearing at a pond that was being searched for anthrax spores. Although advised by colleagues that it would be inappropriate to participate in the investigation in his role as a Red Cross volunteer, he ignored that advice and was present during the search until recognized by an investigator and escorted from the area. Nonetheless, Ivins' provision of scientific expertise in apparent response to the anthrax mailings earned admiration from colleagues and supervisors. In fact, in a public ceremony in 2003, he was awarded the highest US Army Civilian Award, presented personally by the Secretary of the Army.

Absence of evidence, however, is not necessarily evidence of absence. Ivins sometimes evaded opportunities to track his behaviors. For instance, although he had a self-admitted, decades-long history of making midnight drives to other states to burglarize sorority houses, Ivins' wife and family were seemingly unaware of his late night and long-distance travels. He left no credit card records for gasoline or other purchases, and he may in fact have taken further steps to avoid surveillance or obstruct justice. Still, significant behavioral and transactional evidence was amassed as part of the investigation, and that evidence, mapped along temporal and geographic axes with the help of contemporary visualization tools and techniques, would likely reveal patterns unnoticed by investigators at the time of the case and therefore unavailable to behavioral analysts. Even simple visualizations in the form of timelines, maps, scatterplots, and charts can serve to focus investigators' attention. If dense, complex information related to Ivins' activities could have been compared visually against the recorded actions of other scientists under investigation in his lab—or even against his own behavior in less pressured periods—anomalies suggesting fruitful lines of inquiry might have emerged sooner.

However, just as we find in stylometric and sentiment analysis that the very "complexity of language implies that automated content analysis methods will never replace careful and close reading of texts" (Grimmer and Stewart, 2013), data visualization, too, must be understood as a complex, humanistic act depending on and demanding interpretation. Like the human beings whose behaviors they attempt to represent, algorithmic data visualizations can overemphasize and obscure information, both inadvertently and by design. The well-known work of statistician and political scientist Edward Tufte on visualization and information design is foundational here (Tufte, 1997, 2001), as is Johanna Drucker's warning that technologies of display borrowed from the natural and social sciences can render those who study humanistic datasets "ready and eager to suspend critical judgment in a rush to visualization" (Drucker, 2011). Drucker holds that all human-generated data must instead be understood as capta—not as something rationally observed, neutrally presented, and given, but rather as that which is taken, in the form of subjective representations demonstrating and demanding the "situated, partial, and constitutive character of knowledge production, the recognition that knowledge is constructed" by people with inherent, inescapable agendas or biases, blind spots, and points of view (Drucker, 2011).

FINAL WORDS: INTERPRETATION AND INSIDER THREAT

Why are the concerns we highlight here particularly relevant to insider threat cases in a Big Data age? What qualities of these investigations demonstrate how algorithmic data analysis is simultaneously promising—indeed necessary, as crimes are committed in an increasingly networked, digital world—and yet clearly in need of further critical examination? We have used the 2001 Amerithrax case to demonstrate how insider threat investigations pose examples of individuals behaving in traceably anomalous ways, often within groups whose sensitive missions open them to a particularly high level of monitoring and data collection. Cases such as these demand that investigators visualize and identify patterns emerging from dense, rich, and very large sets of behavioral and transactional data that play out across metadata-bearing axes such as space and time. They also provide opportunities for computational techniques possible within smaller sample sets—such as sentiment analysis and forensic authorship attribution—to be tested and refined now that mass-digitized textual corpora are available for comparison, experimentation, and advancement of machine learning and natural language processing.

Most interesting to us, however, as behavioral analysts and law enforcement agencies continue to add algorithmic approaches to their investigatory toolsets, are not questions about what is possible, but about what is advisable. The Ivins case, which ended in the suicide of a suspect under investigation and subsequent, costly, and time-consuming rounds of scientific and psychological review, proves useful in foregrounding the concerns that insider threat investigations raise with regard to data collection, interpretation, ethics, and use. Just as life scientists are examining their ethical obligations vis-à-vis dual use research in an age of bioterrorism (Kuhlau et al., 2008; Somerville and Atlas, 2005), forensic investigators should operate within and advocate for rigorous legal and ethical constraints. To date, debates about psychological ethics and national security have focused largely on the involvement of mental health professionals in prisoner interrogation (APA, 2013; Ackerman, 2014). A concomitant conversation should be opened about the ethics of Big Data use in forensic psychiatry and criminal profiling.

Critical here will be an effort to broaden the understanding that algorithmic data analysis and visualization are no substitute for close reading and interpretation by trained and intuitive psychiatric professionals. These techniques are rather an aid to elucidation, serving to focus investigators' attention and provide further forms of evidence that *must be interpreted* as to behavior and psychological state. Here, we can usefully bring to bear lessons learned from the application of computing to interpretive problems in humanities scholarship. These range from the impact of implicit assumptions and biases on research questions and the assembly of datasets (Sculley and Pasanek, 2008; see also Chapters 17 and 18) to the reminder that subjective and objective concerns must be kept in useful tension in text analysis, data mining, and visualization (Clement, 2013).

A comprehensive review by the Council on Library and Information Resources of eight large-scale digital humanities projects funded under an international Digging into Data Challenge scheme in 2009 and 2011 found that "humanistic inquiry," like human behavior, is "freeform, fluid, and exploratory; not easily translatable into a computationally reproducible set of actions." This review identified a characteristic need that data-driven projects in the humanities share with the application of data analytics to investigations of insider threat: the need to address inevitable gaps "between automated computational analysis and interpretive reasoning" that can "make allowances for doubt, uncertainty, and/or multiple possibilities" (Williford and Henry, 2012). Forensic behavioral scientists, like other investigators of crimes, must recognize the potential of data science to resolve insider threat cases more quickly and effectively, adding crucial evidence to the positive identification of perpetrators and perhaps saving lives. However, they should feel an equally great responsibility to employ new technologies wisely, in accordance with the law and their professional ethics, and in ways that augment rather than supplant close reading and interpretive expertise.

REFERENCES

Ackerman, S., 2014. CIA's Brutal and Ineffective Use of Torture Revealed in Landmark Report. [Online] The Guardian. http://www.theguardian.com/us-news/2014/dec/09/cia-torture-report-released [accessed 09.12.2014].

American Libraries Magazine, August 6, 2008. FBI Seizes Library Computers; Anthrax-case Link Suspected. [Online] American libraries magazine. http://www.americanlibrariesmagazine.org/archive/2008/august2008/anthraxcomputersseized [accessed 09.08.2014].

American Psychological Association (APA), 2013. Policy related to psychologists' work in national security settings and reaffirmation of the APA position against torture and other cruel, inhuman, or degrading treatment or punishment. In: Council Policy Manual [Online]. Available from http://www.apa.org/about/policy/national-security.aspx [accessed 06.09.2014].

boyd, D., Crawford, K., 2012. Critical questions for big data. Information, Communication & Society 15 (5), 662–679.

Chaski, C.E., 2005. Who's at the keyboard: authorship attribution in digital evidence investigations. International Journal of Digital Evidence 4 (1).

Chessick, R.D., 1990. Hermeneutics for Psychotherapists. American Journal of Psychotherapy 44 (2), 256–273.

Clement, T., 2013. Text analysis, data mining, and visualizations in literary scholarship. In: Price, K., Siemens, R. (Eds.), Literary Studies in a Digital Age: A Methodological Primer. MLACommons, New York.

CNN, Wednesday 5 February 2003. Transcript of Powell's U.N. Presentation—Part 5: Biological Weapons Program. CNN. [Online]. Available from http://edition.cnn.com/2003/US/02/05/sprj.irq.powell.transcript.05/. [accessed 24.08.2014].

Data & Society Research Institute, 2014. Event Summary: The Social, Cultural, & Ethical Dimensions of "Big Data. Data & Society Research Institute. Available from http://www.datasociety.net/pubs/2014-0317/BigData ConferenceSummary.pdf.

Drucker, J., 2011. Humanities approaches to graphical display. Digital Humanities Quarterly 5 (11).

George, G., Haas, M.R., Pentland, A., 2014. Big data and management. Academy of Management Journal 57, 321–326. ISSN:0001-4273.

Gold, M.K. (Ed.), 2012. Debates in the Digital Humanities. University of Minnesota Press, Minneapolis.

Grimmer, J., Stewart, B.M., 2013. Text as data: the promise and pitfalls of automatic content analysis methods for political texts. Political Analysis: Oxford Journals. http://dx.doi.org/10.1093/pan/mps028.

Juola, P., 2006. Authorship attribution. Foundations and Trends in Information Retrieval 1 (3), 233–334. http://dx.doi.org/10.1561/1500000005.

Juola, P., 2014. The rowling case: a proposed standard analytic protocol for authorship questions. In: Digital Humanities 2014 Lausanne, Switzerland.

Kuhlau, F., et al., 2008. Taking due care: moral obligations in dual use research. Bioethics 22 (9), 477–487. http://dx.doi.org/10.1111/j.1467-8519.2008.00695.x.

Lennon, B., 2014. The digital humanities and national security. differences: A Journal of Feminist Cultural Study 25 (1), 132–155.

Lichtblau, E., August 08, 2008. Scientist Officially Exonerated in Anthrax Attacks. New York Times. [Online]. Available from http://www.nytimes.com/2008/08/09/washington/09anthrax.html. [accessed 09.08.2014].

Liu, B., 2010. Sentiment analysis and subjectivity. In: Indurkhya, N., Damerau, F.J. (Eds.), Handbook of Natural Language Processing, second ed.

Moretti, F., 2005. Graphs, Maps, Trees: Abstract Models for a Literary History. Verso Books, London.

Moretti, F., 2013. Distant Reading. Verso Books, London.

Mosteller, F., Wallace, D., 1964. Inference and Disputed Authorship: The Federalist Papers. Addison-Wesley, Reading, MA.

National Research Council, 2011. Review of the Scientific Approaches Used During the FBI's Investigation of the 2001 Anthrax Letters. The National Academies Press, Washington, DC.

Nowviskie, B., 2014a. Algorithm. In: Emerson, L., Robertson, B., Ryan, M.-L. (Eds.), The Johns Hopkins Guide to Digital Media. The Johns Hopkins University Press, Baltimore.

Nowviskie, B., 2014b. Ludic algorithms. In: Kee, K. (Ed.), PastPlay: Teaching and Learning History with Technology. University of Michigan Press, Ann Arbor.

Nunan, D., Di Domenico, M., 2013. Market research and the ethics of big data. International Journal of Market Research 55 (4), 2–13.

Pallen, M.J., Wren, B.W., 2007. Bacterial pathogenomics. Nature 449, 835–842. http://dx.doi.org/10.1038/nature06248.

Pasternack, A., 2014. In Our Google Searches, Researchers See a Post-Snowden Chilling Effect, Motherboard. [Online]. Available from http://motherboard.vice.com/read/nsa-chilling-effect [accessed 01.09.2014].

Saathoff, G., DeFrancisco, J., August 2010. The amerithrax case: report of the expert behavioral analysis panel. In: Research Strategies Network.

Sculley, D., Pasanek, B., 2008. Meaning and mining: the impact of implicit assumptions in data mining for the humanities. Literary and Linguistic Computing 23 (4), 409–424.

Shaw, E.,D., Fischer, L.F., Rose, A.,E., 2009. Insider Risk Evaluation and Audit Technical Report 09-02. United States Department of Defense. Available from http://www.dhra.mil/perserec/reports/tr09-02.pdf. [accessed 01.09.2014].

Silowash, G., Cappelli, D., Moore, A., Trzeciak, R., Shimeall, T., Flynn, L., 2012. Common Sense Guide to Mitigating Insider Threats 4th Edition (Technical Report CMU/SEI-2012-TR-012). Software Engineering Institute, Carnegie Mellon University. Available from http://resources.sei.cmu.edu/library/asset-view.cfm?AssetID=34017. [accessed 01.09.2014].

Somerville, M., Atlas, R., 2005. Ethics: a weapon to counter bioterrorism. Science 307 (5717), 1881–1882.

Tufte, E., 1997. Visual Explanations: Images and Quantities, Evidence and Narrative. Graphics Press, Cheshire, CT.

Tufte, E., 2001. The Visual Display of Quantitative Information, Second ed. Graphics Press, Cheshire, CT.

The United States Department of Justice (DOJ), February 19, 2010. Amerithrax Investigative Summary. The United States Department of Justice (DOJ). Available from http://www.justice.gov/archive/amerithrax/docs/amx-investigative-summary.pdf. [accessed 09.08.2014].

United States Federal Bureau of Investigation (FBI), 2011. FBI and Justice Department Response to NAS Review of Scientific Approaches Used During the Investigation of the 2001 Anthrax Letters. [Online] Available from http://www.fbi.gov/news/pressrel/press-releases/fbi-and-justice-department-response-to-nas-review-of-scientific-approaches-used-during-the-investigation-of-the-2001-anthrax-letters [accessed 06.09.2014].

Weisman, S.R., Friday 9 September 2005. Powell Calls His U.N. Speech a Lasting Blot on His Record. New York Times. [Online]. Available from http://www.nytimes.com/2005/09/09/politics/09powell.html. [accessed 24.08.2014].

Williford, C., Henry, C., 2012. One Culture: Computationally Intensive Research in the Humanities and Social Sciences: A Report on the Experiences of First Respondents to the Digging into Data Challenge. Council on Library and Information Resources, Washington, DC. Available from http://www.clir.org/pubs/reports/pub151. [accessed 06.09.2014].

CRITICAL INFRASTRUCTURE PROTECTION BY HARNESSING BIG DATA

6

Laurence Marzell

INTRODUCTION

This chapter looks at the relevance, benefits, and application of Big Data for enhancing the protection and resilience of critical infrastructure (CI). CI is an integral part of an interconnected "system of systems" that affects the health, wealth, and well-being of the communities it touches and in which we all live, also affecting the resilience of the wider society, which depends on it for its essential needs such as transport, food, utilities, and finance.

WHAT IS A CI SYSTEM?

CI is often described as a "system of systems" that functions with the support of large, complex, widely distributed, and mutually supportive supply chains and networks. Such systems are intimately linked with the economic and social well-being and security of the communities they serve. They include not just infrastructure, but also networks and supply chains that support the delivery of an essential product or service.

A "system of systems" is most commonly described at national level, but it also operates locally. For example, the interdependencies of an oil refinery extend equally to the services that support the well-being and social cohesion of its local workforce, such as health, education, and transport, which in turn employ local people, as they do at the shipping lanes that bring in the crude oil, the roads that take the fuel away, and the telecommunications that link all of these elements together. They are not bound by the immediate geography of the refinery itself or necessarily linked directly to its operational role.

As a complex, interdependent "system of systems," the challenges faced by CI, whether from natural or man-made hazards, are shared across the entire system, and its organizational structure and cannot be viewed in isolation.

To understand the relevance of Big Data and its application to the security and resilience of CI, related communities, and wider society, one must also understand the underlying structural makeup of this complex, interconnected system of systems in which all moving parts and stakeholders—CI operators, citizens, business, emergency services, essential service providers, municipal authorities, etc.— are intrinsically linked through a myriad of often hidden and unseen dependencies and interdependencies. Within this system of systems, local communities are not one single homogeneous entity, but take on the shape and characteristics of dynamic ecosystems through their diverse, multilayered human and societal makeup and needs.

The relevance, application, and benefit of Big Data to the security and resilience needs of both the CI and related communities can therefore only be understood within the context of these system of systems and the community ecosystems in which it must be applied, and to which end users of Big Data must operate in their capacity for "protecting citizens from harm and for promoting their well-being."

In acknowledging this system-wide interconnectivity and the interdependencies and dependencies throughout the system, and that risks and harm do not respect man-made borders and boundaries, this chapter also proposes that Big Data should not be considered separate from the rest of the system. Instead, it should be considered part of an integrated supply chain that needs to coexist alongside and interact with all of the other supply chains in the system, whether physical or virtual.

In doing so, Big Data can provide far-reaching benefits to the safety, security, and resilience of the CI-related communities and society, if viewed and considered as part of one unified framework: supporting a top-down–bottom-up and holistic view of the system and of all of its moving parts, players, and needs.

UNDERSTANDING THE STRATEGIC LANDSCAPE INTO WHICH BIG DATA MUST BE APPLIED

Emergencies and threats are continually evolving, leaving CI and communities vulnerable to attacks, hazards, and threats that can disrupt critical systems. More than ever, our CI and communities depend on technologies and information exchange across both physical and virtual supply chains. These are rapidly changing, borderless, and often unpredictable.

All aspects of our CI and of the communities in which we live are affected by continuously shifting environments; the security and resilience of our CI and communities require the development of more efficient and effective mechanisms, processes, and guidelines that mirror and counter these changes in the strategic landscape, to protect and make more resilient those things on which we depend and the way of life to which our communities and society have become accustomed.

CI functions with the support of large, complex, widely distributed, and mutually supportive supply chains and networks. Such systems are intimately linked to the economic and social well-being and security of the communities in which they are located and whom they serve, and with the wider societal reliance for such essential services as food, utilities, transport, and finance.

They include not only infrastructure but also networks and supply chains, both physical and virtual, that support the delivery of an essential product or service.

Future threats and hazards, particularly those caused by the impacts of climate change, have the potential to disable CI sites to the same if not greater degree as a terrorist attack or insider threat. The impact of severe weather such as flooding or heavy snow may disrupt the operation of sites directly or indirectly through supply chain and transport disruption. In addition, the tendency to elevate terrorism as the main threat rather than to consider the full range of hazards from which modern society is at risk results in site-specific plans that assume damage will be the result of acts targeted directly at the critical facility—either a physical attack or an insider threat—rather than a side effect of a wider natural hazard or other non-terrorism–related event affecting either the geographical location in which the CI is located or the interconnected supply chains on which it depends.

The individual assets, services, and supply chains that make up the CI will, in their various forms, sit either directly within a community or straddle and impact multiple communities depending on the sector or the services provided.

As with the CI and its interdependent supply chains, where once geographic boundaries were the only means of describing a community, in our modern interconnected world, a community may and indeed often does extend beyond recognized boundaries, embracing those of like-minded interests or dispositions through shared values and concerns wherever they may be, locally, regionally, nationally, or internationally.

These communities are not static, homogeneous entities, easily described with their entire essential needs catered for by those responsible and then set in stone and left. A community is fluid and constantly changes, as do its needs, across and between the many different layers from which the whole is made. A community has discrete communities within it and further ones within those. A community and its behavior and interactions both within itself and with other communities, and with its dependent relationship with the CI, can more easily be described as an ecosystem.

The following Wikipedia definition of an ecosystem (Wikipedia, 2014) is useful to allow us to picture and compare the value of using such a description:

> An ecosystem is a community of living organisms (plants, animals and microbes – read people) in conjunction with the non-living components of their environment (things like air, water and mineral soil—read CI and essential services), interacting as a system). These components are regarded as linked together through nutrient cycles and energy flows. As ecosystems are defined by the network of interactions among organisms, and between organisms and their environment, they can be of any size but usually encompass specific, limited spaces although some scientists say that the entire planet is an ecosystem. (For the CI, communities and the essential services and supply chain upon which they rely, these nutrient cycles, energy flows and network of interactions represent our modern interconnected and interdependent world).
>
> Ecosystems are controlled both by external and internal factors. External factors such as climate, the parent material which forms the soil and topography, control the overall structure of an ecosystem and the way things work within it, but are not themselves influenced by the ecosystem. Ecosystems are dynamic entities—invariably, they are subject to periodic disturbances and are in the process of recovering from some past disturbance. (For the CI and communities, read man made, natural or malicious events).

As our reliance on the networked world increases unabated, modern society will become ever more complex, ever more interconnected, and ever more dependent on essential technology and services. We are no longer aware of the origin of these critical dependencies; nor do we exert any control or influence over them. In the developed world, there is an ever-downward pressure on cost and need for efficiency in both the public and private sectors. This is making supply chains more complex, increasing their fragmentation and interdependency and making those who depend on them, citizens and their community ecosystems, more fragile and less resilient to shock.

The security and resilience of the CI and of communities are key challenges for nations and those responsible. A collaborative and shared approach among all affected stakeholders, whether public, private, community, or voluntary sector and across artificial and man-made borders and boundaries, is now recognized as the most effective means by which to enhance security and resilience to counter this complexity. The application of Big Data to improve the security and resilience of the CI and related communities could provide a step change in helping to achieve this. However, this can happen only if those responsible for our protection from harm and promotion of well-being become, along with the application of the Big Data itself, as interconnected and interoperable as the CI system of systems and the community ecosystems are themselves.

Alongside the need to understand the structure and makeup of the CI system of systems and community ecosystems before Big Data can be meaningfully applied, it is equally critical to understand the issues and challenges facing those responsible for security and resilience planning, preparedness, response, and recovery: the resilience practitioners, emergency responders, CI operators, and policy makers. Their issues and challenges are intrinsically linked to the ability to enhance the security and resilience of the CI and communities.

It is accepted thinking that the ability of nation states, and indeed of broader institutions such as the European Union, to increase resilience to crisis and disasters cannot be achieved in isolation; it requires all stakeholders, including emergency responders, government, communities, regulators, infrastructure operators, media, and business, to work together. CI and security sectors need to understand the context and relationship of their roles and responsibilities within this interconnected system. This complex "system" of stakeholders and sectors can result in duplication of effort, missed opportunities, and security and resilience gaps, especially where each stakeholder organization has a starting point of viewing risk through its own individual perspective. When greater collaboration and a more collective effort are required, this tends to drive an insular approach when actually it is the opposite that is required.

Where they do consider this "wider system," and the nuclear industry is particularly good in this respect, other factors such as a lack of internal or regulatory integration or a holistic approach to understanding the human elements as they relate to governance, shared risks, and threats and policy undermine this wider view.

An example is recent events in Japan after the devastating earthquake and tsunami that damaged the nuclear power plant at Fukushima Dai-ichi. The natural disaster damaged not only the reactors, but also the primary and secondary power supplies meant to prevent contamination, and the road network, which prevented timely support from reaching the site quickly.

In this instance, safety and security in the nuclear industry have traditionally been regulated and managed in isolation. Safety management has been the responsibility of operators, engineers, safety managers, and scientists, whereas security tends to be the responsibility of a separate function frequently led by ex-military and police personnel with different professional backgrounds and competencies. Similarly, regulators for safety and security are traditionally separate organizations.

The complex, interconnected nature of safety, security, and emergency management requires convergence; without it, serious gaps in capability and response will persist. Although this approach would not have prevented the devastation at Fukushima, had the regulators of safety and security been integrated into mainstream organizational management and development, because it is neither efficient nor effective to consider nuclear safety cases, security vulnerability assessments, and financial and reputational risk separately, certainly some of the consequences at Fukushima could have been mitigated, as the work of the World Institute of Nuclear Security clearly articulates in their International Best Practice Guides.[1]

Much of the debate on CI security and resilience centers on the critical national infrastructure, i.e., the people, assets, and infrastructure essential to a country's stability and prosperity. However, what

---

[1] https://www.wins.org/index.php?article_id=120.

seems evident is that much of what is critical to a nation sits within local communities, often with a strong influence over their economic and social well-being. Disruption to that infrastructure, whether man-made or natural, not only has an impact across a country, but can seriously undermine communities, some of which may already be fragile economically or socially.

CI operators and those in authority charged with keeping the community safe recognize the integral role that CI and its operators have in the local communities upon which they have an effect. In this respect, the term "critical local infrastructure" might be more meaningful because it highlights the importance of involving local people in aspects of emergency preparedness planning and training regarding elements of the CI based in their communities.

A more collective approach and ownership of large-scale, collective risk is essential to meet twenty first–century challenges. The challenges facing a fragmented community not only affect operational effectiveness—in the worst case putting lives at risk—they also result in inefficiencies and duplications that are hard to identify and hard to improve or remove. Natural disasters, industrial accidents, and deliberate attacks do not recognize geographic or organizational borders and the weakness at these interchanges might themselves present weaknesses and vulnerabilities that can be exploited. Risks that appear to be nobody's responsibility have the potential to affect everyone.

Therefore, it should also be clear that the requirement to make appropriate risk assessments needs to be a coherent and integrated process involving all sectors, agencies, and organizations, and which includes the ability to prioritize the risks identified. Such an approach would, for example, enable a collective assessment to be made not only of which risks are greatest, but which risks might be acceptable and which are not, with procurement within and between organizations made, or at least discussed on this basis.

The need for a collective effort to achieve the combined effect between all of the stakeholders in a community, both the consumers and providers (i.e., citizens, CI, and responders), across the spectrum of "harm and well-being", has never been more apparent. Achieving a common scalable and transferable means to better understand, plan for, and counter these complex interdependencies and their inherent vulnerabilities to the consequences of cascading effects, whatever their origin or cause, has never been more critical.

Despite their varying social, cultural, geographic, and ethnic differences citizens and their communities have shared needs in their desire for safety, security, and well-being. The CI, too, despite its operational, geographic, and networked diversity, has a shared need across its different sectors and supply chains for a greater, more enhanced view of the risks and threats it faces, especially from the hidden, unseen interdependencies, and how these can be managed in a more coherent, cohesive, effective, and efficient way.

This shared means, whatever the size, makeup, and location of a community, and from whichever touch point a citizen has engagement, can be described as its strategic community requirement (SCR). Without such a means to achieve this combined effect, our modern society and the millions of individual communities from which it is made can only become less resilient to shocks, whether man-made, natural, or malicious; less cohesive to increasing social tensions; and increasingly unable to provide the quality of life expectations of citizens that our politicians so espouse.

Despite the structural complexity of both community ecosystems and CI system of systems, with the inherent difficulty of understanding how they coexist and interact, with their shared needs for safety, security, resilience, and well-being, this SCR provides commonality and overarching consistency; giving an opportunity to support greater visibility and enhanced cohesion and coherence to improve resilience across the many different moving parts and players.

Use of an overarching architecture to achieve this would enable a single, unified view of the world from which a shared, collective approach to enhancing the security and resilience of the CI and communities can be carried out under a common SCR framework. Within this framework, the application of Big Data by end users can be meaningfully undertaken to maximize and achieve the benefits sought.

WHAT IS MEANT BY AN OVERARCHING ARCHITECTURE?

The architecture is an enabling tool to support the CI, community, and responder organizations in understanding and managing the complexity of the systems in which they operate and are tasked to protect us. It can be used to represent an integrated model of the system, or the community, from the operational and business aspects to the technologies and systems that provide capability. By covering both the operational and technical aspects across such a system, the architecture enables all communities of interest to gain the essential common understanding needed to deliver benefits that are required from the application of Big Data.

One of the main focuses of the architecture in this effort is to present a clear vision of the system in all of its dimensions and complexity in terms of its existing state and its desired or future state(s). The result can support all aspects of the requirement for the use of Big Data including:

- Governance and policy
- Strategic planning
- Tactical planning and operations (front line and logistics)
- Automation of processes
- Capability/requirements capture

THE SCR

Two concepts underpin the SCR, each mutually supporting the other for maximum effect. These concepts are protection from harm and promotion of well-being and combined effect.

Protection from Harm and Promotion of Well Being

Those things that can harm us, or which we perceive to cause us harm, either as individuals or as part of the community in which we live, can be described in high-level terms as:

- Terrorism
- Civil emergency—natural
- Civil emergency—man-made
- Organized crime
- Public order
- Cyber

Aspects that touch our everyday journey as citizens, that can either positively or adversely affect our well-being and quality of life, will to varying degrees sit within the following categories:

- Political
- Cultural
- Environment

- Economic
- Social

As citizens, we expect those responsible in authority to be able to keep us from harm from any of these threats. We also expect those responsible to broadly promote policies that support our well-being across the categories shown.

However, in the complex, interconnected ecosystems in which we reside, and the far wider system of systems in which our CI and communities exist, harm and well-being are intrinsically linked by the myriad of hidden and unseen interdependencies previously described. These might, for example, encompass physical or virtual supply chains of information, essential services, or other critical dependencies. For those in authority, these interdependencies drive unseen gaps, overlaps, and disparities in how they understand, plan for, and provide for our harm and well-being needs. These interdependent, interconnected risks are in turn compounded by the single view of the world approach to risk adopted by the many individual organizations and agencies upon which we rely to keep us safe and provide for our essential needs and life support systems.

As individual citizens coexisting within these complex community ecosystems, we are all consumers of harm and well-being needs: even those in authority charged with providing them. As society gets ever more reliant upon complex, interconnected, unseen, and increasingly stretched dependencies, the need for a collective citizen- and community-centric approach to understand, plan, and manage the shared outcomes and effects we seek has never been greater. The ability for all community stakeholders, wherever they sit on the supply or demand side of harm and well-being, to join together to meet these challenges in a cohesive and coherent way and deliver these shared outcomes through the combined effect of their collective efforts is paramount.

Combined Effect

Within the common framework of shared harm and well-being that straddles both CI and communities, however they are described, their varied, dynamic, and multilayered nature will, of course, dictate locally specific priorities. Four core themes within the SCR framework that will accommodate these and facilitate the collective effort of stakeholders to achieve such a combined effect are:

- Collective view of risks
- Interconnected journey touch points and interfaces
- Shared ownership
- Capability and capacity negotiation

Through these themes, stakeholders charged with meeting our harm and well-being needs can come together and use the SCR architecture framework (SCAF) to deliver the combined effect of their collective effort to understand, plan, and manage the issues and challenges to the CI and communities in a joined up, coherent, and cohesive way. This would include a greater focus on the viewpoint of the citizen, one that understands how citizens interface with these harm and well-being needs in their daily lives and how they expect them to be provided in a seamless manner.

This Combined Effect approach was set out in the joint RUSI/Serco White Paper 'Combined Effect: A New Approach to Resilience' (Cole and Marzell, 2010), published in late 2010, which encouraged a more holistic, collaborative approach to resilience planning. Its aim is to help to bring together public and private sector resilience stakeholders officially designated Category 1 and 2 responders under the

Civil Contingencies Act 2004, the private sector suppliers, operators and contractors, as well as the volunteer organizations and community groups that support them. Importantly, the methodology seeks to identify where gaps in current knowledge, understanding and capability exist so that they can be more easily addressed.

This approach also supports the essential dialogue across and among all relevant and interested community stakeholders wishing to become involved and support the enhanced security and resilience of their communities in a more meaningful way; part of a wider community engagement throughout the ecosystem that is deemed essential by governments in informing and countering many of the societal challenges of policing ethnically and culturally diverse communities.

The overarching SCAF enables the Combined Effect approach to span the spectrum of harm and well-being, whether this is planning and preparing for terrorism, flood or youth offending or providing appropriate access to health care, education, and employment opportunities to those most in need. Often, these involve similar issues and organizations, seeking similar outcomes. Previously, there has been neither the shared visibility nor the collective means to have meaningful discussions on a shared risk, ownership, and outcome approach: an experience that citizens and their communities both expect and seek across the touch points they encounter daily.

A Combined Effect approach provides the wherewithal, the concepts and doctrine to identify, understand, and mitigate the impacts from the system of systems interdependencies, with supporting tools, techniques, and information to mitigate the often hidden or unseen vulnerabilities, threats, risks, and harm they foster. Combined Effect would use intelligence provided by Big Data through the SCAF to inform and improve the collective effort of stakeholders for the security and resilience of the CI and communities.

The diagram in Figure 6.1 illustrates the spectrum of harm and well-being in relation to other elements of the SCR.

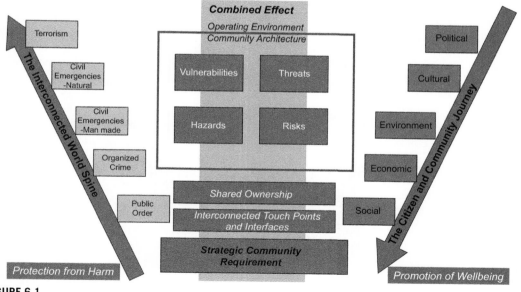

FIGURE 6.1

Strategic Community Requirement: harm and well-being.

UNDERPINNING THE SCR

The challenges these different organizations face in coming together to achieve such a collective effort, let alone the need to embrace citizens more completely in the process, can be achieved through a more informed understanding of the capabilities within the four key capability areas that underpin all aspects of an individual organization's service delivery. Under the SCR framework, these same capabilities would also underpin a collective, Combined Effect approach: governance, people, processes, and systems (technology).

Adoption of such a shared risk approach would enable the gaps, disparities, overlaps, and duplication that exist among different organizations when they come together to be identified, planned for, and managed. Once in place, this would underpin meaningful, evidence-based negotiations among stakeholders regarding how such a Combined Effect undertaking can be achieved. Achieving Combined Effect does not preclude individual organizations from planning for and managing their own individually identified risks, which, when done under the umbrella of the SCR framework to enhance collective security and resilience through a shared risk approach, will provide more effective and efficient benefits across the system and for all as a result.

The diagram in Figure 6.2 outlines these key capability areas and how they fit together to underpin the SCR, relevant stakeholders, and shared risk and outcomes approach.

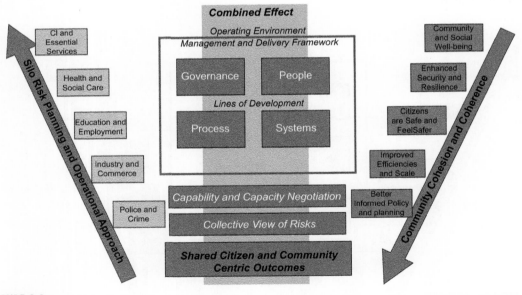

FIGURE 6.2

Shared citizen- and community-centric outcomes.

STRATEGIC COMMUNITY ARCHITECTURE FRAMEWORK

The SCAF will give relevant community stakeholders, such as the police, other emergency responders, and municipal authorities, a shared framework of governance, a concept of operations, and the enabling tools and technology to support closer collaboration for greater, more effective, and efficient community-based security and resilience that is Combined Effect.

The SCAF will enable users at varying levels—strategy and policy, command layers, and operational delivery on the ground—to have a community-wide, holistic understanding and view of the risks, threats, and hazards that they collectively face. The SCAF will support understanding, collation, and coordination of the collective capabilities and capacities that all members of the community—public and private, voluntary and citizens—can bring to bear in support of their collective effort, safety, security, and well-being.

The SCAF will support an informatics capability to ensure that the myriad of informal, formal, and social information and communications channels that now reside within and across communities is fully understood, embedded, and exploited. Visualization and associated modeling and gaming techniques will allow for the dynamic testing and exercising of concepts; drive an iterative process of feedback into CI and community end users; and then continue onward for scalable and transferable exploitation elsewhere.

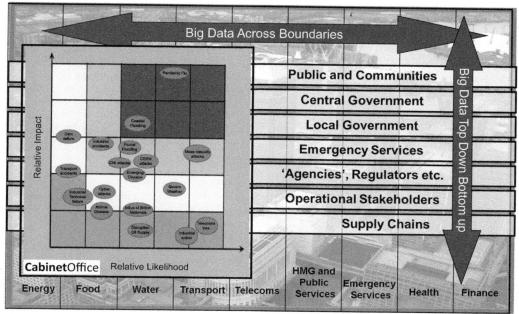

FIGURE 6.3

Building trust and common purpose.

The SCAF will provide the wherewithal and means to understand where and how the application of Big Data in the security and resilience of the CI and communities can be best achieved, supporting the greater collective effort of stakeholders and end users responsible in a joined and coherent fashion.

For example, Big Data can be used to support the security and resilience of the CI and of communities in the following ways:

- Build trust and common purpose among individual citizens, communities, the police, responder and authority groups, and the CI to plan for, prepare for, respond to, and recover from threats, risks, vulnerabilities, and hazards that can harm them and affect their well-being (see Figure 6.3).
- Enable empirical and intelligence-led discussions within and across the community and its stakeholders, as well as regionally or nationally, regarding the benefits and value of shared resources, greater cooperation, and joint working/interoperability to meet identified shared risks and threats through the greater cohesion and coherence of a Combined Effect approach (see Figure 6.4).
- Support iterative processes to feed into local (and, where appropriate, national) policy and strategy planning to inform the creation of a new, dynamic, best-practice, collectively shared safety, security, and resilience plan (see Figures 6.5 and 6.6).

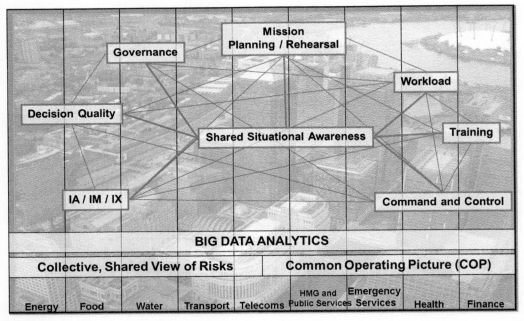

FIGURE 6.4

Big Data: cohesion, coherence and interoperability.

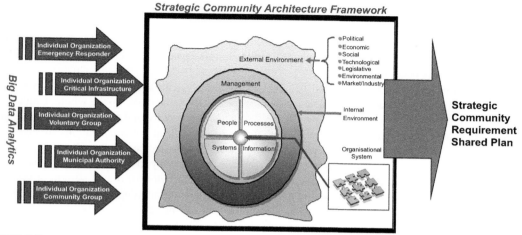

FIGURE 6.5

Shared safety, security, and resilience plan.

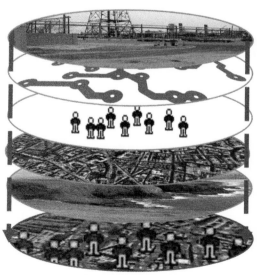

Infrastructure and processes

Systems and technology

Policies, strategies, processes and human factors

Built environment risks and threats

Natural hazards

Shared and common system views in a Strategic Community Architecture Framework vs. current and future threats

Big Data Analytics

FIGURE 6.6

Shared local plans informing wider policy.

CONCLUSIONS

Big Data brings enormous benefits to society through its ability to amalgamate and aggregate the myriad datasets and sources for meaningful application. In this instance, protection of our CI, citizens and communities has been discussed.

Similar to Big Data (see Chapters 1 and 10), the CI system of systems and the community ecosystems are complex and have a myriad dependencies and interdependencies that make up the whole. Unlike Big Data, however, these are not clearly understood; no mechanisms currently make sense of the whole in a coherent and cohesive way and too many individual, fragmented and different organizations are involved, which essentially makes it a largely ungoverned space from a governance perspective. It would be difficult to apply Big Data to such an incoherent space in any meaningful way to make a real difference.

Big Data itself is part of the solution to creating a shared, unified view of the CI system of systems and community ecosystem where all moving parts—the dependencies, interdependencies, and organizational borders and boundaries and stakeholder capabilities—all can be seen within the one architecture framework (SCAF). In creating such a view for the SCR, Big Data may used in a meaningful way to provide real value and benefits to stakeholders charged with keeping us, the CI, and our communities safe, secure, and more resilient through the combined effect of their collective effort.

REFERENCES

Wikipedia, 2014. Ecosystem (Online). Available from: https://en.wikipedia.org/wiki/Ecosystem.
Cole, J., Marzell, L., 2010. Combined Effect: A New Approach to Resilience, Serco. https://www.rusi.org/search?
    cx=018021167295652412753%3Aqkpw7gvgvey&cof=FORID%3A11&ie=UTF-8&q=combined+
    effect&siteurl=www.rusi.org%2F...%2FCombined_Effect_White_Paper__for_web_2.pdf&ref=&ss=
    2587j618183j15&sa.x=0&sa.y=0.

MILITARY AND BIG DATA REVOLUTION

7

Jean Brunet, Nicolas Claudon

RISK OF COLLAPSE

For a number of countries, military forces could miss out and be left unable to meet the ambitions of their mission. The armed forces know how essential their intelligence agencies are to the preparation and success in a battle. Today, any action or decision is preceded by intelligence action. However, the more data you have, the more difficult it is to extract useful information from it. As this book is being written, most intelligence services are struggling with the capabilities required to collect, filter, aggregate, archive, compute, correlate, and analyze the tremendous quantity of data available. The only solution is often a choice between an arbitrary sub-set of data or ignoring some essential business rules. If the human intelligence gathered by a single individual in a location deemed dangerous is still decisive for the success of an operation, the digging and analyzing of the dust of data is secretly done by ordinary citizens assisted by an exponentially growing number of computers. These "armies of the shadow" have become the formidable tool of intelligence services.

Requests for "actionable information[1]" are recurrent. Actionable information is required at every level by military forces, so that well-informed decisions can be made. However, these requests are difficult to meet within a suitable timeframe, and the information often arrives too late for the execution of specific missions, which are defined by speed, lack of casualties, clear and instant information on the battle field, and a restricted budget. Maximizing and optimizing a mission requires additional and efficient data processing. The data processing chain consists, at first sight, of simple operations: filtering, merging, aggregating, and simple correlation of data. These are simple processing operations, but have to be applied on a different scale with low latency to achieve the level of intelligence required by today's missions.

Beyond intelligence requirements, the huge quantity of data available on a battlefield is a consequence of the ever increasing use of sensors, technologies essential in warfare such as nano network sensors, tactical sensors, global positioning systems for vehicles and men, and tags/codes and communications.

The military looks for an agile, responsive, and swift reaction, because this is usually a decisive element for victory. But that is not all. A battlefield is not isolated from its geopolitical, social, and cultural environment. The preparation of military action is based on thorough intelligence groundwork requiring the gathering of a large quantity of data from the environment surrounding the battlefield. Asymmetrical wars have reinforced these links. It is therefore also a matter of processing data

---

[1] Actionable information means having the necessary information immediately available to deal with the situation at hand.

originating worldwide: from the web, social networks, communication flows; i.e., from a "sea of data," which provides a digital picture of the world updated every second with hundreds of thousands of events. The COP[2]—a tool favored by the military when making decisions, giving orders or taking action—is a snapshot that is valued only because it is up-to-date. Such a snapshot is even more difficult to obtain due to primary event flows that are rocketing in terms of quantity and speed.

Even if the Big Data field brings solutions to this new situation, the military knows that technology cannot solve everything on its own. A major risk arises if the data is analyzed by people without experience of analyzing 3'Vs data[3] or without the right tools and modes of data visualization. The human factor is crucial when interpreting complex data structures (see also Chapters 17 and 18). Let us imagine that instead of handling a few hundreds or thousands of lines in an Excel spreadsheet with sorting macros and filters, it is necessary to analyze manually several thousand Excel spreadsheets with hundreds of thousands of lines. For instance, a paper by the UK's Government Business Council estimates that the number of unmanned aerial systems (UAS) in use has risen from 50 a decade ago to "thousands" now, with spending on them increasing from less than $300 million in 2002 to more than $4 billion in 2011. These UAS, it is estimated, have flown more than one million combat hours during this period.

At the more global level, it took years of effort to set up "network centric warfare" (NCW). It is a concept popularized under the name of networked warfare, which appeared in military doctrines at the end of the 20th century. As a term of American origin, it describes a way to conduct military operations by using the capabilities of the information systems and networks available at the time. The main evolution in relation to the prior doctrines concerns the sharing of information. It is about the capacity to link together the different armed forces (Army, Air Force, Navy), as well as armed forces of allied countries, to gather information using drones or satellites and to disseminate it to units in real-time so as to strike quicker and more efficiently. During the past few years, the network centric concept has expanded into the civil and business sector in the United States, and today, it supports the US influence in large companies and international organizations.

Unfortunately, the twilight of the concept began in 2010 for several reasons: the cost of such a system, the complexity of its implementation, and, finally, the nature of complex threats that do not seem, at first sight, to be consistent with the concept. However, a large amount of military needs have been formalized in NCW, and today some elements are extracted by armed forces. These armed forces are also, by indirect means, in possession of a light version of NCW. We feel that the advent of Big Data updates NCW under new auspices. Our objectives are more specifically to allow the rapid rise of networked warfare best practices, at a low cost and adapted to the new threats: agility, swift reaction, and short loops between sensors and effectors.

INTO THE BIG DATA ARENA

The General Atomics MQ-9 Reaper is a surveillance and combat drone built by General Atomics for the US Air Force, the US Navy, the Aeronautica Militare, the Royal Air Force, and the French Air Force. During a mission, the MQ-9 Reaper generates the equivalent of 20 Tbytes of data. A report by

---

[2] Common operational picture.
[3] Volume, velocity, and variety called 3'Vs.

former processing officers reveals that 95% of the videos are never viewed. The continuous rise of connected objects worldwide and on the battlefield is going to increase the gap between an abundance of data and the ability to use this information. It becomes obvious then, that for the armed forces, the risk of errors has to be taken into consideration.

In this chapter, instead of focusing only on Big Data's theoretical capacity to meet needs or on evaluating the positive impact of technology on the military profession, we will focus on a very specific vision of a Big Data system rendered usable by integrating use cases and construction within the same thinking process. This chapter proposes a solution, aiming for quick implementation and immediate cost-effective benefits. In a time of austerity in military budgets, it becomes even more interesting to set priorities with results achievable in less than 18 months and then evolve in increments without forgetting the long-term vision. Wanting to design a full Big Data system can be extremely expensive. It is preferable to set priorities and implement them in stages. For example, it is better to make concessions on precision/accuracy rather than computation time, and then with longer calculation time to increase the result's degree of accuracy. Actions on the ground require a short loop of less than 2 minutes. In that case, any result, however partial, is meaningful, as long as it is delivered swiftly. This is the reason why we are looking to use Big Data systems, which are presently capable of providing results in quasi real-time, and then gradually improve either the precision or the richness of the results.

We will explain how to create a system capable of processing around 10,000 to 1 million events per second. Processing means to filter, enrich, and correlate data sufficiently to obtain results useful on the battlefield. With 3'Vs flows, this system is designed to process an event with a low latency, of about a few seconds, to execute simple or complex business rules, and run machine learning on the fly. We will also explain how to make the system flexible, fault tolerant, and capable of evolving. We shall give a few examples highlighting the advantages of the type of architecture, which will be developed.

In its final stage, a Big Data solution has to be compared to a reactive weapon system that has flexibility and adaptability when faced with rapid threat. It is modular, and it grows incrementally in power and service. The implementation and configuration of thousands of computer nodes is not trivial, but it is possible today. A soldier still finds it difficult to compare the value of a fighter plane and that of a super-scalar Big Data datacenter. It is an old debate, illustrated during past conflicts such as World War II, when the tenacious work of a British team of cryptanalysts averted two years of war.

Finally, it is to be noticed that police force intelligence and military intelligence tend to work more closely together than before. In this time of austerity, it is reasonable to assume that the sharing of means and sources of intelligence will become more common within the same country, while agreements with allied private operators will continue to increase. In other words, what we describe here can also be implemented for police intelligence or for the collaboration of both.

SIMPLE TO COMPLEX USE CASES

To provide the military with the benefits of an intelligence system based on Big Data, one of the main difficulties is the need for diverse information. It is almost limitless in its form and expression, because it is changing constantly. There are two main classes of use cases, which can be differentiated mostly by their processing time/latency and their accuracy/quality. We aim to capture these use cases by means of a classification, which matches with different capabilities and capacities of Big Data systems.

The first class (class I) consists of the use cases already known and implemented in conventional applications that are struggling with the amount of data. It is a matter of adapting these applications or running them after applying some other treatments first, so as to reduce the magnitude with different processing treatments. It is also through Big Data batch processing that it is possible to rewrite part of these applications. These technologies are well known in the Big Data field, and a part of them are described later in the technical chapters (see Chapters 9–14).

As noted, the ability to process Big Data opens horizons inaccessible until now. Information, which used to be hidden in the sea of data, becomes accessible thanks to simple or complex treatments run mostly in MapReduce. This first class is well known, and the "conventional" Big Data systems based on large warehouses and batch processing are fairly well mastered. It is, nevertheless, necessary to review the algorithms to recode them in parallel mode. The infrastructures also need to be fully reviewed and resized to receive Big Data treatments.

The increasing number of events (data points) provided by sensors and other means, which describe individuals and their environment improves the digital version of the world. The challenge is to exploit it through Big Data. The different stages of the processing chain decrease the magnitude of the information along with the enrichment process, so that once it has reached the user's desk, it can be handled, analyzed, and interpreted. This first stage already allows, for instance, the analyst to take all the videos recorded during the MQ-9 Reaper's flight (not just 5%) and to apply treatments for filtering, shape recognition, analysis of differences between two missions, etc. The treatments, applied to each image of the video, are parallelized. For each image, the results are compared with the subsequent computation cycle, until they provide information of interest for the analyst. Although the treatments do not replace the human eyes and brain, they can highlight specific sequences containing relevant elements. To summarize, only a minute fraction of the video will be viewed by the analyst, but it will be the right one. Nonetheless, these treatments are applied after the flight, with batch processing with a duration that will vary from a few minutes to several hours.

Use cases in class II attempt to exploit the sea of available data within a fixed period. This second class regroups use cases that were inaccessible until now, thanks to technologies able to process flows "on the fly," i.e., streaming processing. These use cases are characterized by short processing time and short latency. The computation is applied on a subset of data: The most recent data is used in streaming processing. They are kept within a time window that moves continuously, defined by the current time T and T-delta. Delta can vary from a few minutes to a few hours.

Let us return to the video recording of the MQ-9 Reaper's mission. Imagine that a radio channel enables the retrieval of the images in streaming mode. This flow of images is analyzed in real-time. Each image injected in the Big Data system is processed immediately. As the images are being processed, the results are compared with each previous image. The algorithms of the image analysis are prioritized according to operational priorities: Which strategic information, even incomplete, does the soldier need before taking action? Is it enough to r-program the flight of the drone?

"On the fly" processing provides tactical information, which is at the heart of what is happening on the battlefield and to the action. You need to know about it is at the time the event occurs. Big Data are progressively building up toward the real-time analysis of data. Since 2007, Big Data technologies and systems allow the processing of all data over periods that vary from a few minutes to several hours. Over the past three years, with ever increasing volumes of data, the need of the market is moving toward a demand for reactive systems and short processing times. A need for interactivity with the data is growing beyond batch treatments, because these are not in the "battle rhythm." This requires system architectures and new technologies, which are gradually emerging, to:

- Treat flows before archiving them in a warehouse;
- Maximize the use of servers' RAM;
- Create capacity to trigger treatments on event arrival;
- Optimize the recognition of required treatments and data;
- Transform specific analysis algorithms, so as to deliver useful information as soon as possible;
- Create specific analysis algorithms, which produce increasing accuracy as the computation time increases.

To make the most of real-time mass processing, the implementation of Big Data causes a radical change in the way a need is expressed. This change seems close to the military's operational concerns.

The more data you have, the more difficult it is to extract specific information.

The collection of structured and unstructured datasets involves reconsidering the way data are gradually distilled through several stages, until information for decision-making is produced. To benefit better from it, it is always important to know whether all the data is necessary. A particular organization of the data in RAM could provide useful results with a sufficient degree of accuracy and quality.

Sacrificing accuracy for actionable information to stay in the battle rhythm.

Depending on the case, it is not always necessary to obtain maximum accuracy for "actionable information." The needs should be recorded and then prioritized.

Waiting too long sometimes means being too late.

It is possible to obtain an interesting result without realizing all iterations of the calculation on the whole data. This is why it is desirable to determine and prioritize the needs according to the objective to be achieved.

The better Big Data is explained and used, the more effective is the response to military requirements.

Faced with the Big Data phenomenon, we are trying to build systems, methods, and processes at the crossroad of the constraints of the military profession and the constraints of the computer systems. The subclasses in Figure 7.1 are now described from a different angle:

- *"Global analytic vision" subclass:* This subclass brings together the needs for a global vision of intelligence, of a clarified situation, directions to follow, trends, or behaviors. The results are sufficiently informative. They rely on a large sub-set of data, but computations can be improved, for instance by sampling, to reduce processing time and by reducing the reading time if the data can fit in the RAM. The use of machine learning algorithms can detect information by relying on this sampling.
- *"Deep analytics vision" subclass:* This subclass brings together the needs for an in-depth and detailed vision of intelligence. All requested data are involved in producing the result. The reports are full and detailed, and the analyses are accurate and 100% reliable. The computations are made, if necessary, over the whole set of data. The accuracy and quality of the results are maximized. It usually takes several hours to get them. The treatments are usually of the batch type.

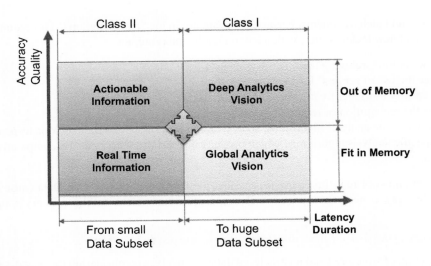

FIGURE 7.1

Use cases classification processing.

- *"Real-time information" subclass:* This subclass brings together the needs for instantly useable information. The processing time is short (from a few milliseconds to a few tens of seconds), and the latency is very low (once collected, the data are processed immediately) and guaranteed. Each fraction of time saved is important when extracting urgent information needed to guide future decisions. The data used are the most recent ones (within a range of a few minutes to a few hours); the algorithms are not always deterministic, insofar as all data are not available. The algorithms are simple, or they are designed to provide a result that is less accurate, but useable nevertheless by setting, if possible, a confidence interval. It often concerns individual, specific information, such as the geographical position of an entity on the ground at a specific time whose identity needs to be confirmed within a few minutes of identification.
- *"Actionable information" subclass:* This subclass brings together the needs associated with the "actionable information" type: high accuracy and quality with short response times (i.e., latency <100 ms). This can be done by simple filtering, merging, or enrichment operations, and by complex algorithms such as space–time correlation or machine learning in streaming mode.

In Figure 7.1, we also note that the separation into subclasses is linked to the localization of the data either in RAM or externally, i.e., stored on disk or accessible through the network on another physical server. The larger the amount of data used for processing located in memory, the quicker the treatments. Conversely, the larger the amount of data stored on disk or remotely, the longer it takes to access it. Depending on this localization, we can notice that the accessible subclasses are different. The size of the data sets used also determines which subclasses are accessible. Obviously, the larger the set, the slower the treatments on a Big Data scale.

CANONIC USE CASES

Hundreds of use cases have been analyzed. Here are some of the categories:

- International common operational picture;
- Troop movements, terror movements;
- Terror threat, terror cells;
- Defense of own troops, protection;
- Prediction of abnormal situation, change detection;
- Local and international media context color detection;
- Mission preparation.

A vast majority of these cases has been collected into 20 canonic cases. These 20 cases determine the architecture and the function of components of the system to be built. They are divided into the classes and subclasses described above.

The system we describe later is capable of handling these canonic use cases (see Table 7.1). It is highly likely that more than 80% of a military intelligence agency's needs can be met by this system. The rest can be met by additional applications included in this system.

In the remaining part of the chapter, we present several canonic use cases to highlight the importance of some components.

No.	Canonic Use Cases
	**Table 7.1 Canonic Use Cases to Gather Constraints on the Real-Time Big Data System**
1	Correlation on the fly in a sliding window
2	Correlation of data over space and time
3	Simple filtering of events with black or white lists
4	Enrichment of content on the fly and immediate notification
5	Enrichment of content on the fly with past knowledge and immediately notification
6	Spread of an interesting result in all the grid computing
7	Notify-alert based on an event with few criteria
8	Notify-alert based on abnormal reality (machine learning) on the fly
9	Numbers called by an identifier in the last hours
10	Numbers called by an identifier over 1 year without the last hours
11	Numbers called by an identifier over 1 year including the last hours
12	Top 50 of called numbers for any identifier over one year including the last hours
13	Provide for one identifier all the communications in the last 3 weeks
14	Provide all identifier in a location at time t
15	Audit why the systems fails to extract information
16	Request: *Quality = F(duration)*
17	Geo fencing
18	Ad-hoc interactivity request on a sub-set of data
19	*Query = F(all data)*
20	Read a big graph and relations

FILTERING

Governments have to implement democratic rules regarding the protection of their citizens' private data. To do so, they need to be able to filter any data protected by specific rules. The excluded data must be destroyed even before they are archived on disk. Military interventions proceed in the same way, but with rules specific to the conflict and to international or strategic agreements. For instance, during an intervention by NATO forces in a conflict, diplomatic relations and agreements between involved forces necessitate filtering the data with the appropriate security mechanisms.

When an event is captured, it can be filtered by applying more or less complex filtering rules. No delay is allowed for the processing; i.e., the processing latency is very low, and no event can be left waiting. In case of the breakdown of one of the system's components, the recovery should be quasi-immediate. It is therefore necessary to include regular checkpoints. The treatments do not need to use past events.

Remember that the flow of events to be filtered ranges from approximately 10,000 events/sec to 1,000,000 events/sec. Over 24h, the number can be as high as 100 billion events per day, while the volume to be stored is 30 Terabytes approximately. These are quantities large enough to explain the fact that solutions are still rare. The system we are describing for these new needs is scalable. The building concepts and principles are all the more valid for a system 1000 times smaller.

CORRELATION OF DATA OVER SPACE AND TIME

As explained above, time is critical, and it is not acceptable for a query to take minutes or even hours. Two approaches are possible to query all data with an almost instant response. The first approach is to answer the query globally. This means that for a query, the computation will be done over the whole data, and the results will be published for all the possible queries. For example, to answer the request of someone's top 50 called numbers, for each individual number a computation will be done and the result will be stored.

- *Benefits:* Best response time to a query.
- *Concerns:* Each query must be programmed.

The second approach is to prepare the result over all the data, but not to get the final answer. The ideal is to compute a grouping that will get answers to many queries. The final answer will be a fast computation on a small sub-set of the data by making operations on the grouping. For example, if you need to create a top 50 of numbers called by a person, the computation over all the data would be to group all numbers that have been called by this person and only store this result. The final answer would be a computation summing each called number only for the person you are interested in, then to order and select only the top 50.

- *Benefits:* The schema is adaptable to queries, so you can answer another query with such a model.
- *Concerns:* A small computation must be done before returning results. It could be difficult to find a global schema to answer many questions.

Query = F(All data) refers literally to making an arbitrary query involving all the data. This is how Nathan Marz (author of "Storm a Big Data Event Processing Technology," 2012) depicts the capabilities of a Real-Time Big Data system such as we describe later. This theoretical capability is actually achievable. Large companies such as Twitter, Facebook, LinkedIn, Google, and others already implement the capability that we are developing and adapting to meet military requirements.

MORE ON THE DIGITAL VERSION OF THE REAL WORLD (SEE THE WORLD AS EVENTS)

In the last decades, increasingly sophisticated calculations have allowed the growth of reading, interpreting and forecasting capabilities. Although the calculations are still useful, the systems are faced with an explosion of 3'Vs data. They are either unable to perform, or it is necessary to choose a sampling mode, which allows a reduction in the number of events on entry—a difficult operation in itself.

One has to consider that this data explosion is also an opportunity, because the world has never been digitalized to such an extent. To mention only one sub-set, our communications and movements, as well as the behaviors of the connected objects that we use, all generate a constantly updated digital image of the world. Not only is the volume of data huge, but reconstituting the real world is difficult; because event sources are diverse, some of those captured are of an uneven quality, are captured with a time lag, or come from different geographical locations.

We have identified an intermediary stage, which consists in rebuilding a coherent digital version of the real world. The construction of a digital version of the world is feasible, if we consider that:

- The digital version can be effective without being complete,
- It specializes in a specific domain such as military intelligence,
- It is based on data, which should be captured with a specific intent/for a specific aim,
- It is based on algorithms ranging from the simplest to the most complex, which—once they have been parallelized—are capable of partially reconstructing a digital version closely resembling the real world for military requirements, and
- The minimal digital version of the world is shared by all downstream processing. All analytical processing, from the simplest to the most complex, aims to gain a better knowledge of reality.

The soldier of today and tomorrow uses more and more connected objects and sensors. Soldiers are now able to shoot at enemies without seeing them directly by using augmented reality glasses connected to his or her viewfinder. It is conceivable that part of the augmented digital world could be superimposed onto these glasses. Within a few seconds, it is possible to provide additional information in the viewfinder by using massive real-time processing to clarify images of newly discovered enemy positions.

The sensors of the soldier's Nano network not only inform the soldier directly, but they also provide data about the environment that could only be correlated by central systems. From a more thorough perspective:

- The world is considered as a set of events.
- Parts of these events are included in the digital version of the world.
- The capture and immediate processing of these events are two conditions, which will result in the creation of an added value that is both complementary to and different from a chain, which archives events and performs deferred batch processing.

There are some paradoxes, which are not only constraints but also strengths:

- The more numerous, specific, and powerful the sensors are, the closer to the real world will be the data collected by these sensors.
- As the 3'Vs data increase in volume, it becomes more difficult to build systems capable of supporting the processing.

To address these paradoxes, we use a building device. "On the fly" processing or streaming allows the launch of immediate processing on the flow of events describing one part of the real world. The resulting information may be partial or complete, partially reliable or totally reliable. However, at the time, it may prove vital to the success of an operation. Indeed, the early emergence of a piece of tactical information enables the early preparation of the means, of the decision to open fire or not, the prepositioning of forces, the selection of targets, etc. It is therefore natural to design processing, which ranges from the simplest to the most complex and from the quickest to the slowest. For example, upstream of the processing, the data are purged by filtering the nonuseful events, sorting or counting them. By examining only a few fields of the event, it is possible to quickly identify the useful events, so as to regroup and correlate them. At every stage, added value appears, which brings more elements to support the decision.

QUALITY OF DATA, METADATA, AND CONTENT

Originating for the most part from varied sources (sensors, Open Source Intelligence (OSINT),[4] websites, social media, communications, SMS, etc.), the data is extremely diverse. It usually takes the form of several streams of files from which the intercepted events are extracted. These events consist of metadata and content. For instance, a communication consists of, on one hand, the sender, the receiver, the start and end dates of the communication, geographical details, etc. On the other hand, there is the content of the communication. Some events contain only metadata. Metadata is small in size (a few hundreds of bytes), whereas the content can reach several tens or hundreds of megabytes in size.

It is important to take into account this difference in size, because the mixing of metadata and content within the same pipeline is to be avoided, because the processes to be applied differ in nature.

To give an idea of the range, the system studied in this chapter is able to process hundreds of thousands of events per second. The average size of an event is in the 500-byte range. This system is mainly concerned with problems related to the processing of metadata. The processing chain for content contains other difficulties, which can be handled by mechanisms already designed within the metadata processing system and by the mechanisms of more conventional systems.

Data sources are imperfect, sensors have limited capabilities, and data transmission can be random. Between the source of the generated event and the data center, it is therefore not unusual for the data to be incomplete, partial, damaged, lost, badly coded, imperfectly decrypted, unsynchronized, or delayed. It is an illusion to want to build a Real-Time Big Data system without taking this situation into account. This is the reason why the concept of constructing a digital image of the world that is being continuously updated is of particular importance. The architecture has to include the different cases of damage to the data, some mechanisms to partially remedy it, and some rules to rectify the situation logically and

---

[4]Open source Intelligence (OSINT) collected from publicly available sources. In the intelligence community (IC), the term "open" refers to overt, publicly available sources (as opposed to covert or clandestine sources). It is not related to open-source software or public intelligence.

progressively to improve the digital world used as a unique source for the processing. The impact on the profession is patent: A method of reflection should be established so as to evaluate how analysts at their desks and soldiers on the ground learn to deal with quantified uncertainty and possible damage to the digital image.

REAL-TIME BIG DATA SYSTEMS
APPLICATION PRINCIPLES AND CONSTRAINTS

The concepts and constraints originate from the needs and use cases described above, namely:

- The digital version of the real world is built in real-time. The necessary and sufficient digital version is formed progressively.
- The continuous digitalization of the world produces new data in real-time, immediately available for real-time enrichment processing.
- As soon as an event is collected, it is processed before being archived.
- The processing time is guaranteed. The latency is as low as possible.
- An immediate partial result is often more interesting than the full result, which requires more calculation time.
- It implements the canonic use cases.
- It contributes highly to the "battle rhythm" by means of reducing the computation time in the same scale as the communication components.

It is a "Real-Time Big Data System" because:

- Events originating from the world and the battlefield are processed immediately. One level of real-time analysis should cover 80% of needs. (It is an approximation, which is to be adjusted according to the operational contexts.)
- It integrates data sources such as geographical data systems, weather forecast services, and civilian or military databases.
- The system is scalable; it increases or reduces in size based on the amount of data, the latency, and the processing times required.
- Within the intelligence chain, it is located between the event sources and the data analysis applications. It is a subsystem of the global system.
- A short loop is available thanks to the "real-time" component of the system.
- It can be highly available (option of a total 24/24 availability).
- In case of recovery, there is no loss of data (option depending on the financial investment).

Each component of the system is justified by:

- The generic use cases;
- The processing time constraints, volume of data, and diverse nature of the data;
- The architectural principles of Big Data computer systems.

In Figure 7.2, which is inspired by the centric warfare concept, sensors generate events consisting in metadata and structured and unstructured contents of varied nature. Sources can also include satellite or ground communication networks, as well as OSINT. Social networks are rich in data, which are useful for

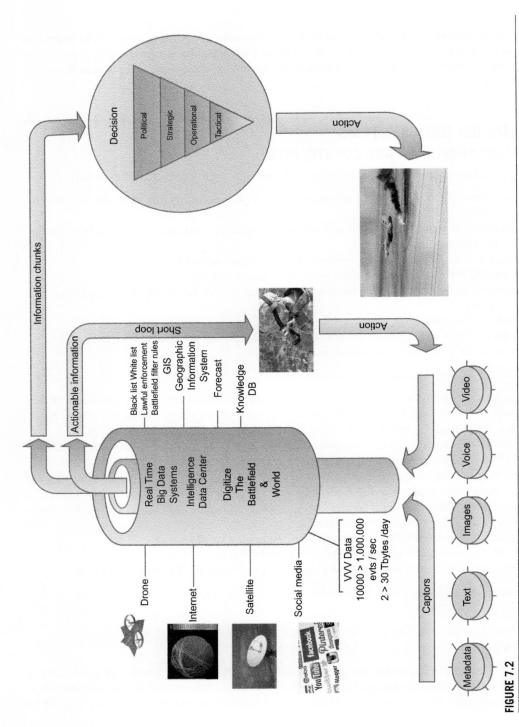

FIGURE 7.2

World and battlefield are made of events to compute into a real-time big data system.

preparing missions and for the "battle rhythm." Military data repositories are also used in combination with other sources such as weather stations or airline or Geographic Information System (GIS) data.

LOGICAL VIEW

The macro logical view gives an overview of a viable real-time Big Data system. The diagram in Figure 7.3 is split into large logical components to get closer to the real system, which is to be built with the relevant technologies. The system is scalable and modular by nature. It is strongly advised that the system be developed in successive increments. It is possible to start by processing a sub-set of data in streaming mode. This, for example, represents about 10% of the proposed system. And yet, it contains all the basic principles, which will allow the system to be developed in several stages. For instance, results are at first accessible only in the form of predetermined alerts. It is possible to program as many alerts as necessary from queries with a shorter or longer response time according to the confidence interval that is to be obtained.

From the left side, accessible data sources generate a few thousand to several millions events per second. They depict the real world, but some of them are polluters or background noise. Others have not been used, or a rule prevents them from being used. The filtering and elimination processing of data has to be updated to a scale suitable to their number, their diversity, and their immediate or delayed use.

In the next stage, these events, still mostly unusable, are transformed into a unique format while retaining their diversity and content. As sources or sensors produce, albeit at different speeds and different places, events describing the same phenomenon (e.g., a communication or an entity's movements), it is necessary to resynchronize, correlate, and aggregate them to reconstruct a coherent image of the real world. This component continuously computes the world in real-time. The digital world is constantly updated by sources and sensors. Only the most recent part is stored in memory, within what is called "the stream of coherent and rectified events," which is then injected in real-time processing and stored on disk. From storage on disk, it is always possible to extract any images from the past. Events are immutable. and they are never deleted.

The "streaming layer" component performs real-time processing triggered on receipt of new events originating from the digital world. Two types of engines are required to meet different needs. The first one is a "pure event processor" engine, able to trigger processing for each event received. The second engine proceeds by aggregating a relatively small number of events to apply the same processing to all of them simultaneously. The latency is potentially higher, but among the use cases "machine learning" is particularly suitable for this engine. The "streaming layer" immediately transfers the results into "real-time views," which index them. These results can be accessed via the "publishing results layer." The "subscribing layers" are notified, and alerts are then dispatched under different forms to terminals such as workstations, tablets, mobile phones, or effectors.

While the "streaming layer" deals only with the latest updates of the digital world, the "batch layer" covers the whole history. This capability is essential when wanting to apply deterministic processing. Class I of the generic use cases is based on batch processing. These types of processing are batch-related, because they last from several minutes to several hours. Thanks to this layer, it is always possible to reconstruct all results from the repository containing the event history. Results produced by the "batch layer" are indexed in batch views accessible via the "publishing layer." The digital world is fully accessible through the "publishing layer" by reuniting the history accessible through the "batch views" and the most recent events, which are flowing into the "streaming layer" via the "real-time views."

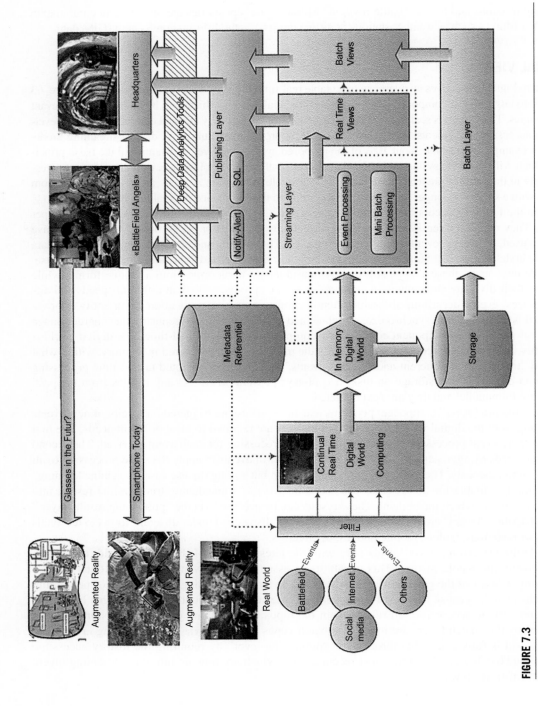

FIGURE 7.3

Real-time big data system view.

IMPLEMENTING THE REAL-TIME BIG DATA SYSTEM

In the following, we explain how and with which technology such a system can be built. We chose the open-source option, but other solutions exist, supplied by publishers such as IBM, HP, Oracle, etc. Our system is a true real-time system. The coupling of three layers (streaming, batch, and publishing) ensures a wider range than what real-time allows in terms of results and access to all data. This range is expressed by the need equation analyzed previously: *Query = Function(All Data)*. In the following, we introduce the optimum choices based on open-source software. The open-source option is a realistic choice also made by the biggest social media and internet players, such as Twitter, Facebook, Netflix, LinkedIn, and others for their own real-time Big Data systems.

The batch, streaming, and publishing layers are loosely coupled with strong coherency between updating and data timeline coverage. Beyond the field of streaming capabilities, all layers give access to the 20 canonic uses cases over the whole data. The most generic of capabilities is contained in the equation: *Query = F(All Data)*. We explain hereafter the optimum choices for the layers with the best Big Data open-source software.

BATCH PROCESSING (INTO THE "BATCH LAYER")

Today, "Big Data" is a trending term associated with the idea that it will solve recurrent problems of existing systems: data warehouse approach brings high maintenance, too much time spent on ETL, increased loading time, etc. Behind the concept, the reality is a little different. The volume, variety, and velocity illustrate what Big Data means: a lot of sensors bringing too much data in a wide range of nonstandardized formats within a few seconds. If making sense of all this data is impossible using a classical approach, because of the long processing time and large data volumes to store, a batch-oriented architecture should be considered.

The storage layer must be able to store petabytes of data effectively under the constraint that costs and performance should stay linear. Instead of using a storage area network, the cost of which will grow exponentially until it has reached a set limit, a distributed file system offers a substantial benefit by only adding servers to a cluster and using their disks as a distributed storage. The storage layer is mostly based on the Hadoop distributed file system (HDFS). The benefits of HDFSs are: they are cheap to maintain; data is replicated and stored in blocks to limit overhead; and access is I/O parallel.

PROCESSING LAYER (INTO THE "BATCH LAYER")

Two main open-source solutions exist today to process large batches of data: Hadoop with MapReduce and Spark. Hadoop has been on the market for a few years. The Apache Software Foundation released the second version of Hadoop during summer 2013. The major improvement has been to split the Job Tracker into two different daemons: the resource manager and the job scheduling/monitoring. This approach, called YARN, allows the resource manager to dedicate resources to application managers that can be a simple MapReduce job or a more complicated DAG job. This has led to the rise of multiple frameworks.

In a Hadoop cluster, data are distributed over all nodes. A MapReduce job is defined as a mapper operation, sometimes a combiner, and finally a reducer, which processes the job result. Ideally, the mapper is executed on each node with the data stored locally on the node. The mapper is a parallel operation, which will produce a tuple with a key and value. The combiner operation happens at the end of the mapper operation. It is also parallelized and in general used to precompute intermediate results. Finally, the reducer will sort the data on the grouped key and will process it.

A MapReduce job is a bit tedious to write. Therefore frameworks have been developed to facilitate this step. Three frameworks should be considered. The first is *Apache Pig*, which is a logical expression of the data pipeline to be created for a job. The Pig execution engine will transform a Pig script as a sequence of M/R jobs.[5] The processing is expressed in the Pig Latin language, and extensions needed such as custom reader or writer must be expressed in a user defined function. (Since the release, 0.12 users can write them in Java (preferred choice), Python (for Hadoop 1.0), Jython, Ruby (experimental), or Javascript (experimental).)

Another approach is to use *Cascalog*, which is similar to Apache Pig, because it enables the developer to express jobs in terms of logical blocks. The processing can be expressed using Clojure or Java.

Apache Hive, as the third framework, is a better approach for non-developers, because it enables users to express queries in a language close to SQL. The purpose of the Stinger initiative, which came out in Hive version 0.13, is to have a full SQL support, meaning that existing SQL applications could be plugged over Hive, and thus accelerate queries by a factor of 100. To do so, queries are now running in memory with Tez.

Tez is an extension to Hadoop developed and supported by Hortonworks. The purpose of Tez is to accelerate and break constraints of the MapReduce by eliminating constraints such as synchronization and read and write to HDFS between jobs. It is an execution engine that can process complex DAG that will be submitted to YARN for resources allocation. Therefore it is highly suitable for Apache Pig and Apache Hive. First results show an improvement by almost 100 times on HiveQL queries (see Stinger initiative from Hortonworks).

Another framework that is getting much attention in the last few months is Spark. Spark is an open source project developed by the Apache Software Foundation.

SPARK

Spark is a distributed execution engine, which works with HDFS to load data and store results. It allows the developer to express a pipeline of instructions easily in Java, Scala, or Python that will be transformed into a DAG job by the execution engine. It is similar to what can be done with Hadoop, but its mechanism of caching the data significantly increases the performance of iterative algorithms. The pipeline of instructions is made possible by the RDD structure. RDD stands for "resilient distributed dataset" and defines an object as a distributed collection over the cluster with operations and actions, which can be applied to the RDD to filter or act on each element (see the operation and actions list in spark.apache.org/docs). The first operation is to load data to an RDD. The easiest way is to use the HadoopRDD that has a method to parse lines from a text file. Once this is done, many operations can be applied, such as a map that means a function will transform each data inside the collection, a filter that also takes a function to keep only the interesting data for the algorithm, a group by key that will help group data according to a field, a join that will help joining two RDD collection on a key, etc.

---

[5] M/R stands for MapReduce. MapReduce is done in several steps. Typically, map computations are parallelized and distributed across the cluster, and the reduce computation aggregate map computation results.

Spark internals

Spark works with three main components. The *Spark master* manages the cluster made of *Spark workers*, which are executing a program driven by an application master called the *driver*. The role of the driver is to submit jobs to the cluster, so if a job fails it will not interfere with other submitted jobs to the cluster from different drivers.

The driver is built with four main components: RDD graph, scheduler, block tracker, and shuffle tracker.

- The RDD graph is the representation of operators applied to data in RDD.
- The schedulers for DAG and tasks in charge of DAG creation and tasks execution.
- The block manager is a "write-once" key-value stored on each worker, which serves shuffle data and cached RDD.
- The shuffle tracker enables retry from shuffle outputs written to RAM/disk.

Once built, the application is executed on the master node in charge to manage the application execution on the Spark cluster. The execution follows a scheduling process in four steps: the DAG scheduler is the component that will interpret the program and create a DAG job that will be split into stages of tasks and then submit each stage as ready. It knows dependencies between operations at the partition level. A partition is a set of tasks defined by an operation on each data element. Its roles are to do the pipelining of partition operations and turn partitions into tasks. Tasks are then grouped into stages for optimization and synchronization. An example of stages is to wait for the map to finish before starting the reduce side. Each stage will be submitted to the task scheduler. The task scheduler's job is to get tasks done. It takes the independent tasks of a stage and submits them to the worker, which will return a failed task if something goes wrong, such as an unavailable or too slow node. The workers have multiples threads to execute the given tasks and a block manager to store and serve blocks to different machines.

Spark stack

The company Databricks is behind the development of the Spark stack. The purpose of Spark stack is to bring many transformation bricks to perform data analysis in a faster way than Hadoop MapReduce. In May 2014, the Spark engine reached its maturity, as the version 1.0.0 was released. Now Spark is also an ecosystem with the help of Spark Streaming, which is able to process streams of data. Spark SQL allows relational queries expressed in SQL, HiveQL, or Scala to be executed using the Spark engine. The machine learning library provides the common implementation of algorithms such as clustering, collaborative filtering, classification, etc. Finally, the stack includes GraphX for graph processing. A resilient distributed property graph extends the abstract RDD, which represents an oriented graph with properties attached to each vertex and edges. The RDD supports fundamental operations to perform graph analysis like reversion, subgraph, and join on vertices.

DATA STREAM PROCESSING (INTO THE "STREAMING LAYER")

Storm—a pure complex event processing

Storm is a distributed streaming engine that could be considered as a pure complex event processing framework, since computing starts when events happen. A *Spout* that will emit tuples to computing units called *Bolts* reads data representing events. A streaming workflow in Storm is called a topology.

A topology is described as a set of Spouts reading events and sets of Bolts that can subscribe to events emitted by Spout and other Bolts. The fault tolerance mechanism is based on the Spout behavior that flags emitted tuples. Each Bolt will acknowledge each received tuple once it has been processed. The DAG job is considered completed once each Bolt has acknowledged the tuple. Then the Spout will consider the events as treated. After a certain timeout, the Spout will emit again the tuple for processing and retry a defined number of times.

Trident over storm

Trident is a logical layer based on the Spouts and Bolts mechanisms described above. Using Trident, the developer expresses the processing based on logical instructions instead of a streaming workflow. Trident is equivalent to Apache Pig for Storm. Tuples are treated in a batch manner inducing a bit of processing latency. It is important to understand that if a tuple fails, the whole batch the tuple belongs to will be replayed by the fault tolerant mechanism. Furthermore, the stream is made up of multiple batches that are sequentially ordered. If a batch fails, it will not be possible to process the subsequent batches. Storm is part of the Apache Software Foundation as an incubating project. The current version is Apache Storm 0.9.1. It has been tested and considered as very stable.

Spark streaming simulating real-time with mini-batches

As a new candidate, Spark Streaming seems promising, because it builds over the Spark engine. The approach is the opposite of the Storm processing, because events are not brought to the processing. Rather they are aggregated in small batches that will last at least for a second. The processing then happens inside a mini-batch in the same way it would happen inside a regular Spark code application. Instead of manipulating an RDD directly, a structure called a DStream (districtized stream) is used, which is a succession of RDD that can be access using a special operation called foreachRDD. Each RDD in a DStream represents data from a certain interval of time. Any operation done on the DStream will be executed on all the RDD composing it by the Spark engine. Operations on a DStream are very similar to the regular Spark API, but can use an updateByKey, which will take a function to update each key. Finally an interesting feature of Spark Streaming is the ability to use sliding windows that will help compute results over several mini-batches (count, reduce, reducebykey).

ALERTS AND NOTIFICATIONS (INTO THE "PUBLISHING LAYER")

As soon as a result is available, users are notified via subscribed applications: popup, graphic alerts in a window, an additional line on a dashboard, a signal over a map, etc. This component must be able to notify a number of results, not only to the end user, but also to other analytics applications in real-time. Between computing an event and the notification on a screen the latency should be less than a second. To ensure the transfer from computing nodes dealing with up to one million of events per second to the users, the "publishing layer" must convert speed and throughput for the slower applications and users.

FILTERING PROCESSING FITTING IN MEMORY (INTO THE "STREAMING LAYER")

Input data should be injected into a messaging queue. Apache Kafka is perfect for the role, because it is a distributed messaging queue serving messages from memory that will fall back to disk storage and cached data. Messages are published to a topic that is distributed to Kafka servers called brokers.

A topic is made of multiple partitions that are each sequentially ordered and to which only data can be append. Reading from Kafka brokers is fast, because it reads from all available partitions. It is the job of the consumer to keep track of what has been read. This helps the broker to keep a low load. The producer, as the name suggests, reads data from a source and then produces messages to a topic. For parallelization, the producer will use all available partitions.

Filtering of stream jobs consists of reading from a Kafka source representing the most recent events and reacting to them. Usually a filtering job will have a collection such as a HashMap that will know, which data should be filtered and which tags should be added to the event that will be distributed across all computing nodes. Once the event matches the filtering map, it will be processed accordingly, which can mean adding tags, transforming the events, and finally publishing it to a Kafka topic called alerts or sending an email if the number of matches is reasonable.

The interesting fact is that, once an event is filtered, it could trigger other processing steps just by being read from the alert topic. This setup provides a true event processing model inside the "streaming layer."

MACHINE LEARNING AND FILTERING (INTO THE "BATCH AND STREAMING LAYERS")

Let us consider distributed denial of service attacks as a use case. A list of vital interest organizations must be monitored for national security purposes, and we are going to describe a basic approach using open-source software instead of network devices to illustrate a possible setup to protect such organizations. This example is to illustrate the filtering method, but would not be as efficient as a specific DDOS[6] network device. A sensor is plugged-in on the national network backbone that delivers Internet traffic to national providers, which are routing it to the vital interest organizations. The sensor is acting as a deep packet inspection and will deliver meta-information and content to our filtering system. Meta-information is small datasets that describe the content that has been generated. Meta-information will provide at least a source IP-address representing the potential threat and a destination IP-address representing our national organization we need to protect.

The first step consists of filtering the massive traffic, i.e., dropping everything that does not target our limited destination IP-address. Using Storm, we are implementing a topology with a spout that will read a Kafka topic with the meta-information. The topology contains three Bolts:

- Destination filtering Bolt, which knows the destination IP-address;
- Request filtering;
- Results write to Kafka Bolt.

The only treatment of the filtering destination Bolt is to look for the destination IP-address. If it is known, it will send a tuple to the filtering request Bolt. Two interesting implementations are worth mentioning. First, if there are a lot of IP-addresses to monitor, it might be interesting to use a bloom filter instead of a HashMap for better performance. Second, if there is a dynamic list of IP-addresses to monitor, it might be interesting to implement a second spout that will read a Kafka topic, which is hosting add and delete actions for monitored IP-addresses. The destination-filtering Bolt will subscribe to the monitored IP-addresses spout and will update its reference table accordingly. The request-filtering job will only look for request types and will drop anything that is not request related. If this is the case,

---

[6] Distributed denial of service attack.

then it will send a tuple to the final Bolt for writing to Kafka. The result Bolt to Kafka exists only because we do not want the request Bolt to wait for a replication acknowledgment from Kafka to be able to process more incoming tuples (events).

To filter the number of requests made by an IP-address, we are going to implement a frequency requests monitoring algorithm. The algorithm will learn from the context. For each mini-batch (lasting a second), the request frequency is calculated for each IP-address, similarly to a word-count. The IP-address will serve as a key, and a tuple will be emitted for each request. The tuple is reduced by the IP-address, and then each bucket is counted. Once the IP-address count is known, it is divided by the number of batches since the beginning or since a specific period to be monitored (sliding window of time), which results in the frequency. The last step is to compare the frequency to the threshold. If it is higher, the requests will be dropped. Such an algorithm should be implemented before the filtering method described above, because it will drop unnecessary traffic to be processed by the Storm topology.

Using the Spark streaming, you are reading a Kafka topic with a Kafka input stream receiver, which provides a DStream of events. We are going to split the events on the separator and drop everything else than our column of interest, the source IP-address. Next we are grouping all events by IP-address and reduce on it. Spark streaming already has implemented a reducekey operation, which takes a function. This function should be associative for parallel computation. We are transforming our DStream with the use of the reduceykey using the addition function, which will give us a new DStream providing a count per IP-address. The frequency is then calculated by dividing it with the number of batches. Finally, we are filtering the DStream with a function that compares the frequency with the threshold. This gives us the final DStream. On the final DStream, we are going to act on each element to produce a Kafka topic. We can make this algorithm "stateful" by remembering the frequency each time or "forgetful" by recomputing it each time.

ONLINE CLUSTERING (INTO THE "STREAMING LAYER")

The online KMeans, which allows clustering data on the fly by reading a stream, is a technique that should be explored. Currently in Spark, the machine learning library is not compatible with the Spark Streaming. Here is an explanation of how to use it.

Data are read from a Kafka topic and then split into different events. These events are dealt with in minibatches; i.e., each batch will cluster its events and then update the centroids. Events are considered as vectors inside a DStream. For each mini-batch, vectors are broken down into k clusters by a function that computes the average distance between a vector and the centroids. Once all vectors are assigned to a cluster, we proceed to compute the intermediate centroid for each cluster. Finally, to get the new centroids, we compute for each cluster the new centroid by weighting the intermediate centroid by the number of vectors that were used to compute it, then add it to the weighted old centroid with the total number of vectors that were used to compute it divided by the total weight of old centroid and intermediate centroid.

RESULTS PUBLICATION

Top 50 source IP-addresses for a destination IP-address in 1 year without the last hour

Let us assume that the batch processing took less than an hour; then the accurate result lies inside the batch view. Therefore a simple query to the publication system should only query the batch processing view and return its results.

Top 50 source IP-addresses for a destination IP-address in the last hour

To build on our example, the batch view has been computed, but it missed the last hour. Therefore the publication system needs to query the last hour of the streaming, view results, and return the result to the user.

Top 50 source IP-addresses for a destination IP-address in 1 year including the last hour

Finally, if the user wants the result to a query, which requires the whole history including the last hour, the publication system should be able to aggregate the results of both views produced above.

BUILD THE LAYERS

As we have seen over the previous pages, the "batch layer" is a collection of events from a large period. In contrast, the data "stream layer" is a collection of events, which are acted on in near real-time (a few milliseconds to a few seconds maximum). For each processing, results are lying in each layer. At times, it will be enough to just query one layer; at others, it may be better to query both layers. If we build on the filtering example, analysts may want to query the top 50 source IP-addresses that have queried one particular host in the last three months, including today and current events that have just happened when the query was made.

The first step is to query the batch layer with Apache Pig. For this, you will load the events stored in HDFS with a load instruction in a relation. Then every field not needed is dropped to keep only the important ones, such as the IP-address (our key), the date of the event, etc. This will limit the size of the data going through the pipeline and will significantly accelerate our Pig script. This is done with the help of the *foreach* instruction for each relation, which generates a list of fields separated by commas. The next step is to group the data by source IP-address. The relation will then contain bags of events, in which the key is the source IP-address. For each bag, we will then count the number of elements. Finally, the list is ordered by count and filtered for the 50 first results. Because the code is pretty simple and can be written in less than 10 lines of Pig script, we added it below as a reference:

```
rawdata=LOAD 'myhdfsevent' AS (srcip, evtdate,dstip);
ipaddresses=FOREACH rawdata GENERATE srcip, evtdate;
grps=GROUP ipaddresses BY srcip;
count=FOREACH grps GENERATE count(ipadresses) as frequency, ipadresses.srcip;
order=ORDER count BY frequency DESC;
result=LIMIT order 50

STORE result INTO 'output' USING PigStorage(';');
```

Depending on the amount of data stored in HDFS and the number of nodes in a cluster, the batch processing time could exceed hours. Therefore a query regarding past and today's events will not be accurate only using results processed by the batch; i.e., the batch view is only accurate during the processing of a batch, and for the time the views are published to a database. To respect the CAP theorem, the database needs to be available and partition tolerant to user requests. Therefore a batch view will replace an older batch view and switch only when it is absolutely certain that it has been totally uploaded. An important feature for such databases is that they must be able to do random reads, once writable, as well as be scalable and fault tolerant.

In case of a DDOS attack, the source IP-address might change during the attack. If this is happening, the top 50 might change radically. Therefore a topology or a job is needed that will compute the same results, but for the last hours including only events since the last batch starting time. With such an approach, there will be redundant algorithms expressed in different technologies. Efforts are being made to limit algorithm implementations.[7]

Such results should be stored in a database like Cassandra or HBase, which are capable of storing a large number of results and be queried very fast, if the schema is designed in accordance to the queries. In general, NoSQL databases like the ones mentioned previously are made to support large amounts of data, and contrary to the SQL model, "denormalization" is here the main principle. Therefore schemas for fast queries can be designed, which do not care about the amount of data stored in a system. Of course there should be a tradeoff between the number of times information is stored and the requests, which cannot wait for replies. The drawback of such a database is that it needs to retain indexes. Therefore appending is easy, but updating and removing is dangerous.

When a top-50 request is made, the system will ask the batch view and the data stream view for the top 50 results since the last batch start time. The system will then compare the last entry of the batch view results and the first results of the data stream view. If the data stream results do not differ, it will return the response directly; otherwise, it will recompute the new response before returning it back to the user.

Another approach would be to use only the Spark stack with a Spark Streaming and to join them with a Spark Batch to publish the results. At the time of writing, this setup has not yet been tested, but this should be done soon.

INSIGHT INTO DEEP DATA ANALYTICS TOOLS AND REAL-TIME BIG DATA SYSTEMS

The best intelligence systems are very sophisticated. Many highly performing analytics or data-mining engines are used: correlation engines, predictive analytics, or monitored machine learning algorithms. SAAS, SPSS, KXen, Cognos, and numerous other tools have been used over the years to perform complex data analyses to produce results. I2 Analyst's Notebook and Palantir are also used to handle and visualize information. *We are not questioning these tools and their necessity.* On the contrary, they belong to the tools located downstream of the system proposed in this book. *Still, none of them can handle one-thousandth of the flows considered.* Moreover, they are also not designed to operate in a "streaming" mode, which consists in executing algorithms iteratively on part of the data while taking earlier computations into account. Generally, to execute analyses or classification algorithms, these tools require all the data on entry. It is only recently that several new open-source projects have started to bring batch algorithms into new frameworks to process in streaming mode. This computation mode is essential, and we shall see how it is implemented later.

---

[7] Twitter has developed a framework in Scala to develop a logical job only once that will be executed in Storm and in MapReduce. This framework is called SummingBird. The source is available on github (https://github.com/twitter/summingbird) and is working over Tez.

For these tools to support the heavy load of these data, three options are available:

1. The publishers transform part of the software to adapt them to Big Data using NoSQL data bases, streaming mode, parallelism, and scalability. This is a real challenge, presently not sufficiently met in roadmaps.
2. Only part of the data flow is accessible through the tools, the rest is sacrificed. The tool's role is restricted/limited, and the analyst's field is reduced in the case of correlation or obtaining specific query results. The results are partial or not reliable due to a lack of original/primary data.
3. Upstream enrichment processing is performed in Big Data to reduce the cardinality of the data injected in the tools.

We recommend option 3. It is necessary to apply part of the business rules upstream in the Big Data system. For conventional data mining tools, this option presents some difficulties on entry with regard to the integration and understanding of the added value and use of intermediate results.

ADD FAULT TOLERANCE

Each technology mentioned above has its own mechanism of fault tolerance that will replay data if a node fails. But what if your application is trying to aggregate events by time and by space—meaning you are not working anymore on a single event, but rather are waiting for multiple events to happen before getting a result? In this case you will have to keep the data until each event happened or before a timeout occurred. This timeout should be tuned to the algorithm. Such algorithms require a system that supports random reads and random write updates and deletes data very fast. At the same time, it should not keep data very long. A good candidate is Memcached, a distributed key-value store with load-balancing capacities. Because the open-source community lacks such solutions, we can mention commercial solutions such as VoltDB and SQL Fire.

In a time and space aggregation algorithm, you will store in Memcached the bucket (usually a Hashmap), which stores the waiting events. In case of a node failure, buckets will not be lost; instead they would simply be reloaded into a new node. To reload the bucket, the newly started node should request the key at initialization from Memcached, which will return the bucket list. The drawback of this method is that the bucket list should be serializable. Clearly, there is a trade-off between performance and missing elements. If you want best performance you will use an asynchronization client for Memcached. In this case, if a node fails, the most recent events would not be in sync. Therefore, when a node starts again you might have lost some information. In contrast, if 100% recovery is required, performance will be impacted.

SECURITY

The Big Data world is still recent, and as such, technologies are not focusing their main efforts on the security aspects. Currently, the batch processing view supports communication security. Hadoop v2 Hbase and Cassandra have implemented encrypted communication with the help of certificates and Kerberos realm. However, looking at the streaming view, technologies are not security mature. Apache Kafka has just released a specification for the security aspect, but does not include it yet in the roadmap. Apache Storm and Spark do not include communication security. Therefore, security should be implemented at organizational level and technical level focusing on network security, isolation, and operating system hardening.

ADDING FLEXIBILITY AND ADAPTATION

When working with a large stack of middleware, there is a need to react quickly when facing event overloads. As cloud solutions are adopted more and more, such tools now exist, and it should be easy to obtain at least a configured operating system on demand. It is important to build the cloud catalogue services, because this will help provisioning snapshots in a short period. For each Big Data technology in a cluster, all nodes' hostnames must be held in a configuration file. With the help of suites such as Chef, Puppet, and even Salt, it becomes increasingly easier to deploy the software mentioned above, because most of them have existing contributed modules. Therefore the combination of a cloudstack and a puppet suite helps the provisioning and reconfiguration of a cluster. The cluster orchestration should be developed according to procedures. It should support start, stop, and update at any time without impacting the production of Cloud and SaaS added values.

VERY SHORT LOOP AND BATTLEFIELD BIG DATA DATACENTERS

It is likely that the digitalization of the battlefield will lead armed forces to install, in the field, computational means and devices powerful enough to meet the requirements and the data flow generated by all sources present on the battlefield. The anticipation of means/devices, which will allow a better view of the hidden reality through the digital world, more accurate predictions of movements, a monitoring of the operational level of fuel, batteries, remaining ammunition, as well as of the troops' state of health and fatigue in real-time, will result in improved leadership in battle, improved conduct of operations, reduced loss of life, less disrupted supply chains, etc.

This is the reason why it is recommended that a superscalar datacenter (see Figure 7.4) be made available on the battlefield to drastically shorten the loop between sensors and users and to obtain real-time results with very low latency. Services rendered by the datacenter are so important that any break in the link with a central level becomes critical. Consequently, a loose cooperative mode is envisaged between the main datacenter and the battlefield datacenter, as well as a disconnected operational mode. In that case, there is an impact on the use: any user should be informed of the operational status of the systems used for the conduct of operations.

CONCLUSIONS

The Big Data field includes 3'Vs data, technologies and systems built with these technologies, and a specific architecture. To fully exploit the data, we have shown that the military can greatly benefit from reconsidering the quality and accuracy of the results according to the type of requirements. It is not a weakness, but a different relationship with time, space, and the digital world. Knowing how to obtain instantaneous results that are immediately useable from so much data becomes a strength. Then, as the duration of computation lengthens, the results increase in richness and accuracy, and they progressively enrich decisions and actions without any wasted time. There is no longer any waiting at the end of a long tunnel of computation, but a number of stages in step with the battle rhythm. The military analyst in his or her office and the troops on the ground penetrate more deeply into the digital world for a sharper view of the battlefield and its surroundings.

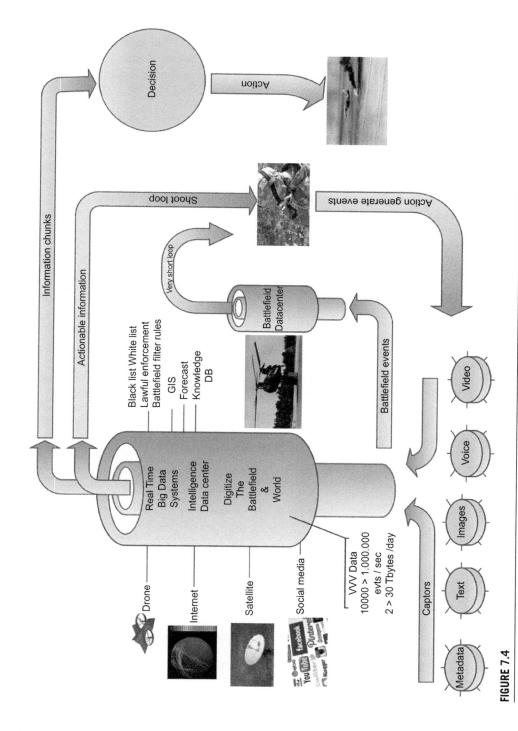

FIGURE 7.4

Drop of a superscalar datacenter on the battlefield.

The Big Data technologies we have briefly described are operational. The architecture of the proposed system combine these technologies to bring them to the attention of our readers and provide pointers on how to build the new generation of Big Data systems, capable of processing the large quantities of data available within a time scale ranging from tenths of a second to several minutes. This chapter opens the way to quickly implemented solutions, sometimes breaking away from the traditional approaches of military intelligence, command systems, and logistics systems.

Breaking away does not mean throwing out existing applications, but rather replacing or building some radically different links, as well as dealing with the change in the approach to the battlefield. This change of approach has the support of the younger soldiers, who are familiar with the digital world and fully used to superposing it onto the real world of action and the triggering of fire. It is also certain that the multiplication of data sources—as previously described—is accompanied by a multiplication of ways to use the results of Big Data processing at all levels in the armed forces. The mobility of sources and terminals is an essential element, which should be factored into the impact of Big Data when exploiting results. Thanks to its potential capability for zero latency, the real-time Big Data system, as described in this chapter, adds decisive sharpness and augmented reality to the battlefield if, but only if, the information is instantly exploited by military analysts in an operation center and by troops close to the frontline.

FURTHER READING

Apache Software Foundation, 2014a. Apache Storm. [Online] Available from: http://storm.incubator.apache.org/documentation/Home.html.

Apache Software Foundation, 2014b. Apache Spark. [Online] Available from: http://spark.apache.org/docs/latest/.

Barlow, M., 2013. Real Time Big Data Analytics: Emerging Architecture. O'Reilly Media, Sebastopol, CA.

Bloem, J., van Doorn, M., Duivestein, S., van Manen, T., van Ommeren, E., Sachdeva, S., 2013. No More Secret with Big Data Analytics. VINT SOGETI. Available from: http://vint.sogeti.com/wp-content/uploads/2013/11/Sogeti_NoMoreSecrets.pdf.

Dimiduk, N., Khurana, A., 2013. HBase in Action. Manning Publications Co., Shelter Island, NY.

Holmes, A., 2012. Hadoop in Practice. Manning Publications Co., Shelter Island, NY.

Hortonworks, 2014. Stinger. Next: Enterprise SQL at Hadoop Cale. [Online] Available from: http://hortonworks.com/labs/stinger/.

Kuhn, R., Allen, J., 2014. Reactive Design Patterns. Manning Early Access Program (MEAP). Manning Publications.

Luckham, D., 2002. The Power of Events: An Introduction to Complex Event Processing in Distributed Enterprise Systems. Addison Wesley.

Marz, N., Warren, J., 2012. Big Data Principles and Best Practices of Scalable Realtime data Systems. Manning Early Access Program (MEAP). Manning Publications Co.

Opher, E., Niblett, P., 2011. Event Processing in Action. Manning Publications Co., Stamford, CT.

Office of Science and Technology Policy. Obama Administration Unveils "Big Data" Initiative: Announces $200 Millions in New R&D Investment R&D 2012. Office of Science and Technology Policy Executive Office of the President of the United States. Available from: http://www.whitehouse.gov/sites/default/files/microsites/ostp/big_data_press_release.pdf.

Pearce, R., Wednesday 13 March 2013. How Defence Tackles the Challenge of Big Data with Machine Learning. Computerworld. [Online] Available from: http://www.computerworld.com.au/article/456194/how_defence_tackles_challenge_big_data_machine_learning/.

Torruela, R., December 1, 2006. Managing the battle rhythm. [PowerPoint presentation] In: Presented at the 12th International Command and Control Research and Technology Symposium (ICCRTS) at Newport, Rhode Island. Available from: http://www.dodccrp.org/events/12th_ICCRTS/CD/html/presentations/132.pdf.

Wikipedia, 2014a. Network Centric Warfare. [Online] Available from: http://fr.wikipedia.org/wiki/Network_Centric_Warfare.

Wikipedia, 2014b. Actionable Information Logistics. [Online] Available from: http://en.wikipedia.org/wiki/Actionable_information_logistics.

Wikipedia, 2014c. Complex Event Processing. [Online] Available from: http://fr.wikipedia.org/wiki/Complex_event_processing.

CYBERCRIME: ATTACK MOTIVATIONS AND IMPLICATIONS FOR BIG DATA AND NATIONAL SECURITY

8

Ben Brewster, Benn Kemp, Sara Galehbakhtiari, Babak Akhgar

INTRODUCTION

Organizations are increasingly turning to the immeasurable quantities of data available through open-source mediums such as the web and social media to enhance their analytical capability and ultimately improve the quality and quantity of the information they have available to make decisions. Law enforcement agencies (LEAs) are no exception to this trend, with efforts being made to use open-source data to supplement traditional forms of intelligence commonly used in crime prevention and response. In this chapter, one specific facet of this capability is discussed: the use of open-source data and analytical tools to detect criminal motivation and intention in open sources to commit cybercrime and cyberterrorism related offenses. More specifically, the chapter discusses and profiles the various types of attack and the tools used to facilitate them towards developing a comprehensive insight into the underlying motivations of cyberattackers.

It is becoming more and more difficult to escape the notion of "big data" in all facets of modern life, a term that has become synonymous with any and all attempts to exploit and use large datasets for competitive advantage. This trend can be observed across all industries and sectors, through the use of data-mining techniques, textual and predicative analytics, and a host of other business intelligence (BI)-associated technologies. Increasingly, as covered in this particular volume, LEAs have begun to explore the potential uses of big data to enhance their own capabilities through instilling science and computational technology into their analytical, operational, and policymaking operations. The application of these tools aims to enable the more effective and efficient investigation, response, prediction, and even prevention of a host of criminal activities, as they gradually come to terms with the overwhelming increase in information available to them and the tools needed to draw information from these data. With this increase, traditional, established sources of information used by LEAs are fast being outpaced by the vociferous nature of the Internet and the amount of data to which it provides access. Despite the widespread use of these tools within the private sector, LEAs are still lagging behind in their use and understanding of big data and, as a result, are not exploiting it to its full potential. LEAs have long been extremely capable in their data-collection activities; however, they have not always exhibited the same level of competence in analyzing it and subsequently converting it into usable intelligence (Thomson Reuters, 2014).

Within England and Wales, law enforcement has undergone significant budget reductions of up to 20%, with further cuts planned for 2015. Because approximately 80% of police budgets are spent on staffing, this has meant that in real terms England and Wales have nearly 16,000 fewer officers in 2014 than they did in 2009, with some forces reporting significant cuts in preventative policing areas in particular (Travis, Thursday, July 18, 2013). These reductions have been generally achieved through restructuring and merging services with other forces and partners. While this has proved challenging, it has also provided an entry platform for the integration of big data analysis techniques and the information and intelligence that can be derived from them, with a number of police forces turning to big data analysis tools to maximize the effectiveness of their remaining resources.

Big Data is widely integrated into UK preventative policing deployment plans around acquisitive crime such as burglary and theft from vehicles, to assist and maximize the impact of operational officers on the ground. This approach has removed the unscientific, "tacit" nature of this type of policing—often referred to as the "bobby's nose," which is heavily dependent on the skill and experiences of one person. This more experiential style of practice, and the knowledge embedded within it, is difficult to capture and share with other stakeholders, and its effectiveness is often difficult to quantify (Brewster et al., 2014a; Glomseth et al., 2007). This approach is often also largely dependent on the detailed geographical and offender knowledge of the officer and cannot be easily transferred to other officers and areas of policing. Using data already within existing policing systems such as historical crime statistics, associated crime within the area, and other intelligence available, police forces have been able to predict with some accuracy areas where there is a high probability of offences occurring between specific times, enabling suitable intervention mechanisms to be put in place to prevent and detect them. Approaches such as this have been integrated across international policing to reduce crimes such as burglary and armed robbery (Haberman and Ratcliffe, 2012; Perry et al., 2013) and have proven to have a quantifiable impact on crime, as demonstrated by West Yorkshire Police's "Operation Optimal," a community policing based initiative targeted toward combatting burglary. This, and similar approaches have led to offense reduction rates of up to 50% in some communities in the UK (BBC News, Wednesday, November 7, 2012).

As these approaches continue to demonstrate practical value, they are certain to be regarded as key tools within the law enforcement "toolbox", and questions will follow regarding their application in other areas of law enforcement. The wider challenge remains for these tools to be embedded within policing to exploit the data available to them into their other core business functions, such as over the course of a complex criminal investigation or public disorder incident, cognizant of the legal framework and ethical requirements imposed on and expected of LEAs operating within these contexts (see Chapters 15 and 16).

One such example of this is the EU, FP7 funded ePOOLICE (Early Pursuit Against Organized Crime Using Environmental Scanning, the Law and Intelligence Systems) project. ePOOLICE seeks to develop a software system, and supporting methodology, that scans the open-source environment to strategically identify, prevent, and even predict emergent organized criminal threats. The project aims to meet these objectives through the analysis of two key types of data, that which directly indicates the presence or possible presence of illicit activity and that which contributes to the creation of an environment that facilitates crime, such as political and economic instability or social unrest (Brewster et al., 2014b). One potential use case that can be used to demonstrate the utility of this and similar approaches is the trafficking of human beings.

Similarly to the approaches used to combat burglary and armed robbery, capability can be enhanced through examining the factors that are present in existing and previous forms of human trafficking,

FIGURE 8.1

Linear trafficking model.

making it possible to identify patterns that may be repeated elsewhere. Using a basic model of the trafficking process (Figure 8.1), it is clear to see stages of the crime and how at specific stages "big" and open-source data can improve the quantity and quality of information available to LEAs.

The crawling and analysis of localized news articles, social media, and other Web data enables the identification of weak signals, such as events and seizures that may allude to the presence and emergence of trafficking in specific locations, or at a more strategic level, the presence of economic, social, and political conditions that provide a fertile environment for the supply of trafficking victims or demand for illicit services such as prostitution and forced labor.

Further, traditional, "physical" crimes, such as that of human trafficking, present the possibility to use data from open sources, such as the Web, to identify specific factors that may provide signals of illicit activity. These signals range from high-level, strategic information such as the fact that locations that are considered to be politically unstable or that those with low gross domestic product (GDP) have an increased propensity to be supply locations of trafficking victims (United Nations Office on Drugs and Crime, 2009), to lower-level, operational indictors, such as observations that indicate staff that at a particular business appear to be under the legal working age or appear to have been physically and/or sexually abused (ILO/International Labour Office, 2009).

Further, the use of social media and other big data sources in enhancing the situational awareness and decision-making capability of blue light services is increasingly evident in other areas. For example, in policing football matches and other large-scale events with potential for public order issues, social media can be mined for sentiment to identify indicators of crowd tension or incidents enabling policing resources to be deployed more intelligently during the events and for future deployments to be strategically informed by historical data. Similarly, geo-tagged data from smart devices used to connect with social media may be used to identify potential witnesses to serious and organized crime incidents, through identifying accounts or individuals that were in close proximity to a specific event at a specific time. The use of data in this way by blue light services goes beyond crime prevention and response, with its use in crisis management as a means of enhancing the awareness and communicative capability of command and control and first-response services to assist citizens in a range of disaster events, from natural disasters, terrorism attacks, and large-scale public disorder events (Andrews et al., 2013). However, when considering cybercrimes and criminal behavior committed through the use of the Internet, the use and utility of open-source-derived data by LEAs must evolve to enable understanding of the motivations behind them and factors that enable these incidents to take place.

DEFINING CYBERCRIME AND CYBERTERRORISM

Near ubiquitous access to vast quantities of data, ideas, and research has made the Internet a vital source of information and a pervasive part of everyday life for individuals and organizations across the world. However, despite the wealth of opportunity and positive potential it offers, it also has a dark underbelly that presents individuals and criminal groups with new avenues for exploitation. A major and increasingly pertinent aspect of this "dark side" of the Internet is growing threats of cybercrime and cyberterrorism, phrases that we are becoming more accustomed to hearing, with reported attacks becoming ever more frequent and severe in their impact. Cybercrime costs the global economy, its people, and businesses billions of dollars each year. With the impact and severity of these attacks becoming ever higher, the requirement for innovation in the field of cybersecurity has grown exponentially to aid in the mitigation of increased threat levels (Elis, 2014).

Attempts to reach a universally agreed definition for cybercrime have been met with considerable challenge (Brenner, 2004). Existing definitions range from those describing it as any crime facilitated through the use of a computer to those that are facilitated through the use of computer networks, with some reports prefixing any crime that involves the use of a computer in some capacity with "cyber." The United Kingdom's Home Office, in a report published in October 2013, defined two types of cybercrime, cyber-enabled crimes and cyber-dependent crimes. Cyber-enabled crimes such as fraud and theft can be committed without the use of Information & Communication Technology (ICT); however, the scale or reach of these crimes is increased by the use of computers, networks, and other forms of ICT. On the other hand, cyber-dependent crimes can only be committed using a computer, computer networks, or other forms of ICT (McGuire and Dowling, 2013). In the latter, the motivations are largely focused on personal profit or monetary gain or in a form of protest and/or criminal damage. In the United States, the US Federal Bureau of Investigation (FBI) uses the notion of "high-tech" crimes to encompass cyberterrorism, cyberespionage, computer intrusion, and cyberfraud (Federal Bureau of Investigation, 2014). In this chapter, a synthesis of these definitions will be used to describe what will be referred to as cybercrime.

The Internet provides a platform for attacks such as cybercrime, cyberterrorism, cyberwarfare, and hactivism to grow. It is sometimes difficult to distinguish and draw a line between these concepts, because there are similarities and overlaps in the characteristics of the attacks, the motivations behind them, and the individuals and groups who initiate them. In this chapter, we aim to identify and categorize these motivations, briefly assessing other categories when there is an overlap, while discussing their implications on national security and the potential role of big data in combatting them.

ATTACK CLASSIFICATION AND PARAMETERS

In this section, attack characteristics, such as the types of cyberattack and the tools and techniques used to facilitate them, are outlined to aid in the identification of patterns and subsequently develop classification types for the motivations that underpin them. The concept of cybercrime carries a certain degree of contextual variety that subsequently contributes to its imprecision. The term has become synonymous with crime that takes place within "cyberspace," i.e. on the Web, and the transformation of criminal behavior through the use of computer networks (Fafinski et al., 2010).

Cybercrime imposes what can be considered as a key threat on national and economic security, a threat that continues to cost consumers and business billions of dollars annually (Finklea and Theohary, 2012). This threat increases the pressure on corporate and government computer networks and further undermines worldwide confidence in international financial systems. The threat on national security of cyber-oriented threats is further enhanced by the secrecy of institutions, such as those in the financial sector, which rarely disclose the fact that they have been subjected to, or compromised by cyberattacks, often with either no, or extremely limited public visibility, such as unexplained service or Website outages (Finkle and Henry, 2012). Despite institutions spending more than ever on securing their systems and data, the scale of criminal activity is also seemingly up-scaled, as transnational organized groups and even governments invest heavily in enhancing their cyber capability to realize financial gains and better inform their own intelligence efforts (The Economist, 2013).

When discussing nation states and governments, an additional dimension of cyber-related activity must be considered, that of cyberwarfare. The rise in prominence of cyberwarfare is typified by the US Air Force, which in 2006 adopted a new mission statement pledging to fight (and win) in "air, space, and cyberspace" (US Air Force, 2014). Cyberwarfare is the reapplication of cyberattacks for the purposes of espionage, sabotage, or to conduct attacks on a target's strategic and tactical resources (Manoske, 2013). Nations have begun to use cyberattacks as an additional facet of their military armory, to achieve the same objectives as they would normally pursue through the use of military force: to achieve competitive advantage over rival nation states or to prevent rivals from achieving the same objectives (Brenner, 2007). Western governments and NATO are becoming increasingly aware and concerned about growing international cyber threats originating from countries such as China, attacks targeting key government and intelligence networks (Schneier, 2014). Cyberwarfare is acknowledged, with terrorism, to be one of the most serious national security threats facing western nations (Gercke, 2012).

As an additional facet of cybercrime, and more specifically the combative nature of cyberwarfare, it is possible to introduce the concept of cyberterrorism. After 9/11, the use of information technology by terrorists is increasingly being considered as part of an intensive discussion around the continued threat of international terrorism as a whole. Cyberterrorism has the potential to impact a range of critical national infrastructures (Jalil, 2003). However, it is also necessary to distinguish between cyberterrorism, that is, the direct use of cyber-related attacks to damage national infrastructures, and other terrorist uses of ICT, such as for propaganda, information/intelligence acquisition, planning and preparation of physical attacks, dissemination of radicalized material, communication, and financing (Gercke, 2012).

Cyberterrorists and criminals use computer technology in similar ways to the way in which more traditional weapons are used, with the aim of undermining citizens' faith in their government's ability to maintain the integrity of the systems, services, and infrastructure that make up the fabric of their everyday lives (Brenner, 2007). The evolution of terrorism into the virtual world has been foreseen since the 1980s, resulting in the formation of a dedicated definition of cyberterrorism as the use of network tools to shutdown critical national infrastructure or to coerce or intimidate a government or civilian population (US Department of Justice (2011)).

The categories of cybercrime, cyberterrorism, and cyberwarfare can be used as holistic terms to classify the overarching reasons behind cyberattacks. However, within these terms, it is necessary to acknowledge a number of subcategories that can exist within them. One such category is that of cyberespionage. Cyberespionage is, in many ways, similar to traditional forms of espionage, i.e., the unauthorized access to confidential information by an individual or government. Espionage in this way can be undertaken for a variety of reasons, such as for intelligence-gathering purposes, financial gain, or a combination of the two (Finklea and Theohary, 2012). The United States in particular has acknowledged the growing threat of foreign economic, industrial, and military espionage to national security and to the continued prosperity of the affected nation (Council on Foreign Relations, 2014). The tools used to conduct cyberspying can be the same as those used to commit a host of disruptive or destructive acts ranging from online activism to criminal activity and conceivably even an act of war. Due to the politically sensitive nature of these types of attacks, concrete examples are few and far between, and instead it is necessary to rely on alleged actions as opposed to factual reports to demonstrate their existence. As a recent example, there have been a number of accusations from the United States and China in recent years regarding the alleged hacking of industrial secrets and intent to commit economic espionage on the part of the other (Kaiman, Tuesday, May 20, 2014).

A further subcategorization of cyber-related crime is that of "hactivism." Hactivism is concerned with the hacking of computer systems and networks in social, political and economic protest. However, the growing profile, and significance of these attacks in recent years has turned these attacks, in the eyes of some, from straddling the line between legitimate protest and basic criminal behavior, into a legitimate threat pon national security in the eyes of security professionals (Sterner, 2012). Perhaps the most contemporary example of a hactivist group is Anonymous, a group of individuals that has become synonymous with numerous attacks over the last decade, designed around the defense of online freedom and Internet neutrality. These individuals are motivated by sociopolitical issues such as the promotion of access to information, free speech, and transparency (Australian National Computer Emergency Response Team, 2013; Lockley and Akhgar, 2014). As one example of an attack by Anonymous in support of their campaign for Internet neutrality, four individuals operating under the moniker "Operation Paypack" carried out a number of distributed denial of service (DDoS) attacks on antipiracy organizations and banks that had withdrawn services from proprietors of the infamous WikiLeaks site (Addley and Halliday, Wednesday, December 8, 2010).

WHO PERPETRATES THESE ATTACKS?

As the previous section demonstrated, cyberattacks are undertaken to achieve a variety of underlying objectives, from those simply aiming to extort financial benefits to those seeking to protest perceived injustices or those acting on behalf of governments aiming to create competitive advantage over and gather intelligence on rival nations. To truly understand the core underlying motivations behind attacks, it is first necessary to profile those who perpetrate them.

One such taxonomical categorization of cyberattacks has identified what it refers to as "actors" (van Heerden et al., 2012). In this classification, the following were identified as being potential originators of cyberattacks: commercial competitors, hackers, "script kiddies," skilled hackers, insiders, admin insiders, normal insiders, organized crime groups, and protest groups; this classification adds value when considering the profile of the individuals and groups behind cyberattacks such as differentiating between insider and external attackers, protestors, criminals, and commercial competition. However, the following narrative deconstructs this classification further, to derive further insight into to underlying motivations that underpin cyber-attacks.

SCRIPT KIDDIES

Script kiddies, or "skiddies," is a term used to describe groups of amateur hackers, often students with some, but limited knowledge of hacking who conduct attacks with the intention of impressing peers and gaining kudos among online enthusiast communities (Millar, Tuesday, June 5, 2001). There are a number of prominent examples of these types of attacks from over the last 20 years. Some of the most notable are the cases of Michael Calce, also known as "Mafiaboy," a Canadian high school student who in 2000 was responsible for a number of DDoS attacks on websites such as Yahoo, eBay, and CNN.

Another notable attack was that conducted by Jeffrey Lee Parson, an 18-year-old high school student from Minnesota, who was responsible for spreading a variant of the infamous "Blaster" worm. The program was part of a DDoS attack against computers using the Microsoft Windows operating system. He was sentenced to 18 months in prison in 2005 (NBC News, 2003). Denial of service or distributed denial of service attacks (DoS and DDoS) relate to the flooding of Internet servers with so many requests that they are unable to respond quickly enough. In both of these instances, Calce and Parson used their, at the time, limited knowledge to use existing tools written by others to carry out new attacks. Similarly, in both cases the individual showed an "extracurricular" interest in hacking, carrying out their attacks partly out of curiosity and partly to impress and gain the respect of their peers and members of online hacking communities.

WEB DEFACERS

Another of the more specialized groups are web defacers, who, as their name suggests, set out with the intention of penetrating and changing the content displayed on Websites, often to relay political or protest messages against their targets. In one such example, hacking group Anonymous carried out a series of Website defacement attacks in the build up to the 2014 World Cup in Brazil. The attacks were carried out in protest against the alleged social injustices and uneven distribution of wealth in the nation that was causing civil unrest and public disorder events in the lead up to the tournament (Guerrini, 2014).

HACKERS

As the most generic of the categories identified, "hackers" has become an umbrella term for those who commit cyber-related crimes that do not necessarily fit into one of the more specialized categories. Hackers generally fall within two categories: "white hat," i.e., those who use their expertise to defend networks and systems, and "black hat," those who set out with the objective to destroy or damage them. Increasingly, companies and security agencies are turning to black hat hackers, recruiting them to aid in enhancing their own cyber defense capability. George Hotz, or "GeoHot" as he is more commonly known within online communities, is one example of this. Hotz, the hacker responsible for exposing security flaws in both Sony's Playstation and the Apple iPhone, was recruited by Google in 2014 to identify security flaws within their software (BBC News, Wednesday, July 16, 2014).

PIRATES

Pirates are individuals or groups that unlawfully create and distribute copies of copyrighted materials, such as software, films, and music. Although the issue of digital piracy goes beyond that of cybercrime, pirates regularly circumvent and seek to find gaps in the security and encryption that protects copyrighted material to distribute and resell such content. DrinkOrDie is one of the most notable examples of a piracy group. Active throughout the 1990s, DrinkOrDie established significant online notoriety for using the Internet as a platform to illegally reproduce and distribute games, movies, and software. The group's own code of practice prevented its members from seeking financial gain from the activities. Instead their aim was to compete with rival piracy groups and achieve recognition among enthusiast communities (Broadhurst et al., 2014).

PHONE PHREAKERS

Phone phreaking is concerned with the hacking of telephone systems. The concept of phreaking origi-nated in the 1950s in the United States, where "phone phreaks" decoded the tones used to route phone calls to avoid the tolling charges for making long distance calls (Rustad, 2001). However, phreaking is now commonly associated with phone hacking and the social engineering of telephone support lines to facilitate unauthorized access to information and other crimes. Matthew Weigman, an American with a heightened sense of hearing, is a well-known convicted phone hacker. Weigman used a combi-nation of his ability to unscramble in-band phone signals and social engineering skills to make fraudu-lent SWAT calls and commit a range of other offenses, including gaining access to unauthorized information and cutting the lines of other telephone service subscribers (Schneier, 2009). Unlike Weigman, who does not attest to having any malicious intention, hacking network Anonymous is alleged to have unlawfully accessed and released a conference call between the FBI and the UK police, within which they discussed efforts against criminal hackers. The call covers the tracking of Anonymous and similar groups, dates of planned arrests, and details of evidence held (BBC News, Friday, February 3, 2012).

Assessing the types of attacks that are undertaken and the underlying reasons as to why they are carried out provides some initial elucidation as to the motivations behind cyberattacks and those who facilitate them. However, to develop a deeper understanding, it is first necessary to look into the types of tools used by these attacks, the characteristics of which provide further insights into the underlying motivations of attackers.

TOOLS USED TO FACILITATE ATTACKS

The individuals who conduct cyberattacks use a range of different tools to facilitate them, with each having differing potential impacts and characteristics. One such tool is malware, malicious software that interferes with a computer's ability to operate correctly. Malware commonly delete files or causes system crashes, but can also be used to steal users' personal information. The concept of malware can be further subdivided into a number of other categories (McGuire and Dowling, 2013).

One such sub category is viruses. Viruses can cause damage ranging from mild computer dysfunc-tion to more severe effects that cause systems to become inoperable. Viruses install themselves onto the user's hardware without consent and cause damage by self-replicating. In 2013, the Massachusetts State Police Department fell victim to what is known is a "ransomware" virus. In this instance, the software infected the target machine, demanding that the users pay a ransom using the online "Bitcoin" currency to have access to their machines restored (Winter, 2013).

Worms, similarly to viruses, also cause damage through self-replication; however, they differ in characteristics because they commonly spread and cause damage to networks rather than spe-cific machines and do not need to latch on to existing pieces of software as viruses do. In 2010, the computer worm Stuxnet was discovered. Stuxnet was designed to attack industrial systems, such as those used to control machinery in factory assembly operations. The main victim of the attack in 2010 was Iran and in particular its nuclear enrichment facilitates; speculation around the origin of the attack still continues to this day (Kushner, 2013). Worms are viruses that have the potential to have a range of differing impacts, from demanding and stealing money to rendering systems inoperable.

Trojans, as their name suggests, take a slightly different approach. These programs pose as legitimate pieces of software, which, once installed by the user, can be used to facilitate illegal access to the compute, and in turn used to steal information and disrupt the computers operations without the user's knowledge or consent. Twenty-three-year-old Edward Pearson of York (UK), used variants of existing Trojan viruses to gain access to thousands of credit card details and the postcodes, passwords, names, and dates of birth of more than eight million people. In comments made after his arrest, Pearson was said to be motivated by his thirst for intellectual challenge (Leyden, 2012). These tools can also be used to create botnets on host computers. Botnets are clusters of computers infected by malicious software that are subsequently used to send out spam, phishing emails, or other malicious email traffic automatically and repeatedly to specified targets (McGuire and Dowling, 2013).

Alternatively, spyware, software that infects systems to facilitate the identification and extraction of personal information such as users' login information, Internet habits, and payment information, is a further example of malware. Its activities are often carried out using key-logging software or through rerouting Web traffic from the user's infected computer. Spyware is also often used by legitimate government agencies and law enforcement to intercept suspicious communications. Key-loggers in particular have been used in a number of cases by individuals to collect user information and bank account details.

An alternative approach, hacking, involves the unauthorized use of computers or network resources to exploit identified security vulnerabilities in networks, which can be used to gather personal data/information, to deface websites, or as part of DDoS attacks.

As an example, hacking group Anonymous, through a series of DDoS and Website defacement attacks, protested social injustices surrounding the 2014 World Cup in Brazil, most notably the allegations of alleged corruption in the Brazilian government, and the tournament's organizing body, FIFA (Guerrini, 2014). In this particular instance, the hackers targeted the Brazilian Federal Police in an attempt to draw attention to the political and social issues surrounding the tournament.

In a less direct approach, a tactic referred to as "social engineering" has been used by hackers to gain access to individuals' user accounts, billing information, and other personal data. The case of technology journalist Mat Honan in 2012 demonstrated how using only two key pieces of information, his email address and billing address, hackers were able to bypass the usual password authentication and encryption mechanisms that are used to protect data online. Using the data identified, hackers contacted and manipulated the telephone customer service systems of Apple and Amazon and used it to recover and reset the passwords on the respective accounts (Honan, 2012). Although unconfirmed, a similar approach is suspected to have been used to access and steal private images from a number of high-profile celebrities in 2014, images that were subsequently released online (Profis, 2014).

Phishing attacks, often facilitated using spam email, present a further threat to cybersecurity. Phishing emails have often been used by criminals attempting to steal banking information and login information and to fraudulently generate funds. Phishing emails are commonly sent in bulk to unsuspecting recipients, often posing as official communications from reputable companies asking users to follow web links to enter their login credentials and banking information. In 2010, in the aftermath of the Haiti earthquake, criminals attempted to cash in on sympathizers by seeking funds for bogus charities by sending thousands of emails. Attackers created a webpage asking users to make donations and subsequently used the financial and personal information provided to carry out fraudulent transactions (BBC News, Tuesday, February 16, 2010).

MOTIVATIONS

The distinction between cyber-based malicious acts and crimes such as fraud, espionage, and theft is the attackers' motivation, a characteristic that subsequently influences their goals and objectives. But attribution has always been difficult. Where we think behavior may have come from may not be where it actually originated. It is for these reasons that the development of taxonomy to align and categorize the motivations behind cyberattacks truly demonstrates its value. The motivations behind rule-breaking have not changed significantly, despite the rapid evolution and revolution in the ways in which it can be facilitated, because they arise from the very essence of human nature (Smith et al., 2011). Criminals may be motivated by passion, greed, revenge, curiosity, need, or abnormal perceptions of themselves or society. Some simply enjoy the challenge of offending and not being caught, whereas sometimes rules are broken just because they are not appropriate to the people, the place, or the time they are intended to protect.

To take a holistic view of cybercrime motivations, it is important to duly consider the various facets that may contribute to the underlying notion of motivation. Therefore, although personal and emotional motivations can play a crucial role, political, economic, and social tensions, turbulence, and ideological trends can also drive criminals' desire to commit cybercrime. Recent political pressures within the Korean peninsula, for example, may constitute key drivers for cyber-related attacks, motivations that go well beyond raw human emotion such as hate or the desire to challenge oneself or gain individual recognition within a specific community. Existing taxonomies (van Heerden et al., 2012) have identified the desire for financial gain, personal challenge, protest, spying, and nonfinancially motivated criminal activities as key reasons behind cyberattacks. Within these motivations, it is possible to derive that attacks can be political, financial, or driven by the desire for personal gratification (Fleishman, 2014). This variation may be related to differences in the targets of the attacks. Whether they target individuals, organizations, businesses, governments, or entire nations, the motivations can differ drastically from one to the next. According to the Australian Computer Emergency Response Team (CERT), the motivations or attack reasoning exhibited by organizations range from commercial advantage, malicious damage, using the system for further attacks, personal grievance, hactivism, negligence, illicit financial gain, and random or indiscriminate motive. The majority, if not all, of these motivations can be attributed back to the organizations seeking commercial or competitive advantage, with attacks commonly taking the form of information or intellectual property theft (CERT, 2013).

Cyberattacks, such as those exemplified here, have increasing potential to cause issues of national security, as cyberspace continues to form an important domain that underpins the complex systems that are used in commerce, the provision of critical infrastructure services such as power and water, and the protection of the state through the military and policing services. The growing role of cyberspace serves to amplify the potential impact of cyberattacks and consequently the ability of organizations and nations to function effectively in the aftermath of a serious attack (McGuire and Dowling, 2013).

Further classifications (see Kilger et al., 2004) have focused on the underlying motivations of cyberattackers, identifying causes such as seeking money, entertainment, entry to social cliques, and for status, while others have focused more on emotionally aligned classifications identifying curiosity, boredom, power, recognition, and politics. Of course, there is a clear overlap between psychology and motivation, a link that has been acknowledged, with links established between conditions such as compulsive disorder, narcissism, antisocial personality disorder, Asperger syndrome, and addiction in some instances of cybercrime-related activity (Campbell and Kennedy, 2009). However, these classifications also highlight the deviation between highly personal motives and those of a more commercial nature. For example, those acting on behalf of a nation state may not have any personal motivation for perpetrating an attack and instead may be acting in the interest of a government—and are likely be politically motivated. For example, in October 2010, an attack was discovered on the NASDAQ stock exchange in New York; the reported cause was alleged to have been a military attack by the Russian government with the aim of collecting intelligence on the NASDAQ exchange systems for use within their own Micex and RTS exchanges (Bender and Kelley, 2014).

ATTACK MOTIVATIONS TAXONOMY

Existing classifications have focused mainly on attack characteristics and methods, negating to consider the true motivations and human elements that underpin them. The taxonomy proposed here combines and considers both the human and corporate motivations behind attacks. Human motivations are often more difficult to assess, because they tend to be personal to the attackers themselves by their very definition. For the purposes of the taxonomy, these motivations are grouped under financial, political, personal, and emotional (Dittrich and Himma, 2005), as demonstrated in Figure 8.2. This taxonomy takes influence from the existing works cited previously, with the primary analysis of more than 300 separate cyberattacks.

The proposed taxonomy divides attack motivations into eight categories.

POLITICAL

Political motives refer to those of a corporate nature and can be linked to countering governmental policies or actions such as sabotage, espionage, and propaganda (Lockley and Akhgar, 2014). A prominent example of politically motivated attacks is those that were carried out against Iranian nuclear facilities in 2010. Nicknamed the "Stuxnet" worm, the attacks are widely reported to have been perpetrated by the US and Israeli governments over growing concerns regarding the development of nuclear weapons in the region (Beaumont and Hopkins, 2012). In contrast to the majority of indiscriminate cybercrime threats on the Internet, these attacks were aimed at specific targets, with no obvious financial motivation behind them; the aim instead being to sabotage systems. Concrete examples of politically motivated attacks are hard to come by, as the responsible nations and groups go to great lengths to conceal their activities. This is due to the potential ramifications of such attacks, including increased international tensions, and the threat of counter-attacks that may occur as a result of being explicitly identified. As a result many of the organizations and nations given as examples here, are often as a result of media speculation rather than concrete evidence, and thus should not be assumed to be factual records of the events in question.

Politically motivated attacks form a significant threat to national security, as cyber becomes an increasingly prominent facet of international intelligence and espionage activities. Sri Lankan guerrilla fighters the Tamil Tigers were one of the first terrorist organizations to use cyberattacks to disrupt government communications. In 1998, the Tamil Tigers organized spam attacks flooding Sri Lankan embassies across the globe to disrupt government communications systems (Lockley and Akhgar, 2014).

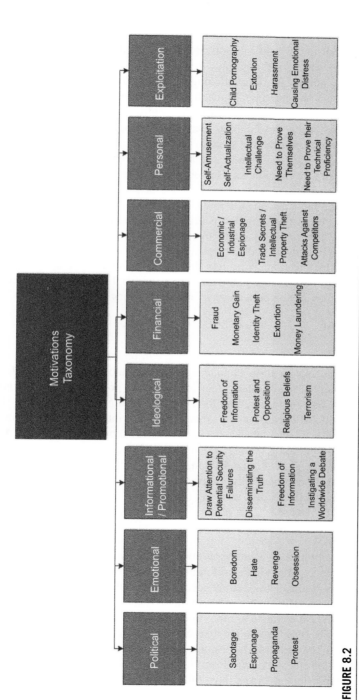

FIGURE 8.2

Cybercrime motivations taxonomy.

IDEOLOGICAL

Although potentially similar to the political motivations described previously in relation to the acts of nation states, governments, and terrorist groups, it is possible to differentiate between them and the ideological motivations of individuals. These ideological motivations can consist of protest and opposition, and religious beliefs. As one example, Mitchell Frost, a 19-year-old college student at the University of Akron, used the school's computer network to control the botnets he had created, targeting conservative Websites supporting the Giuliani election campaign (Brenner, 2012; Dittrich, 2009). Although in this instance the attacks did not seem to pose any direct threat to national security, it serves to demonstrate how individual disillusionment combined with technical capability can create a fertile environment for fairly serious cyberattacks. However, a number of attacks on Russian websites in response to the political crisis in Ukraine show how the acts of individuals can escalate in protest against ideological enemies and subsequently threaten critical infrastructure and motivated attacks are conducted with the goal of impact on national security (Bender and Kelley, 2014).

This networked world of increasingly interconnected states provides a breeding ground for the varied spread of conflicting individual and collective values. Such an environment can result in ideological threats such as that posed by terrorism. A leading threat for British and US national security is that of Al Qaeda, the group believed to be responsible for the September 11 attacks in New York and Virginia and the 7/7 bombings on the London public transportation network (HM Government, 2010).

COMMERCIAL

Commercial hacking is another form of motivation that can underpin a wide range of cyberattacks. Commercially motivated attacks are those conducted with the aim of achieving some form of competitive advantage over commercial rivals. These types of attacks can potentially exhibit some overlap with those of a political nature, as demonstrated by the alleged state-organized attacks by US and Chinese government agencies, each state accusing the other of hacking into industrial systems to steal trade secrets that could potentially aid and enhance the capability of competitors (US Department of Justice (2014)). Due to this cross-pollination between the impacts of commercially and politically motivation attacks, distinguishing the boundary around each may be difficult. Despite this, these types of attacks also establish the potential of commercially motivated attacks to impact national security, due to the inherent ability of confidential intellectual property to expose vulnerabilities in critical infrastructures.

EMOTIONAL

On other occasions, motivations may be more purely emotionally oriented, with feelings such as boredom or the desire for revenge playing a key role in reasons as to why individuals and groups commit cyberattacks. As with each of the classifications identified here, there is potential for overlap between categories, i.e., attacks that initially appear to be emotionally motivated may also be aligned with ideological or political motives. An example are the protests against an FBI seizure of virtual cash on the notorious deep Website "silk road," an online marketplace for the trade of illicit goods. In response to the seizure, enraged users and pro-drug protestors vowed to carry out a series of attacks on the FBI personnel responsible for the site shutdown (Hamill, 2013).

In a broader sense, gaining an understanding of the emotions and psychology of attackers can aid in predicting, and subsequently preventing, acts of hostility and violence. Emotional motivations are an essential means for understanding individual and group behavior. Videos, writings, and recordings of attackers such as Virginia Tech shooter Cho Seung Hui, as well as more historical figures (e.g., Hitler, etc.) have demonstrated how groups and individuals can be motivated and incited to act violently or commit crimes due to flared emotions (Matsumoto et al., 2012).

INFORMATIONAL/PROMOTIONAL

Informational and promotional motivations are those which cumulate in the desire to disseminate information to increase public awareness of a particular issue or event. There is significant overlap between attacks of this kind and those underpinned by ideological or political motives as information is regularly disseminated or released in order to enhance or advance an individuals political or ideological agenda. An example is the case of Chelsea Manning (formerly known as Bradley Manning), the US military analyst responsible for leaking classified military information to the WikiLeaks site (Sanchez, 2013). Edward Snowdon is wanted by the US authorities for committing similar violations of the espionage act in a whistle-blowing incident trying to expose the (allegedly) unethical practices of US and UK intelligence agencies, in specific regard to classified operations facilitating the unlawful surveillance of citizens (Greenwald et al., 2013).

FINANCIAL

Motivations for cyber-dependent crimes tend to focus largely on financial gain. Such attacks may often involve fraud and identity theft. Unlike the other motivations identified, financially motivated attacks are often more easily identifiable in terms of the underlying motive behind them. As an example, in 2014 Russian hacker Evgeniy Bogachev was charged with conspiracy, bank and computer fraud, and money laundering. Bogachev and the organized crime group to which he belonged were members of a crime ring responsible for hacking into financial institutions to access account information. These details were then ultimately used to withdraw millions of dollars from a number of the eight million accounts from which they are alleged to have stolen detail from in the period between January and August 2012. Similar attacks have been reported across global banking systems in recent years, with cyberattacks forming a considerable threat to financial institutions across the globe (Lockley and Akhgar, 2014). The significance and assumed risk of cyberattacks on the financial sector are further increased as the nature and impact of attacks are rarely reported by institutions to avoid causing damage to the company's image and public backlash. This lack of disclosure has the potential to threaten the integrity of the sector as a whole while simultaneously impacting national security (McGuire and Dowling, 2013).

The rise of global financial markets has significantly increased the threat of money laundering, enabling funds to be transferred and deposited around the globe with ease. International crime agencies report that this issue costs the global economy anywhere from $500 billion to $1 trillion per year, a problem that has been exacerbated by use of the Internet as a means of money transmission for criminal and terrorist groups (Kellermann, 2004).

PERSONAL

Personal motivations are those associated with individuals' or groups' desire to prove themselves. Such motivations are often fuelled by the aspiration to be recognized among peers, to prove intellectual and technical capability, or to establish an online reputation. These individuals often spend years among peers trying to establish themselves within online hacking communities. The desire for personal recognition is often combined with other motives, such as the ideologies or objectives of the communities to which they belong. In 2013, hactivist group Lulzsec initiated a cyberattack on the Website of the US Central Intelligence Agency to try to establish a reputation as a group that should be taken seriously among online peers and rival hacking groups (Broadhurst et al., 2014). In another instance, Canadian student Michael Calce carried out a number of DDoS attacks on corporations including Yahoo, eBay, and Amazon in 2000.

Personal motives for cybercrime can be self-amusement, self-actualization, intellectual challenge, need to prove one's self, need to prove technical proficiency, recognition, call for attention, status, and curiosity. When questioned on his motives, Calce cited the desire to establish "dominance" for his hacking group, TNT, among competitor groups, but also curiosity as to whether or not the attacks were actually possible (Calce and Silverman, 2011).

EXPLOITATION

This category contains attacks and attackers motivated by their desire to exploit other individuals, such as to bully, humiliate, or harass others. The threat of these attacks on national security is comparatively minimal when compared to some of the other categories identified. Past examples of such attacks have ranged from the theft and subsequent public release of private photographs and videos of celebrities and other public figures, such as those released in September 2014 (Steinberg, Sunday, August 31, 2014), to the images released by Tyler Schrier, who stole naked photos from the email accounts of male professional poker players to extort them for hundreds of thousands of dollars, to 14 men in a secret and members-only child pornography Website that involved 251 children, mostly boys, across five countries (Federal Bureau of Investigation (2013)). Similarly to the other motivations, extortionists often have other motivations, such as those of a personal nature, to establish a reputation online, or to extort others for financial gain.

DETECTING MOTIVATIONS IN OPEN-SOURCE INFORMATION

As discussed previously, LEAs have taken to using big data derived from open sources to enhance their decision-making capability. However the nuances of cybercrime and cyberterrorism require their own considerations to make use of this vast pool of information more effectively. One such approach involves the potential application of sentiment analysis, a text mining approach concerned with the identification of opinions and emotions through the linguistic analysis of textual data.

Sentiment analysis has been widely adopted in marketing practices to assess customers' brand affections and feelings toward particular products and companies (Kasper and Vela, 2011) to support a number of business functions and ultimately provide another stream of data that can be used to enhance decision-making capability (Cambria et al., 2013). In other instances, it has been applied to predict polling results during political elections through gauging positivity and negativity toward the various candidates (O'Connor et al., 2010). The diversification demonstrated in the application of sentiment analysis in part stems from the rise and near ubiquitous adoption of social media. More recently, research efforts have focused on the development of approaches to use such techniques within differing contexts, dealing with the varying contextual nuance that comes with them. Such examples include the monitoring of public sentiment to establish national and regional "moods" through social media, enabling the identification of swings in public sentiments that may indicate friction in particular areas that could lead to social disorder, such as that which resulted in the London riots in 2011 (Sykora et al., 2013). Further, efforts have also been made to use sentiment mining within the context of national security. For instance, the EU, FP7-funded project ePOOLICE, as one aspect of its environmental scanning toolset, aims to use sentiment mining to visualize sentiment in relation to organized crime threats (ePOOLICE, 2013).

Social media has also been identified as a platform that is being used to radicalize individuals and terrorist groups to spread propaganda and promote extremist ideologies, and for organizing criminal activity (Yang and Ng, 2007). In response, projects led by LEAs have sought to identify means to use social media in more unconventional ways, which do not directly use computational and analytical tools. One such approach has aimed to use social media as a platform for credible voices within communities to provide access to moderate messages to attempt to stem the spread of extremist rhetoric online and particularly in social media, provide support to vulnerable individuals and communities and access to relevant, up-to-date and factual information in response to news and events that attract those with tendencies to spread extreme views (Staniforth and Nitsch, 2014). Reintroducing the notion of big ata and the concept of cybercrime presents the opportunity for the application of sentiment analysis in detecting and analyzing motives and intentions to commit cyberattacks.

Furthermore, the use of big and open-source data opens up a huge debate from an ethical and legal standpoint (see Chapters 15 and 16), an issue that is only re-enforced when considering the allegations that have surrounded Western intelligence agencies in recent years regarding the unlawful surveillance of citizens and the alleged illegal acquisition of personal data. This is, of course, an extremely complex and sensitive discussion, and it is beyond the scope of this particular chapter to present and analyze the various facets of this debate. However, it is important to ensure that this discussion takes place to restore and maintain public faith and confidence in intelligence agencies and the activities that they undertake (Greitzer et al., 2011).

CONCLUSION

This chapter has provided an overview of the growing threat of cybercrime, considering its role and potential impact on businesses, organizations, nations, and wider society. It is clear that cybercrime, cyberterrorism, and cyberwarfare pose a significant threat to national security, with the role of big data analytics and text mining set to form a key component of the armory of LEA in combatting and responding to them. As one facet of this, the taxonomy presented here assesses the motivations of attackers, from those attempting to instill political change through online activism to those merely attempting to gain kudos among their peers, providing a foundation for further research into the use of text mining and sentiment analysis tools in detecting motives, tensions, and indicators in unstructured, disparate data.

REFERENCES

Addley, E., Halliday, J., Wednesday, December 8, 2010. Operation payback cripples MasterCard site in revenge for WikiLeaks ban. The Guardian. [Online]. Available from: http://www.theguardian.com/media/2010/dec/08/operation-payback-mastercard-website-wikileaks (accessed 26.09.14.).
Andrews, S., Yates, S., Akhgar, B., Fortune, D., 2013. The ATHENA project: using formal concept analysis to facilitate the actions of responders in a crisis situation. In: Akhgar, B., Yates, S. (Eds.), Strategic intelligence management: national security imperatives and information and communication technologies. Elsevier, Amsterdam, pp. 167–180.

Australian National Computer Emergency Response Team, 2013. Cyber Crime and Security Survey Report 2013. Available from: https://www.cert.gov.au/system/files/614/679/2013%20CERT%20Australia%20Cyber%20Crime%20%2526%20Security%20Survey%20Report.pdf (accessed 26.09.14.).

BBC News, Wednesday, July 16, 2014. Google takes on top hacker George Hotz for Project Zero. BBC News. [Online]. Available from: http://www.bbc.co.uk/news/technology-28327117 (accessed 26.09.14.).

BBC News, Friday, February 3, 2012a. Anonymous gain access to FBI and scotland yard hacking call. BBC News. [Online]. Available from: http://www.bbc.co.uk/news/world-us-canada-16875921 (accessed 26.09.14.).

BBC News, Wednesday, November 7, 2012b. West Yorkshire PCC candidates: burglary is a priority. BBC News. [Online]. Available from: http://www.bbc.co.uk/news/uk-england-leeds-20243960 (accessed 19.09.14.).

BBC News, Tuesday, February 16, 2010. Haiti earthquake: bogus "charity" uncovered by BBC. BBC News. [Online]. Available from: http://news.bbc.co.uk/1/hi/in_depth/8516115.stm (accessed 26.09.14.).

Beaumont, P., Hopkins, N., 2012. US was "key player in cyber-attacks on Iran's nuclear programme. The Guardian. [Online]. Available from: http://www.theguardian.com/world/2012/jun/01/obama-sped-up-cyberattack-iran (accessed 29.09.14.).

Bender, J., Kelley, M., 2014. The Ukraine-Russia cyber war is heating up. Business Insider India. [Online]. Available from: http://www.businessinsider.in/The-Ukraine-Russia-Cyber-War-Is-Heating-Up/articleshow/31555149.cms (accessed 29.09.14.).

Brenner, S.W., 2012. Bits, bytes, and bicycles: theft and cyber theft. New England Law Review 47, 817–859.

Brenner, S.W., 2007. At light speed: attribution and response to cybercrime/terrorism/warfare. Journal of Criminal Law Criminology 97 (2), 378–476.

Brenner, S.W., 2004. US cybercrime law: defining offenses. Information Systems Frontiers 6 (2), 115–132.

Brewster, B., Akhgar, B., Staniforth, A., Waddington, D., Andrews, S., Johnson-Mitchell, S., Johnson, K., 2014a. Towards a model for the integration of knowledge management in law enforcement agencies. International Journal of Electronic Security and Digital Forensics 6, 1–17.

Brewster, B., Polovina, S., Rankin, G., Andrews, S., 2014b. Knowledge management and human trafficking: using conceptual knowledge representation, text analytics and open-source data to combat organized crime. In: Graph-Based Representation and Reasoning, pp. 104–117.

Broadhurst, R., Grabosky, P., Alazab, M., Chon, S., 2014. Organizations and cyber crime: an analysis of the nature of groups engaged in cyber crime. International Journal of Cyber Criminology 8 (1), 1–20.

Calce, M., Silverman, C., 2011. Mafiaboy: A Portrait of the Hacker as a Young Man. Globe Pequot, United States.

Cambria, E., Schuller, B., Xia, Y., Havasi, C., 2013. New avenues in opinion mining and sentiment analysis. IEEE Intelligent Systems 15–21.

Campbell, Q., Kennedy, D.M., 2009. The psychology of computer criminals. In: Bosworth, S., Kabay, M.E., Whyne, E. (Eds.), Computer Security Handbook. John Wiley and Sons, Inc., New York, NY.

Council on Foreign Relations, 2014. United States of America v. Members of China's People's Liberation Army. [Online]. Available from: http://www.cfr.org/intellectual-property/united-states-america-v-members-chinas-peoples-liberation-army/p32998 (accessed 25.09.14.).

Dittrich, D., 2009. The conflicts facing those responding to cyberconflict. USENIX. Available from: https://www.usenix.org/legacy/publications/login/2009-12/openpdfs/dittrich.pdf (accessed 29.09.14.).

Dittrich, D., Himma, K.E., 2005. Active Response to Computer Intrusions. The Handbook of Information Security, vol. 3, 664–681.

Elis, N., Monday, May 12, 2014. Can big data predict the next cyber attack? Jerusalem Post. [Online]. Available from: http://www.jpost.com/Enviro-Tech/Can-big-data-predict-the-next-cyber-attack-351957 (accessed 29.09.14).

ePOOLICE, 2013. ePOOLICE—about. [Online]. Available from: https://www.epoolice.eu/EPOOLICE/about.jsp (accessed 19.08.13.).

Fafinski, S., Dutton, W.H., Margetts, H., 2010. Mapping and Measuring Cybercrime. OII Forum Discussion Paper No. 18. Oxford Internet Institute, University of Oxford.

Federal Bureau of Investigation, 2013. Two Northern Californian Men in Sextortion Plot Targeting Professional Poker Players Recieve Federal Prison Sentences. [Press Release]. Available from: http://www.fbi.gov/losange les/press-releases/2013/two-northern-california-men-in-sextortion-plot-targeting-professional-poker-players-receive-federal-prison-sentences (accessed 29.09.14.).

Federal Bureau of Investigation, 2014. Cyber Crime. [Online]. Available from: http://www.fbi.gov/about-us/investigate/cyber (accessed 19.09.14.).

Finkle, J., Henry, D., 2012. Bank group warns of heightened risk of cyber attacks. Reuters. [Online]. Available from: http://www.reuters.com/article/2012/09/20/us-jpmorganchase-website-idUSBRE88I16M20120920 (accessed 25.09.12.).

Finklea, K.M., Theohary, C.A., 2012. Cybercrime: conceptual issues for congress and US law enforcement. Congressional Research Service. Available from: http://fas.org/sgp/crs/misc/R42547.pdf (accessed 29.09.14).

Fleishman, G., 2014. Escalating cyber-attacks: it's about time. The Economist. [Online]. Available from: http://www.economist.com/blogs/babbage/2014/02/escalating-cyber-attacks (accessed 26.09.14.).

Gercke, M., 2012. Understanding cybercrime: phenomena, challenges and legal response. International Telecommunication Union. Available from: http://www.itu.int/ITU-D/cyb/cybersecurity/docs/Cybercrime%20legislation%20EV6.pdf.

Glomseth, R., Gottschalk, P., Solli-Sæther, H., 2007. Occupational culture as determinant of knowledge sharing and performance in police investigations. International Journal of the Sociology of Law 35, 96–107.

Greenwald, G., MacAskill, E., Poitras, L., 2013. Edward Snowden: the whistleblower behind the NSA surveillance revelations. The Guardian. [Online]. Available from: http://www.theguardian.com/world/2013/jun/09/edward-snowden-nsa-whistleblower-surveillance.

Greitzer, F.L., Frincke, D.A., Zabriskie, M., 2011. Social/Ethical Issues in Predictive Insider Threat Monitoring (Chapter 7). In: Dark, M.J. (Ed.), Information Assurance and Security Ethics in Complex Systems: Interdisciplinary Perspectives. IGI Global, Hershey, PA, pp. 132–161.

Guerrini, F., Tuesday, June 17, 2014. Brazil's world cup of cyber attacks: from street fighting to online protest. Forbes. [Online]. Available from: http://www.forbes.com/sites/federicoguerrini/2014/06/17/brazils-world-cup-of-cyber-attacks-from-street-fighting-to-online-protest/ (accessed 26.09.14.).

Haberman, C.P., Ratcliffe, J.H., 2012. The predictive policing challenges of near repeat armed street robberies. Policing 6, 151–166.

Hamill, J., 2013. Shadowy Drug Fans Threaten FBI Agents, Vow to "Avenge" Silk Road Shutdown. [Online]. Available from: http://www.theregister.co.uk/2013/10/10/dark_web_plans_revenge_for_dread_pirate_roberts_arrest/ (accessed 29.09.14.).

HM Government, 2010. A strong Britain in an age of uncertainty: the national security strategy. HM Government. Available from: https://www.gov.uk/government/uploads/system/uploads/attachment_data/file/61936/national-security-strategy.pdf.

Honan, M., 2012. How Apple and Amazon security flaws led to my epic hacking. Wired. [Online]. Available from: http://www.wired.com/2012/08/apple-amazon-mat-honan-hacking/all/ (accessed 26.09.14.).

van Heerden, R.P., Irwin, B., Burke, I., 2012. Classifying network attack scenarios using an ontology. In: Proceedings of the 7th International Conference on Information Warfare and Security. University of Washington, Seattle, pp. 311–324. March 22-23, 2012.

ILO (International Labour Office), 2009. Operational Indicators of Traffcking in Human Beings. ILO (International Labour Office). Available from: http://www.ilo.org/wcmsp5/groups/public/---ed_norm/---declaration/documents/publication/wcms_105023.pdf.

Jalil, S.A., 2003. Countering Cyber Terrorism Effectively: Are We Ready to Rumble? GIAC Security Essentials Certification (GSEC) Practical Assignment Version 1.4b, Option 1, [Online] SANS Institute. Available from: http://www.giac.org/paper/gsec/3108/countering-cyber-terrorism-effectively-ready-rumble/105154.

Kaiman, J., Tuesday, May 20, 2014. China reacts furiously to US cyber-espionage. The Guardian. [Online]. Available from: http://www.theguardian.com/world/2014/may/20/china-reacts-furiously-us-cyber-espionage-charges (accessed 25.05.14.).

Kasper, W., Vela, M, 2011. Sentiment analysis for hotel reviews. In: Jassem, K., Fuglewicz, P., Piasecki, M., Przepiorkowski, A. (Eds.), Proceedings of the Computational Linguistics-Applications Conference (CLA–2011), pp. 45–52 Jachranka.

Kellermann, T., 2004. Money laundering in cyberspace. The World Bank. Available from: http://www-wds.worldbank.org/external/default/WDSContentServer/WDSP/IB/2006/04/21/000012009_20060421140305/Rendered/PDF/359050rev0Mone1nCyberspace01PUBLIC1.pdf (accessed 29.09.14.).

Kilger, M., Arkin, O., Stutzman, J., 2004. Profiling. In: The Honeynet Project (Ed.), Know Your Enemy: Learning about Security Threats, second ed. Addison-Wesley Professional, Boston, MA, pp. 505–556.

Kushner, D., 2013. The real story of STUXNET. Spectrum, IEEE 50, 48–53.

Leyden, J., 2012. UK hacker jailed for nicking PayPal, banking data from millions. [Online]. Available from: http://www.theregister.co.uk/2012/04/04/cybercrook_jailed/ (accessed 26.09.14.).

Lockley, E., Akhgar, B., 2014. Understanding the situational awareness in cybercrimes: case studies. In: Akhgar, B., Staniforth, A., Bosco, F. (Eds.), Cyber Crime and Cyber Terrorism Investigators Handbook. Syngress, Elsevier, pp. 101–121.

Matsumoto, D., Hwang, H.S., Frank, M.G., 2012. The role of emotion in predicting Violence. FBI Law Enforcement Bulletin 1–11.

Manoske, A., 2013. How does cyber warfare work? Forbes. [Online]. Available from: http://www.forbes.com/sites/quora/2013/07/18/how-does-cyber-warfare-work/ (accessed 25.09.14.).

McGuire, M., Dowling, S., 2013. Cyber Crime: A Review of the Evidence—Summary of Key Findings and Implications. The UK Home Office. Available from: https://www.gov.uk/government/uploads/system/uploads/attachment_data/file/246749/horr75-summary.pdf.

Millar, S., Tuesday, June 5, 2001. Teenage clicks. The Guardian. [Online]. Available from: http://www.theguardian.com/technology/2001/jun/05/hacking.security (accessed 26.09.14.).

NBC News, 2003. I'm Not the One They Need to Get. [Online]. Available from: http://www.nbcnews.com/id/3078580/ns/technology_and_science-security/t/im-not-one-they-need-get/#.VCU69vldV8E (accessed 26.09.14.).

O'Connor, B., Balasubramanyan, R., Routledge, B.R., Smith, N.A., 2010. From tweets to polls: linking text sentiment to public opinion time series. In: Proceedings of the International AAAI Conference on Weblogs and Social Media (ICWSM 11), Washington, DC, May 2010, pp. 122–129.

Perry, W.L., McInnis, B., Price, C.C., Smith, S.C., Hollywood, J.S., 2013. Predictive Policing: The Role of Crime Forecasting in Law Enforcement Operations. RAND Safety and Justice Program. Available from: https://www.ncjrs.gov/pdffiles1/nij/grants/243830.pdf.

Profis, S., 2014. How those nude photos were leaked (and why you should care). [Online]. Available from: http://www.cnet.com/uk/how-to/how-nude-photos-leaked-protect-icloud-account-security/ (accessed 26.09.14.).

Rustad, M.L., 2001. Private enforcement of cybercrime on the electronic frontier. Southern California Interdisciplinary Law Journal 11, 63–116.

Sanchez, R., 2013. WikiLeaks QandA: Who is Bradley Manning and What Did He Do? [Online]. Available from: http://www.telegraph.co.uk/news/worldnews/wikileaks/10210160/WikiLeaks-Q-and-A-who-is-Bradley-Manning-and-what-did-he-do.html (accessed 29.09.14.).

Schneier, B., 2014. Chinese hacking of the US. Blog. [Online]. Available from: https://www.schneier.com/blog/archives/2014/06/chinese_hacking_1.html (accessed 25.09.14.).

Schneier, B., 2009. Matthew Weigman. Blog. [Online]. Available from: https://www.schneier.com/blog/archives/2009/09/matthew_weigman.html (accessed 26.09.14.).

Smith, R., Grabosky, P., Urbas, G., 2011. Cyber Criminals on Trial. Cambridge University Press, Cambridge.

Staniforth, A., Nitsch, H., 2014. Preventing terrorism together: a framework to provide social media anti-radicalization training for credible community voices. In: Akhgar, B., Arabnia, H.R. (Eds.), Emerging Trends in ICT Security. Morgan Kaufmann, Elsevier, London, pp. 549–556.

Steinberg, J., Sunday, August 31, 2014. Nude photos of Jennifer Lawrence and Kate Upton leak: five important lessons for all of us. Forbes. [Online]. Available from: http://www.forbes.com/sites/josephsteinberg/2014/08/31/nude-photos-of-jessica-lawrence-and-kate-upton-leak-five-important-lessons-for-all-of-us/ (accessed 29.09.14.).

Sterner, E., 2012. Hacktivists' Evolution Changes Cyber Security Threat Environment. Available from: http://www.worldpoliticsreview.com/articles/11864/hacktivists-evolution-changes-cyber-security-threat-environment (accessed 26.09.14.).

Sykora, M.D., Jackson, T.W., OBrien, A., Elayan, S., 2013. National security and social media monitoring: a presentation of the EMOTIVE and related systems. In: Proceedings of the 2013 European Intelligence and Security Informatics Conference, pp. 172–175.

The Economist, 2013. War on terabytes: as banking has gone electronic, it has also become vulnerable. The Economist. [Online]. Available from: http://www.economist.com/news/finance-and-economics/21571152-banking-has-gone-electronic-it-has-also-become-vulnerable-war-terabytes (accessed 29.09.14.).

Thomson Reuters, 2014. Haystacks of needles: law enforcement fights organized crime with smart analytics. Thomson Reuters. Available from: http://www.globalinitiative.net/download/general/global/Thompson%20Reuters%20-%20Smart%20Analytics%20-%20July%202014.pdf.

Travis, A., 2013. Police forces will struggle to make further cuts, says watchdog. The Guardian. [Online]. Available from: http://www.theguardian.com/uk-news/2013/jul/18/police-forces-futher-cuts-watchdog (accessed 29.09.14.).

US Air Force, 2014. Our Mission [Online]. Available from: http://www.airforce.com/learn-about/our-mission/ (accessed 25.09.14.).

U.S. Department of Justice, 2014. US Charges Five Chinese Military Hackers for Cyber Espionage Against US Corporations and a Labor Organization for Commercial Advantage. [Online]. Available from: http://www.justice.gov/opa/pr/us-charges-five-chinese-military-hackers-cyber-espionage-against-us-corporations-and-labor (accessed 29.09.14.).

U.S. Department of Justice, 2011. Cyber terror. [Online] FBI Law Enforcement Bulletin 80 (11). Available from: http://leb.fbi.gov/2011/november/leb-november-2011.

United Nations Office on Drugs and Crime, 2009. Global Report on Trafficking in Persons. United Nations Office on Drugs and Crime. Available from: http://www.unodc.org/documents/Global_Report_on_TIP.pdf.

Winter, R., 2013. Ransonware: protection, prevention and what to do in an attack. The Guardian. [Online]. Available from: http://www.theguardian.com/media-network/media-network-blog/2013/may/31/ransomware-virus-protection-attack (accessed 26.09.14.).

Yang, C.C., Ng, T.D., 2007. Terrorism and crime related Weblog social network: link, content analysis and information visualization. In: IEEE Intelligence and Security Informatics Conference, May 23-24, 2007, New Brunswick, NJ, pp. 55–58.

METHODS AND TECHNOLOGICAL SOLUTIONS

REQUIREMENTS AND CHALLENGES FOR BIG DATA ARCHITECTURES

John Panneerselvam, Lu Liu, Richard Hill

WHAT ARE THE CHALLENGES INVOLVED IN BIG DATA PROCESSING?

Data generated across the society is very much in a raw state and must be processed to transform it into valuable and meaningful information. Raw data always includes dirty data, i.e., data with potential errors, incompleteness, and differential precision, which must be refined. Usually, data reach their most significant value when they are in their refined state. Architectures for processing big data must be scalable to answer the following questions (Fisher et al., 2012):

- How do we capture, store, manage, distribute, secure, govern, and exploit the data?
- How do we create links across the data stored in different locations? The data value explodes when it is interlinked, leading to better data integration.
- How do we develop trust in the data?
- What advanced tools are available for rapid analysis and to derive new insights?

Real-time analytics of all formats of data and of any volume is the ultimate goal of big data analytics. In other words, Big Data solutions require the analysis against the volume, velocity, and variety of data, while the data are still in motion. To facilitate this, the architectural structure requires integrated data, actionable information, insightful knowledge, and real-time wisdom in its processing model (Begoli and Horey, 2012). This is best achieved with a complete hardware and software integrated framework for big data processing.

DEPLOYMENT CONCEPT

It is appropriate to consider the deployment process in accordance with the three major phases (data acquisition, data organization, and data analysis) of the big data infrastructure. Generally speaking, deployment constitutes the way of thinking about the minutia involved in the acquisition, organization, and analysis phases. Usually, enterprises will participate in a predeployment analysis phase to identify the architectural requirements based on the nature of the data, the estimated processing time, the expected confidentiality of the generated results, and the affordability for a particular project. The major challenges to be considered in the deployment process are heterogeneity, timeliness, security, scale in terms of volume, complexity of the data, the expected accuracy of the results, and more importantly the way of enabling human interaction with the data. According to the five-phase process model (Barlow, 2013), real-time processing includes data distillation, model development, validation and

Table 9.1 Big Data Deployment Pipeline

Major Phases	Subprocess	Purpose
Data acquisition	• Acquiring data and recording	• Collects the data from different data sources, and the data are usually loaded in NoSQL databases
	• Architectural analysis	• Based on the acquired data, enterprises analyze the architecture requirements appropriate for processing
Data organization	• Extraction and shaping of the data	• Refine the raw data to extract the required sample data
	• Integration	• Identifying the relationship between the connected data points
	• Aggregation and representation	• Establish a common representation of the connected data
Data analysis	• Analysis and modelling	• Performing the required data analysis
	• Interpretation	• Loading the data in a user-friendly format, into the databases

deployment, real-time scoring, and model refreshing. In simple terms, a big data solution is the art of merging the problem with the platform to achieve productivity.

The deployment pipeline of big data may start from acquiring and recording the data and then move to the analysis of the architecture; extraction of the data; shaping of the data; their integration, aggregation, analysis, and modelling; representation; and finally their interpretation. All of these processes are complex, because a multitude of options and optimization techniques are available in every phase of the deployment pipeline. Choosing and handling the appropriate techniques for every phase depends on the nature of the data and the outcome expected. For ease of understanding, these subprocesses are grouped under the major three phases of the infrastructure. Table 9.1 explains the subprocesses and their respective purposes involved in the deployment pipeline.

TECHNOLOGICAL UNDERPINNING

No single technology can form a complete big data platform. It is the integration of many core technologies that build the big data platform, thus creating a broader enterprise big data model. Yet, rather than viewing the big data solution as an entirely new technology, it is appropriate to see the big data platform as the integrated extension of existing business intelligence (BI) tools. The orchestration of these technologies (Byun et al., 2012), such as real-stream analytics, MapReduce frameworks, and massively parallel processing (MPP) processors, with massive databases scalable for big data, forms an integrative big data solution.

THE CORE TECHNOLOGIES
MapReduce frameworks
The massive parallel processing of big data in a distributed fashion is enabled by MapReduce frameworks. MapReduce (Raden, 2012) is a programming strategy applied to big data for analytics, which

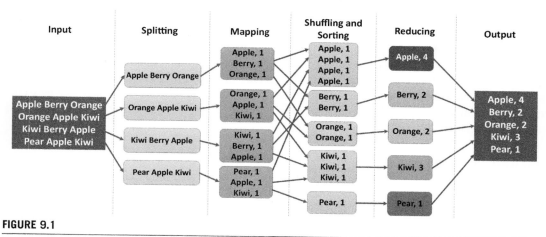

FIGURE 9.1

MapReduce operation for counting the number of objects.

usually divides the workload into subworkloads and separately processes each block of the subunit to generate the output. MapReduce frameworks often depend on Hadoop-like technologies (Shangy et al., 2013), which allows the processing and analysis of data, while the data reside in their original storage location. Hadoop allows the users to load and process the data without the need for any transformation before loading the data into the MapReduce platform.

As its name suggests, the MapReduce process involves two phases, the map phase and the reduce phase. The map phase divides (splits) the workload into subworkloads and assigns tasks to the mapper. The mapper processes each unit of the sub-block and generates a sorted list of key-value pairs that are passed on to the next phase, reduce. The reduce phase merges and analyzes the key-value pairs to produce the final output. MapReduce applications can be programmed in Java or with other higher-level languages like Hive and Pig. A simple MapReduce operation for counting the number of objects from raw data is illustrated in Figure 9.1.

Hadoop distributed file systems

Hadoop distributed file system (HDFS) is a long-term storage option of the Hadoop platform, which is used to capture, store, and retrieve data for later analysis. HDFS is usually configured as direct attached storage (DAS) to Hadoop and facilitates moving data blocks to different distributed servers for processing. HDFS is focused on NoSQL databases, capable of capturing and storing all formats of data without any categorization. The output generated by the Hadoop platform is usually written on the HDFS, which operates in master–slave architecture, with two types of nodes, the name node and the data node. It uses a single name node per cluster, acting as a master, and a number of data nodes performing the read and write requests of the clients. The data nodes store the data blocks in the HDFS, while the name node holds the metadata with the enumeration of the blocks and the list of data nodes in the HDFS cluster. HDFS has the capability of storing data of all formats and of massive sizes. They thus outperform the capabilities of traditional RDBMS, which are limited only to structured data.

HBase

HDFS may include the implementation of HBase, which usually sits on top of the HDFS architecture. HBase is a column-oriented database management system, which provides additional capabilities to HDFS and makes working with HDFS much easier. HBase configuration can be carried out in Java, and its programming functionalities are similar to MapReduce and HDFS. HBase requires the predetermination of the table schema and the column families. However, it provides the advantage that new columns to the families can be added at any time, thus enabling scalability for supporting changes in the application requirements.

Data warehouse and data mart

A data warehouse is a relational database system used to store, query, and analyze the data and to report functions. The data warehousing structure is ideal for analyzing structured data with advanced in-database analytics techniques. In addition to its primary functionalities, data warehouses also include extract-transform-load (ETL) solutions and online analytical processing (OLAP) services. OLAP-based data warehouses have powerful analytical capabilities that can be integrated to generate significant results. Data warehouses are nonvolatile, which means that the data, once entered, cannot be changed, allowing the analysis of what has actually occurred.

There are two approaches to store the data in data warehouses, dimensional and normalized. In the *dimensional approach*, transaction data is partitioned into either facts, which are the transaction data, or dimensions, which are the reference information providing contexts to the facts. The dimensional approach provides an understanding of the data warehouse and facilitates retrieval of the information. Yet, it has complications in loading the data into the data warehouse from different sources and also in the modification of the stored data. In the *normalized approach*, the tables are grouped together by subject areas under defined data categories. This structure divides the data into entities and creates several tables in the form of relational databases. The process of loading information into the data warehouse is thus straightforward, but merging of data from different sources is not an easy task due to the number of tables involved. Also, users may experience difficulties in accessing information in the tables, if they lack precise understanding of the data structure.

The data warehouse architecture may include a data mart, which is an additional layer used to access the data warehouse. Data marts are important for many data warehouses, because they customize various groups within an organization. The data within the data mart is generally tailored according to the specific requirements of an organization.

PLANNING FOR A BIG DATA PLATFORM
INFRASTRUCTURE REQUIREMENTS

Typically, big data analytics work with the principle of ETL. It is the act of pulling the data from the database to an environment where it can be dealt with for further processing. The data value chain defines the processing of any kind of data, flowing from data discovery, integration, and then to data exploitation. It is important to keep in mind that our ultimate target is to achieve easy integration, thereby conducting deeper analytics of the data. In this case, the infrastructure requirements

(Dijcks, 2012; Forsyth, 2012) for the framework to process big data span across three main phases: data acquisition, data organization, and data analysis (Miller and Mork, 2013).

Data acquisition

Trends and policies in acquiring data have changed drastically over the years, and the dynamic nature of big data is forcing enterprises to adapt changes in their infrastructure, mainly in the collection of big data. The infrastructure must show low, predictable latency, not only in capturing the data, but also in executing the process in quick succession. Handling high volumes of transaction data is one of the key characteristics that create the need for infrastructures that are scalable, supporting flexible and dynamic data structures.

In recent years, there has been a transition from SQL databases to NoSQL databases (Kraska, 2013), to capture and store big data. Unlike traditional SQL databases, NoSQL databases show the advantage of capturing the data without any categorization of the collected data. This keeps the storage structure simple and flexible, and thus scalable for dynamic data structures. NoSQL databases do not follow any specific patterns or schemas with respect to relationships between the data. Instead they contain a key to locate the container holding the relevant data. This simple storage strategy avoids costly reorganization of the data for later processing in the data value chain.

Data organization

Data organization is also referred to as data integration. Data integration allows the analysis and the manipulation of the data with data residing (Cleary et al., 2012) in their original storage location. This avoids the complex process of moving huge bulks of data to various places, not only saving processing time, but also costs. Data organization should be managed in such a way that the infrastructure offers higher throughput in handling various formats of data (i.e., from structured to unstructured).

Integrating data is a means of identifying the cross-links between connected data, thereby establishing a common representation of the data. Integration constitutes mapping by defining how the data are related in a common representation. This common representation often depends on the data's syntax, structure, and data semantics and makes the information available usually from a metadata repository. Data integration can be either virtual, through a federated model or physical, usually through a data warehouse. Organizing the data provides ease of storage and facilitates more effective analytics not only in the present, but also in the future.

Data analysis

Data analysis is an important phase in the data management, which leads the way for assisted decision-making in enterprises. From an analysis perspective, the infrastructure must support both statistical analysis and also deeper data mining. Because we are talking about processing the data in its original storage location, a high degree of parallelization is an important criterion that makes the infrastructure scalable. Faster response times, low latency, tolerance to extreme conditions, adaptability to frequent changes, and automated decisions are other important features that make a big data infrastructure more effective.

The purpose of data analysis is to produce a statistically significant result that can be further used by enterprises to make important decisions. Along with the analysis of current data, a combined analysis with older data is important, because this older data could play a vital role in decision making. The interpreted results generated by the analysis phase must be available to the decision maker in a simple and understandable format, usually by providing visualization of the metadata to the interpreter.

Network considerations

Because we process big data in a distributed fashion, the interconnections of the operating nodes within a cluster are crucial, particularly during both the read and write functionalities of the HDFS (Bakshi, 2012) and also the MapReduce metadata communications between the nodes. Every node in HDFS and MapReduce needs low latency and high throughput. In the HDFS framework, the name node should be in a highly connected fashion with the data nodes, to avoid the name node de-listing any data node belonging to its cluster. In a typical Hadoop cluster, the nodes are arranged in racks, and so network traffic from the same rack is more desirable than across the racks. Replication of the name nodes is advantageous because it provides improved fault tolerance.

The network should demonstrate redundancy and should be scalable as the cluster grows. To overcome drawbacks such as single point failure and node block-outs, multiple redundant paths are useful for the operating nodes. At times, the read–write functionalities may involve bottlenecks, leading to packet drops, which in turn forces retransmission of the dropped packets. This leads to longer than usual processing times causing unnecessary delays. Higher network oversubscription may cause packet drops and lower performance, and conversely, lower network oversubscriptions are usually costly to implement. Maintaining lower network latency is always beneficial, and application developers need to consider this when designing solutions. Network bandwidth is another important parameter that has a direct impact on the analytics performance. Because we are moving massive volumes of information from the storage repositories, subscribing to the optimum level of bandwidth is essential.

Performance considerations

When considering performance, the following criteria are relevant:

- *Scalable cluster sizing* of the Hadoop platform allows the cluster to expand as new nodes arrive. Generally speaking, the best way of decreasing the time required for job completion and to offer faster response times is to increase the number of active nodes participating in the cluster.
- *Suitable algorithms* increase the efficiency of the entire data model. The algorithm should be designed in accordance with the input datasets and the expected results. Offloading the computational complexities towards the map phase than that of the reduce phase or vice versa may make the algorithm inefficient. In this sense, the design of the algorithm should be in balance between the two phases of the MapReduce framework.
- *The pipeline* defines how the job task flows from capturing the data until the interpretation of the output. A pipeline with the integration of smaller jobs proves to be more efficient than single larger jobs. This strategy helps in avoiding issues like network bottlenecks, overloading, etc., and thus helps optimization.
- *Scheduling* jobs to a local node offers faster job completion than scheduling to a node located remotely. Assigning tasks normally depends on the instances available in the clusters.

- *Parallel processing* allows MapReduce to process jobs concurrently, e.g., in the form of ETL.
- *Service discovery* helps the master node to identify the required resources for newly submitted jobs. Less sharing of the node clusters ensures node availability for processing the newly submitted jobs, thus achieving better performance.

CAPACITY PLANNING CONSIDERATIONS

Hadoop manages data storage and analytics under the software tier rather than relying on storage options such as SAN and server blades. A typical Hadoop element includes CPU, memory, disk, and the network. The platform requires a partition of the MapReduce intermediate files and the HDFS files, implying that both must be stored in separate locations. Swapping these two memories often degrades the system performance. *In-database analytics techniques* are essential, which takes the processing to the data rather than moving the data to the processing environment. *In-memory computing* should be enabled in relationship with the in-database analytics by providing high-speed analytics for online transaction processing (OLTP) and BI applications. In-memory computing stores the processed data in a memory storage, which is directly addressable using the memory bus of the CPU.

Data stack requirements

Organizations dealing with big data are still faced with significant challenges, both in the way they extract significant value out of the data and the decision, whether it is appropriate to retain the data or not. In some cases, most or all of the data must be processed to extract a valuable sample of data. The "bigness" of the data is determined according to their location in the data stack. The higher the data move up in the stack, the less of the data needs to be actively managed (Barlow, 2013). Often we see data quantities of petabytes and exabytes in the data layer, where it is usually collected. The analytics layer can reduce this data volume to terabytes and gigabytes after refining the raw and dirty data. It is feasible that this data volume is even reduced to megabytes in the integration layer. This architecture manages to reduce data into just kilobytes in the decision layer. Thus the architecture reduces the size of the data by a considerable volume at the top of the data stack. The data stack architecture is illustrated in Figure 9.2.

CLOUD COMPUTING CONSIDERATIONS

Processing big data with cloud computing resources involves the transmission of large volumes of data to the cloud through a network. This highlights the importance of network bandwidth allocation, network congestion, and other network-related issues such as overloading and bottlenecks (KDnuggets, 2012). Enterprises prefer to process their data in an environment that computes the units of data close together rather than distributing them geographically. It is important for enterprises to identify the correct cloud services for their requirements. Another issue in processing big data in clouds is the level of trust in processing the data with the cloud providers. Enterprises should assess the trust level offered by the cloud providers as they are ready to process their confidential data in an environment that is beyond their reach. Before going to the cloud, enterprises should conduct an assessment to evaluate the cloud provider's capacity in satisfying their architectural needs and the application requirements within their inevitable financial constraints.

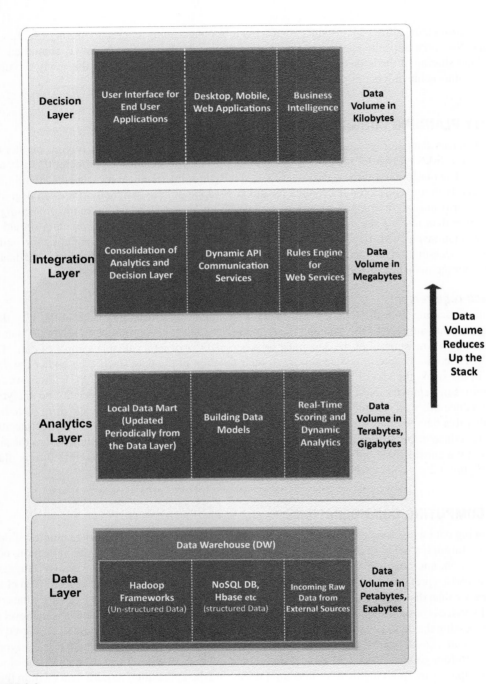

FIGURE 9.2

Data stack architecture.

CONCLUSIONS

Big data analytics illustrates a significant and compelling value, but they also encompass the complexity in every processing step of the analytics platform. The success of the big data concept lies in the potential integration of the supporting technologies that can facilitate the infrastructure requirements of collecting, storing, and analyzing the data. Undoubtedly, the big data implementations require extension or even replacement of the traditional data processing systems. Knowing the significance of big data in the next solid set of years, enterprises have started to adopt big data solutions at a quicker time scale. On the other hand, we see the size of the datasets increasing constantly, and therefore, we need new technologies and new strategies to deal with these data. Thus in the near future, we might need *systems of systems, techniques of techniques, and strategies of strategies* to solve the big data queries. Cloud computing directly underpins big data implementations. On the whole, the dependability of big data requires the incorporation, integration, and matching of suitable techniques and technologies to sustain the promises and potential of big data solutions.

REFERENCES

Bakshi, K., 2012. Considerations for big data: architecture and approach. In: Aerospace Conference, 2012 IEEE. IEEE, Big Sky, pp. 1–7.

Barlow, M., 2013. Real-Time Big Data Analytics: Emerging Architecture. O'Reilly.

Begoli, E., Horey, J., 2012. Design principles for effective knowledge discovery from big data. In: Joint Working Conference on Software Architecture & 6th European Conference on Software Architecture. IEEE, Helsinki, pp. 215–218.

Byun, C., Arcand, W., Bestor, D., Bergeron, B., Hubbell, M., Kepner, J., McCabe, A., Michaleas, P., Mullen, J., O'Gwynn, D., Prout, A., Reuther, A., Rosa, A., Yee, C., 2012. Driving big data with big compute. In: IEEE Conference on High Performance Extreme Computing (HPEC). IEEE, Waltham, pp. 1–6.

Cleary, L., Freed, B., Peterson, E., Media, B., 2012. Big data analytics guide. SAP.

Dijcks, J.P., 2012. Oracle: Big Data for the Enterprise. Oracle Corporation, USA, pp. 1–14.

Fisher, D., DeLine, R., Czerwinski, M., Drucker, S., 2012. Interactions with Big Data Analytics. pp. 50–59.

Forsyth, C., 2012. For big data analytics there's no such thing as too big, the compelling economics and technology of big data computing. Cisco 1–20.

Kraska, T., 2013. Finding the needle in the big data systems haystack. IEEE Internet Comput 17, 84–86.

KDnuggets, 2012. Demystifying Big Data. TechAmerica.

Miller, H., Mork, P., 2013. From data to decisions: a value chain for big. IT Professional 15, 57–59.

Raden, N., 2012. Big data analytics architecture. Hired Brains 1–13.

Shangy, W., Jiangy, Z., Hemmatiy, H., Adamsz, B., Hassany, A., Martin, P., 2013. Assisting developers of big data analytics applications when deploying on hadoop clouds. In: 35th International Conference on Software Engineering (ICSE). IEEE, San Francisco, pp. 402–411.

TOOLS AND TECHNOLOGIES FOR THE IMPLEMENTATION OF BIG DATA

10

Richard J. Self, Dave Voorhis

INTRODUCTION

This chapter provides an overview and critical analysis of the current status and issues likely to affect the development and adoption of Big Data analytics. It covers the conceptual foundations and models of the subject, the varied technologies and tools that are relevant to practitioners, and a range of considerations that affect the effective implementation and delivery of Big Data solutions to organizational strategies and information requirements.

The three V's (Laney, 2001; Gartner, 2011) present inherent technical challenges to managing and analyzing Big Data:

- *Volume* implies that there are too much data to house or process using commodity hardware and software. "Too much" is deliberately vague. What is considered too much grows over time—to date, the upper bound of what can be stored or managed is always increasing—and depends on the requirements and budget. A Big Data volume for a small under-funded charity organization may be considered small and trivially manageable by a large well-funded commercial enterprise with extensive storage capacity.
- *Velocity* implies that new data arrive too quickly to manage or analyze or analysis is required too quickly or too often to support with commodity hardware and software. Of course, "too quickly" is as vague as "too much data."
- *Variety* implies that there is too much variation in data records or too many diverse sources to use conventional commodity software easily. Conventional data analysis software typically assumes data that are consistently formatted or perhaps are already housed in, for example, a structured query language database management system (SQL DBMS).

The presence of any one of the three V's is sufficient to acquire a label of "Big Data" because "big" refers to sizable complexity or difficulty and not necessarily volume. Conversely, if all three aspects of *velocity*, *volume*, and *variety* of data are manageable with conventional commodity hardware and software, by this definition it is not Big Data. It might be "Large Data" (i.e., it occupies a manageable amount of space but presumably is still vast, for some agreeable definition of "vast") or it might just be "data" that are rapidly changing and/or the results are needed in a hurry, but not unfeasibly so, and/or is diverse but not unmanageably so.

"Commodity hardware and software" is not rigorously defined here. It can be taken to mean anything from off-the-shelf desktop data analysis tools such as Microsoft Excel and Access; to enterprise relational DBMSs such as Oracle Database, Microsoft SQL Server, or IBM DB2; to data analysis and business intelligence suites such as SAS by SAS Software or SAP Business Objects. "Big Data" implies, in general, that such tools are inadequate, and so are the techniques on which they are based. As a result, a number of specialized techniques have emerged to tackle Big Data problems. The remainder of this chapter will describe some of these techniques, followed by some of the tools that implement them.

TECHNIQUES

This section is divided into two parts. The first deals primarily with the *volume* aspect of Big Data: how to represent and store it. The second deals essentially with the *velocity* aspect, i.e., methods to produce results in an acceptably timely fashion. Both sections mention, as appropriate, *variety*.

REPRESENTATION, STORAGE, AND DATA MANAGEMENT

This section highlights a representative, rather than comprehensive, selection of techniques used to represent and store Big Data, focusing on approaches that can manage a volume of data that is considered infeasible with conventional database technologies such as SQL DBMSs. In general, as of late 2013, in-memory or direct-attached storage is generally favored over network accessible storage (Webster, 2011).

Distributed Databases

Distributed databases are database systems in which data are stored on multiple computers that may be physically co-located in a cluster or geographically distant. Distributed database systems can include massively parallel processing (MPP) databases and data-mining grids. Distributed database systems typically shield the user from accessing the data storage directly by accessing it via a query language. The *variety* aspect of Big Data can make traditional storage approaches challenging, with the result that column stores or key-value stores—rather than SQL-based storage—are commonplace. Alternatives to SQL are commonly known as NoSQL.

Massively Parallel Processing Databases

Massively parallel processing databases are distributed database systems specifically engineered for parallel data processing. Each server has memory and processing power, which may include both central processing units and graphics processing units (Ectors, 2013), to process data locally (DeWitt and Gray, 1992). All communication is via networking; no disks are shared, in what is termed a "shared nothing" architecture (Stonebraker, 1986). This can help address the *velocity* and *volume* issues of Big Data. Database query languages designed specifically for MPP databases may be employed (Chaiken et al., 2008).

Data-Mining Grids

Unlike a cluster, which is a group of closely coupled computers dedicated to high-performance parallel computing, a grid is a collection of computers that are relatively loosely coupled and that may leave or join the grid arbitrarily, but which collectively (typically via software running on the individual machines) support high-performance, massively parallel computing (Foster and Kesselman, 2004). When this computational capacity is dedicated to data analysis, it is considered a data-mining grid and often takes the form of a collection of tools to facilitate data mining using grid infrastructure (Cannataro and Pugliese, 2004). This can help address the *velocity* and *volume* issues of Big Data.

Distributed File Systems

Distributed file systems are approaches to storing files that involve multiple computers to extend storage capacity, speed, or reliability—typically via redundancy (Levy and Silberschatz, 2009). This can help address the *velocity* and *volume* issues. Unlike distributed database systems, which typically shield the user from direct access to stored data, distributed file systems are specifically designed to give users and their applications direct access to stored data.

Cloud-Based Databases

Cloud-based database systems are distributed database systems specifically designed to run on cloud infrastructure (Amazon, 2013). They may be SQL or NoSQL based.

ANALYSIS

This section presents a selection of Big Data analysis approaches, organized alphabetically. Unless otherwise noted, the assumption is that the data are already stored in or accessible via one of the approaches described in the previous section. The descriptions below are intended to be brief introductions rather than detailed overviews and the focus is generally on categories of analysis rather than specific techniques. The latter would be too extensive to cover here and would only duplicate existing texts on statistics, machine learning, artificial intelligence, business intelligence, and the like.

A/B TESTING

A/B testing is the process of using randomized experiments to verify which of two advertising campaigns or advertising approaches is most effective. For example, a mail campaign soliciting donations may not be sure which wording is best at generating a response: "Donate now, we are counting on your help!" or "We need your donation!" Using A/B testing, a trial batch of envelopes will be sent with the first wording (Group A) and an equivalent batch with the second wording (Group B). A form is included that the recipient must fill out to accompany a donation, which includes some indication—such as an A or B code discretely printed at the bottom—to indicate which wording was used. It is then a simple matter to determine which wording results in the best response. However, this is not Big Data in and of itself.

The same process is often used to test changes to Web sites to gauge their effectiveness (Ozolins, 2012). Given the volume of Web site hits that a popular Web site can receive, it can easily represent a significant volume of data being generated. However, this does not necessarily bring it into the Big Data category. Yet, combined with other analyses of user attributes—such as what country the user is coming from, along with demographic data sourced from a user's account on the given Web site as part of an overall retail analytics strategy—the need to produce results rapidly based on data from a variety of sources including A/B testing may bring it into Big Data territory (Ash, 2008).

ASSOCIATION RULE LEARNING

Association rule learning is a method for discovering relations among variables in databases, based on identifying rules (Agrawal et al., 1993). For example, a database of supermarket sales may record sales of carrots, beans, beer, coffee, peas, and potatoes. Analysis of the data using association rule learning may reveal a rule that a customer who buys carrots and beans is also likely to buy potatoes, and another that a customer who buys beer and coffee is also likely to buy peas. These rules may be used to govern marketing activity. For example, the supermarket may choose to locate carrots and beans in the same freezer and position a poster advertising a particular deal on bulk potatoes (which delivers a high margin) above it.

When the volume of data of data is high—say, generated by Web site visits on a popular site—it may be classified as a Big Data analysis technique.

CLASSIFICATION

Classification is a general term associated with the identification of categories in a database. It is not a single technique, but a category of techniques serving a variety of purposes in the general area of data mining. It may involve statistical, artificial intelligence, machine learning, or pattern recognition techniques, among others (Fayyad, 1996a). Classification is by no means specific to Big Data, but Big Data analysis frequently employs classification techniques as part of an overall suite of analytical processes.

CROWDSOURCING

Crowdsourcing is the use of human effort—typically from an online community—to provide analysis or information rather than using automated processes or traditional employees. This differs from traditional outsourcing in that the humans involved typically do not have a formal employment relationship with the organization that is using them. They may, for example, be recruited online or may simply be casual browsers of a particular Web site. This becomes relevant to Big Data when the diversity of information (i.e., variety) or volume of information to be collected only becomes feasible to collect or process via crowdsourcing (Howe, 2006).

DATA MINING

Like classification, data mining is not a single technique but a variety of techniques for extracting information from a database and presenting it in a useful fashion. Originally, the term "data mining" implied discovery of unanticipated findings, such as patterns revealed or relationships uncovered, but over time the term has come to refer to any form of information processing, particularly that involving statistics, artificial intelligence, machine learning, or business intelligence and data analysis (Fayyad, 1996b).

NATURAL LANGUAGE PROCESSING AND TEXT ANALYSIS

Large volumes or continuous streams of text, such as Twitter feeds (Twitter, 2013), online forum postings, and blogs, have become a popular focus for analysis. Their unconventional variety, at least from a conventional data processing point of view, and size inevitably associate them with Big Data. In general, natural language processing refers to a variety of techniques that rely on automated interpretation of human languages, which (among a variety of purposes) may be used for machine translation of text, virtual online assistants, natural language database queries, or sentiment analysis (see below) (Jurafsky and Martin, 2009).

Text analysis (also known as text mining) is closely related to natural language processing but refers specifically to studying human text for patterns, categories of text, frequencies of words or phrases, or other analysis of text without the express purpose of acting on its meaning (Feldman and Sanger, 2007) (for more details, see Chapters 11–13).

SENTIMENT ANALYSIS

Also known as opinion mining, sentiment analysis combines natural language processing, text processing, and statistical techniques to identify the attitude of a speaker or writer toward a topic (Lipika and Haque, 2008). Of particular interest to large corporations seeking to evaluate and/or manage popular commentary on their products or actions, sentiment analysis has grown in significance along with the popularity of social media. The *volume*, *variety*, and *velocity* of postings on social media—particularly in response to hot topics—brings this firmly into the domain of Big Data.

SIGNAL PROCESSING

The volume of data implied by Big Data leads naturally to considering data as a continuous signal rather than discrete units. Processing vast volumes of data as individual transactions may be nearly intractable, but treating the data as a signal permits the use of established data analysis approaches traditionally associated with processing sound, radio, or images. For example, the detection of threats in social networks may be effectively handled by representing the data as graphs and by identifying graph anomalies using signal detection theory (Miller et al., 2011).

VISUALIZATION

The velocity of Big Data can present particular challenges in terms of analyzing data; traditional approaches of generating tables of figures and a few graphs are too slow, too user-unfriendly, or too demanding of resources to be appropriate. Visualization is the use of graphical summarization to convert significant aspects of data into easily understood pictorial representations (Intel, 2013).

COMPUTATIONAL TOOLS

This section makes no attempt to be comprehensive, but provides a sample of some notable tools (and, in the case of MapReduce, a category of tools) that are particularly recognized in the context of Big Data. The absence of a tool from this section should not be considered a deprecation of its capabilities, nor should the presence of a tool here be considered an endorsement. The tools listed have been chosen at random from a pool identified solely on the basis of being recognizably connected to the field of Big Data.

Notably and intentionally absent are conventional SQL DBMSs, which are appropriate for managing large, structured collections of data, but are generally regarded as unsuitable for the nearly intractable volume and/or variety of Big Data. Furthermore, they are more than adequately described elsewhere (Date, 2003).

HADOOP

Hadoop is open source software designed to support distributed computing (Hadoop, 2013). In particular, it contains two fundamental components that together address the *volume* and *velocity* aspects of Big Data:

1. A distributed file system called HDFS that uses multiple machines to store and retrieve large datasets rapidly.
2. A parallel processing facility called MapReduce (see below) that supports parallel processing of large datasets.

MAPREDUCE

MapReduce is an approach to processing large datasets using a parallel processing, distributing algorithm on a cluster of computers (Shankland, 2008). A MapReduce program consists of two procedures: Map(), which takes the input data and distributes them to nodes in the cluster for processing; and Reduce(), which collects processed data from the nodes and combines them in some way to generate the desired result. A typical production implementation of MapReduce (e.g., Hadoop, which provides MapReduce processing via the identically named MapReduce component) also provides facilities for communications, fault tolerance, data transfer, storage, redundancy, and data management.

APACHE CASSANDRA

Cassandra is an open source, high-performance, distributed Java-based DBMS designed specifically to be fault tolerant on cloud infrastructure (Cassandra, 2013). It is considered an NoSQL database system because it employs standard SQL as a query language but uses an SQL-like query language called CQL. It can integrate with Hadoop. Notably, it does not support joins or sub-queries.

(More details on some of the technical tools and considerations of constructing Big Data system can be found in Chapters 7 and 9.)

IMPLEMENTATION

The development and introduction of new technologies and systems are an uncertain art, as can be seen from the Standish Group Chaos reports and Ciborra (2000). Project success rates are low and levels of cancellation and failure are high. High expectations are endemic and often unrealistic (Gartner, 2012).

Many factors affect the implementation and uptake of new technologies in organizations. Some of the most important ones that will have an impact on Big Data systems are presented and evaluated in this section, which covers critical questions relating to the following major topic areas:

- Implementation issues for new technologies and systems
- Data sources
- Governance/compliance.

The intent of this section is not to provide specific answers or recommendations; rather it is to sensitize all stakeholders involved in Big Data analytics projects to the areas in which risk assessment and mitigation are required to deliver successful, effective systems that deliver benefits.

IMPLEMENTATION ISSUES

Ultimately, technologies and systems projects need to be implemented so that business can be conducted. Project teams continually encounter many pitfalls on the road to implementation.

New Technology Introduction and Expectations

The IT industry is subject to cycles of hyperbole and great expectations. Big Data is one of the latest technologies, which raises the question of whether it is just a fashion or whether there is a degree of reality. Gartner (2012) provides regular evaluations of the hype cycles of a wide range of technologies, including one for the technologies and tools of Big Data.

The Gartner hype cycle is a plot of the levels of expectation associated with a particular technology or concept or product across time. The first phase is called the technology trigger phase, during which the levels of expectation of feasibility and benefits rapidly rise, reaching a peak of inflated expectation. Typically, products then rapidly descend toward the trough of disillusionment as products fail to deliver the promised benefits. Thereafter, a few products and technologies start to climb the slope of enlightenment as they are seen to deliver some of the hyped benefits and capabilities. Eventually, a very few products reach the final phase of the plateau of productivity because they prove effective. The Gartner hype cycle reports also assess when the technology might reach the final productive stage.

Tables 10.1 and 10.2, sourced from Gartner (2012), show that some aspects of Big Data are already in the plateau of productivity.

Thus, it is clear that the field of Big Data passes the test of operational reality, although there are many aspects in which research is required to ensure the feasibility and effectiveness of the tools and techniques before introduction into high-value and high-impact projects.

PROJECT INITIATION AND LAUNCH

Information technology projects are particularly prone to lack of success, The Standish Group has been researching and publishing on this problem since the original CHAOS report (Standish Group, 1994), which first identified the scale of the problem.

There seem to be various causes for the lack of success of IT-related projects. A key cause was identified by Daniel Kahneman (2011) as the *planning fallacy* associated with high degrees of overoptimism and confidence by project planners and sponsoring executives. This is often compounded by the *sunk-cost fallacy*, described by Arkes and Blumer (1985, cited in Kahneman, 2011, p. 253), in which the size of the investment in a failing project prevents the project team from cutting its losses.

Kahneman describes the planning fallacy as a combination of unreasonable optimism about the likely success of the particular project under consideration and a deliberate act of ignoring external evidence about the likely success of the project based on other, similar projects. He provides strong evidence that this is a universal human behavior pattern in both corporate and personal environments, leading to project

Table 10.1 Rising to the Peak of Inflated Expectations

Technologies on the Rise	Time to Deliver, in Years	At the Peak of Inflated Expectations	Time to Deliver, in Years
Information valuation	>10	Dynamic data masking	5–10
High-performance message infrastructure	5–10	Social content	2–5
Predictive modeling solutions	2–5	Claims analytics	2–5
Internet of things	>10	Content analytics	5–10
Search-based data discovery tools	5–10	Context-enriched services	5–10
Video search	5–10	Logical data warehouse	5–10
		NoSQL database management systems	2–5
		Social network analysis	5–10
		Advanced fraud detection and analysis technologies	2–5
		Open SCADA (Supervisory Control And Data Acquisition)	5–10
		Complex-event processing	5–10
		Social analytics	2–5
		Semantic web	>10
		Cloud-based grid computing	2–5
		Cloud collaboration services	5–10
		Cloud parallel processing	5–10
		Geographic information systems for mapping, visualization, and analytics	5–10
		Database platform as a service	2–5
		In-memory database management systems	2–5
		Activity streams	2–5
		IT service root cause analysis tools	5–10
		Open government data	2–5

Sourced from Gartner (2012).

cost overruns of 40% to 1000% and time scale overruns of similar size factors, often compounded by the sunk-cost fallacy. To mitigate the effects of the planning fallacy, Kahneman provides evidence from both the transport (Flyvberg, 2006) and construction industries (Remodeling 2002, cited Kahneman, 2011, p. 250), and from his own teaching and research, that it is critical to obtain an outside view for actual achievements from a wide range of similar projects. This represents the development of reference class forecasting by Bent Flyvberg from a comprehensive analysis of transport projects (Flyvberg, 2006).

A reference class view should encompass a range of comparative metrics of achievements compared with the original plans that were approved at the time of the project launch for as large a collection of projects as possible. This will provide a means of baselining the specific project, which can then be modified in the light of any specific project factors, and which may justify a more optimistic or pessimistic plan.

Table 10.2 Falling from the Peak to Reality

Sliding into the Trough of Disillusionment	Climbing the Slope of Enlightenment	Entering the Plateau of Productivity
Typically 2–5 years delivery		*Typically >2 years delivery*
Telematics	Intelligent electronic devices (2–5)	Web analytics
In-memory data grids	Supply chain analytics (obsolete)	Column-store DBMS
Web experience analytics	Social media monitors (<2)	Predictive analytics
Cloud computing	Speech recognition (2–5)	
Sales analytics (5–10)		
MapReduce and alternatives		
Database software as a service		
In-memory analytics		
Text analytics		
Sourced from Gartner (2012).		

INFORMATION TECHNOLOGY PROJECT REFERENCE CLASS

The Standish Group research identified that in the 19 years since its first report in 1994, the level of successful IT-related projects has averaged approximately 30% of all surveyed projects (on time, to budget, and delivering all specified functionality in relation to the launch contract). This is approximately half the rate of successful projects (defined as meeting their original business goals) in an international survey by the Project Management Institute across all business sectors and types of projects (ESI Int, 2013). Current research has not clearly identified why IT-related projects are so much less successful as a class than other projects.

Whereas the Standish Group reports provided some approaches that are claimed to improve the probabilities of success and reduce the likelihood of outright failure, the overall rates of project success (narrowly defined as on time, to budget, and delivering the full agreed functionality) have not improved significantly since 2002. It is of significant concern that the proportion of failed projects (projects that never achieve implementation) has steadily increased since 2002. Challenged projects are defined as those that are implemented in part, overrun time and cost budgets, and fail to deliver the agreed functionality (i.e., fail to meet the quality target). The definitions are provided in the original 1994 Standish Group report.

A key finding was that projects with a value of over $10 million have a 0% probability of being delivered on time, to budget, and with all contracted functionality, whereas small projects with a total budget of less than $750,000 have a relatively high probability of success, at 55% (Standish Group, 1999). This set of data provides salutary evidence of the continued existence of the planning fallacy among planners and sponsors of IT-related projects.

Those involved in the development and implementation of Big Data analytics projects are therefore strongly encouraged to use these data as a base-level reference class from which to develop their project planning estimates. Continued research is also required to collect the reference class data for Big Data analytics projects to provide a more refined base-level forecast for the future.

MITIGATING FACTORS

The Standish Group also collected data on the top factors reported by chief information officers (CIOs) who completed the Chaos surveys as their assessment of the contributory causes for project success (see Table 10.3).

User involvement has remained a critical factor in the success of projects through the years, as has the importance of the active support of company executives. In addition, it is becoming clear that the agile approach is a factor in successful projects. Owing to the novelty of the field of Big Data analytics, user involvement and agile, exploratory approaches will be necessary to be able to deliver value to the business.

USER FACTORS AND CHANGE MANAGEMENT

It is clear from Table 10.3 that users have always been highly important in contributing to the success of a project. This is reinforced by almost all textbooks and commentaries on the subject of the introduction of changes to the working environment and new business practices. Burnes (2009) provides a particularly good insight into the critical factors for the involvement of users successfully introducing new systems and technology. Because the field of Big Data analytics will involve significant developments of new ways of gathering data and then analyzing and presenting them in ways that provide valuable business insights, it will be especially important for the development team to work closely with users and management to facilitate this process. It will be vital to identify the change champions (Burnes, 2009) from among the users, who have both a deep understanding of the business domain and the corporate strategy, working practices, and internal culture together with a good understanding of the

Table 10.3 Standish Group Success Factors

1994	1999	2001	2004	2010, 2012
1. User involvement	1. User involvement	1. Executive management support	1. User involvement	1. Executive support
2. Executive management support	2. Executive management support	2. User involvement	2. Executive management support	2. User involvement
3. Clear statement of requirements	3. Smaller project milestones	3. Competent staff	3. Smaller project milestones	3. Clear business objectives
4. Proper planning	4. Competent staff	4. Smaller project milestones	4. Hard-working, focused staff	4. Emotional maturity
5. Realistic expectations	5. Ownership	5. Clear vision and objectives	5. Clear vision and objectives	5. Optimizing scope
6. Smaller project milestones				6. Agile process
7. Competent staff				7. Project management expertise
8. Ownership				8. Skilled resources
9. Clear vision and objectives				9. Execution
10. Hard-working, focused staff				10. Tools and infrastructure

capabilities and limitations of information technology. Change champions may not always be senior, but they will have highly developed internal networks and will be highly trusted by their colleagues.

Change champions will need to be introduced to the concepts and objectives of Big Data analytics at an early stage in the project so that they can appreciate the potential of Big Data analytics for the business and can identify critical business insights that can be developed from the data. Their active involvement will help to sell the project to all involved and, as important, to identify areas of change that will need particularly sensitive treatment in the overall change management program.

DATA SOURCES AND ANALYTICS

Big Data analytics can be sourced from a wide variety of environments; however, they can generally be categorized into public sourcing (cloud/crowd) and internal corporate data collection. Different consequences relate to the main sources of Big Data.

CLOUD/CROWD SOURCING

Much of the data involved in Big Data analytics are sourced from social media such as Twitter, Facebook, and YouTube and similar types of systems including text and multimedia (Minelli et al., 2013). These types of sources satisfy all of the V's of the definition of Big Data. The purpose of analytics in this area is to attempt to obtain an understanding of the public's thinking and the impact of its perceptions on business strategy, operations, and tactics using all possible sources including both structured and unstructured data. Corporations will often use these sources to analyze customer perceptions of competitor products and services as well as of their own products and services.

One critical issue of using this type of data is how much trust can be placed on the accuracy of the data and the intended insights to be derived through the analytics process (this relates to the fifth V of Big Data, i.e., *veracity*). Strong anecdotal evidence suggests that much of the data provided by the public on Web pages are deliberately falsified, particularly elements relating to identity and demographic data. Often, these data items are particularly important to the intended analytics exercise.

CORPORATE SYSTEMS

Executive systems within large organizations are another source of Big Data, particularly in the financial services and health care fields (Minelli et al., 2013), where the IT systems collect very large volumes of customer data. Aerospace and car manufacturer companies and their systems suppliers collect large volumes of data relating to the operation and use of their products, such as aircraft and engine performance data. These data are collected by the equipment condition monitoring systems to gain insights at fleet level into how the products are used, with the aim of assisting in the development of revised and new products and diagnosing the causes of specific failures. Equipment operators also use analytics to manage the maintenance and overhaul of their fleet, often using predictive analytics in the process. In the financial services arena, Big Data analytics are often involved in risk analysis and management and in fraud detection and prevention.

Even though the data are derived from the operational systems and processes of the relevant organization, it is not possible to fully trust the accuracy of the data provided to the analytics processes. Corporate data are rarely completely accurate or up-to-date.

An endemic problem in much of the financial services world is the failure of organizations to adequately manage the use of end-user type tools (such as spreadsheets and macros), which are the source of key regulatory reporting data streams (at very high *velocity* and *volume*) and management data (such as real-time capital risk analysis and exposure) in the investment banking field.

Persistent research and many publications have demonstrated that approximately 95% of all complex spreadsheets contain errors (Deloitte, 2010; Panko, 2008; Panko and Port, 2012). In addition, many organizations then link spreadsheets together in large networks of interdependency (Cluster Seven, 2011), which results in the propagation of erroneous information through the network until it is used both executively and in decision making.

Most organizations implementing enterprise resource planning systems have found it vital to carry out extensive data cleansing exercises before transferring the data from the legacy systems into the new systems. Often, 50–70% of all data in the databases are removed. This should be another warning flag to the creators and users of Big Data analytics projects: The critical question is, "Are my data clean enough to give valid insights?" This clearly presents a challenge in relation to the fourth and fifth V's of Big Data (*veracity* and *value*) (see Chapter 1).

ANALYTICS PHILOSOPHY: ANALYSIS OR SYNTHESIS

The core science that supports analytics is statistics. Fundamentally this identifies correlations among factors and data items to identify patterns and trends from historical data. However, correlation and causation are not equivalent. It is also vital to recognize that there is no guarantee that the future will be the same as the past. The use of correlation-based analytics of data (from whatever source) is an exercise in pattern identification from the past. It is also simplistic in its statement that "these two things happen together." The more insightful approach is to develop a clearer understanding of what factor causes the response (causal relationships), because this will enable management to better assess the full business model and business case for actions developed as a consequence of the analysis (see also discussions in Chapter 17 on cultural influences on data patterns).

An example of the problem of understanding the past from analysis of the data is seen in the aftermath of the Credit Crunch in 2008–2009, in the extreme difficulties that the economics profession had in understanding what the levers of control had become for the post–credit crunch economic environment. They found that few if any of the economic correlations and models from the past seemed to apply in understanding the influences and interactions of interest rates, inflation, and employment. The world had changed and a new set of relationships needed to be developed, modeled, and understood; the past was not the same as the future. Part of the problem in this example is that many of the different economic models are based on correlation rather than a fundamental understanding of causal relationships (often because of the extreme complexity of the models and the real world).

The attraction of the statistical analytics approach is that it has the feel and appearance of the scientific process; gather data, analyze according to algorithms, and identify statistically based results that identify the contributing components of the relationships. It is, however, an exercise of thinking within the box, within a single domain of knowledge.

To obtain truly valuable insights, a different approach is often effective. This is the approach of *synthesis*: thinking outside the box and connecting two or more domains of knowledge (Buytendijk, 2010). Incorporating the concept of synthesis into the application of Big Data analytics will be a critical challenge for many organizations.

Success in developing the *synthesis* of concepts and domains to identify the most important insights will be a critical differentiator between organizations that use analytics as a commodity tool and those that are able to generate sustainable strategic advantage (Carr, 2004).

GOVERNANCE AND COMPLIANCE

Information governance and compliance is a well-recognized topic for CIOs (Soares, 2012). Big Data is information technology and is therefore in one sense just business as usual for CIOs and their teams from the perspective of information governance, using frameworks such as International Organization for Standardization 27001/27002 or Control Objectives for Information and Related Technology to define their information governance strategy. However, specific issues may be significant challenges in meeting data protection requirements in many legal jurisdictions (see Chapters 15 and 16).

DATA PROTECTION REQUIREMENTS AND PRIVACY

Within the European Union (EU), the data protection regime is strict about the collection, storage, protection, and use of data that can be linked to identifiable citizens (Data Protection Directive 95/46/EC), which is currently implemented via national legislation in each EU country. The EU is in the process of revising this directive to recognize the impact of new factors such as globalization, the cloud, and social networks to create a general data protection regulation to provide a unifying framework for the whole EU. The planned timescale is to introduce it in 2014 and for it take effect in 2016 (EU, 2012).

The impact of the restrictions in the current regime on the transfer of personal data to third countries is particularly significant in its effect on cloud-based processing, where it may not be easy or even feasible to determine the location of the storage and processing and whether it meets EU requirements. In theory, the United States (US) Safe Harbor framework (US Dept of Commerce, 2013) meets many of the requirements of the EU framework. However, there are still significant differences between the two regimes, especially in the level and type of access to personal data by government agencies.

In principle, the EU position is that general access by government agencies is highly regulated and permissible only in the course of investigating a specific crime, whereas the US principle is far more relaxed and operates with relatively few constraints. The decision of the Society for Worldwide Interbank Financial Telecommunication network to re-engineer its systems in 2009 to separate EU and non-EU data processing, to ensure that financial data relating to EU organizations were not accessible to the US agencies (SWIFT, 2008) illustrates the difficulties for Big Data users in a highly interconnected global world.

The disclosures in the *Guardian* (Greenwald et al., 2013) provided by Edward Snowden identified the levels and types of access to personally identifiable data in many jurisdictions. Whereas many of his disclosures relate to the US, some also relate to apparent issues in the EU. The impact of this, now public domain knowledge, raises significant questions related to an organization's ability to comply with the European Data Protection Act (DPA) regime.

One of the criteria of the EU regime is the agreement by the data subject to the collection and use of the data (Article 7). This has consequences that are not currently clear for the collection and processing (analytics) of social media sources such as Twitter or the use of personal and location data by Google in the direction of advertisements toward the users of its services (Davis, 2012). The fundamental questions are who actually owns the personal data, who has the right to use it, and to what purpose. The current EU DPA regime is clear that it lies with the data subject; however, in practice many organizations take the ethically suspect position that they can use it to provided added value to their customers and users.

REFERENCES

Agrawal, R., Imieliński, T., Swami, A., 1993. Mining association rules between sets of items in large databases. In: Proceedings of the 1993 ACM SIGMOD International Conference on Management of Data – SIGMOD '93, p. 207.

Amazon, 2013. Amazon Relational Database Service (Amazon RDS). http://aws.amazon.com/rds/ (retrieved 11.09.13.).

Ash, T., 2008. Landing Page Optimization. Wiley Publishing.

Burnes, B., 2009. Managing Change, fifth ed. Financial Times/Prentice Hall.

Buytendijk, F., 2010. Dealing with Dilemmas: Where Business Analytics Fall Short. John Wiley & Sons.

Cannataro, M., Pugliese, A., 2004. Distributed data mining on grids: services, tools, and applications. IEEE Transactions on Systems, Man, and Czybernetics 34 (6).

Carr, N., 2004. Does It Matter? Information Technology and the Corrosion of Competitive Advantage. Harvard Business School Press, Boston.

Cassandra, 2013. Welcome to ApacheTM Cassandra®. http://cassandra.apache.org/ (accessed 11.09.13.).

Chaiken, R., Jenkins, B., Larson, P.-Å., Ramsey, B., Shakib, D., Weaver, S., Zhou, J., 2008. SCOPE: easy and efficient parallel processing of massive data sets. Proceedings of the VLDB Endowment 1 (2), 1265–1276.

Ciborra, C., 2000. From Control to Drift: The Dynamics of Corporate Information Infrastructures. OUP.

Cluster Seven, 2011. Cluster Seven Spider Map. http://www.clusterseven.com/spreadsheet-links-map/ (accessed 09.09.13.).

Date, C.J., 2003. An Introduction to Database Systems, eighth ed. Addison Wesley.

Davis, K., 2012. Ethics of Big Data: Balancing Risk and Innovation. O'Reilly Media.

Deloitte, 2010. Spreadsheet Management: Not what You Figured. Deloitte LLP. http://www.deloitte.com/assets/Dcom-UnitedStates/Local%20Assets/Documents/AERS/us_aers_Spreadsheet_eBrochure_070710.pdf (accessed 10.09.13.).

DeWitt, D., Gray, J., 1992. Parallel database systems: the future of high performance database systems. Communications of the ACM 35 (6), 85–98.

Ectors, M., 2013. MapD – Massively Parallel GPU-Based Database. http://telruptive.com/2013/05/13/mapd-massively-parallel-gpu-based-database/ (retrieved 22.08.13.).

ESI Int, 2013. Ticking Time Bomb for Project Management. Raconteur (8.07.13.) http://theraconteur.co.uk/why-professional-project-managers-are-worth-their-weight-in-gold/ (accessed 10.07.13.).

EU, January 25, 2012. Proposal for the EU General Data Protection Regulation. European Commission. http://ec.europa.eu/justice/data-protection/document/review2012/com_2012_11_en.pdf (accessed 09.09.13.).

Fayyad, U., Piatetsky-Shapiro, G., Smyth, P., 1996a. From data mining to knowledge discovery in databases. AI Magazine 17 (3), 37–54.

Fayyad, U., Piatetsky-Shapiro, G., Smyth, P., Uthurusamy, R., 1996b. Advances in Knowledge Discovery and Data Mining. AAAI Press.

Feldman, R., Sanger, J., 2007. The Text Mining Handbook. Cambridge University Press.

Flyvberg, B., 2006. From Nobel Prize to project management: getting risks right. Project Management Journal 37, 5–15.

Foster, I., Kesselman, C. (Eds.), 2004. The Grid 2. Elsevier Inc.

Gartner, 2011. Gartner Says Solving "Big Data" Challenge Involves More than Just Managing Volumes of Data. http://www.gartner.com/newsroom/id/1731916 (accessed 20.08.13.).

Gartner, 2012. Hype Cycle for Big Data. Gartner Research. http://www.gartner.com/DisplayDocument?doc_cd=235042 (accessed 16.07.13.).

Greenwald, G., MacAskill, E., Poitras, L., June 10, 2013. Edward Snowden: The Whistleblower behind the NSA Surveillance Revelations. The Guardian.

Hadoop, 2013. Welcome to Apache™ Hadoop®. http://hadoop.apache.org (accessed 11.09.13.).

Howe, J., 2006. The Rise of Crowdsourcing. Iss 14.06. Wired.

Intel IT Center, 2013. Turning Big Data into Big Insights. White Paper. http://www.intel.co.uk/content/dam/www/public/us/en/documents/white-papers/big-data-visualization-turning-big-data-into-big-insights.pdf (retrieved 11.09.13.).

Jurafsky, D., Martin, J., 2009. Speech and Language Processing. Prentice Hall.

Kahneman, D., 2011. Thinking, Fast and Slow. Allen Lane.

Laney, D., 2001. 3D Data Management: Controlling Data Volume, Velocity, and Variety. Meta Group (Now Gartner). http://blogs.gartner.com/doug-laney/files/2012/01/ad949-3D-Data-Management-Controlling-Data-Volume-Velocity-and-Variety.pdf (accessed 02.08.13.).

Levy, E., Silberschatz, A., 2009. Distributed file systems: concepts and examples. ACM Computing Surveys 22 (4), 321–374.

Lipika, D., Haque, S.K.M., 2008. Opinion mining from noisy text data. In: Proceedings of the Second Workshop on Analytics for Noisy Unstructured Text Data, pp. 83–90.

Miller, B., Beard, M., Bliss, N., 2011. Eigenspace Analysis for Threat Detection in Social Networks, 14th International Conference on Information Fusion. Chicago, Illinois, USA.

Minelli, M., Chambers, M., Dhiraj, A., 2013. Big Data, Big Analytics: Emerging Business Intelligence and Analytic Trends for Today's Businesses. John Wiley & Sons.

Ozolins, M., 2012. Run More Tests, Run the Right Tests. http://www.webics.com.au/blog/google-adwords/split-testing-guide-for-online-retailers/ (accessed 02.09.13.).

Panko, R.R., Port, D.N., January 2012. End user computing: dark matter (and dark energy) of corporate IT. In: Proceedings of the 45th Hawaii International Conference on System Sciences Maui, Hawaii.

Panko, R.R., 2008. What we know about spreadsheet errors. Journal of End User Computing 10 (2), 15–21. Spring 1998 (revised May 2008). http://panko.shidler.hawaii.edu/My%20Publications/Whatknow.htm (accessed 28.04.12.).

Shankland, S., 2008. Google Spotlights Data Center Inner Workings. http://news.cnet.com/8301-10784_3-9955184-7.html (accessed 08.09.13.).

Soares, S., 2012. Big Data Governance: An Emerging Imperative. MC PRESS.

Standish Group, 1994. The Chaos Report. The Standish Group International Inc.

Standish Group, 1999. Chaos: A Recipe for Success. The Standish Group International Inc.

Stonebraker, M., 1986. The case for shared nothing. Database Engineering 9, 4–9.

SWIFT, 2008. SWIFT: SIBOS Issues. SWIFT. September 16, 2008. p. 12. http://www.swift.com/sibos2008/sibos_2008_learn_discuss_debate/sibos_issues/Sibos_Issues_20080916.pdf (accessed 09.09.13.).

Twitter, 2013. https://twitter.com (accessed 11.09.13.).

US Dept of Commerce, 2013. Safe Harbor. http://export.gov/safeharbor/index.asp (accessed 09.09.13.).

Webster, 2011. Storage Area Networks Need Not Apply. CNET. http://news.cnet.com/8301-21546_3-20049693-10253464.html (accessed 20.08.13.).

MINING SOCIAL MEDIA: ARCHITECTURE, TOOLS, AND APPROACHES TO DETECTING CRIMINAL ACTIVITY

11

Marcello Trovati

INTRODUCTION

In his famous article, "Computing Machinery and Intelligence," Turing (1950) begins by introducing the question, "Can machines think?"

Since the dawn of artificial intelligence research, the possibility of creating machines able to interact and ultimately contribute to our society has been at its core. Despite the enormous progress made in several aspects within this ambitious goal, language acquisition and its understanding has proved to be probably the most complex task of all. The act of making sense of the complicated and often ambiguous information captured by language comes naturally to us humans, but its intrinsic and inexplicable complexity is extremely hard to assess and manage digitally.

The development of the Internet has created a wide variety of new opportunities as well as challenges for our societies. Since their introduction, social media have increasingly become an extension of the way human beings interact with each other, providing a multitude of platforms on which individuals can communicate, exchange information, and create business revenue without geographical and temporal constraints. As a consequence, this new technology is very much part of the fabric of our societies, shaping our needs and ambitions as well as our personality (McKenna, 2004). In particular, social media have redefined and shifted our ways of manipulating and generating information, collaborating, and deciding what personal details to share and how.

It is not difficult to imagine that social media are extremely complex systems based on interwoven connections that are continuously changing and evolving. To harness their power, there has been much research to scientifically describe their properties in a rigorous yet efficient manner. Owing to their multidisciplinary nature, researchers from a variety of fields have united their efforts to produce mathematical models to capture, predict, and analyze how information spreads and its perception and management as it travels across social media. When we think of Facebook, LinkedIn, or Twitter, we tend to picture a huge tapestry of relations linking individuals, companies, entities, and countries, to name but a few. A specific representation of such systems is social networks, a concept with which most of us are familiar, and which many people associate with social media. The formal definition of social networks is intuitive. They consist of nodes (such as individuals) and edges, representing the mutual relationships (for an example, see Figure 11.1).

Although it appears to be an overly simple definition, it has a powerful modeling ability to describe the behavior of social networks. They are, in fact, not about individuality. They are about mass

155

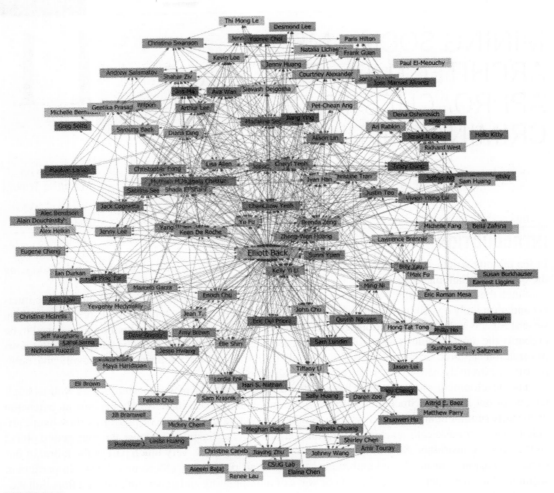

FIGURE 11.1

One of many examples of a social network freely available online.

http://www.digitaltrainingacademy.com/socialmedia/2009/06/social_networking_map.php.

information interpretation and perception. They are about collective intelligence, the cognitive process created by collective interactive systems (Schoder et al., 2013); in other words:

> It is a form of universally distributed intelligence, constantly enhanced, coordinated in real time, and resulting in the effective mobilization of skills.
>
> **Lévy, 1994, p. 13**

Furthermore, how social networks change and adapt to new information is what shapes the way we interact, behave, and use social networks.

MINING OF SOCIAL NETWORKS FOR CRIME

The introduction of social media and social networks in particular has changed not only the opportunities available to us, but also the type of threats of which we need to be aware. The wealth of information available within any social networking scenario is valuable to criminals, who use individuals' personal details and information to their advantage. There has been a worrying upward trend of alleged crimes linked to the use of social networks, which poses a new challenge to identify and prioritize social networking crimes linked to genuine harm without restricting freedom of speech. For example, police forces around the United Kingdom (UK) have seen a 780% increase in 4 years of potential criminal activity linked to Facebook and Twitter (The Guardian, 2012).

A dramatic surge in terrorist attacks has caused drastic and long-lasting effects on many aspects of our society. Furthermore, there has been exponential growth in the number of large-scale cybercrimes, which cause considerable financial loss to organizations and businesses. Cybercriminals tend to collaborate, exchange data and information, and create new tools via the dark markets available on online social media (Lau et al., 2014). On the other hand, it offers the possibility of obtaining relevant information about these criminal networks to create new methods and tools to obtain intelligence on cybercrime activities.

Experts from a variety of fields have increasingly contributed to improving the techniques and methods for enhancing the ability to fight criminal activity. In particular, data mining techniques can be applied to assessing information sharing and collaboration as well as their classification and clustering both in spatial and temporal terms (Chen, 2008).

One of the most dangerous and insidious aspects of cybercrime is related to the concept of social engineering. It refers to the ability of obtaining information from systems and data by exploiting human psychology rather than by using a direct approach. A social engineer would find, assess, and combine information to obtain the crucial insight that would lead to getting inside the system. For example, rather than finding software vulnerabilities, a social engineer would obtain sensitive information by deceit, such as obtaining the trust of one or more individuals who might have valuable information. As a consequence, there is an increasing emphasis on specific penetration test techniques, which analyze information available on social network sites to assess several types of related criminal activity.

In work by Jakobsson (2005), an investigation on spear phishing, or context aware phishing, is discussed, detailing a network-based model in which the ability to linking e-mail addresses to potential victims is shown to increase the phishing outcome, urging more sophisticated and effective tools (Dhamija and Tygar, 2005; Dhamija et al., 2006). In April 2011, a variety of companies including Citibank, Disney, JPMorgan Chase, The Home Shopping Network, and Hilton were affected by a security breach into the Internet company Epsilon, which exposed e-mail details of millions of users (Schwartz, 2011). This was one example of collaborative phishing, in which multiple data sources are analyzed to identify specific patterns that will be used to infer statistical information via sophisticated algorithms (Shashidhar and Chen, 2011). As a consequence, criminal network analysis based on social network techniques has been shown to provide effective tools for the investigation, prediction, and management of crime. In fact, the amount of information flowing and propagating across social networks is astonishing. Such information contains a wealth of data encapsulating human activity, individual and general emotions and opinions, as well as intentions to plan or pursue specific activities.

Therefore, social network mining provides an important tool for discovering, analyzing, and visualizing networked criminal activity. Because of the complexity of the task, the numerous research efforts that have been carried out and implemented have achieved only partial success. Therefore, the collective goal is to improve state-of-the-art technology to produce a comprehensive approach to extracting relevant and accurate information to provide criminal network analysis intelligence.

Most information embedded in social networks is in the form of unstructured textual data such as e-mails, chat messages and text documents. The manual extraction of relevant information from textual sources, which can be subsequently turned into a suitable structured database for further analysis, is certainly inefficient and error prone especially when big, if not huge, textual datasets need to be addressed. Therefore, the automation of this process would enable a more efficient approach to social network (and media) mining for criminal activity as well as hypothesis generation to identify potential relationships among the members of specified networks.

TEXT MINING

Text mining, often referred to as natural language processing (NLP), consists of a range of computational techniques to analyze human language using linguistic analysis for a range of tasks or applications. In particular, such techniques have been shown to have a crucial role in how we can represent knowledge described by the interactions between computers and human (natural) languages. The main goal of NLP is to extend its methods to incorporate any language, mode, or genre used by humans to interact with one another, to achieve a better understanding of the information captured by human communication (Liddy, 2001).

Language is based on grammatical and syntactic rules that fall into patterns or templates that sentences with similar structure follow. Such language formats allow us to construct complex sentences as well as frame the complexity of language. For example, the ability to determine the subject and the object of a particular action described by a sentence has heavily contributed to human evolution and the flourishing of all civilizations (see also Chapter 13).

NATURAL LANGUAGE METHODS

NLP methods have been developed to embrace a variety of techniques that can be grouped into four categories: symbolic, statistical, connectionist, and hybrid. In this section we will briefly discuss these approaches in terms of their main features and suitability with respect to the tasks requiring implementation.

SYMBOLIC APPROACH

In this method, linguistic phenomena are investigated that consist of explicit representations of facts about language via precise and well-understood knowledge representations (Laporte, 2005). Symbolic systems evolve from human-developed rules and lexicons, which generate the relevant information on which this approach is based. Once the rules have been defined and identified, a document is analyzed to pinpoint the exact conditions, which validates them. All such rules associated with semantic objects generate networks describing their hierarchical structure. In fact, highly associated concepts exhibit directly linked properties, whereas moderately or weakly related concepts are linked through other semantic objects. Symbolic methods have been widely exploited in a variety of research contexts such as information extraction, text categorization, ambiguity resolution, explanation-based learning, decision trees, and conceptual clustering.

STATISTICAL APPROACH

This approach is based on observable data and large documents to develop generalized models based on smaller knowledge datasets and significant linguistic or world knowledge (Manning and Schütze, 1999). The set of states is associated with probabilities. Several techniques can be used to investigate their structures, such as the hidden Markov model, in which the set of status is regarded as not directly observable. The techniques have many applications such as parsing rule analysis, statistical grammar learning, and statistical machine translation, to name but a few.

CONNECTIONIST APPROACH

This approach combines statistical learning with representation techniques to allow an integration of statistical tools with logic-based rule manipulation, generating a network of interconnected simple processing units (often associated with concepts) with edge weights representing knowledge. This typically creates a rich system with an interesting dynamical global behavior induced by the semantic propagation rules. In Troussov et al. (2010), a connectionist distributed model is investigated pointing toward a dynamical generalization of syntactic parsing, limited domain translation tasks, and associative retrieval.

GENERAL ARCHITECTURE AND VARIOUS COMPONENTS OF TEXT MINING

In linguistics, a (formal) grammar is a set of determined rules that govern how words and sentences are combined according to a specific syntax. A grammar does not describe the meaning of a set of words or sentences; it only addresses the construction of sentences according to the syntactic structure of words. Semantics, on the other hand, refers to the meaning of a sentence (Manning and Schütze, 1999). In computational linguistics, semantic analysis is a much more complex task because it is based on the unique identification of the meaning of sentences.

Any text mining process consists of a number of steps to identify and classify sentences according to specific patterns, to analyze a textual source (see Figure 11.2). Broadly speaking, to achieve this, we need to follow these general steps:

1. Fragments of text are divided into manageable components, usually words, that can be subsequently syntactically analyzed.
2. The above components, forming a tokenized text fragment, are then analyzed according to the rules of a formal grammar. The output is a parsing tree—in other words, an ordered tree representing the hierarchical syntactic structure of a sentence.
3. Once we have isolated the syntactic structure of a text fragment, we are in the position of extracting relevant information, such as specific relationships and sentiment analysis.

More specifically, the main components of text mining are as follows:

LEXICAL ANALYSIS

The most basic level in an NLP system is based on lexical analysis, which deals with words regarded as the atomic structure of text documents; in particular, it is the process that takes place when the basic components of a text are analyzed and grouped into tokens, which are sequences of characters with a

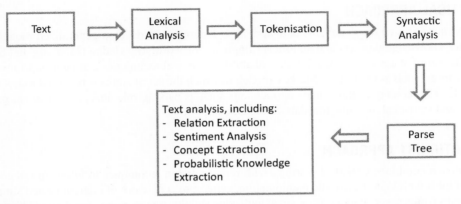

FIGURE 11.2

Steps to identify and classify sentences.

collective meaning (Dale et al., 2000). In other words, lexical analysis techniques identify the meaning of individual words, which are assigned to a single part-of-speech (POS) tag. Lexical analysis may require a lexicon, which is usually determined by the particular approach used in a suitably defined NLP system as well as the nature and extent of information inherent in the lexicon. Mainly, lexicons may vary in terms of their complexity because they can contain information about the semantic information related to a word. Moreover accurate and comprehensive sub-categorization lexicons are extremely important for the development of parsing technology as well as for any NLP application that relies on the structure of information related to predicate-argument structure. More research is currently being carried out to provide better tools for analyzing words in semantic contexts (see Korhonen et al., 2006 for an overview).

POS TAGGING

POS tagging is one of the first steps in text analysis because it allows us to attach a specific syntactic definition (noun, verb, adjective, etc.) to the words that are part of a sentence. This task tends to be accurate because it relies on a set of rules that are usually unambiguously defined. Consider the word "book." Depending on the sentence to which it belongs, it might be a verb or a noun. Consider "a book on a chair" and "I will book a table at the restaurant." The presence of specific keywords such as "a" in the former and "I will" in the latter provides important clues as to the syntactic role that "book" has in the two sentences. One of the main reasons for the overall accuracy of POS tagging is that a semantic analysis is often not required. It is based only on the position of the word and its neighboring words.

PARSING

Once the POS tagging of a sentence has identified the syntactic roles of each word, we can consider such a sentence in its entirety. The main difference with POS tagging is that parsing enables the identification of the hierarchical syntactic structure of a sentence. Consider, for example, the parsing tree

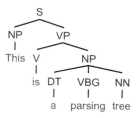

FIGURE 11.3

Parsing tree of the sentence "This is a parsing tree."

structure of the sentence "This is a parsing tree," depicted in Figure 11.3. Each word is associated with a POS symbol that corresponds to its syntactic role (Manning and Schütze, 1999).

NAMED ENTITY RECOGNITION

An important aspect of text analysis is the ability to determine the type of the entities within a text fragment. More specifically, determining whether a noun refers to a person, an organization, or a geographical location (to name but a few) substantially contributes to the extraction of accurate information and provides the tools for a deeper understanding. For example, the analysis of "Dogs and cats are the most popular pets in the UK" would identify that dogs and cats are animals and the UK is a country. Clearly, there are many instances where this depends on the context. Think of "India lives in Manchester." Anyone reading such a sentence would interpret India as the name of a specific person, and rightly so. However, a computer might not be able to do so and may decide that it is a country. We know that a country would not be able to "live" in a city. It is just common sense. Unfortunately, computers do not have the ability to discern what common sense is. They might be able to guess according to the structure of a sentence or the presence of specific keywords. Nevertheless, it is precisely that—a guess. This is an effective example of semantic understanding, which comes naturally to humans but is a complex, if impossible, task for computers.

CO-REFERENCE RESOLUTION

Co-reference resolution is the task of determining, which words refer to the same objects. An example is anaphora resolution, which is specifically concerned with the nouns or names to which words refer. Another instance of co-reference resolution is relation resolution, which attempts to identify to which individual entities or objects a relation refers. Consider the following sentence: "We are looking for a corrupted member of the panel." Here, we are not looking for just any corrupted member of the panel, but for a specific individual.

RELATION EXTRACTION

The identification of relations among different entities within a text provides useful information that can be used to disambiguate subcomponents of the text fragment as well as determine quantitative and qualitative information linking such entities. For example, consider the sentence "Smoking potentially causes lung cancer." Here, the act of smoking is linked to lung cancer by a causal relationship.

CONCEPT EXTRACTION

A crucial task in information extraction from textual sources is concept identification, which is typically defined as one or more keywords or textual definitions. The two main approaches in this task are supervised and unsupervised concept identification, depending on the level of human intervention in the system.

In particular, formal concept analysis (FCA) provides a set of robust data and text mining tools to facilitate the identification of key concepts relevant to a specific topical area (Stumme, 2002). Broadly speaking, unstructured textual datasets are analyzed to isolate clusters of terms and definitions referring to the same concepts, which can be grouped together. One of the main features of FCA is that it is human-centered, so that user(s) can actively interact with the system to determine the most appropriate parameters and starting points of such classifications.

In work by Poelmans et al. (2010), a case study describing the extraction of domestic violence intelligence from a dataset of unstructured Dutch police reports is analyzed by applying FCA. The aim is to determine the concepts defined by terms, which are clustered together. Figure 11.4 depicts the main architecture of this approach. As this figure demonstrates, FCA provides a useful and powerful platform to visualize and capture the main factors in crime detection.

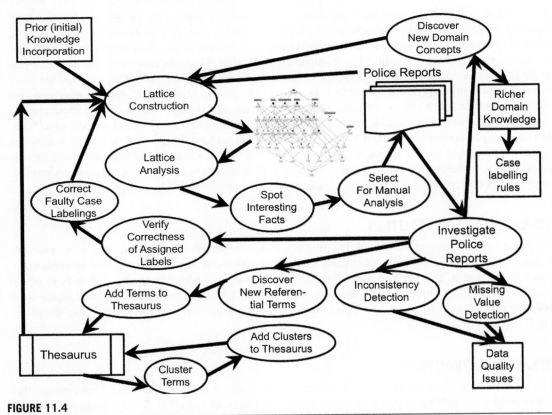

FIGURE 11.4

Example of a detailed human-centered knowledge discovery process for crime detection using formal concept analysis (FCA) (as described in Chen, 2008).

TOPIC RECOGNITION

This procedure attempts to identify the general topic of a text by grouping a set of keywords that appear frequently in the documents. These are then associated with one or more concepts to determine the general concept trend.

SENTIMENT ANALYSIS

This is a particular example of information extraction from text, which focuses on identifying trends of opinions across a population in social media. Broadly speaking, its aim is to determine the polarity of a given text, which identifies whether the opinion expressed is positive, negative, or neutral. This includes emotional states such as anger, sadness, and happiness, as well as intent: for example, planning and researching. Sentiment analysis can be an important tool in obtaining insight into criminal activity because it can detect a general state of mind shared by a group of individuals via their blog entries and social network discussions. A variety of tools are used in crime detection as well as prosecution that can automate law enforcement across several social media, including Web sites, e-mails, personal blogs, and video uploaded onto social platforms (Dale et al., 2000).

SEMANTIC ANALYSIS

Semantic analysis determines the possible meanings of a sentence by investigating interactions among word-level meanings in the sentence. This approach can also incorporate the semantic disambiguation of words with multiple senses. Semantic disambiguation allows selection of the sense of ambiguous words, so that they can be included in the appropriate semantic representation of the sentence (Wilks and Stevenson, 1998). This is particularly relevant in any information retrieval and processing system based on ambiguous and partially known knowledge. Disambiguation techniques usually require specific information about the frequency with which each sense occurs in a particular document, as well as an analysis of the local context and the use of pragmatic knowledge of the domain of the document. An interesting aspect of this research field is concerned with the purposeful use of language in which the use of a context within the text is exploited to explain how extra meaning is part of some documents without actually being constructed in them. Clearly this is still being developed, because it requires an incredibly wide knowledge dealing with intentions, plans, and objectives (Manning and Schütze, 1999). Extremely useful applications in NLP can be seen in inferencing techniques, in which extra information derived from a wider context successfully addresses statistical properties (Kuipers, 1984).

MACHINE TRANSLATION

The automatic translation of a text from one language into another one provides users with the ability to read texts quickly and fairly accurately in a variety of languages. This is a complex task involving several challenges, from mapping different syntactic structures to semantic interpretation and disambiguation.

BAYESIAN NETWORKS

Bayesian networks (BNs) are graphical models that capture independence relationships among random variables, based on a basic law of probability called Bayes' rule (Pearl, 1998). They are a popular modeling framework in risk and decision analysis and have been used in a variety of applications such as safety assessment of nuclear power plants, risk evaluation of a supply chain, and medical decision support tools (Nielsen and Verner Jensen, 2009). More specifically, BNs are composed of a graph whose nodes represent objects based on a level of uncertainty, also called random variables, and whose edges indicate interdependence among them. In addition to this graphical representation, BNs contain quantitative information that represents a factorization of the joint probability distribution of all variables in the network. In fact, each node has an associated conditional probability table that captures the probability distribution associated with the node conditional for each possibility.

Suppose, for example, we want to explore the chance of finding wet grass on any given day. In particular, assume the following:

1. A cloudy sky is associated with a higher chance of rain.
2. A cloudy sky affects whether the sprinkler system is triggered.
3. Both the sprinkler system and rain have an effect on the chance of finding wet grass.

In this particular example, no probabilistic information is given. The resulting BN is depicted in Figure 11.5.

Such graphical representations provide an intuitive way to depict the dependence relations among variables.

In BN modeling, the strong statements are not about dependencies, but rather about independences (i.e., absence of edges at the graph level), because it is always possible to capture them through the conditional probability tables when an edge is present, even though the reverse is not true.

The construction of a BN can be done either through data or, when unavailable, through literature review or expert elicitation. Whereas the first approach can be automated, the other two require a significant amount of manual work, which can make them impractical on a large scale. There is extensive research on BNs, and in particular their extraction from text corpora is increasingly gaining attention. For example, Sanchez-Graillet and Poesio (2004) suggested a domain-independent method for acquiring text causal knowledge to generate BNs. Their approach is based on a classification of lexico-syntactic patterns, which refer to causation, in which automatic detection of causal patterns and semi-validation of their ambiguity is carried out. Similarly, in work by Kuipers (1984), a supervised method for the detection and extraction of causal relations from open domain texts is presented. The authors provide an in-depth analysis of verbs and cue phrases that encode causality and, to a lesser extent, influence.

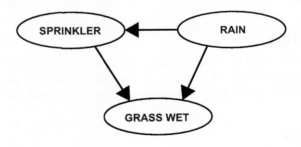

FIGURE 11.5

Bayesian network resulting from the given example.

AUTOMATIC EXTRACTION OF BNs FROM TEXT

Because of the mathematical constraints posed by Bayes' rule and general probability theory, identification of suitable BNs is often carried out by human intervention in the form of a modeler who identifies the relevant information. However, this can be time-consuming and may use only specific, often limited, sources depending on the modeler's expertise. On the other hand, it is enormously valuable to be able to extract the relevant data automatically, in terms of increased efficiency and scalability to the process of defining and populating BNs. However, extracting both explicit and implicit information and making sense of partial or contradictory data can be demanding challenges. More specifically, elements of the quantitative layer depend on the graphical layer; in other words, the structure of the conditional probability tables depends on the parents of each node. Therefore, it is necessary to determine the structure of the BN before populating it with quantitative information. Figure 11.6 depicts the most important components of the general architecture in the automatic extraction of BNs from text.

DEPENDENCE RELATION EXTRACTION FROM TEXT

Nodes in BNs, which are connected by edges, imply that the corresponding random variables are dependent. Such dependence relations must therefore be extracted from textual information when they are present. The conditional dependencies in a BN are often based on known statistical and computational techniques. One of their strengths is the combination of methods from graph theory, probability theory, computer science, and statistics. Linguistically speaking, a dependence relation contains specific keywords that indicate that two concepts are related to a certain degree. Consider the sentence "Lung cancer is more common among smokers." There is little doubt that we would interpret this as a clear relation linking lung cancer with smoking. However, there is not a precise linguistic definition to determine a relationship between two concepts from the text. The reason is that it depends on the context.

When full automation of the process of textual information extraction is carried out, a clear and unambiguous set of rules ensures a reasonably good level of accuracy. As a consequence, it is usually advisable to consider causal relationships. Causal inference is one stage of a crucial reasoning process (Pearl, 1998) that has a fundamental role in any question-answering technique with interesting artifical intelligence applications such as decision making in BNs. Despite this, they convey a much stronger statement, because causal

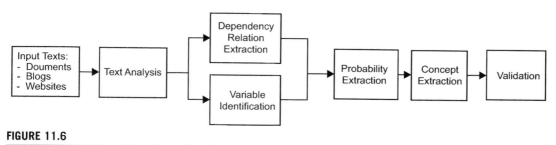

FIGURE 11.6

Architecture of Bayesian network extraction from textual information.

relations are often regarded as a subgroup of dependence relations; they are more easily spotted owing to a more limited set of linguistic rules that characterize them. Going back to the above example, saying that smoking causes lung cancer assumes a direct link between them. We cannot arguably say the contrary, but there are other cases in which there is a less marked cutoff. If we are looking only for causal relationships when populating a BN, we might miss several dependence relations. However, accuracy is much more preferable. In fact, integrating an automatic BN extraction with human intervention usually addresses this issue. Therefore, the identification of causal relationships between concepts is an essential stage of the extraction of BNs from text.

Causal learning often focuses on long-run predictions through estimating the parameters of causal BN structural learning. An interesting approach is described in Danks et al. (2002), in which people's short-term behavior is modeled through a dynamic version of the current approaches. Moreover, the limitation of a merely static investigation is addressed by a dynamical approach based on BN methods. Their result applies only to a particular scenario, but it offers a new perspective and shows huge research potential in this area.

VARIABLES IDENTIFICATION

Mapping a representative to a specific variable is closely linked to the task of relations extraction. However, this is partially a modeling choice by the user based on the set of concepts in which she or he is interested. Consider again the sentence "Smoking causes lung cancer." If this were rephrased as "Smokers are more likely to develop lung cancer," we would need to ensure that "smoking" and "smokers" are identified as a single variable associated with the act of smoking. In a variety of cases, this can be addressed by considering synonymy. However, as in our example, it might also happen that they refer to the same concept, rather than being the same concept. FCA is a computational technique that can be successfully applied in this particular context.

BN STRUCTURE DEFINITION

This step aggregates the information gathered in the previous two steps to output the structure of the BN. This includes evaluating the credibility of each dependence relation, determining whether the dependence stated is direct or indirect, and ensuring that no cycles are created in the process of orienting the edges.

PROBABILITY INFORMATION EXTRACTION

This step involves processing the textual sources to extract information about the probability of variables. This includes the search for both numerical information and quantitative statements such as "Smoking increases the chances of lung cancer" and "Nonsmokers are less likely to get lung cancer."

AGGREGATION OF STRUCTURAL AND PROBABILISTIC DATA

This step obtains a fully defined BN network automatically, typically with the help of the user. This also includes state identification and combining conflicting and partial information in a rigorous way.

BNs AND CRIME DETECTION

As discussed above, BN modeling is an efficient and powerful tool for defining and investigating systems consisting of phenomena with a level of uncertainty. Because BNs combine expert knowledge with observational and empirical data, they provide a platform that can facilitate decision making. As a consequence, BNs have been successfully applied to crime detection, prevention, and management (Ghazi et al., 2006). In particular, the extraction of BNs from textual sources associated with social networks, and social media in general, can improve the overall modeling power of BNs by enabling the acquisition of large amounts of information and its management with limited human intervention.

An example of BN modeling applied to crime activity detection includes fraudulent transaction identification. In fact, BNs have the distinct advantage of adapting in real time, which enables probabilistic data to be updated while fraud analysts determine whether specific transactions are either fraudulent or legitimate. Furthermore, the process of assessing the quantitative information from each transaction is facilitated by the relative approachability of Bayesian probability evaluation.

Psychological and social profiling of criminal suspects can also benefit from the use of BNs (Stahlschmidt and Tausendteufel, 2013). More specifically, known characteristics of an offender can identify the number of potential suspects by removing individuals who are not likely to have those features, with obvious advantages in terms of time and cost efficiency. Using specific BN modeling can be applied to understanding the structure of an unknown domain as well as for profile prediction. Profilers could, for example, obtain a prediction of the offender's age and thereby reduce the number of suspects substantially by adding evidence found in the crime scene to an appropriate BN. As part of their investigation, they ascertain that offenders are likely to meet their victims in unfamiliar surroundings, preferring to travel a long distance to avoid obvious exposure of their crime and showing a high level of forensic awareness. On the other hand, more impulsive offenders are likely to commit a crime closer to their familiar environment. The use of BNs in this research field has also facilitated the creation of a probabilistic model to visualize the main factors and parameters in sex-related homicides. Figure 11.7 depicts an example which provides a user-friendly yet rigorous platform to support and facilitate the decision-making progress.

GENERAL ARCHITECTURE

The general architecture of the extraction of BNs from social media for detecting and assessing criminal activity typically consists of the following components (see also Figure 11.8):

1. Existing and predefined information about criminal activity would be incorporated into a database or knowledge database (KDB) consisting of:
   a. Historical data from structured databases
   b. BNs built on existing data
   c. Data entered by modeler(s) and manually validated
   The KDB is an important component because it is based on information that is deemed reliable. In a variety of cases, the KDB is maintained by modeling experts to ensure that the data are regularly updated to prevent inconsistency and ambiguity.
2. The user would interact with the system by specifying social media textual sources such as Web pages, blogs, and general data on the structure of social interactions.

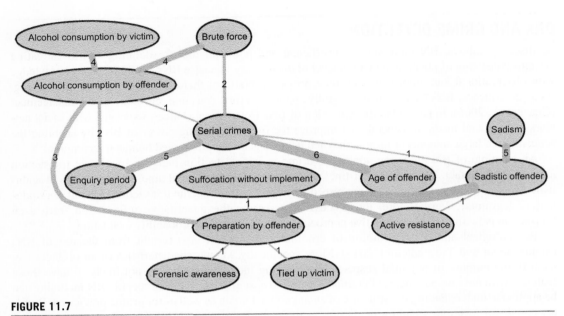

FIGURE 11.7

Main variables identifying the difference between an offender and situation-driven crime.

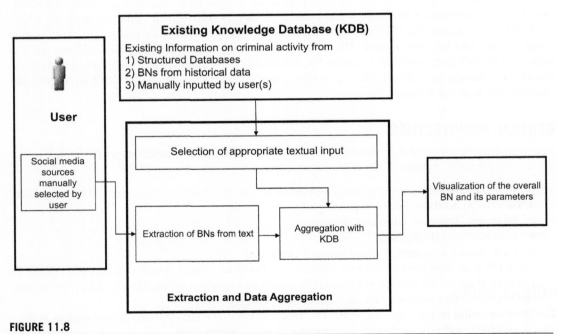

FIGURE 11.8

General architecture of Bayesian networks (BNs) for crime detection.

3. The extraction and data aggregation stage consists of identifying appropriate textual data associated with the social media sources and standardization of their format. For example, if a Web page contains multimedia data along with some text, only the latter would be considered. This would enable the extraction of a BN both as an unsupervised and semi-supervised process. This would be integrated with a combination of different information from the KDB with extraction of the sources identified by the user and the removal of any data duplication. An essential part of this process is to address data inconsistency at both a qualitative and quantitative level. As discussed above, BNs have strict mathematical constraints that make any fully unsupervised automatic extraction prone to inaccuracies and inconsistencies. As a consequence, human intervention is often advisable to minimize error.

4. Finally, the BN is visualized, providing:
   a. Relevant information on the structure of the BN
   b. Description of the different parameters
   c. Any required action to address inconsistency that could not be resolved automatically. This is typically an interactive step in which the result can be updated by the user and focused on a specific part of the BN.

EXAMPLE OF BN APPLICATION TO CRIME DETECTION: COVERT NETWORKS

Automatic extraction of relevant information to define and populate BNs has a variety of applications in crime detection and management. Furthermore, the huge potential offered by the investigation of Big Data can provide critical insight into criminal activities. However, the extraction, assessment, and management of datasets that are continuously created poses challenges that have to be addressed to provide a valuable platform.

A relevant scenario in which BNs provide a useful tool in criminal detection is described in Smith et al. (2013), who discuss criminal detection within covert communities. A well-known example is the terrorist network that carried out the 9/11 attack in the United States. In fact, it exhibited the property that members of the different cells were kept unconnected, which ensured that the structure of the network was unknown by its components (Krebs, 2002). These types of networks tend to be defined by a tree, as shown in Figure 11.9.

Despite the difficulties in the assessment and criminal detection of such networks, covert communities tend to be discoverable during any activity they may carry out, even for a short amount of time. In particular, this allows the different components and their interconnections to be fully observable, which suggests that BNs can successfully model such scenarios correlating a priori information regarding the observed network connections. All relevant information can be gathered from both structured and unstructured Big Datasets, including surveillance and reconnaissance sensors such as wide-area motion imagery, and textual information from the Web (Smith et al., 2013).

CONCLUSIONS

The ability to mine social media to extract relevant information provides a crucial tool in crime detection. A wealth of emerging techniques has been successfully applied in this field and has led to increased multidisciplinary collaboration among academics and practitioners. In particular, because a great

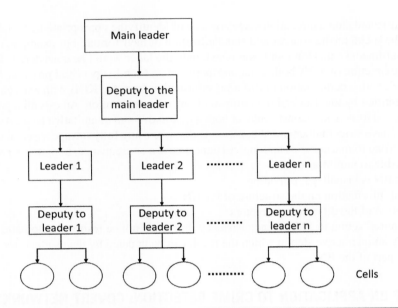

FIGURE 11.9

Example of the tree structure of a covert network.

proportion of relevant information contained in social media is in the form of unstructured data, there is a common effort to provide state-of-the-art tools and techniques to automatically collect and assess intelligence on criminal activity.

Furthermore, since the birth of Big Data, the availability of increasingly large datasets has introduced huge potential in crime detection. However, this raises several difficulties in identifying relevant and accurate information and its assessment. In fact, any information extraction from Big Data sets is highly inefficient and error prone when it is addressed manually. Therefore, the creation of specific approaches to automated mining of social media for criminal activity and the assessment of complex systems with a level of uncertainty allow the retrieval, management, and analysis of Big Datasets with small human intervention (see Chapter 3). This facilitates the decision-making process supported by both observed and inferred knowledge, which is of paramount importance when determining and isolating criminal activity.

REFERENCES

Chen, H., 2008. Homeland security data mining using social network analysis. In: Ortiz-Arroyo, D., Larsen, H.L., Zend, D.D., Hicks, D., Wagner, G. (Eds.), IEEE Intelligence and Security Informatics Lecture Notes in Computer Science, vol. 5376. Springer.

Dale, R., Moisl, H., Somers, H.L., 2000. Handbook of Natural Language Processing. Marcel Dekker, New York.

Danks, D., Griffiths, T.L., Tenenbaum, J.B., 2002. Dynamical causal learning. In: Becker, S., Thrun, S., Obermayer, K. (Eds.), Advances in Neural Information Processing Systems, vol. 15. MIT Press, Cambridge, MA., pp. 67–74.

Dhamija, R., Tygar, J.D., Hearst, M., April 22–27, 2006. Why phishing works. In: CHI 2006 Montreal, Canada.

Dhamija, R., Tygar, J.D., July 2005. The battle against phishing: dynamic security skins. In: SOUPS 2005: Proceedings of the 2005 ACM Symposium on Usable Security and Privacy, ACM International Conference Proceedings Series. ACM Press, pp. 77–88.

Ghazi, A., Laskey, K., Wang, X., Barbará, D., Shackelford, T., Wright, E., Fitzgerald, J., 2006. Detecting threatening behavior using Bayesian networks. In: Conference on Behavioral Representation in Modeling and Simulation.

The Guardian, Thursday, December 27, 2012. The Guardian. [Online]. Available from: http://www.theguardian.com/media/2012/dec/27/social-media-crime-facebook-twitter (accessed 24.06.14.).

Jakobsson, M., 2005. Modeling and preventing phishing attacks. In: Patrick, A.S., Yung, M. (Eds.), FC 2005. LNCS, vol. 3570. Springer, Heidelberg.

Korhonen, A., Krymolowski, Y., Briscoe, T., 2006. A large subcategorisation lexicon for natural language processing applications. In: Proceedings of the 5th International Conference on Language Resources and Evaluation.

Krebs, V.E., 2002. Uncloaking terrorist networks. First Monday 7 (4).

Kuipers, B.J., 1984. Causal reasoning in medicine: analysis of a protocol. Cognitive Science 8, 363–385.

Laporte, E., 2005. Symbolic natural language processing. In: Lothaire (Ed.), Applied Combinatorics on Words. Cambridge University Press, pp. 164–209.

Lau, R.Y., Yunqing, X., Yunming, Y., 2014. A probabilistic generative model for mining cybercriminal networks from online social Media. Computational Intelligence Magazine 9 (1), 31–43.

Lévy, P., 1994. Collective Intelligence: Mankind's Emerging World in Cyberspace. Basic Books.

Liddy, E.D., 2001. A robust risk minimization based named entity recognition system. In: Encyclopedia of Library and Information Science. Marcel Decker, Inc.

Manning, C.D., Schütze, H., 1999. Foundations of Statistical Natural Language Processing. MIT Press.

McKenna, J.A., 2004. The internet and social life. Annual Review of Psychology 55, 573–590.

Nielsen, T.D., Verner Jensen, F., 2009. Bayesian Networks and Decision Graphs. Springer Science & Business Media.

Pearl, J., 1998. Probabilistic Reasoning in Intelligent Systems: Networks of Plausible Inference. Morgan Kaufmann Publishers Inc., San Francisco.

Poelmans, J., Elzinga, P., Viaene, S., Dedene, G., 2010. Formal concept analysis in knowledge discovery: a survey. In: Croituru, M., Ferré, S., Lukose, D. (Eds.), ICCS 2010, LNAI 6208. Springer-Verlag Berlin Heidelberg, pp. 139–153.

Sanchez-Graillet, O., Poesio, M., 2004. Acquiring Bayesian Networks from Text. LREC 2004, Lisbon, Portugal.

Schoder, D., Gloor, P., Metaxas, P., 2013. Social media and collective intelligence – ongoing and future research streams. KI – Künstliche Intelligenz 27 (1), 9–15.

Schwartz, M.J., Friday, November 4, 2011. Epsilon Fell to Spear-Phishing Attack. Information Week. [Online]. Available from: http://www.darkreading.com/attacks-and-breaches/epsilon-fell-to-spear-phishing-attack/d/d-id/1097119? (accessed 17.06.14.).

Shashidhar, J., Chen, N., 2011. A phishing model and its applications to evaluating phishing attacks. In: Proceedings of the 2nd International Cyber Resilience Conference, Perth, Australia, August 1–2, 2011.

Smith, S.T., Senne, K.D., Philips, S., Kao, E.K., Bernstein, G., 2013. Covert network detection. Lincoln Laboratory Journal 20 (1).

Stahlschmidt, S., Tausendteufel, H., 2013. Bayesian networks for sex-related homicides: structure learning and prediction. Journal of Applied Statistics 40 (6), 1155–1171.

Stumme, G., 2002. Efficient Data Mining Based on Formal Concept Analysis. Lecture Notes in Computer Science, vol. 2453, Springer Berlin Heidelberg.

Troussov, A., Levner, E., Bogdan, C., Judge, J., Botvich, D., 2010. Spreading activation methods. In: Dynamic and Advanced Data Mining for Progressing Technological Development: Innovations and Systemic Approaches, pp. 136–167.

Turing, A.M., 1950. Computing machinery and intelligence. Mind 49, 433–460.

Wilks, Y., Stevenson, M., 1998. The grammar of sense: using part-of-speech tags as a first step in semantic disambiguation. Natural Language Engineering 4, 135–143.

MAKING SENSE OF UNSTRUCTURED NATURAL LANGUAGE INFORMATION

12

Kellyn Rein

INTRODUCTION

> Information is of great value when a deduction of some sort can be drawn from it. This may occur as a result of its association with some other information already received.
>
> **AJP 2.0 Allied Joint Intelligence, Counter Intelligence and Security Doctrine (NATO, 2003)**

The Holy Grail of Big Data is making sense of the overwhelming mountains of information available. This information is generated by a variety of devices such as video cameras, motion sensors, acoustic sensors, satellites, and global positioning systems (GPS), as well as by humans in written and spoken form. Automatic processing of data derived from devices uses powerful mathematical algorithms that manipulate the data and are often capable of running in parallel on multitudes of servers to produce more timely results.

Unstructured information—that is, information that is not stored in a structured format such as a database or an ontology, but is formulated in natural language such as social media, blogs, government documents, research papers, intelligence reports, and so on—poses some hurdles that do not exist for device-derived data: A thermometer delivers a value that we know represents a temperature, an acoustic sensor delivers data that we know represent sound waves, and the output of a GPS system is the location where we currently find ourselves. Although some interpretation (usually in the form of an algorithm) is needed to make sense of the data received from devices, we do not try to interpret a GPS reading as a temperature.

In contrast, a human being delivers data in the form of natural language formulations, which can represent a wide range of information (including temperatures, sounds, and locations). Furthermore, each human chooses any of a number of human languages in which to describe those temperatures, sounds, or locations. Thus the first objective may be to determine which natural language has been used to describe the information (Spanish? Chinese? English?); the next objective is to determine the focus of the information (e.g., temperature, sounds, locations, persons, events). In other words, we know fairly precisely what information to expect from a given device, but a human may deliver a wide and diverse set of topics, including something new and unexpected.

Unfortunately for understanding unstructured natural language, not only are there many natural languages in which this information can be formulated, there are variations within each language for the representation of that information (dialect and synonymic formulations). For example, when describing the detonation of a bomb, various words and phrases may be used: "blew up," "exploded," "went off," and so on. Although a speaker of that language would understand that these can all be used to describe the same event, automated processing requires the system to be able to recognize this as well.

Furthermore, any data received from a device are always historical in the sense that the data represent something that the device has observed and recorded. Using these historical data, algorithms may project future conditions—for example, the projected flight path of an airplane being tracked by radar—but this projection is based on historical data and algorithmic programming. Much of what is formulated in natural language reflects observations made in the past, but there is also a significant amount of inference and speculation about future events. Similarly, reporting on events that occurred in the past may include interpretation or speculation on the part of the reporter rather than statements of fact. Complicating things even further, the speaker may pass on information received via a third party such as another person, a news report, or blog, rather than simply reporting something personally witnessed. Finally, the speaker may lie, tell partial truths, or distort the facts. Although a device may sometimes fail or be negatively influenced by environmental factors such as heat or humidity, and although the object of observation by a device may employ diversionary tactics to evade identification, the device never makes a decision to intentionally deceive.

Thus, for the security and intelligence communities, sense making includes sifting through signals expressed in natural language by human sensors who pass on hearsay, conceal, intentionally distort, lie, and conjecture in words that are ambiguous, vague, and imprecise, looking for clues to anticipate and hostile actions. Credibility of information is not based on calibrations achieved by testing under various conditions, but on examining the sources of that information and the clues to veracity that these sources embed in their communications.

Current technologies in text analytics have made some inroads into dealing with the complexities of natural language data. However, many challenges remain for efficient and effective processing of this information. This chapter examines a number of these technologies and discusses an approach to processing natural language communications, which provides a high level of flexibility.

BIG DATA AND UNSTRUCTURED DATA

"Big Data" is an umbrella term that covers datasets so immense that they require special methodologies such as massively parallel systems and algorithms to be processed. Digital data are being generated and collected at unprecedented rates. Big science accounts for a huge volume of data: for example, in 2010, *Economist* reported that "When the Sloan Digital Sky Survey started work in 2000, its telescope in New Mexico collected more data in its first few weeks than had been amassed in the entire history of astronomy" (Economist, 2010). Big business accounts for another huge chunk of Big Data: Retailers, banks and credit card companies collect and analyze vast amounts of customer data daily for processing. Security cameras capture our daily movements, mobile telephone companies identify our locations and contacts, and we even self-report via social media.

Unstructured data are data that are not stored in a structured format such as a database or ontology. They are generally understood to include such diverse forms as e-mails, word processing documents, multimedia, video, PDF files, spreadsheets, text messaging content, digital pictures and graphics, mobile phone GPS records, and social media content (Roe, 2012).

Exploitation of these unstructured data depends on the type of unstructured data. Some require specialized algorithms such as image processing or analysis of acoustic data. Others require preprocessing; for example, PDF files are often converted to normal text files to run more standard text analytic algorithms. In many cases, unstructured data may be structured to make them more processable (see Chapters 2 and 10).

ASPECTS OF UNCERTAINTY IN SENSE MAKING

Regardless of the source of the data we receive, these data cannot always be taken at face value. Sometimes we know a lot about the source of the data we received; i.e., we know exactly what make and model of sensor we have placed where, we have calibration and reliability information about that particular type of sensor, and we know how it reacts under various types of environmental conditions (rain, heat, night, etc.). Therefore, knowing the time, weather conditions, and so on, we will have some idea of the reliability of the information that the sensor delivers, as well as precisely where the data have been gathered.

Humans, on the other hand, are mobile and able to insert new information into the system from a variety of locations; i.e., a blogger may blog from anywhere in the world in which the Internet is accessible and the blog post may contain information about events happening far distant from the blogger's physical location. Even if the blogger tells us (truthfully) in the text where he is currently located, we may actually access that text at an entirely different time, rendering the information useless except for historical purposes.

Ultimately, five aspects of uncertainty need to be considered in analyzing and aggregating information (Kruger, 2008; Kruger et al., 2008; Rein and Schade, 2009; Rein et al., 2010):

1. *Source uncertainty:* How reliable is the source of the information? How much do we trust this source? Is this eyewitness information or are there indications that the source is relating information derived from another source (hearsay)?
2. *Content uncertainty*: How credible do we believe the content, which the source has delivered, to be? Does it have to be confirmed by other sources? Does it fit with other data or is it anomalous? If the source is an algorithm (the result of other preprocessing), does the algorithm give us an estimate of the certainty of its results?
3. *Correlation uncertainty*: How certain are we that various pieces of information are related? When dealing with natural language information, we are often confronted with vague or imprecise formulations. How confident are we that reports concerning "several large vehicles" and "five tanks" are referring to the same thing?
4. *Evidential uncertainty*: How strongly does our information indicate a specific threat or behavior in which we are interested? Although the purchase of 50 kg of a chemical fertilizer may indicate that a homemade bomb is being built, it is much less shaky as evidence than the same individual acquiring a significant amount of, say, plastique.
5. *Model uncertainty*: Even with all factors present, how certain are we that the model mirrors reality— for instance, when there is constant behavior modification on the parts of foes who seek to evade discovery?

In making sense of text-based data, we need to take all of these various types of uncertainty into consideration; otherwise both the data upon which we base information and the assumptions we make about the connections among the various pieces of information are compromised (Dragos and Rein, 2014).

SITUATION AWARENESS AND INTELLIGENCE

Sense making can mean different things in different contexts. In numerous domains such as the military, air traffic control, harbor security, emergency services (crisis management), and public safety, sense making is generally synonymous with situation awareness, with emphasis on threat recognition and decision support. Situation awareness, particularly in the military domain, is an ongoing overview of important environmental elements within the area of interest, such as the locations of military units, both friendly and hostile, tracking personnel and equipment movements, and locations and conditions of facilities. On an intelligence level this may also include information on nonmilitary or paramilitary activities such as refugee movement, political climate, and tribal coalitions. Often this information is captured and displayed visually on maps in the command and control systems being used to give decision makers an overview of the current state of affairs. In the case of trackable changes such as the movements of individuals, vehicles, or military units, there will generally be some projection as to a future state (e.g., "where that column of tanks may be 1 h from now"). Such situational awareness is generally restricted as to the timeline (current state plus projections that may forecast second, minutes, or perhaps hours). Decision support under these circumstances will affect the assignment of resources, aid in detecting developing problems, and support the protection of life and property.

SITUATION AWARENESS: SHORT TIMELINES, SMALL FOOTPRINT

Situation awareness depends on knowing or predicting the state of the elements of interest in the (complex) environment under consideration. According to Endsley (1988), situation awareness is "the perception of elements in the environment within a volume of time and space, the comprehension of their meaning, and the projection of their status in the near future" (p. 792).

The timeline is generally relatively limited, the geographical area likewise usually restricted, and the possible threats relatively well understood or defined by experience. Often a significant percentage of the information underlying the situation awareness picture comes from devices such as video and still cameras, motion detection sensors, acoustic sensors, and radar. Algorithms to make sense of the data produced by the devices are continuously improving.

Natural language information for situation awareness often concerns movements or changes within the area of interest, and text analytic processing used to update the situation awareness may be relatively lightweight.

INTELLIGENCE: LONG(ER) TIMELINES, LARGER FOOTPRINT

Sense making for intelligence purposes, whether military, national security, or business, often involves timelines that are much longer, covering weeks, months, or years instead of microseconds, minutes, or hours. Intelligence sense making over longer periods will often rely on information that is text based. Much intelligence work is carried out over longer periods during which assets may be acquired and set in motion. The data collected via assets may include focused reports from intelligence assets, but also many types of open sources including news sources, government documents, and research results. Thus, environmental scanning may be subtle and complex, involving political and cultural changes, economic shifts, and other trends, which may indicate activities that pose threats. In such cases, open sources such as newspapers, television, government reports, blogs, and social media as well as reports from intelligence assets and analysts are useful. However, the information in these sources must first be understood and then collated and examined for (repetitive) patterns of behavior that indicate developing threats.

PROCESSING NATURAL LANGUAGE DATA

Natural language processing uses a number of techniques to analyze the individual parts of sentences in an attempt to make sense of them. Parsing analysis will use grammatical rules to identify the parts of speech contained within the sentence (subject, verb, and direct and indirect objects) as well as identify adjectives, adverbs, prepositional phrases, and other constructs of which the sentence is composed.

Text mining, popularly referred to as "text analytics," encompasses a variety of different techniques for analyzing natural language text to cull information from documents at hand. Using analysis techniques based on lexical and grammatical patterns in the language employed, sentences can be parsed so that information about documents as well as individual structures within documents and sentences (and, to a small extent, between sentences) may be discovered. These techniques include (but are not limited to):

- *Document classification:* Using a variety of techniques based on linguistic and statistical analysis, documents may be classified (type of content, human language used, etc.), summarized (what the document is about), or clustered (based on a classification).
- *Named entity recognition/pattern recognition:* Useful patterns such as proper names of individuals or organizations, telephone numbers, or e-mail addresses may be recognized and extracted.
- *Co-reference identification*: Alternate names for the same object may be identified through correlation analysis: "Barack Obama," "President Obama," "the US President," "the 44th president," and "44" all refer to the current president of the United States.
- *Sentiment analysis:* Using emotive words and phrases buried within the text, hints as to sentiment, emotion, or opinion may be culled. This has been recently most extensively used in social media analysis.
- *Relationship and event extraction:* Relationships among objects found in the text ("Susan works at ABC Company," "Jane is the sister of Bob," and "Mozart died in 1791") may be discovered.

The results of the extraction processes are then available for use in logic models and algorithms, which will look for yet more complex and subtle relationships among the entities that have been discovered. Some of this will serve as background information for context, i.e., to aid in disambiguation (e.g., helping to determine when "44" refers to Mr. Obama and when it refers to, say, someone's age). Other algorithms combine the extracted information: "Susan Smith works for ABC Company" and "Sam Brown works for ABC Company" establishes a link between Susan Smith and Sam Brown.

Much of the information thus extracted is stored in databases and, increasingly for large volumes of data, a specialized type of storage called a triple store, which has been designed to efficiently store and retrieve triples consisting of subject–predicate–object. These will be discussed in more depth in the following section.

STRUCTURING NATURAL LANGUAGE DATA

Extracted text-based information may be stored in structured formats for processing and access. Currently, structures for storage of text-based information for automatic processing generally fall into two categories: ontologies and databases/triple stores, the latter of which are a special kind of database. Each of these has its strengths and weaknesses for sense making, which we will discuss in this section (see also Chapter 12).

Ontologies contain information about the characteristics of and relationships among different classes of objects within a specific domain: that is, a definition of a shared concept of the objects in the domain. For example, within a domain containing human beings, a "parent" is a (human) object that has at least one instance of an object called "child." A "mother" is a special subclass of parent with the extra characteristic that she also has the gender "female," and so on. Thus, when an object is described as a specific class within the domain of interest, there is knowledge about some aspects of the object ("Mary must be female because she is a mother") and relationships between objects ("If Mary is Susan's mother, then Susan is Mary's child"). Ontologies have the advantage in that we have defined in advance exactly what each class of objects is and how it relates to all other objects within our domain of interest. However, although we use an ontology to store information about the characteristics of the concept "mother" in the domain, information on individual instances of each classes is usually stored using other methods to store the actual objects—for example, databases.

Databases are useful for storing large amounts of often complex information about specific instances of objects within the domain of interest. Generally, the information contained within databases is contained within files of similar objects, often presented as tables, which may be interrelated to reduce data redundancy, speed up processing, and structure results. Files contain records in which the data for numerous instances of similar item are stored as named and typed fields describing the important characteristics of the objects in the file. Within a single file, the record structures are identical. Retrieving information relies on knowledge about the structures within the various files as well as the relationships among them. Structures for the files are determined before filling in information on individual instances, thus ensuring conformity to ease retrieval. However, determining the structure ahead of time means that the analysts have made a priori decisions as to what information is needed and what information belongs together. Later changes to the structures within the database are possible but not always easy to effect.

A special variant of databases known as a triple store is a potential solution. A *triple store* contains atomic information contained in triples rather than as records inside of more complexly structured files. A triple is a three-part data entity in the form subject–predicate–object: "1-800-555-1234 is a telephone number," "Susan Smith works at ABC Company," "ABC Company produces widgets," etc. In a triple store, each triple is an autonomous piece of information that does not rely on structures such as a database record format to provide some context for the information. There are advantages to this, one of which is that record formats and schema do not need to be modified if there are changes and updates to the type of information being stored. Another advantage is that queries are simplified because one does not need to know the names of files and fields to make a query. Yet another advantage is that the presentation of a query is easily shown in a graph format, facilitating visualization of the query results.

TWO SIGNIFICANT WEAKNESSES

Two weaknesses in current text analytics processing should be taken into account for appropriate intelligence exploitation and decision making. The first is that embedded non-content information, which provides clues as to the true source of the content (first person, hearsay, speculation, etc.) and to the credibility of the information, is being ignored. The second is that extraction of information and storage out of their original context may result in information being lost or subtly altered. These two areas of concern are discussed in detail below.

IGNORING LEXICAL CLUES ON CREDIBILITY AND RELIABILITY

Humans do not simply communicate factual observations; they relate information received from other sources, they speculate and infer, they tell partial truths, and they discuss events that might take place in the future. North Atlantic Treaty Organization (NATO) intelligence organizations often use the A1-F6 designations described in the Joint Consultation, Command and Control Information Exchange Data Model (JC3IEDM) for source reliability and information credibility. Not only are these designators relatively broad ("report plausible" or "confirmed by at least three sources"), they are often assigned to a complete report and not to individual facts (or speculations) within the report, but also are usually assigned by an analyst (i.e., not automatically generated) and are therefore also subject to that analyst's knowledge or interpretation. Automated text analytic processing generally looks for certain types of patterns and simply ignores other elements of the texts.

Specific content within a given statement is often packed with lexical elements that indicate in some manner the uncertainty of the content itself or that indicate the original source of information. Take, for example, the following sentences:

1. John is a terrorist.
2. The Central Intelligence Agency (CIA) has concluded that John is a terrorist.
3. I believe that John is a terrorist.
4. My neighbor thinks John is a terrorist.
5. It has been definitely disproved that John is a terrorist.

In each of these sentences, the relationship ("fact") pattern of the sentence would produce the relation *John IS-A terrorist*. However, the lexical clues surrounding this "fact" weaken the belief in its veracity. In (1) there are no lexical clues as to what the writer believes, but in (2) and (4) there are indicators of third-party information (which may or may not have been repeated accurately); (2) indicates an inference; (3) and (4) indicate belief rather than knowledge; and (5) could be an unidentified third-party source, but the conclusion is a contradiction of the extracted "fact" of John being a terrorist.

Humans also chain multiple indicators of uncertainty into a single statement. For example, by adding the adverb "probably" to (2), the resulting "fact" of John being a terrorist is even weaker.

2. The CIA has concluded that John is a terrorist.
6. The CIA has concluded that John is probably a terrorist.

Appropriate decision making depends on knowledge of the quality of the intelligence upon which the decision rests. Natural language processing algorithms, which identify parts of speech, can identify adjectives, adverbs, and other constructs in which expressions of uncertainty are embedded; the results from text analytic processes that extract information from natural language text should be expanded to include the analysis of such embedded information to the fusion algorithms and models that predict threats.

OUT OF CONTEXT, OUT OF MIND

Over time, those who pose a threat to the security and well-being of citizens learn and modify their behavior to escape detection. This means that tools and behavioral expectations that are created today may well be outdated tomorrow. This also means that information we find unimportant today may be highly significant tomorrow. In addition, patterns of activity may become more nuanced and complex over time; we may not always know in advance what we are looking for.

Extracting isolated pieces of information out of the context in which they were stated may result in incorrect information being stored. Consider the following sentences:

7. Elaine flew from London to Stockholm via Amsterdam on 17 November.
8. Wolfgang gave Johanna Petra's book.

From (7) we can, of course, extract triples such as "Elaine flew to Stockholm," "Elaine flew via Amsterdam," and "Elaine flew on 17 November." However, if we are looking for patterns of behavior, it may turn out that the most interesting information is that Elaine flew via Amsterdam on that particular date (perhaps because another person of interest also was at Amsterdam airport on that day)—something that would be hard to reconstruct unless this information remains connected.

The second sentence, (8), contains both a direct object (Petra's book) and an indirect object (Johanna), which means that there are (at least) four major components to this statement, rendering it impossible to represent as a triple as it stands. Either we make inferences about some of the information in this statement (Wolfgang is somehow connected to Johanna, and Johanna has Petra's book) to force a triple or we store this information in another format. A database could be suitable, but then we must anticipate in advance which information we will store and under what format, and the database must be flexible enough to accommodate all possible formulations: for example, the ability to store information about multiple "via" stops, should Elaine's next suspicious trip include more than one stopover.

AN ALTERNATIVE REPRESENTATION FOR FLEXIBILITY

Originally designed for commanding simulated units, BML is a standardized language for military communication (orders, requests, and reports) that has been developed under the aegis of the NATO MSG-048 "Coalition BML" and has been expanded to communicate not only orders but also requests and reports. BML is based on JC3IEDM (NATO Multilateral Interoperability Program (MIP), 2005), which is used by all participating NATO partners. As NATO standard (STANAG 5525), JC3IEDM defines terms for elements of military operations, whether wartime or non-war, and thus provides a vocabulary sufficiently expressive to formulate both military and nonmilitary communications for a variety of different deployment types. It also provides a basis for standardized reporting among NATO coalition partners. Although BML has been predominantly developed for use by the military, the principles underlying the grammar and standardized representation of natural language text can be expanded into any domain. Extensions of BML for other domains such as crisis management (CML), police investigations (IML), and e-government (C2LG) already exist or are in development.

BML has been designed as a controlled language (Huijsen, 1998) based on a formal grammar (Schade and Hieb, 2006; Schade et al., 2010). This grammar was designed after one of the most prominent grammars from the field of computational linguistics, Lexical Functional Grammar (Bresnan, 2001). As a result, BML is an unambiguous language that can easily be processed automatically.

As described in Schade and Hieb (2006) and in Schade and Hieb (2007), a basic report in BML delivers a statement about an individual task (action), event, or status. A task report is about a military action either observed or undertaken. An event report contains information on nonmilitary non-perpetrator occurrences such as flooding, earthquakes, political demonstrations, or traffic accidents. Event reports may provide important background information for a particular threat: For example, a traffic accident may be the precursor of an improvised explosive device detonation. Status reports provide information on personnel, materiel, facilities, etc., whether own, enemy, or civilian, such as the number of injured, amount of ammunition available, and condition of an airfield or bridge.

Using various natural language processing techniques and text analytics as described previously, natural language statements can be processed and converted to BML (Jenge et al., 2009). BML has an advantage in that the production rules of the underlying grammar capture all of the content information held in context. Clues as to source type (e.g., eyewitness or third-party) as well as linguistic clues as to uncertainty of the information (e.g., "possibly," "probably," "might be") are reduced to information concerning source type and reliability, credibility of the information, and a label, which among other things establishes provenance because it is generated based on time/date information.

The statement "*Coalition forces report the detonation of a bomb at the Old Market in XY City at shortly past 4 PM today*" would be represented as a BML string (Figure 12.1, bottom) and can be implemented as a feature-value (structured) matrix (Figure 12.1, top) or other structured form for use.

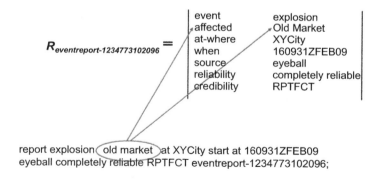

FIGURE 12.1

Representation of the report "*Coalition forces report the detonation of a bomb at the Old Market in XY City at shortly past 4 PM today*" as a BML string (bottom) and implemented as a feature-value (structured) matrix. Note that indicators of source type ("eyeball" meaning "eyewitness") and reliability ("completely reliable") and content credibility ("RPTFCT" indicating "reported considered fact") are attached to the statement, as well as a provenance marker (the final position in the string at bottom).

Note that the information remains in context, but also that the simplified representation of the statement as a BML string means that this representation is implementation independent and therefore can be easily mapped into other formats such as XML as needed for further processing (Jenge et al., 2009; Rein, 2013).

To date, this data representation is used for multilevel fusion, including within a NATO research group (IST-106) as a means to bridge the gap between information generated by devices and by algorithms (which present their results in BML) to fuse both hard and soft data, as well as for low-level and high-level fusion results (Biermann et al., 2014; Rein et al., 2012; Rein and Schade, 2012). Furthermore, the underlying concept may be used to enable information fusion across multiple natural languages by converting and mapping to the (English-like) BML, thus lowering the barrier of multilingual information (Rein and Schade, 2012; Kawaletz and Rein, 2010).

CONCLUSIONS

Natural language data are exploding and are increasingly important; yet, making sense of them remains problematic. Many inroads have been made into techniques for limited extraction of information from text, but two major weaknesses remain: insufficient analysis of embedded linguistic clues concerning the certainty (truth) of the statements, and loss of information owing to removed context. We have discussed these problems as well an alternative representation to current popular techniques, which would resolve or minimize these problems.

REFERENCES

Bresnan, J., 2001. Lexical-Functional Syntax. Blackwell, Malden, MA.

Biermann, J., Garcia, J., Krenc, K., Nimier, V., Rein, K., Snidaro, L., July, 2014. Multi-level fusion of hard and soft information. In: Proceedings Fusion 2014. Salamanca.

Dragos, V., Rein, K., 2014. Integration of soft data for information fusion: pitfalls, challenges and trends. In: Proceedings of Fusion 2014, Salamanca.

Endsley, M.R., 1988. Situation awareness global assessment technique (SAGAT). In: Proceedings of the National Aerospace and Electronics Conference (NAECON). IEEE, New York, pp. 789–795. http://dx.doi.org/10.1109/NAECON.1988.195097.

Huijsen, W.-O., May, 1998. Controlled language—an introduction. In: Proceedings of the Second International Workshop on Controlled Language Applications (CLAW98). Language Technologies Institute, Carnegie Mellon University, Pittsburgh, PA, pp. 1–15.

Jenge, C., Kawaletz, S., Schade, U., October, 2009. Combining different NLP methods for HUMINT report analysis. In: NATO RTO IST Panel Symposium, Stockholm, Sweden.

Kruger, K., 2008. Two "Maybes," one "Probably" and one "Confirmed" equals what? Evaluating uncertainty in information fusion for threat recognition. In: Proceedings of MCC 08, Cracow.

Kruger, K., Schade, U., Ziegler, J., July, 2008. Uncertainty in the fusion of information from multiple diverse sources for situation awareness. In: Proceedings of the 11th International Conference on Information Fusion (Cologne).

Kawaletz, S., Rein, K., September 2010. Methodology for standardizing content of military reports generated in different natural languages. In: Proceedings of MCC 2010, Wroclaw, Poland.

NATO, 2003. AJP 2.0 Allied Joint Intelligence, Counter Intelligence and Security Doctrine, NATO/PfP Unclassified, Ratification Draft 2.

NATO Multilateral Interoperability Programme (MIP), 2005. JC3IEDM–Metamodel–IPT3 V3.1.4 Multilateral Interoperability Programme (MIP) the Joint C3 Information Exchange Data Model Metamodel (JC3IEDM Metamodel). NATO Multilateral Interoperability Programme (MIP). Available from https://mipsite.lsec.dnd.ca/Public%20Document%20Library/04-Baseline_3.1/Interface-Specification/JC3IEDM/JC3IEDM-Metamodel-Specification-3.1.4.pdf.

Roe, C., 2012. The Growth of Unstructured Data: What to Do with All Those Zettabytes? [Online] Dataversity. Available from: http://www.dataversity.net/the-growth-of-unstructured-data-what-are-we-going-to-do-with-all-those-zettabytes/.

Rein, K., Schade, U., 2009. How certain is certain? Evaluation of uncertainty in the fusion of information derived from diverse sources. In: Proceedings of ISIF Fusion 2009, Seattle.

Rein, K., Schade, U., Kawaletz, S., 2010. Uncertainty estimation in the fusion of text-based information for situation awareness. In: Proceedings of 13th International Conference on Information Processing and Management of Uncertainty in Knowledge-based Systems, Dortmund, Germany, June 28–July 2, 2010. Springer Verlag.

Rein, K., 2013. Re-thinking standardization for interagency information sharing. In: Akhgar, B. (Ed.), Strategic Intelligence Management: National Security Imperatives and Information and Communications Technologies. Elsevier, Boston.

Rein, K., Schade, U., Remmersmann, T., Spring, 2012. Using battle management language to support all source integration. In: NATO RTO IST-112 Joint Symposium. Quebec City, Canada.

Rein, K., Schade, U., March, 2012. Battle management language as a "Lingua Franca" for situation awareness. In: Proceedings of IEEE CogSiMa 2012, New Orleans.

Schade, U., Hieb, M.R., 2006. Development of formal grammars to support coalition command and control: a battle management language for orders, requests, and reports. In: 11th International Command and Control Research and Technology Symposium (ICCRTS). Cambridge, UK.

Schade, U., Hieb, M., Frey, M., Rein, K., June 2010. Command and Control Lexical Grammar (C2LG) Specification. Version 1.3. FKIE Technical Report ITF/2010/02 Available at: http://c4i.gmu.edu/eventsInfo/conferences/2011/BMLsymposium2011/papers/BML-Symposium-Schade.pdf.

Schade, U., Hieb, M.R., March, 2007. Battle management language: a grammar for specifying reports. In: 2007 Spring Simulation Interoperability Workshop (Paper 07S-siw-036). Norfolk, VA.

The Economist, 2003. Data, Data Everywhere. Special report. The Economist. February 25, 2010. Available at: http://www.economist.com/node/15557443.

LITERATURE MINING AND ONTOLOGY MAPPING APPLIED TO BIG DATA

13

Vida Abedi, Mohammed Yeasin, Ramin Zand

INTRODUCTION

The effective mining of literature can provide a range of services such as *hypothesis generation* or find *semantic-sensitive* networks of *association from Big Data such as* PubMed, which has more than 24 million citations of biomedical literature (http://www.pubmed.org) and increases by roughly 30,000 per day. This may also help in understanding the potential confluence among different entities or concepts of interest. A well-designed and fully integrated text analytic tool can bridge the gap between the generation and consumption of Big Data and increase its usefulness in the sense of usability and scalability. A plethora of state-of-the-art applications were reported in the contemporary literature and succinctly reviewed in a recent survey by Lu (2011). A total of 28 tools targeted to specific needs of a scientific community were reviewed to compare functionality and performance. Common underlying themes of the tools were to:

1. Improve the relevance of search results
2. Provide better quality of service
3. Enhance user experience with PubMed

Although these applications were developed to minimize information overload, the questions of scalability and finding networks of semantic associations to gather actionable knowledge.

Traditional literature mining frameworks rely on keyword-based approaches and are not suitable for capturing meaningful associations to reduce information overload or generate new hypotheses, let alone find networks of semantic relations. Existing techniques lack the ability to present biological data effectively in an easy-to-use form (Altman et al., 2008) to further knowledge discovery (KD) by integrating heterogenous data. To reduce information overload effectively and complement traditional means of knowledge dissemination, it is imperative to develop robust and scalable KD tools that are versatile enough to meet the needs of a diverse community. The utility of such a system would be greatly enhanced with the added capability of finding semantically similar concepts related to various risk factors, side effects, symptoms, and diseases. There are a number of challenges to developing such a robust yet versatile tool. A key problem is to create a fully integrated and functional system that is specific to a targeted audience, yet flexible enough to be creatively employed by a diverse range of users. To be effective, it is necessary to map the range of concepts using a set of criteria to a dictionary that is specific to the community. Second, it is important to ensure that the KD process is scalable with the growing size of data and dynamic terminology, and is effective in capturing the semantic relationships and network of concepts.

In essence, because biology and medicine are rich in terminology, KD has to overcome specific challenges. For instance, in pathology reports and medical records, 12,000 medical abbreviations have been identified (Berman, 2004). In addition, this large vocabulary is dynamic and new terms emerge rapidly. Furthermore, the same object may have several names, or distinct objects can be identified with the same name; in the former case the names are synonyms, whereas in the latter case the objects are homonyms. Consequently, literature mining of biological and medical text becomes a challenging task and the terms that suffer the most are gene and protein names (Hirschman et al., 2002; Wilbur et al., 1999). Alternatively, to design and implement a more accurate system, it is important to understand and tackle these challenges at their root level. However, even more challenging is implementing the information extraction, also known as deep parsing.

Deep parsing is built on formal mathematical models, attempting to describe how text is generated in the human mind (i.e., formal grammar). Deterministic or probabilistic context-free grammars are probably the most popular formal grammars (Wilbur et al., 1999). Grammar-based information extraction techniques are computationally expensive because they require the evaluation of alternative ways to generate the same sentence. Grammar-based information could therefore be more precise but at the cost of reduced processing speed (Rzhetsky et al., 2008). An alternative to grammar-based approaches is semantic methods such as latent semantic analysis (LSA) (Landauer and Dumais, 1997). The LSA-based methods use a bag-of-word model to capture statistical co-occurrences. These techniques are computationally efficient and are suitable for finding direct and indirect associations among entities.

BACKGROUND

Latent semantic analysis is a well-known technique that has been applied to many areas in data science. In the LSA framework (Landauer and Dumais, 1997), a word document matrix (also known as TD–IDF matrix) is commonly used to represent a collection of text (corpus). The LSA extracts the statistical relations among entities based on their second-order co-occurrences in the corpus. Arguably, LSA captures some semantic relations among various concepts based on their distance in the eigenspace (Berry and Browne, 1999). The most common measure used to rank the vectors is the cosine similarity measure (Berry and Browne, 1999). The three main steps of LSA are summarized from Landauer and Dumais (1997) for the sake of clarity:

1. *Term-Document Matrix*: Text documents are represented using a bag-of-words model. This representation creates a term-document matrix in which the rows are the words (dictionary), the columns are the documents, and the individual cell contains the frequency of the term appearance in the particular document. Term frequency (TF) and inverse document frequency (IDF) are used to create the TF–IDF matrix.
2. *Singular Value Decomposition (SVD)*: SVD or sparse SVD (approximation of SVD) is performed on the TF–IDF matrix and the k largest *eigen*vectors are retained. This k-dimensional matrix (encoding matrix) captures the relationship among words based on first- and second-order statistical co-occurrences.
3. *Information Retrieval*: Information related to a query can be retrieved by first translating the query into the LSA space. A ranking measure such as cosine is used to compute the similarity between the data representation and the query.

PARAMETER OPTIMIZED LATENT SEMANTIC ANALYSIS

Although LSA has been applied to many areas in bioinformatics, the LSA models have been based on ad hoc principles. A systematic study was performed on the parameters affecting the performance of LSA to develop a parameter optimized latent semantic analysis (POLSA) (Yeasin et al., 2009). The various parameters examined were corpus content, text preprocessing, sparseness of data vectors, feature selection, influence of the first eigenvector, and ranking of the encoding matrix. The optimized parameters should be chosen whenever possible.

IMPROVING THE SEMANTIC MEANING OF THE POLSA FRAMEWORK

Methods such as LSA have been successful in finding direct and indirect associations among various entities. However, these methods still use bag-of-words concepts; therefore, they do not take into account the order of words, and hence the meaning of such words is often lost. Using multi-gram words would alleviate some of the problems of the bag-of-words model. In a multi-gram dictionary (MGD) the words "vascular accident" (which is a synonym of "stroke") would be differentiated from "accident," which could also mean "car accident" in a different context. However, it is challenging to generate such a dictionary. If all combinatorial words in the English dictionary are chosen, the size of such a dictionary would be considerably large—even if one considers only up to three-gram words. A larger dictionary implies also increased sparsity in the TF–IDF matrix. A possible solution is to construct the dictionary based on combinations of words that are biologically relevant for the case of biological text mining. Identification of biologically relevant word combinations can be derived from biological ontologies such as gene ontology (www.geneontology.org) or Medical Subject Headings (MeSH) (http://www.ncbi.nlm.nih.gov/mesh). Using an MGD could in principle improve the accuracy of vector-based frameworks such as the LSA that rely only on bag-of-words models. Use of an MGD provides also a means of extracting associations based on higher-order co-occurrences.

WEB SERVICES

It would be ineffective to build an integrated system unless researchers could interact with the system and obtain valuable information directly. Hence, for a system to be used by experts it is imperative to have a robust and practical application tool. There are four key advantages in using a Web service (WS) framework compared with a Web-based application (Papazoglou, 2008):

1. WS can act as client or server and can respond to a request from an automated application without human intervention. This feature provides a great level of flexibility and adaptability.
2. Web services are modular and self-descriptive: The required inputs and the expected output are well defined in advance.
3. Web services are manageable in a more standard approach. Even when an WS is hosted in a remote location, accessible only through the network, and written in an unfamiliar language, it is still possible to monitor and manage it using external application management and workflow systems.
4. An WS can be used by other applications when similar tasks need to be executed. This is important because more tools are being developed and soon integrated to provide improved services.

5. Finally, WS are the next generation of Web-based technology and applications. They provide a new and improved way for applications to communicate and integrate with one another (Papazoglou, 2008). The implications of this transition are profound, especially with the growing body of data and available tools.

ARIANA: ADAPTIVE ROBUST INTEGRATIVE ANALYSIS FOR FINDING NOVEL ASSOCIATIONS

Adaptive Robust Integrative Analysis for Finding Novel Associations (ARIANA) is an efficient and scalable KD tool providing a range of WS in the general area of text analytics in biomedicine. The core of ARIANA is built by integrating semantic-sensitive analysis of text data through ontology mapping (OM), which is critical for preserving specificity of the application and ensuring the creation of a representative database from an ocean of data for a robust model. In particular, the Medical Subject Headings ontology was used to create a dynamic data-driven (DDD) dictionary specific to the domain of application, as well as a representative database for the system. The semantic relationships among the entities or concepts are captured through a POLSA. The KD and the association of concepts were captured using a relevance model (RM). The input to ARIANA can be one or multiple keywords selected from the custom-designed dictionary, and the output is a set of associated entities for each query.

The DDD concepts were introduced starting from the domain-specific "dictionary creation" to the "database selection" and to the "threshold selection" for KD using the RM. The key idea is to make the system adaptive to the growing amounts of data and to the creative needs of diverse users. Key features distinguishing this work from closely related works are (but are not limited to):

1. Flexibility in the level of abstraction based on the user's insight and need
2. Broad range of literature selected in creating the KD module
3. Domain specificity through a mapping ontology to create DDD and an application-specific dictionary and its integration with POLSA
4. Presentation of results in an easy-to-understand form through RM
5. Implementation of DDD concepts and modular design throughout the process
6. Extraction of hidden knowledge and promotion of data reuse by designing a system with modular visualization engine; for instance, ARIANA allows users to expand certain nodes or collapse a sub-network, or stretch some components of the network for better visual clarity

In essence, ARIANA attempts to bridge the gap between creation and dissemination of knowledge by building a framework that ensures adaptiveness, scalability, robustness, context specificity, modularity, and DDD constructs (see Figure 13.1). Case studies were performed to evaluate the efficacy of the computed results.

CONCEPTUAL FRAMEWORK OF ARIANA

ARIANA is built on the backbone of the hypothesis generation framework (Abedi et al., 2012). It implements a system that is modular, robust, adaptive, context-specific, scalable, and DDD. The current system uses 50 years of literature from the PubMed (http://www.pubmed.org/) database. It can find

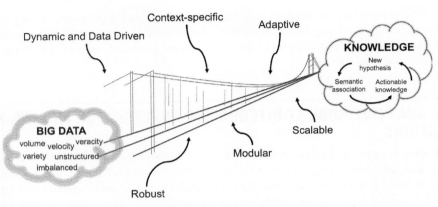

FIGURE 13.1

Bridging the gap between Big Data and knowledge.

associations linking disease and non-disease traits—also referred to as concepts or MeSH. In addition, it can identify direct and indirect associations between traits. From the user's perspective, ARIANA is an WS that can uncover knowledge from literature. Empirical studies suggest that the system can capture novel associations and provide innovative services. These results may have broader impact on gathering actionable knowledge and the generating of hypotheses. ARIANA is a customizable technology that can fit many specialized fields, when appropriate measures are considered. For instance, text-mining methods have been applied to the following fields:

1. Link and content analysis of extremist groups on the Web (Reid, 2005)
2. Public health rumors from linguistic signals on the Web (Collier et al., 2008)
3. Medical intelligence for monitoring disease epidemics (Steinberger et al., 2008)
4. Opinion mining and sentiment analysis (Nasukawa and Yi, 2003; Pang and Lee, 2008)

The expanded system, significantly evolved and fine-tuned over the past years, integrates semantic-sensitive analysis of text data through OM with database search technology to ensure the specificity required to create a robust model in finding relevant information from Big Data. There are five components as building blocks:

1. OM and MGD creation
2. Data Stratification and POLSA
3. RM
4. Reverse ontology mapping
5. Interface and visualization (I&V)

In biomedicine applications, an important addition to the system was the integration of the Online Mendelian Inheritance in Man (OMIM) database (http://www.ncbi.nlm.nih.gov/omim), a flat list of human-curated gene diseases, and MeSH, a hierarchical database of Medical Subject Headings, to provide gene–trait associations. Figure 13.2 summarizes these modules and their main functionalities. In the following section we will elaborate on each of the modules and their main objectives.

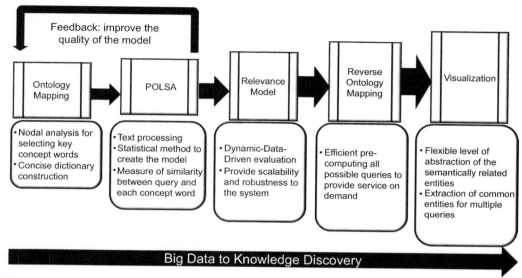

FIGURE 13.2

Main modules of the ARIANA system.

ONTOLOGY MAPPING

The main objective of the OM module is to create a model that is modular, scalable, and domain specific. These characteristics will reduce noise and enhance the overall quality of the system. Because the data is broad and voluminous, attention must be paid to reduce the different sources of noise and bias in the system. By employing a domain-specific ontology to create the model, biases in the data can be minimized. The two functions of OM are to create a concise dictionary, preferably multi-gram, and to facilitate extraction of key concept words in the field. A domain-specific concise dictionary will be used in the statistical LSA and its quality will translate directly to the system's performance. Furthermore, the selection of key concept words is important to reduce systemic bias that is integral to all statistical text analytic methods. Figure 13.3 summarizes the steps in OM customized for biomedical applications.

Systemic bias is mainly characterized by imbalanced data. As in many applications, there are large numbers of examples for some cases, yet there are few examples for other situations. For instance, there are a significantly higher number of people without migraine compared with the proportion of the population with migraine. The systemic bias is more pronounced for cases in which there are only few examples, such as rare conditions. In addition to systemic bias, subject-level bias can introduce noise into the system. For instance, if concept words were selected by an individual, the model would be biased toward the personal preference of that individual. Automatic selection of concept words based on a domain-specific ontology would greatly reduce this bias in the system.

DATA STRATIFICATION AND POLSA

A context-specific ontology (such as MeSH) is the main input to the POLSA module. Concept words and the MGD, obtained from the OM module, are both input to the POLSA framework. Text data,

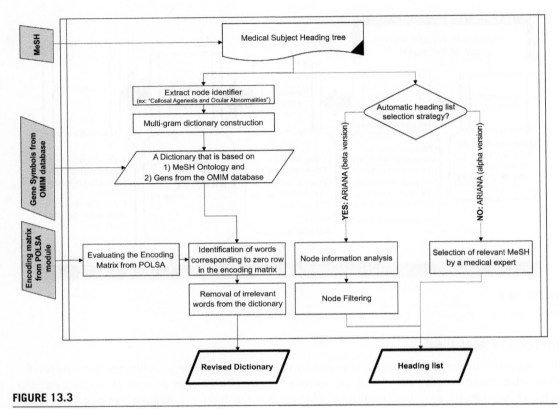

FIGURE 13.3

Ontology mapping for biomedical applications.

which can be in form of short texts or text fragments, is downloaded and stratified based on concept words. For instance, all of the text data extracted for the word "stroke" are collectively organized in the database as one document. Concept words have to be specific enough to extract specific text; however, they have to be general enough to secure enough related text to minimize problems resulting from data imbalance and systemic bias. The POLSA framework will produce a ranked list of concepts along with the respective similarity measure for any given user's query, which will be fed to the RM. Figure 13.4 summarizes the steps in the POLSA module.

RELEVANCE MODEL

The RM is a logical extension of the disease model reported in our previous work (Abedi et al., 2012). It is an intuitive, simple, and easy-to-use statistical analysis of rank values to compute the strongly related, related, and not related concepts (or risk factors) with respect to a user query. Figure 13.5 illustrates the core concept of a disease model hypothesis. The implicit assumption in this model is that if associated factors of a disease are well known, a large body of literature will be available to corroborate the existence of such associations. On the other hand, if associated factors of a disease are not well documented, the factors are weakly associated with the disease, with few factors displaying a high level of

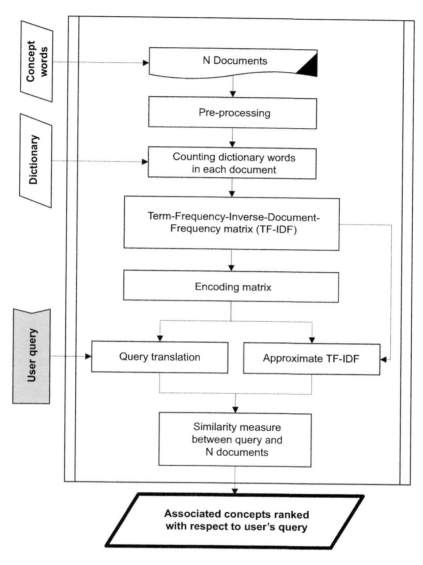

FIGURE 13.4

Flowchart outlining steps involved in the POLSA module.

association. In general, we expect the distributions to be uneven, and the largest distribution to correspond to the set of risk factors that are not known to be associated with the disease. The disease model can be applied in many fields and facilitate grouping of associated entities into three or more bins.

In essence, if one accepts this assumption, the distribution of associated factors follows a tri-modal distribution and it will be intuitive to measure the level of association for different factors with respect to a given disease. Use of a disease model (by a tri-modal distribution) allows better identification of the three sets of factors: unknown associations, potential associations, and established associations.

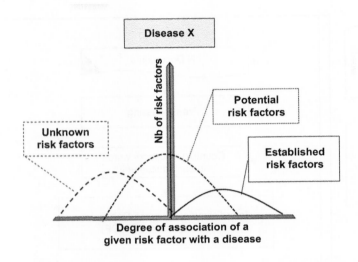

FIGURE 13.5

Disease model based on literature evidence (the horizontal axis represents the similarity measure between the query—in this case, "disease x"—and concept words (risk factors); the vertical axis represents the number of concept words with a given similarity measure).

Estimating the parameters of the tri-modal distribution can be computationally expensive for real-time services. In addition, fuzzy c-mean clustering can be applied to the similarity scores to group the scores into three bins. This DDD process provides robustness and scalability to the system and can group concepts without requiring a fixed threshold. Furthermore, because the distribution of relevance scores is a function of user queries, the cutoff value to separate highly, possible, and weakly associated headings will be determined dynamically.

REVERSE ONTOLOGY MAPPING

Because the visualization of semantically related concepts is an important component of KD, a modular framework is designed to map the highly associated concepts for a given query to the context-specific ontology. This will provide the basis for a flexible and user-centric visualization module.

VISUALIZATION AND INTERFACE

A flexible visualization engine is implemented to facilitate a user's interaction with the system. The key idea is to use the hierarchical structure of the context-specific ontology to present results to the user in a way that would enhance the user's experience and interests. The network representation makes it easier to interact with the results and generate new hypotheses. For example, the interface of ARIANA is designed to give the user the option to expand or collapse a node of interest and capture knowledge at various levels of abstraction.

To present the results in a graphical representation, JavaScript Object Notation (JSON) objects are created for a user's query to create the network of associations. Figure 13.6 summarizes the steps

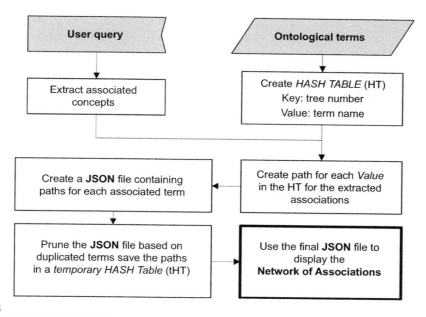

FIGURE 13.6

Steps in generating JSON files for network visualization.

of the process. To represent the JSON objects as graphical forms, D3 library (http://d3js.org/) is used to implement the collapsibility and expandability of each node. Main advantages of using this representation are:

1. Compliant computing in the World Wide Web Consortium, the main international standards organization for the World Wide Web
2. Use of the widely implemented Scalable Vector Graphics
3. HTML5, JavaScript, and Cascading Style Sheets standards
4. Control over the final visual product

Features that were critical in this project were event handlers such as collapsibility and expandability features. Finally, to represent the network of associations for every query in the system, JSON objects were created and displayed.

IMPLEMENTATION OF ARIANA FOR BIOMEDICAL APPLICATIONS

ARIANA is an efficient and scalable KD tool providing a range of services in the general areas of text analytics. Here, we showcase how ARIANA can be used as a tool in mining biomedical literature—although the system can also be customized for other uses relevant to national security, such as link, opinion, or sentiment analysis. We will refer to the system as applied in biomedicine as ARIANA+. The core of ARIANA+ is built by integrating semantic-sensitive analysis of text data through OM, which is critical to preserve the specificity of the application and ensure the creation of a representative database from millions of publications for a robust model. In particular, the MeSH ontology was used to create a DDD dictionary specific to the domain of application, as well as a representative database for the system. Semantic relationships among the entities or concepts are captured through a POLSA. The KD and the association of concepts were captured using an RM. The input to ARIANA+ can be one or multiple keywords selected from the MeSH and the output is a set of associated entities for each query. The system can be used to identify hidden associations among biomedical entities, facilitate hypothesis generation, and accelerate KD. ARIANA+ can aid in identifying key players in national and international emergencies such as pandemics (e.g., swine flu or Ebola). In essence, the system can help authorities in critical decision-making situations by providing a robust source of knowledge. In particular, we will show how ARIANA+ was able to bring forward critical missed associations in clinical trials.

In the following section we will elaborate technical details of ARIANA+ for each component and highlight key features that provide adaptiveness, robustness, scalability, specificity, and modularity to the system.

OM AND MGD CREATION

Based on the domain knowledge, a very large database was stratified using concepts and entities with a broad coverage. The selection of concept words (referred to as heading selection) was fully automated to reduce bias and noise while improving the scalability and robustness of the model. The current version of the system (ARIANA+) is mainly based on our work (Abedi et al., 2014) and has a modular design that is reconfigurable. An alpha prototype was developed and reported in a pilot study (Abedi et al., 2012).

The OM provides a systematic way to fine-tune and refine the different features of the system. One of the key functions of the OM is to filter redundant dictionary terms to refine the encoding matrix. This refinement process helped create a rank full-encoding matrix from the TF–IDF matrix that is extremely sparse in nature. The MGD has been also optimized accordingly to overcome the limitations of LSA-based techniques. The two key paths in the OM are to create a revised MGD that is concise and domain specific and to select a heading list with a broad-based coverage. In ARIANA+, node information from MeSH ontology was extracted to stratify the database (see section on heading selection below) and to create the model.

The key input to the OM is the MeSH ontology. Medical Subject Headings provide a hierarchical structure of terms. For instance "Ebolavirus" has two paths in the MeSH hierarchy:

1. Viruses [B04] > RNA Viruses [B04.820] > Mononegavirales [B04.820.455] > Filoviridae [B04.820.455.300] > Ebolavirus [B04.820.455.300.200]
2. Viruses [B04] > Vertebrate Viruses [B04.909] > RNA Viruses [B04.909.777] > Mononegavirales [B04.909.777.455] > Filoviridae [B04.909.777.455.300] > Ebolavirus [B04.909.777.455.300.200].

Therefore, extracting the associations among elements requires evaluating the exact level of specificity and key relations with respect to other elements in the field. It also requires use of a common language to avoid misinterpreting and misrepresenting information.

The hierarchical structure of MeSH is used to extract node identifiers. For instance, "Ebolavirus" or "RNA Viruses" are node identifiers. Based on this information, first an MGD is constructed (see the section on MGD construction below). Parallel to that, a series of nodes from all MeSH nodes is selected (referred to as headings) to create the model through a systematic process (see Automatic Heading Selection below). The selected headings are used in the POLSA module to extract and organize the literature data by creating an encoding matrix. The encoding matrix is evaluated for sparsity and refined accordingly. This refinement process will produce a more concise dictionary of terms by filtering irrelevant words—words that add no new information to the model.

CREATION OF THE MGD

The MeSH ontology was used to create a concise domain-specific dictionary. Creation of a meaningful dictionary is important in developing a data-driven model to find novel associations through higher-order co-occurrences. A context-specific MGD ensures some level of semantics based on the order of words, which is lost in statistical models that are based on bag-of-words. To create the context-specific MGD, first MeSH node identifiers are extracted and then, using a Perl script, the text file containing node identifiers is parsed to construct the multi-grams. Duplicates, stop words, words starting with a stop word or number, and all words of length two or fewer characters were removed in the filtering stage. The size of the dictionary after the first pass was 39,107 words. Gene symbols from the OMIM database were added to this dictionary. An iterative process was employed to fine-tune the dictionary. The refinement involved iterative removal of null rows (filled with zeros) from the encoding matrix. The final size of the dictionary after this process became 17,074 words that contain mono-, bi-, and tri-grams.

The automated process to generate dictionary words and concept words, here referred to as the heading list, provides robustness and scalability to the system. It also adds a layer of modularity and facilitates integration of the system with other ongoing efforts in the field. Having the same language as the community is important in sustainability and future development.

DATA STRATIFICATION AND POLSA

Data stratification

ARIANA+ includes literature data for 2,545 automatically selected headings (see Automatic Heading Selection below). These headings are the main input to the POLSA module. In addition, the MGD was enriched with all of the gene symbols from the OMIM database and represented the second input. Using the selected headings, titles and abstracts of publications of the past 50 years were downloaded from PubMed and stored in an MySQL database on a server. The database construction was simple yet efficient. There is an advantage to using a database to store the data: Because the relationship between the abstract and headings is many to one, by saving the data into a database each abstract will only be downloaded once, which saves significant amount of storage space.

Three tables are used to construct the database for the MeSH-based concepts: (1) Factor table, (2) FactorPMID table, and (3) PMIDContent table. Factor table contains basic information regarding the 2,545 headings, such as Name, ID, and "Most recent article (year)"; the latter is used to update the entry in the database more efficiently. FactorPMID contains information needed to link the factor to PubMed abstracts using PMIDs (unique identifies of PubMed abstracts). PMIDContent contains all of the information about each abstract, such as PMID, Title, Abstract, Year, and MeSH tags. In fact, every article in PubMed is tagged with one or more MeSH to facilitate searches.

The number of items in the corpus was the same as the number of elements in the heading list (2,545 headings). Each of the 2,545 items was parsed to create a TF–IDF matrix using the words in the refined and representative dictionary. The preprocessing step was customized to suit the structure of the dictionary, because it contained multi-gram words. For instance, (1) stemming was not necessary because multi-gram words were not stemmed; (2) stop word removal was also not necessary because the multi-gram words had stop words within them in some cases. In addition, use of the POLSA framework provided scalability to the system.

Automatic heading selection

Automatic heading selection for ARIANA+ was achieved through a statistical filtering process. The key selection criterion was to use a subset of MeSH headings that provides relatively broad coverage. It was critical to choose representative data while creating a balanced dataset from the unstructured abstracts. Eight categories from the MeSH tree were selected based on the application constraints and domain knowledge: Diseases (C); Chemicals and Drugs (D); Psychiatry and Psychology (F); Phenomena and Processes (G); Anthropology, Education, Sociology, and Social Phenomena (I); Technology, Industry, and Agriculture (J); Named Groups (M); and Health Care (N). These categories were subject to filtering, and about 2.5–17% of their descendant nodes were selected in the final list. Three features were used in the filtering process: (1) number of abstracts for each heading, (2) number of descendant nodes associated with each heading, and (3) ratio of the number of abstracts between child to parent node (also referred to as fold change). Finally, 2,545 headings from a total of 38,618 were selected to populate the database.

Heading selection rules were progressive and were fine-tuned with heuristic rules consistent with different categories. Table 13.1 summarizes the rules applied to the eight distinct categories. These rules were adjusted for each category to include concepts from a wide range of fields while keeping a higher number of headings from the disease class. The disease class included the MeSH from the C category and the non-disease class contained headings from the remaining seven categories. Furthermore, inclusion criteria were continuously adjusted to reduce the skewness in the dataset. For instance,

Table 13.1 Progressive Filtering Rules Applied to the Eight MeSH Categories

Medical Subject Heading Categories	Number of Selected Headings	Progressive Selection Rules		
		Abstracts/Headings	Descendant Node/ Heading	Fold Change
C: Diseases	1,828	1,000–50,000	1–100	<10
D: Chemicals and Drugs	475	5,000–10,000	1–100	<5
F: Psychiatry and Psychology	128	1,000–30,000	1–10	<10
G: Phenomena and Processes	242	1,000–20,000	2–50	<10
I: Anthropology, Education, Sociology, and Social Phenomena	31	1,000–10,000	1–10	<10
J: Technology, Industry, and Agriculture	66	1,000–10,000	1–10	<10
M: Named Groups	13	1,000–20,000	1–5	<5
N: Health Care	63	5,000–10,000	1–10	<10

some categories were very large—Chemicals and Drugs had over 20,000 subheadings—whereas others were small—Named Groups had 190 subheadings. Therefore, the selection criteria were progressively adjusted to reduce the bias in the dataset. A total of 475 out of 20,015 subheadings were selected from the Chemicals and Drugs category (only 2% coverage), whereas a total of 13 out of 190 (or 7% coverage) were selected from the Named Groups category. Progressive heading selection rules were important in providing robust and context specificity of the system.

The main constraint in this model was to select more than 50% of headings from the Diseases category. In essence, key objectives of the project were to determine disease networks, identify associated risk factors for a disease, and highlight traits that were directly or indirectly associated with a disease, to aid in our understanding of disease mechanisms. The three features (number of abstracts for each heading, number of descendant nodes associated with each heading, and fold change) were used to create the heuristic that would measure the specificity (as an estimated measure of level of abstraction) of the headings and facilitate the selection. A total of 1,828 headings were therefore selected, representing 17% coverage and accounting for 64% of the total number of headings in the ARIANA+ database.

The *Chemical and Drugs* category was one of the largest MeSH categories, with 20,015 headings. Selection criteria for this category were therefore stringent. One of the main objectives was to select headings that would represent a maximum of 50% from the non-disease group. A total of 475 headings were selected, representing 47% of the headings from the non-disease group. The Psychiatry and Psychology category had only 1,050 headings. Selection criteria were adjusted to keep roughly 10% of the best representative headings from this category. These headings had a wide range; among other measures, the number of abstracts for each heading in this category ranged from one to 859,564. The filtering process attempted to select the most homogenous headings to minimize systemic bias and noise. The *G* category (Phenomena and Processes) was relatively large, with 3,164 headings. A total of 242 headings were selected from this category to represent 24% of the non-disease class in the database.

Other categories such as *I* (Anthropology, Education, Sociology, and Social Phenomena) and *J* (Technology, Industry, and Agriculture) had similar characteristics, with 559 and 558 headings, respectively. Category *I* had an average of 7,374 and category *J* an average of 7,290 abstracts per heading. Similarly, category *I* had an average of 1.7 child nodes whereas category *J* had an average of 1.6 child nodes. Finally, categories *I* and *J* had an average of 114 and 99 fold changes per heading, respectively. The selection rules were adjusted in a similar manner, with the ultimate goal to select about 100 nodes to populate roughly 10% of the non-disease category. By applying the filtering process, the average number of abstracts was reduced to 5,520 in category *I* and 4,787 in category *J*. Similarly, the average number of child nodes after filtering was 2.2 in category *I* and 1.6 in category *J*; finally the average fold changes per heading were reduced to 3.5 in category *I* and 3.1 in category *J*. These numbers demonstrate that a progressive filtering process can be beneficial, and fold change in this case had a more discriminative power. In fact, the average number of abstracts was reduced only by 25% and 34% after filtering for *I* and *J* categories, respectively. However, average fold change was reduced by 97% for both categories.

The *M* category (*Named Groups*) was small, with only 190 headings. The selection process filtered this category in a way to include only a small subset of headings in the non-disease class. Although this category had a limited number of headings, variation in terms of the specificity of topics was large. After filtering, 13 headings were selected to be in the non-disease class. The inclusion of a small representative sample from this category can be important, because these were potentially interesting headings for epidemiological studies, such as: "Hispanic Americans," "Twins," and

"Emergency Responders." The *Health Care* category had 2,207 headings with a large range of specificity. This filtering process created a small subset of headings from this category (for a total of 63, or 6% of the non-disease group). This selection process ensured the inclusion of headings with moderate specificity, therefore reducing systemic bias in the dataset.

Once the headings were selected, the duplicates were removed. In MeSH, some nodes are duplicated because their parent node is different. However, the documents retrieved for both duplicated nodes were identical; hence, duplicates were removed without causing inconsistency. A total of 301 headings were duplicated from the following categories: 218 (or 12%) from the *C* category, 39 (8%) from the *D* category, 7 (5%) from the *F* category, 32 (13%) from the *G* category, 2 (3%) from the *J* category, and 3 (or 4%) from the *N* category. This final step in heading selection reduced the list from 2,846 to 2,545.

PARAMETER OPTIMIZED LATENT SEMANTIC ANALYSIS

Using 2545 headings, the TF-IDF matrix was employed to generate the encoding matrix. Dimensionality was reduced to cover 95% of the total energy. In particular, dimensionality was reduced from 2,545 to 1,400 headings to create the encoding matrix. Using the encoding matrix, the query was translated into the eigenspace to rank the headings based on the cosine similarity measure. This process was applied iteratively to fine-tune the dictionary, which was used to generate a final encoding matrix. The iterative fine-tuning provides robustness and DDD property to the system.

Fine-tuning the encoding

After the analysis of the initial encoding matrix obtained by POLSA, it was observed that many of the entries (rows) were zero. Removing these rows made the dictionary more concise and relevant to the data. It also helped create a full rank-encoding matrix that improved the robustness of the system by capturing meaningful semantic associations.

RELEVANCE MODEL

The list of associated headings that are ranked with respect to a user query is used as input to the RM. The top-ranked headings are strongly associated with the query, and the headings ranked at the bottom do not have significant evidence to support their association with the query. The headings that are between the two extremes are those that might or might not be associated with the query, because there is some supportive evidence for their association. These weak associations are important in the KD process and call for further investigation by domain experts. In essence, the RM is an intuitive and easy-to-use statistical analysis strategy of rank and group similarity scores of associated headings. The goal is to group related headings into three bins: namely strongly related, possibly related, and unrelated headings.

The underlying assumption is that if concepts (also referred to as headings) are highly associated, a large body of literature is available to corroborate existence of their association. Similarly, if two headings or biological entities are not well documented, they are only weakly associated. Furthermore, because the distribution of relevance scores is a function of user queries, the cutoff value to separate highly, possible, and weakly associated headings must be determined dynamically. This requires a simplified yet effective model to ensure scalability; therefore, it was assumed that the distribution of the ranked list can be viewed as a Gaussian mixture model and the partition can be computed using the DDD threshold estimation. In particular, the distribution of relevance scores of the headings for a given query was approximated as a tri-modal Gaussian distribution. The separation of the three distributions allowed implementation of the DDD cutoff system. A curve-fitting approach can be used to estimate the parameter of the tri-modal distribution and determine two cutoff values to separate the three groups. However, the estimation process can be computationally expensive. A more practical approach is to use a fuzzy c-mean clustering approach to group the scores. The latter is more robust and scalable and can provide a finely tuned means to evaluate the results on demand. Furthermore, this DDD cutoff value determination can also be integrated in other information retrieval (IR) systems.

Fuzzy c-means clustering is applied to group associated headings using the MATLAB built-in function. Using the clustering, the scores are first grouped into two clusters based on the membership values of these two clusters, Algorithm 1 is used to assign each heading to one of the three groups in the RM. The cosine cutoff values estimated through this process are DDD; hence, the cutoffs are subject to change as the dataset expands. The input is the limit defined by an expert to separate the known and unknown headings and place them into the possible heading group (i.e., the gray zone). A conservative limit threshold of 0.9 was chosen to analyze the results (value of j in Algorithm 1).

SET a and b as cluster membership for headings such that

sum(a)≥sum(b)

SET j as the limit to select headings in gray zone

FOR each heading

   IF a≤ b   *THEN SET c to 1;   END IF*

   IF abs(a-b) ≤j   *THEN SET d to 1;   END IF*

END FOR

FOR each heading

   IF c=1   *THEN SET group to high_Assoc;*

   ELSIF d=1   *THEN SET group to possible_Assoc;*

   ELSE   *SET group to no_Assoc;*

   END IF

END FOR

Algorithm 1. Grouping Headings by fuzzy c-mean clustering.

The RM was applied to the top 750 headings (30%), assuming the number of highly and possibly associated headings is less than 20% or 500 headings. In cases in which the number of associated headings would be higher, the initial query must be revised because it likely represents a generic term such as "disease" or "medicine." As also indicated in our empirical study, finding a novel association with no citation in the database required analyzing the top 10% of the headings. In that specific case (see Empirical Studies section below) five associated headings leading to a new hypothesis were among the top 10% of the ranked list. The RM is one of the key modules that ensure the DDD property of the system while providing a robust and scalable framework.

REVERSE ONTOLOGY MAPPING AND I&V

Reverse ontology mapping maps back the semantically associated concepts to the MeSH tree to create the network of associations for a given query. It is easy to interact with and understand the network representation. It also helped to implement flexible visualization, in which users can expand or collapse nodes to interact with the captured knowledge at various levels of abstraction.

To present the results in a graphical representation, JSON objects are created for a user's query to create the network of associations. At the first stage, MeSH terms are used to create a Hash Table (HT). For instance, "dementia" is an MeSH identifier and is identified in MeSH as F03.087.400, meaning that "dementia" is a third-level node in the MeSH tree in the F category. In the HT, "dementia" has a key that corresponds to its tree number and a value, which is its identifier (i.e., "dementia"). Similarly, highly and possibly associated headings with a user's query are identified. For each associated heading, a path is created for each value in the HT. For instance, if an associated heading to a user query includes "dementia," a path is created for that heading; in this case, the path for "dementia" is "Root > Mental Disorders > Delirium, Dementia, Amnestic, Cognitive Disorders > Dementia." After the path is generated, JSON files are constructed with paths for each associated heading. Then the JSON files are pruned to remove duplicated terms. The final JSON files are used to create the networks using the D3 library.

Users can interact with the tool and explore different queries. For instance, in the case of "caffeine," the tree will be crowded and can be partially expanded to allow users to explore topics of interest. Associated concepts related to "caffeine" are diverse, ranging from "leisure activities" such as "relaxation" and "skin disease" such as "pigmentation disorder" to "acyclic acids" such as "maleimides." Considering the example in which the query is "iron metabolism." There are four associated headings: "Iron Overload," "Growth Disorders," "Pigmentation Disorders," and "Myelodysplastic Syndromes." All of these detected associations have supporting evidence in PubMed. In essence, ARIANA+ provides a global view based on a reliable source of information. Furthermore, exploration of weakly related entities could bring forward new emerging research trends and potential new hypotheses. To explore weakly associated concepts, users can download the ranked list of associated headings and their relative cosine scores. In addition, users can perform multiple search queries simultaneously and extract common associated headings instantaneously.

Reverse ontology mapping and V&I are important components of the system; they provide adaptive specificity and modularity. ARIANA+ could be further expanded and customized in specialized fields using the described framework with minor modifications.

In the following section, case studies are presented to illustrate the potentials of this tool.

CASE STUDIES

To develop the ARIANA+ system, two pilot studies were performed to identify and address challenges and design a robust and scalable system. In the initial study (Abedi et al., 2012), 96 concepts were considered and 20 years of literature were analyzed. In the second stage of the system, 276 concepts were considered and the past 50 years of literature were analyzed (Abedi et al., 2014). Even in those smaller-scale studies, interesting observations were made. However, the most important KD case occurred when we expanded the system to incorporate 2,545 concepts from MeSH and fine-tuned the system at different levels. For instance, we identified the association between the drug hexamethonium and pulmonary inflammation and fibrosis, which in 2001 caused the tragic death of a healthy volunteer who was enrolled in an asthma study. The system was also able to identify a link between Alzheimer disease (AD) and tuberculosis (TB), two distant conditions.

CASE STUDY I: KD: LETHAL DRUG INTERACTION

In 2001, an asthma research team at the Johns Hopkins University used the drug hexamethonium on a young healthy volunteer, which ended in the death of the woman as a result of pulmonary inflammation and fibrosis. Hexamethonium was a drug used mainly to treat chronic hypertension and was proposed as a potential drug to treat asthma; however, the non-specificity of its action led to its use being discontinued (Nishida et al., 2012; Toda, 1995). During the course of the asthma study, a healthy volunteer, Ellen Roche, died only a few days after inhaling this drug. She was diagnosed with pulmonary inflammation and fibrosis based on chest imaging and an autopsy report after her death. The autopsy report stated the following facts: "The microscopic examination of the lungs later revealed extensive, diffuse loss of alveolar space with marked fibrosis and fibrin thrombi involving all lobes. There was also evidence of alveolar cell hyperplasia as well as chronic inflammation compatible with an organizing stage of diffuse alveolar damage. There was no evidence of bacteria, fungal organisms, or viral inclusions on routine or special stains" (Internal Investigative Committee Membership, 2001). The principal investigator made a good-faith effort to research the drug's (hexamethonium's) adverse effects, mainly by focusing on a limited number of resources, including the PubMed database, and the ethics panel subsequently approved the safety of the drug. This tragedy highlights the importance of a literature search in designing experiments and enrolling healthy individuals in control groups.

The volunteer was a young healthy person with no lung or kidney problems. One day after enrolling in the study she developed a dry cough and dyspnea and 2 days after she developed flu-like symptoms. Her forced expiratory volume in the first second was reduced. On May 9, 2001, she became febrile and was admitted to the Johns Hopkins Bayview Medical Center. The chest X-ray revealed streaky densities in the right perihilar region. Arterial oxygen saturation fell to 84% after she walked a short distance. She was in critical condition and 3 days after was referred to the intensive care unit, where she was intubated and ventilated. She experienced bilateral pneumothoraces and presented a clinical picture of adult respiratory distress syndrome. She died on June 2, 2001. However, this accident could have been prevented if the researcher had known of a case report published in 1955 (Robillard et al., 1955) or extracted the association using ARIANA+.

Interestingly, a literature (PubMed) search of "Hexamethonium" and "pulmonary fibrosis" returns (as verified in August 2014) four hits, none of them with available abstracts online. One of the publications is in the Russian language, published in 1967 (Malaia et al., 1967). The other three were published 60 to 30 years ago (Brettner et al., 1970; Cockersole and Park, 1956; Stableforth, 1979). Searching individual entries returned 21,167 record for "pulmonary fibrosis" and 7,102 entries for "Hexametho-nium." However, to date there is limited direct evidence of the toxicity of this drug in PubMed. The PDF of the case report published in 1955 can be found in PubMed today; however, many data mining tools including ARIANA+ do not take into account PDFs of very old articles. Nonetheless, ARIANA+ was able to capture this association.

The analysis revealed five clear indications among the top 10% of the ranked headings, providing strong evidence for such an association. ARIANA+ was able to extract this information from 50 years of literature, even though the 1955 case report (Robillard et al., 1955) was not in the database. Of 2,545 concepts in the system, ARIANA+ ranked "Scleroderma, Systemic" as the 13th ranked concept, "Neoplasms, Fibrous Tissue" as the 16th, "Pneumonia" as the 38th, "Neoplasms, Connective and Soft Tissue > Neoplasms, Connective Tissue > Neoplasms, Fibrous" as the 174th, and finally, "Pulmonary Fibrosis" as the 257th. ARIANA+ captured this association and could have prevented the volunteer's death.

CASE STUDY II: DATA REPURPOSING: AD STUDY

The identification of networks of semantically related entities with a single or double query can uncover hidden knowledge and facilitate data reuse among other things. AD is a debilitating disease of the nervous system. It mostly affects the older population. ARIANA+ captured some of the obvious associations, such as "Tauopathies," "Proteostasis Deficiencies," "Amyloidosis," "Cerebral Arterial Diseases," "Multiple System Atrophy," and "Agnosia." It also identified some of the less obvious associations, such as "Tissue Inhibitor of Metalloproteinases" (Ridnour et al., 2012; Wollmer et al., 2002). Using "TB" as a second query, a common entity was recognized to be linked to both AD and TB. "*Proteostasis Deficiencies > Amyloidosis*" is highly related (cosine score of 0.5651) to TB and moderately related (cosine score of 0.0734) to AD. Further investigation by experts revealed that AD and TB could be indirectly related through matrix metalloproteinase (MMP) gene family members.

MMPs are zinc-binding endopeptidases that degrade various components of the extracellular matrix (Brinckerhoff and Matrisian, 2002; Davidson, 1990). They are believed to be implicated in TB by the concept of matrix degrading phenotype (Elkington et al., 2011). Various studies in human cells, animal models, as well as gene profiling studies support the association of MMPs and TB and involvement of TB-driven lung matrix deconstruction (Berry et al., 2010; Mehra et al., 2010; Russell et al., 2010; Thuong et al., 2008; van der Sar et al., 2009). MMPs are also implicated in AD (Yong et al., 1998). In fact, MMP proteins can breakdown amyloid proteins (Yan et al., 2006) that are present in the brain of AD patients. Therefore, this association is advantageous.

In summary, there is literature evidence for the link between MMP genes and AD, in which MMP genes are beneficial; and similarly between MMP genes and TB, in which MMP genes have a negative effect. However, the connection between AD and TB through MMP genes is extracted by a global analysis of the literature, facilitated by visual inspection of the network of semantically related entities.

DISCUSSION

ARIANA is a system targeting a large scientific community: medical researchers, epidemiologists, biomedical scientific groups, high-level decision makers in crisis management, and junior researchers with focused interests. The tool can be used as a guide to broaden one's horizon by identifying seemingly unrelated entities. ARIANA+ provides relations between query word(s) and 2,545 headings using 50 years of literature data from PubMed. The design is efficient, modular, robust, context specific, dynamic, and scalable. The framework can be expanded to incorporate a much larger set of headings from the MeSH or any other domain-specific ontology. In addition, a DDD system is implemented to group ranked headings into three groups for every query. The DDD system can be applied in other systems to improve the quality of information retrieval. As a consequence of incorporating a context-specific MGD, the sparsity of the data model is lower and the size of the dictionary is significantly smaller than if all combination of English words were taken into consideration.

The features and functionalities of the system are compared and contrasted with state-of-the-art systems. In a survey in which 28 applications were reviewed (Lu, 2011), five used clustering to group search results into topics and another five used different techniques to summarize results and present a semantic overview of the retrieved documents. The tools that are based on clustering are fundamentally different from ARIANA+, whereas the rest of the tools have some similarities in their scopes and designs.

One of the systems, Anne O'Tate (Smalheiser et al., 2008) uses post-processing to group the results of literature searches into predefined categories such as MeSH topics, author names, and year of publication. Although this tool can be helpful in presenting results to the user, it does not provide the additional steps to extract semantic relationships.

The McSyBi (Yamamoto and Takagi, 2007) clusters results to provide an overview of the search and to show relationships among retrieved documents. It is reported that LSA is used with limited implementation details; furthermore, only the top 10,000 publications are analyzed. ARIANA+ analyzes over eight million publications. XplorMed (Perez-Iratxeta et al., 2001) allows users to further explore the subjects and keywords of interest. MedEvi (Kim et al., 2008) provides 10 concept variables as semantic queries. XplorMed puts a significant limit (no more than 500) on the number of abstracts to analyze. MEDIE (Ohta et al., 2006) provides utilities for semantic searches based on deep-parsing and returns text fragments to the user. This is conceptually different from ARIANA+. EBIMED (Rebholz-Schuhmann et al., 2007) extracts proteins, gene ontology, drugs, and species, and identifies relationships among these concepts based on co-occurrence analysis.

Among all reviewed tools (Lu, 2011), EBIMED is most comparable to ARIANA+; yet, that system focuses only on proteins, gene ontology annotations, drugs, and species as concepts. ARIANA+ differs from EBIMED in a number of ways. First, ARIANA+ provides systematic data stratification based on domain knowledge and application constraints. Second, it uses OM to create a robust dictionary, which in turn produces a better model and also helps in finding crisp associations of concepts. Third, it computes the associations based on higher-order co-occurrence analysis and the introduction of an RM to present the results into an easy-to-use and understandable manner. In addition, Because MeSH provides a hierarchical structure, ARIANA+ could be expanded to include a large number of headings.

In summary, the ARIANA system with only 276 MeSH (Abedi et al., 2014) was able to extract interesting knowledge, such as the association between sexually transmitted diseases and migraine: an association that was published after we downloaded the abstracts from PubMed (Kirkland et al., 2012). The expanded and fine-tuned ARIANA+ (with 2,545 headings) was able to extract even more valuable information, leading toward actionable knowledge. Among the refinement steps, the headings selection process created a balanced representative dataset across all selected categories, in which noise and systemic bias were minimized. This fine-grain filtering process provided a stratified data, and specificity measures were used to create a robust model. In addition to a strong data model, the interactive visualization and interface module gives control to users to view only associations that are relevant to them, by collapsing irrelevant topics. The visualization module was based on the use of a hierarchical structure to represent the terms. In this case, using MeSH has the advantage of also providing modularity and scalability to the framework. In addition, the interactive system empowers users with more search options, such as multi-query search. The latter will translate to wider usage and exploration of the tool by inter- and multidisciplinary teams.

Finally, the path from *Big Data* to *actionable knowledge* is multidimensional and nonlinear. However, the investigation of cause–effect relationships in translational research could be a step toward *bridging* that gap. This study shows that a custom-designed literature mining tool can be successful in the discovery of semantically related networks of associations. In an empirical study, it was shown that ARIANA+ can capture the hidden association of *"Pulmonary Fibrosis"* and *"Hexamethonium,"* even though such an association is still not evident in a PubMed search.

With the current version of the system, once an association is found, the user's expertise will guide the search direction. The user can use that information and search an array of databases and explore various tools such as PubMed, OMIM, and Phenotype Genotype Integrator (PheGenI), all maintained by the National Center for Biotechnology Information; GeneMANIA (Zuberi et al., 2013); Gene Ontology (Ashburner et al., 2000); STRING (Franceschini et al., 2013); and so forth, to further refine the hypothesis. Interestingly, the current version of PheGenI accepts MeSH as input and can extract associated genetic information from NHGRI genome-wide association study catalog data and other databases such as Gene, the database of Genotypes and Phenotypes (dbGaP), OMIM, GTEx, and dbSNP. The comprehensive system uses the dbGaP, which was developed to facilitate research in clinical and epidemiological fields. The modularity provided by ARIANA+ will further integrative analysis. In essence, in the case of an indirect association, more in-depth analysis of available data will be needed to understand the intriguing mechanism linking two or more traits. In essence, no one tool or technique can best extract knowledge from an ocean of information; however, literature data could provide a starting point and additional sources can aid in the quest for *actionable knowledge.*

CONCLUSIONS

Strategic reading, searching, and filtering have been the norm in gaining perspectives from the ocean of data in the field of biomedicine and beyond. Intriguingly, information overload has contributed to widening the knowledge gap; therefore, more data do not translate to more knowledge directly. It is widely acknowledged that efficient mining of biological literature could provide a variety of services (Rzhetsky et al., 2008) such as hypothesis generation (Abedi et al., 2012) and semantic-sensitive KD. The same is true for national security applications such as link and content analysis of extremist groups on the Web (Reid, 2005), public health rumors from linguistic signals on the Web (Collier et al., 2008), or opinion mining and sentiment analysis (Nasukawa and Yi, 2003; Pang and Lee, 2008).

Traditionally, literature mining tools focus on text summarization and clustering techniques (Lu, 2011) with the goal of reducing data overload and with the ability to read and synthesize more information in a shorter time. It was argued that a text analytic tool capable of extracting networks of semantically related associations may help bridge knowledge gaps by using humans' unique visual capacity and information-seeking behavior. For instance, in a study, 16,169 articles were chosen to create a visual representation of main concepts, creating a visual map of verbal information (Landauer et al.,

2004). In that analysis, "verbal presentation offers more precise information […], whereas the visual presentation offers a more flexible style of exploration that better shows multiple, fuzzy, and intermixed and complexly patterned relations among the documents." In addition, literature mining tools that can capture semantic relationships could in principle connect disjoint entities among different research fields.

ARIANA+ can uncover networks of semantic associations and provide WS to generate hypotheses. In addition, because of its modular design, it can be integrated with additional tools and be designed to provide complementary information to refine the hypotheses. In essence, ARIANA+ will enable exploration of literature to find answers to questions that we did not know how to ask. We are still working to enhance the visualization module to enrich the user's overall interactive experience. Ongoing effort is focusing on integrating ARIANA+ with other tools that provide complementary information to generate actionable knowledge.

Finally, in critical situations such as crisis management and epidemic monitoring, time becomes the most crucial parameter; understanding and extracting meaningful associations and exploring various hypotheses simultaneously can save human lives and expedite the process of rescue. In essence, in time-critical circumstances rapid response is needed to preserve national security at many levels (also see Chapters 4 and 5). However, in today's fast-paced and globally interconnected world, public health experts who historically have been trained in medical or epidemiological fields are from diverse backgrounds including anthropology, economics, sociology, and engineering (Garcia et al., 2014). Therefore, policy decision makers from diverse backgrounds have to navigate through large and complex literature evidence of varying quality and relevance to make important decisions quickly (Cockcroft et al., 2014). A tool such as ARIANA to extract knowledge and summarize the literature has great value in providing evidence-based decision support systems to government agencies and decision makers. The presented framework can be a great tool in KD, hypothesis generation, and data repurposing. In addition, identification of potential hypotheses for a fast response to pandemics can be of great importance. Furthermore, a customized system can be implemented to analyze different types of short text data in the English language or any other language, such as e-mail or other types of communications, reports, or Web-based information. The system can be configured to address other areas of concern for national security, such as law and order or combating terrorism.

ACKNOWLEDGMENT

This work was supported by the Electrical and Computer Engineering Department and Bioinformatics Program at the University of Memphis; by the University of Tennessee Health Science Center; and by NSF Grant NSF-IIS-0746790. The authors thank Faruk Ahmed, Shahinur Alam, Hossein Taghizad, and Karthika Ramani Muthukuri for programming support and implementation of the Web tool for the ARIANA+ system.

REFERENCES

Abedi, V., Yeasin, M., Zand, R., 2014. ARIANA: adaptive robust and integrative analysis for finding novel associations. In: The 2014 International Conference on Advances in Big Data Analytics. Las Vegas, NV.

Abedi, V., Zand, R., Yeasin, M., Faisal, F.E., 2012. An automated framework for hypotheses generation using literature. BioData Mining 5, 13. http://dx.doi.org/10.1186/1756-0381-5-13.

Altman, R.B., Bergman, C.M., Blake, J., Blaschke, C., Cohen, A., Gannon, F., Grivell, L., Hahn, U., Hersh, W., Hirschman, L., Jensen, L.J., Krallinger, M., Mons, B., O'Donoghue, S.I., Peitsch, M.C., Rebholz-Schuhmann, D., Shatkay, H., Valencia, A., 2008. Text mining for biology–the way forward: opinions from leading scientists. Genome Biology 9 (Suppl. 2), S7. http://dx.doi.org/10.1186/gb-2008-9-s2-s7.

Ashburner, M., Ball, C.A., Blake, J.A., Botstein, D., Butler, H., Cherry, J.M., Davis, A.P., Dolinski, K., Dwight, S.S., Eppig, J.T., Harris, M.A., Hill, D.P., Issel-Tarver, L., Kasarskis, A., Lewis, S., Matese, J.C., Richardson, J.E., Ringwald, M., Rubin, G.M., Sherlock, G., 2000. Gene ontology: tool for the unification of biology. The gene ontology consortium. Nature Genetics. 25, 25–29. http://dx.doi.org/10.1038/75556. Gene.

Berman, J.J., 2004. Pathology abbreviated: a long review of short terms. Archives of Pathology & Laboratory Medicine 128, 347–352. http://dx.doi.org/10.1043/1543-2165(2004)128<347:PAALRO>2.0.CO;2.

Berry, M.P.R., Graham, C.M., McNab, F.W., Xu, Z., Bloch, S.A.A., Oni, T., Wilkinson, K.A., Banchereau, R., Skinner, J., Wilkinson, R.J., Quinn, C., Blankenship, D., Dhawan, R., Cush, J.J., Mejias, A., Ramilo, O., Kon, O.M., Pascual, V., Banchereau, J., Chaussabel, D., O'Garra, A., 2010. An interferon-inducible neutrophil-driven blood transcriptional signature in human tuberculosis. Nature 466, 973–977. http://dx.doi.org/10.1542/peds.2011-2107LLLL.

Berry, W.M., Browne, M., 1999. Understanding Search Engines: Mathematical Modeling and Text Retrieval. Society for Industrial and Applied Mathematics Philadelphia, Philadelphia, PA, USA.

Brettner, A., Heitzman, E.R., Woodin, W.G., 1970. Pulmonary complications of drug therapy. Radiology 96, 31–38. http://dx.doi.org/10.1148/96.1.31.

Brinckerhoff, C.E., Matrisian, L.M., 2002. Matrix metalloproteinases: a tail of a frog that became a prince. Nature Reviews Molecular Cell Biology 3, 207–214. http://dx.doi.org/10.1038/nrm763.

Cockcroft, A., Masisi, M., Thabane, L., Andersson, N., 2014. Science Communication. legislators learning to interpret evidence for policy. Science 345, 1244–1245. http://dx.doi.org/10.1126/science.1256911.

Cockersole, F.J., Park, W.W., 1956. Hexamethonium lung; report of a case associated with pregnancy. Journal of Obstetrics and Gynaecology of the British Empire 63, 728–734.

Collier, N., Doan, S., Kawazoe, A., Goodwin, R.M., Conway, M., Tateno, Y., Ngo, Q.-H., Dien, D., Kawtrakul, A., Takeuchi, K., Shigematsu, M., Taniguchi, K., 2008. BioCaster: detecting public health rumors with a Web-based text mining system. Bioinformatics 24, 2940–2941. http://dx.doi.org/10.1093/bioinformatics/btn534.

Davidson, J.M., 1990. Biochemistry and turnover of lung interstitium. European Respiratory Journal 3, 1048–1063.

Elkington, P.T., Ugarte-Gil, C.A., Friedland, J.S., 2011. Matrix metalloproteinases in tuberculosis. European Respiratory Journal 38, 456–464. http://dx.doi.org/10.1183/09031936.00015411.

Franceschini, A., Szklarczyk, D., Frankild, S., Kuhn, M., Simonovic, M., Roth, A., Lin, J., Minguez, P., Bork, P., von Mering, C., Jensen, L.J., 2013. STRING v9.1: protein-protein interaction networks, with increased coverage and integration. Nucleic Acids Research 41, D808–D815. http://dx.doi.org/10.1093/nar/gks1094.

Garcia, P., Armstrong, R., Zaman, M.H., 2014. Models of education in medicine, public health, and engineering. Science 345, 1281–1283. http://dx.doi.org/10.1126/science.1258782.

Hirschman, L., Morgan, A.A., Yeh, A.S., 2002. Rutabaga by any other name: extracting biological names. Journal of Biomedical Informatics 35, 247–259.

Internal Investigative Committee Membership, 2001. Report of Internal Investigation into the Death of a Volunteer Research Subject. [Online] Available from: http://www.hopkinsmedicine.org/press/2001/july/report_of_internal_investigation.htm.

Kim, J.-J., Pezik, P., Rebholz-Schuhmann, D., 2008. MedEvi: retrieving textual evidence of relations between biomedical concepts from Medline. Bioinformatics 24, 1410–1412. http://dx.doi.org/10.1093/bioinformatics/btn117.

Kirkland, K.E., Kirkland, K., Many, W.J., Smitherman, T.A., 2012. Headache among patients with HIV disease: prevalence, characteristics, and associations. Headache 52, 455–466. http://dx.doi.org/10.1111/j.1526-4610.2011.02025.x.

Landauer, T.K., Dumais, S.T., 1997. A solution to Plato's problem: the latent semantic analysis theory of acquisition, induction, and representation of knowledge. Psychological Review 104, 211–240. http://dx.doi.org/10.1037/0033-295X.104.2.211.

Landauer, T.K., Laham, D., Derr, M., 2004. From paragraph to graph: latent semantic analysis for information visualization. Proceedings of the National Academy of Sciences 101, 5214–5219. http://dx.doi.org/10.1073/pnas.0400341101.

Lu, Z., 2011. PubMed and beyond: a survey of web tools for searching biomedical literature. Database (Oxford) baq036. http://dx.doi.org/10.1093/database/baq036.

Malaia, L.T., Shalimov, A.A., Dushanin, S.A., Liashenko, M.M., Zverev, V.V., 1967. Catheterization of veins and selective angiopulmonography in comparison with several indices of the functional state of the external respiratory apparatus and blood circulation during chronic lung diseases. Kardiologiia 7, 112–119.

Mehra, S., Pahar, B., Dutta, N.K., Conerly, C.N., Philippi-Falkenstein, K., Alvarez, X., Kaushal, D., 2010. Transcriptional reprogramming in nonhuman primate (Rhesus Macaque) tuberculosis granulomas. PLoS One 5. http://dx.doi.org/10.1371/journal.pone.0012266.

Nasukawa, T., Yi, J., 2003. Sentiment analysis. In: Proceedings of the International Conference on Knowledge Capture - K-cap '03. ACM Press, New York, USA, p. 70. http://dx.doi.org/10.1145/945645.945658.

National Center for Biotechnology Information, n.d. Phenotype-genotype Integrator [Online]. Available from: http://www.ncbi.nlm.nih.gov/gap/phegeni.

Nishida, Y., Tandai-Hiruma, M., Kemuriyama, T., Hagisawa, K., 2012. Long-term blood pressure control: is there a set-point in the brain? Journal Of Physiological Sciences 62, 147–161. http://dx.doi.org/10.1007/s12576-012-0192-0.

Ohta, T., Masuda, K., Hara, T., Tsujii, J., Tsuruoka, Y., Takeuchi, J., Kim, J.-D., Miyao, Y., Yakushiji, A., Yoshida, K., Tateisi, Y., Ninomiya, T., 2006. An intelligent search engine and GUI-based efficient MEDLINE search tool based on deep syntactic parsing. In: Proceedings of the COLING/ACL on Interactive Presentation Sessions. Association for Computational Linguistics, Morristown, NJ, USA, pp. 17–20. http://dx.doi.org/10.3115/1225403.1225408.

Pang, B., Lee, L., 2008. Opinion mining and sentiment analysis. Foundations and Trends® in Information Retrieval 2, 1–135. http://dx.doi.org/10.1561/1500000011.

Papazoglou, M., 2008. Web Services: Principles and Technology. 752.

Perez-Iratxeta, C., Bork, P., Andrade, M.A., 2001. XplorMed: a tool for exploring MEDLINE abstracts. Trends in Biochemical Sciences 26, 573–575.

Rebholz-Schuhmann, D., Kirsch, H., Arregui, M., Gaudan, S., Riethoven, M., Stoehr, P., 2007. EBIMed–text crunching to gather facts for proteins from Medline. Bioinformatics 23, e237–e244. http://dx.doi.org/10.1093/bioinformatics/btl302.

Reid, E., 2005. US domestic extremist groups on the web: link and content analysis. IEEE Intelligent Systems 20, 44–51. http://dx.doi.org/10.1109/MIS.2005.96.

Ridnour, L.a, Dhanapal, S., Hoos, M., Wilson, J., Lee, J., Cheng, R.Y.S., Brueggemann, E.E., Hines, H.B., Wilcock, D.M., Vitek, M.P., Wink, D.a, Colton, C.a, 2012. Nitric oxide-mediated regulation of β-amyloid clearance via alterations of MMP-9/TIMP-1. Journal of Neurochemistry 123, 736–749. http://dx.doi.org/10.1111/jnc.12028.

Robillard, R., Riopelle, J.L., Adamkiewicz, L., Tremblay, G., Genest, J., 1955. Pulmonary complications during treatment with hexamethonium. Canadian Medical Association Journal 72, 448–451.

Russell, D.G., VanderVen, B.C., Lee, W., Abramovitch, R.B., Kim, M., Homolka, S., Niemann, S., Rohde, K.H., 2010. Mycobacterium tuberculosis wears what it eats. Cell Host Microbe 8, 68–76. http://dx.doi.org/10.1016/j.chom.2010.06.002.

Rzhetsky, A., Seringhaus, M., Gerstein, M., 2008. Seeking a new biology through text mining. Cell 134, 9–13. http://dx.doi.org/10.1016/j.cell.2008.06.029.

Smalheiser, N.R., Zhou, W., Torvik, V.I., 2008. Anne O'Tate: a tool to support user-driven summarization, drill-down and browsing of PubMed search results. Journal of Biomedical Discovery and Collaboration 3, 2. http://dx.doi.org/10.1186/1747-5333-3-2.

Stableforth, D.E., 1979. Chronic lung disease. Pulmonary fibrosis. British journal of hospital medicine 22 (128), 132–135.

Steinberger, R., Fuart, F., Goot, E., Van Der, Best, C., 2008. Text Mining from the Web for Medical Intelligence. Heal, San Fr. http://dx.doi.org/10.3233/978-1-58603-898-4-295. 295–310.

Thuong, N.T.T., Dunstan, S.J., Chau, T.T.H., Thorsson, V., Simmons, C.P., Quyen, N.T.H., Thwaites, G.E., Lan, N.T.N., Hibberd, M., Teo, Y.Y., Seielstad, M., Aderem, A., Farrar, J.J., Hawn, T.R., 2008. Identification of tuberculosis susceptibility genes with human macrophage gene expression profiles. PLoS Pathogens 4. http://dx.doi.org/10.1371/journal.ppat.1000229.

Toda, N., 1995. Regulation of blood pressure by nitroxidergic nerve. Journal Of Diabetes And Its Complications 9, 200–202.

Van der Sar, A.M., Spaink, H.P., Zakrzewska, A., Bitter, W., Meijer, A.H., 2009. Specificity of the zebrafish host transcriptome response to acute and chronic mycobacterial infection and the role of innate and adaptive immune components. Molecular Immunology 46, 2317–2332. http://dx.doi.org/10.1016/j.molimm.2009.03.024.

Wilbur, W.J., Hazard, G.F., Divita, G., Mork, J.G., Aronson, A.R., Browne, A.C., 1999. Analysis of biomedical text for chemical names: a comparison of three methods. Proceedings of AMIA Symposium 176–180.

Wollmer, M.A., Papassotiropoulos, A., Streffer, J.R., Grimaldi, L.M.E., Kapaki, E., Salani, G., Paraskevas, G.P., Maddalena, A., de Quervain, D., Bieber, C., Umbricht, D., Lemke, U., Bosshardt, S., Degonda, N., Henke, K., Hegi, T., Jung, H.H., Pasch, T., Hock, C., Nitsch, R.M., 2002. Genetic polymorphisms and cerebrospinal fluid levels of tissue inhibitor of metalloproteinases 1 in sporadic Alzheimer's disease. Psychiatric Genetics 12, 155–160.

Yamamoto, Y., Takagi, T., 2007. Biomedical knowledge navigation by literature clustering. Journal of Biomedical Informatics 40, 114–130. http://dx.doi.org/10.1016/j.jbi.2006.07.004.

Yan, P., Hu, X., Song, H., Yin, K., Bateman, R.J., Cirrito, J.R., Xiao, Q., Hsu, F.F., Turk, J.W., Xu, J., Hsu, C.Y., Holtzman, D.M., Lee, J.-M., 2006. Matrix metalloproteinase-9 degrades amyloid-beta fibrils in vitro and compact plaques in situ. Journal of Biological Chemistry 281, 24566–24574. http://dx.doi.org/10.1074/jbc.M602440200.

Yeasin, M., Malempati, H., Homayouni, R., Sorower, M., 2009. A systematic study on latent semantic analysis model parameters for mining biomedical literature. BMC Bioinformatics 10, A6. http://dx.doi.org/10.1186/1471-2105-10-S7-A6.

Yong, V.W., Krekoski, C.A., Forsyth, P.A., Bell, R., Edwards, D.R., 1998. Matrix metalloproteinases and diseases of the CNS. Trends in Neuroscience 21, 75–80. http://dx.doi.org/10.1016/S0166-2236(97)01169-7.

Zuberi, K., Franz, M., Rodriguez, H., Montojo, J., Lopes, C.T., Bader, G.D., Morris, Q., 2013. GeneMANIA prediction server 2013 update. Nucleic Acids Research 41, W115–W122. http://dx.doi.org/10.1093/nar/gkt533.

BIG DATA CONCERNS IN AUTONOMOUS AI SYSTEMS

James A. Crowder, John N. Carbone

INTRODUCTION

To be truly autonomous, an artificially intelligent system (AIS) must be provided with real-time cognition-based information discovery, decomposition, reduction, normalization, encoding, and memory recall (i.e., knowledge construction) to improve understanding and context-based decision making for autonomous robotic systems. Cognitive systems must be able to integrate information into their current cognitive conceptual ontology (Crowder et al., 2012) to be able to "think" about, correlate, and integrate the information into the overall AIS memories. When describing how science integrates with information theory, Brillouin (2004) defined knowledge succinctly as resulting from a certain amount of thinking and as distinct from information, which had no value, was the "result of choice," and was the raw material consisting of a mere collection of data. In addition, Brillouin concluded that 100 random sentences from a newspaper, a line of Shakespeare, or even a theorem of Einstein have exactly the same information value. Therefore, information content has no value until it has been thought about and thus turned into knowledge within a given context.

Decision making is of great concern because of the handling of ambiguity and the ramifications of erroneous inferences. Often there can be serious consequences, when actions are taken based on incorrect recommendations (Crowder, 1996) and misunderstanding of context, which can influence decision making before the inaccurate inferences can be detected or even corrected. Underlying the data fusion domain is the challenge of creating actionable knowledge from information content harnessed from an environment of vast, exponentially growing structured and unstructured sources of rich, complex, interrelated cross-domain data. This is a major challenge for autonomous artificially intelligent (AI) systems that must deal with ambiguity without the advantage of operator-based assistance.

Dourish (2004a) stated that the scientific community has debated definitions of context and its uses for many years. He discussed two notions of context—technical, for conceptualizing human–action relationships between the action and the system, and social science—and reported that "ideas need to be understood in the intellectual frames that give them meaning." Hence, he described features of the environment, where activity takes place (Dourish, 2004b). Alternatively, Torralba (2003) derived context-based object recognition from real-world scenes and said that one form of performing the task was to define the "context" of an object in a scene in terms of other previously recognized objects. The author concluded that a strong relationship exists between the environment and the objects found within and that increased evidence exists of early human perception of contextual information.

Dey (2001) presented a context toolkit architecture that supported the building of more optimal context-aware applications because, he argued, context was a poorly used resource of information in computing environments, and information must be used to characterize the collection of states—or, as he called it, the "situation abstraction" of a person, place, or object relevant to the interaction between a user and the application. Similarly, when describing a conceptual framework for context-aware systems, Coutaz et al. (2005) concluded that context informs recognition and mapping by providing a structured, unified view of the world in which a system operates. The authors provided a framework with an onto-logical foundation, an architectural foundation, and an approach to adaptation that supposedly scale alongside the richness of the environment. The authors further concluded that context was critical in understanding and developing information systems. Winograd (2001) noted that intention could be determined only through inferences based on context. Hong and Landay (2001) described context as knowing the answers to the "W" questions (e.g., Where are the movie theaters?). Similarly, Howard and Qusibaty (2004) described context for decision making using the interrogatory 5WH model (who, what, when, where, why, and how). Finally, Ejigu et al. (2008) presented a collaborative context-aware service platform based on a developed hybrid context management model. The goal was to sense context during execution along with internal states and user interactions by using context as a function of collecting, organizing, storing, presenting, and representing hierarchies, relations, axioms, and metadata.

These discussions outline the need for an AIS cognitive framework that can analyze and process knowledge and context (Crowder and Carbone, 2012) and represent context in a knowledge management framework composed of processes, collection, preprocessing, integration, modeling, and representation, thus enabling the transition from data, information, and knowledge to new knowledge. Described in this chapter is a cognition-based processing framework and memory management encoding and storage meth-odology for capturing contextual knowledge, thus providing decision-making support in the form of a knowledge thread repository that depicts the relationships corresponding to specific context instances.

ARTIFICIALLY INTELLIGENT SYSTEM MEMORY MANAGEMENT
SENSORY MEMORIES

The sensory memory within the AIS memory system is memory registers in which raw, unprocessed information is ingested via AIS environmental sensors and is buffered to begin initial processing. The AIS sensory memory system has a large capacity to accommodate large quantities of possibly disparate and diverse information from a variety of sources (Crowder, 2010b). Although it has large capacity, it has short duration. The information buffered in this sensory memory must be sorted, categorized, and turned into information fragments, metadata, contextual threads, and attributes (including emotional attributes), and then sent on to the working memory (short-term memory (STM)) for initial cognitive processing. This cognitive processing is known as recombinant knowledge assimilation (RNA), in which raw infor-mation content is discovered from the information domain and is decomposed, reduced, compared, contrasted, and associated into new relationship threads within a temporary working knowledge domain and subsequently normalized into a pedigree within the knowledge domain for future use (Crowder and Carbone, 2011b). Hence, based on the information gathered in initial sensory memory processing, cog-nitive perceptrons, manifested as intelligence information software agents (ISAs), are spawned as in relative size swarms to create initial "thoughts" about the data. Subsequently, hypotheses are generated by the ISAs. The thought process information and ISA sensory information is then sent to a working memory region that will alert the artificial cognition processes within the AIS to begin processing (Crowder and Friess, 2012) Figure 14.1 illustrates the sensory memory lower ontology.

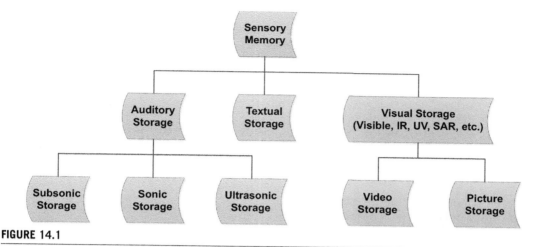

FIGURE 14.1

Sensory memory lower ontology.

SHORT-TERM ARTIFICIAL MEMORIES

Short-term or working memory within the AIS is where new information is transitionally stored in a temporary knowledge domain (Crowder and Carbone, 2011a) while it is processed into new knowledge. This follows the paradigm that information content has no value until it is thought about (Brillouin, 2004). Short-term memory is where most reasoning within the AIS happens. Short-term memory provides a major functionality called rehearsals, which allows the AIS to continually refresh or rehearse STMs while they are being processed and reasoned about, so that memories do not degrade until they can be sent on to long-term memory (LTM) and acted upon by the artificial consciousness processes within the AIS's cognitive framework (Crowder and Carbone, 2011a).

Short-term memory is much smaller in relative space compared with LTM. Short-term memory should not necessarily be perceived as a physical location, as in the human brain, but rather as the rapid and continuous processing of information content relative to a specific AIS directive or current undertaking. One must remember that STM, which includes all external and internal sensory inputs, will trigger a rehearsal if the AIS discovers a relationship to a previously interred piece of information content in either STM or LTM. Figure 14.2 illustrates the STM lower ontology for the AIS.

LONG-TERM ARTIFICIAL MEMORIES

In the simplest sense, LTM is the permanent knowledge domain where we assimilate our memories (Crowder and Carbone, 2011a). If the information we take in through our senses does not make it to LTM, we cannot and do not remember it. Information that is processed in the STM makes it to LTM through the process of rehearsal, processing, and encoding, and then by creating associations with other memories. In the brain, memories are not stored in files or in a database. In fact, memories are not stored whole at all, but instead are stored as information fragments. The process of recall, or remembering, constructs memories from these information fragments that, depending on the type of information, are stored in various regions of the brain.

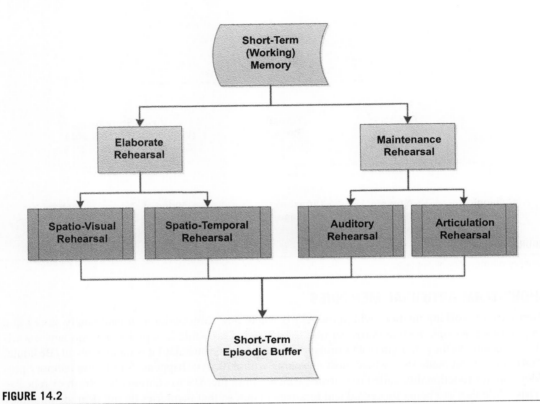

FIGURE 14.2

Artificially intelligent system short-term memory (STM) lower ontology.

To create our AIS in a way that mimics human reasoning, we follow the process of storing information fragments and their respective encoding in different ways, depending on the type and context of the information. Each simple discrete fragment of objective knowledge includes an n-dimensional set of quantum mechanics–based mathematical relationships to other fragments/objects bundled in the form of eigenvector-optimized knowledge relativity threads (KRT) (Crowder and Carbone, 2011a). These KRT bundles include closeness and relative importance value, among others. This importance is tightly coupled to the AIS emotional storage as a function of desire or need, as described in Figure 14.3, in which the LTM lower ontology is illustrated. There are three main types of LTM (Crowder, 2010a): explicit or declarative memories, implicit memories, and emotional memories.

ARTIFICIAL MEMORY PROCESSING AND ENCODING
SHORT-TERM ARTIFICIAL MEMORY PROCESSING

In the human brain, STM corresponds to the area of memory associated with active consciousness and is where most cognitive processing takes place. It is also a temporary storage and requires rehearsal to keep it fresh until it is compiled into LTM. In the AIS, the memory system does not decay over time; however, the notion of memory refresh or rehearsal is still a valid concept because artificial

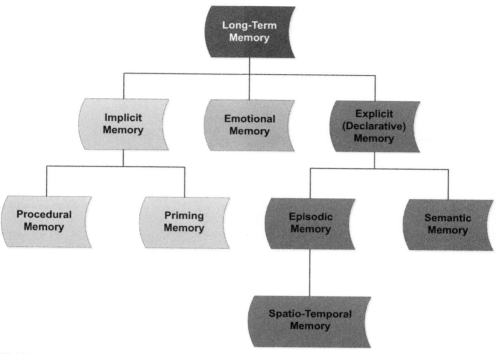

FIGURE 14.3

Artificial long-term memory (LTM) lower ontology.

cognitive processes work on this information. However, the notion of rehearsal means keeping track of versions of STM as it is being processed and evaluated by artificial cognition algorithms, which is why it appears to feed back onto itself (rehearsal loop). This is illustrated in Figure 14.4, the AIS STM attention loop. Three distinct processes are handled within the STM that determine where information is transferred after cognitive processing (Crowder, 2010a). This processing is shown in Figure 14.5.

Artificial STM processing steps are:

- *Information fragment selection*: This process involves filtering incoming information from the AIS artificial preconscious buffers into separable information fragments and then determining which information fragments are relevant to be further processed, stored, and acted upon by the cognitive processes of the AIS as a whole. Once information fragments are created from incoming sensory information, they are analyzed and encoded with initial topical information as well as metadata attributes that allow the cognitive processes to organize and integrate incoming information fragments into the AIS's overall LTM system. Information Fragment encoding creates a small information fragment cognitive map that will be used for organization and integration functions.
- *Information fragment organization*: These processes within the artificial cognition framework create additional attributes within the information fragment cognitive map that allow it to be organized for integration into the overall AIS LTM framework. These attributes have to do with how the information will be represented in LTM and determine how these memory fragments will be used to

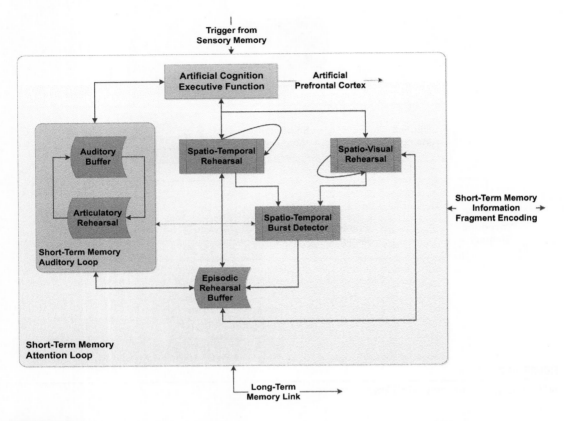

FIGURE 14.4

Short-term artificial memory attention loop.

construct new memories or recall memories later as needed by the AIS. This step uses Knowledge Relativity Thread (KRT) representation to capture the context of the information fragment and each of its qualitative relationships to other fragments and/or bundles of fragments already created.

- *Information fragment integration*: Once information fragments within the STM have been KRT encoded, they are compared, associated, and attached to larger topical cognitive maps that represent relevant subjects or topics within the AIS's LTM system. Once these information fragment cognitive maps have been integrated, processed, and reasoned about, including emotional triggers or emotional memory information, they are sent on to the LTM system as well as the AIS artificial prefrontal cortex to determine whether actions are required.

One of the major functions within the STM attention loop is the spatiotemporal burst detector. Within these processes, binary information fragments (BIFs) are ordered in terms of their spatial and temporal characteristics. Spatial[1] and temporal transitions states are measured in terms of mean, mode,

---

[1] Spatial in this context can refer to geographic locations (either two- or three-dimensional), cyber-locations, or other characteristics that may be considered spatial references or characteristics.

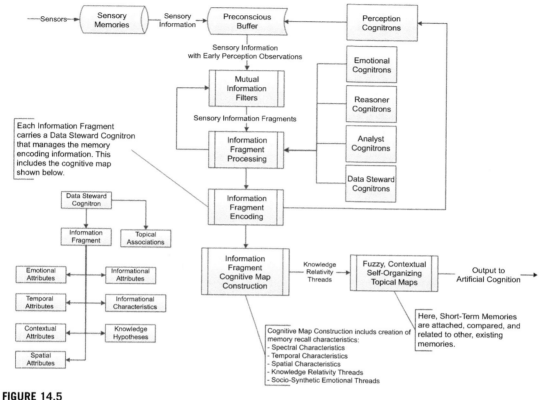

FIGURE 14.5

Artificially intelligent systems information fragment encoding.

median, velocity, and acceleration and are correlated between their spatial and temporal characteristics and measurements. Rather than just looking at frequencies of occurrence within information, we also look for rapid increases in temporal or spatial characteristics that may trigger an inference or emotional response from the cognitive processes.

An AIS system does not process information content differently based on how rapidly content is ingested; an AIS must be able to recognize instances when information content might seem out of place within the context of a situation (e.g., a single speeding car within a crowd of hundreds of other cars). An AIS not only optimizes its processing on the supply side of the knowledge economy, it has to recognize, infer, and avoid distractions on what focuses the demand side of its knowledge economy upon operations and directives. State transition bursts are ranked according to their weighting (velocity and acceleration) together with the associated temporal and/or spatial characteristics and any triggers that might have resulted from this burst processing (LaBar and Cabeza, 2006). This burst detection and processing may help identify relevant topics, concepts, or inferences that may need further processing by the artificial prefrontal cortex and/or cognitive consciousness processes (Crowder and Friess, 2012).

Once processing within the STM system has been completed and all memories are encoded, mapped to topical associations and with their contexts captured, their KRT bundled representations are created and sent on to the cognitive processing engine. Memories that are deemed relevant to remember are then integrated into the LTM system.

LONG-TERM ARTIFICIAL MEMORY PROCESSING

The overall AIS high-level memory architecture is shown in Figure 14.6. One thing to note is the connection between emotional memories and both explicit and implicit memories. Emotional memory carries both explicit and implicit characteristics.

Explicit or declarative memory is used to store conscious memories or conscious thoughts. Explicit memory carries information fragments that are used to create what most people would think of when

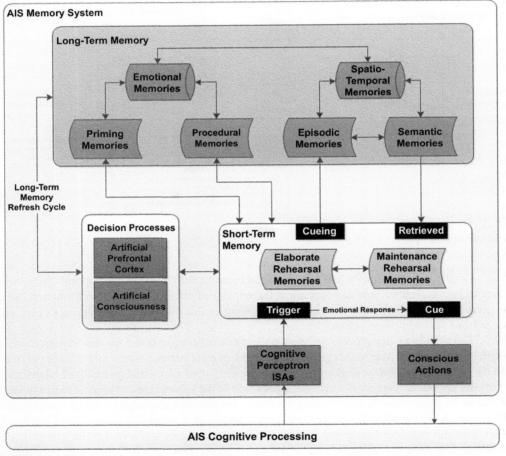

FIGURE 14.6

High-level artificial memory architecture.

they envision a memory. Explicit memory stores things such as objects and events, i.e., things that are experienced in the person's environment. Information fragments stored in explicit memory are normally stored in association with other information fragments that relate in some fashion. The more meaningful the association, the stronger the memory and the easier it is to reconstruct or recall the memory when you choose to (Yang and Raine, 2009). In our AIS, explicit memory is divided into different regions, depending on the type or source of information. Regions are divided because different types of information fragments within the AIS memories are encoded and represented differently, each with their own characteristics, which makes it easier to construct or recall the memories, when the AIS later needs the memories. In the AIS LTM, we use fuzzy, self-organizing, contextual topical maps to associate currently processed information fragments from the STM with memories stored in the LTM (Crowder and Carbone, 2011a).

Long-term memory information fragments are not stored in databases or as files, but are encoded and stored as a triple helix of continuously recombinant binary neural fiber threads that represent:

- The BIF object along with the BIF binary attribute objects
- The BIF RNA binary relativity objects
- The binary security encryption threads

Built into the RNA binary relativity objects are binary memory reconstruction objects, based on the type and source of BIF, that allow memories to be constructed for recall purposes.

There are several types of binary memory reconstruction objects:

- Spectral eigenvectors that allow memory reconstruction using implicit and biographical LTM BIFs
- Polynomial eigenvectors that allow memory reconstruction using episodic LTM BIFs
- Socio-synthetic autonomic nervous system arousal state vectors that allow memory reconstruction using emotional LTM BIFs
- Temporal confluence and spatial resonance coefficients that allow memory reconstruction using spatiotemporal episodic LTM BIFs
- Knowledge relativity and contextual gravitation coefficients that allow memory reconstruction using semantic LTM BIFs

IMPLICIT BIOGRAPHICAL MEMORY RECALL/RECONSTRUCTION USING SPECTRAL DECOMPOSITION MAPPING

We create a nonuniform expanding fractal decomposition of the image to be remembered. We use the right and left eigenvectors of the Pollicott–Ruelle resonances to determine the separable pictorial information fragment (PIF) objects. The resulting singular fractal functions form fractal spectral representations of the PIFs. These binary fractal representations are stored as the binary information fragments for the image. The reconstruction uses these PIFs to create a piecewise linear image memory reconstruction, although the individual PIFs can be used in other memory and cognitive processes, such as to perform pattern matching and/or pattern discovery. The proposed high-level architecture for the ISA cognition and memory system is illustrated in Figure 14.7.

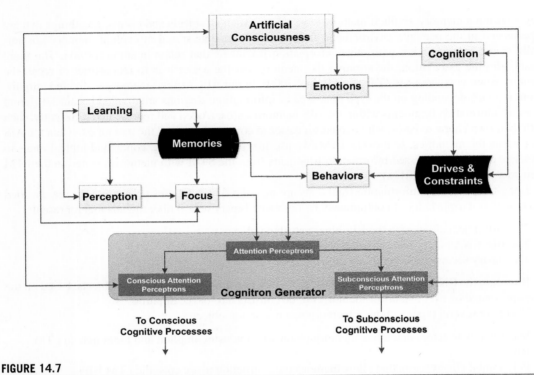

FIGURE 14.7

Artificially intelligent system high-level cognitive architecture.

CONSTRUCTIVIST LEARNING

A major issue in Big Data is the need to learn continually as more information and knowledge is gained as the volume of processed data increases. This leads us to look at constructivist learning as a construct for Big Data processing. In the view of constructivists, learning is a constructive process in which the learner builds an internal illustration of knowledge, a personal interpretation of experience. This representation is continually open to modification—its structure and linkages forming the ground to which other knowledge structures are attached. Learning is an active process in which meaning is accomplished on the basis of experience. This view of knowledge does not reject the existence of the real world and agrees that reality places constraints on what is possible; contending that all we know of the real world are the human interpretations of their experiences. Conceptual growth comes from the sharing of various perspectives and the simultaneous changing of our internal representations in response to those perspectives as well as through cumulative experience (Bednar et al., 1998).

When considering Big Data in light of an AIS, we have to ask ourselves, "What is reality?" Here we take our queue about humans. Each person has experiences of an event. Each person will see reality differently and uniquely. There is also world reality. This world reality may be based on fact or perception of fact. In fact, we construct our view of the world, of reality, from our memories, our experiences. For further thought, let us then consider construct psychology. According to the *Internet Encyclopedia of Personal Construct Psychology*, the constructivist philosophy is interested more in people's construction of the world than they are in evaluating the extent to which such constructions are true in representing a presumable external reality. It makes sense to look at this in the form of legitimacies. What is true is factual legitimate, and what is people's construction of the external reality is another form of legitimacy. Later, we can consider the locus of control in relation to internal and external legitimacies or realities.

An AIS is not human and does not have human perceptions. Artificially cognitive systems may have their own perceptions and realities, and it is important that the cognitive systems and memories have the abilities to construct correct views of the world around it, if we are to rely on them. Thus, a mentor will be necessary. That mentor will need to understand the artificial cognitive system, the AIS, and be able to understand the AIS in a human way, a human reality. After all, is this not this what makes the AIS autonomous?

Constructive psychology is a meta-theory that integrates different schools of thought. According to Bednar (Bednar et al., 1998):

Hans Vaihinger (1852–1933) asserted that people develop "workable fictions." This is his philosophy of "As if" such as mathematical infinity or God. Alfred Korzybski's (1879–1950) system of semantics focused on the role of the speaker in assigning meaning to events. Thus constructivists thought that human beings operated on the basis of symbolic or linguistic constructs that help navigate the world without contacting it in any simple or direct way. Postmodern thinkers assert that constructions are viable to the extent that they help us live our lives meaningfully and find validation in shared understandings of others. We live in a world constituted by multiple social realities, no one of which can claim to be "objectively" true across persons, cultures, or historical epochs. Instead, the constructions on the basis of which we live are at best provisional ways of organizing our "selves" and our activities, which could under other circumstances be constituted quite differently.

According to *Adlerian Therapy as a Relational Constructivist Approach*, the Adlerian perspective affirms the emphasis on the importance of humans as active agents creatively involved in the construction of their own psychology. Here, the position is that "although humans exist in a socio-cultural world of persons, a distinguishing characteristic of personhood is the possession of an individual agentic consciousness." The article goes on to say, "If there is no self-reflexive individual and situatedness is indeed inescapable, then it is a spurious notion to think we can engage in what can be called the 'emancipator potential of discourse analysis, that is inquiry which causes us to reflect critically and creatively on our own forms of life.'" Also, Adlerian therapy accounts for both the social-embedded nature of human knowledge and the personal agency of creative and self-reflective individuals within relationships.

According to *Personal Construct Psychology, Constructivism, and Postmodern Thought* (Luis Botella at http://www.massey.ac.nz/-alock/virtual/Construc.htm), there are three main areas to consider: psychological knowledge, psychological practice, and psychological research. First, we consider psychological knowledge. In his article, Mahoney (2003) said: "knowledge cannot be disentangled from the process of knowing, and all human knowing is based in value-generated processes" (p. 451). Next we consider psychological research. In postmodern terms, research is not viewed as a mapping of some objective reality, but as an interactive co-construction of the subject investigated (Kvale, 1992). This conversational and interpretive view of psychological research requires a multi-method approach, fostering the use of hermeneutic, phenomenological, and narrative methodologies.

For the Big Data concerns of AIS in terms of constructivist learning, the AI cognitive learning process is a building (or construction) process in which the AI's cognitive system builds an internal illustration of knowledge based on its experiences and personal interpretation (fuzzy inferences) of experience. The knowledge representation and KRTs within the cognitive system's memories are continually open to modification and the structure and linkages formed within the AI's STM, LTM, and emotional memories, along with the contextual KRTs, form the bases for which knowledge structures are created and attached to the BIF. Learning becomes an active process in which meaning is accomplished through experience, combining structural knowledge (knowledge provided in the beginning) with constructivist knowledge to provide the AIS' view of the real world around it. Conceptual growth within the autonomous AIS would come from collaboration among all AIS ISAs within the system, sharing their experiences and inferences—the total of which creates changing interpretations of their environment through their collective, cumulative experiences.

Therefore, one result of the constructivist learning process within the AIS is to gradually change the locus of control from external (the system needing external input to make sense or infer about its environment) to internal (the system has a cumulative constructive knowledge base of information, knowledge, context, and inferences to handle a given situation internally, meaning it is able to make relevant and meaningful decisions and inferences about a situation without outside knowledge or involvement).

It might be possible to pose specific goals for the AIS to cause it to construct knowledge about a subject or situation incrementally as data are added, to aid in its learning process as the system evolves. It may be possible to provide a real-world context for the AIS, giving it the cognitive knowledge to understand whether its locus of control should be internal or external, and when it can make that shift in its understanding.

ADAPTATION OF CONSTRUCTIVIST LEARNING CONCEPTS FOR BIG DATA IN AN AIS

- Learning to strengthen knowledge (gain a better understanding of things, topics, etc. that have been learned)
  - *Role of learning management systems*: Administering learning goals and constraints
  - *Role of learning algorithms*: Measures of effectiveness against goals and constraints
    - Uses hypothesis testing from hypotheses generated by knowledge acquisition learning system
  - *Function of learning in this role*: Increase in stimulus–response feedback for this strengthened knowledge within the cognitive conceptual ontology
  - *Focus*: Addition of behaviors/information to current memories; addition of contextual threads to current memories; addition of emotional memory triggers; addition of procedural memories
- Learning to acquire knowledge (understanding new information, new topics, etc. that have not been previously experienced or learned)
  - *Role of learning management system*: Present new information/concepts to be learned from sensor information correlated with current conceptual ontology
  - *Role of learning algorithms*: Receive and process information to form new concept(s) that must be included in conceptual ontology (Occam learning algorithms)
  - *Function of learning in this role*: Create new concepts, find fundamental concept that can be learned about this new information, and generate hypotheses about concept for knowledge strengthening learning system to use when new information is available.
  - *Focus*: Creation of procedural memories; creation of initial information fragments

- Learning to construct knowledge (create a knowledge representation in our memories; create meaningful connections between knowledge)
  - *Role of learning management system*: Cognitive guidance and modeling; deconstruct information into manageable information fragments, correlation (integration) into current memory fragment structure; encoding of memory fragments, based on RNA threads and information encoding schemas
  - *Role of learning algorithms*: Reasoning and analysis of data to determine stimulus/response to goals and constraints; making sense of information and constructing knowledge representations
  - *Functions of learning in this role*: Create meaningful information fragment representations and contextual threads that allow assimilation into LTMs; memory organization and integration
  - *Focus*: Constructivist learning (active learning) using a variety of cognitive processes (reasoner and analyst agents) during the learning process; construction of emotional contexts

PRACTICAL SOLUTIONS FOR SECURE KNOWLEDGE DEVELOPMENT IN BIG DATA ENVIRONMENTS

As expressed previously, constructing qualitative knowledge is a function of meaningful information content management and the ability of the system to develop high-fidelity weighted n-dimensional value within Big Data storage environments of systems. The practical reality of system solutions is that they must be (S)ecure, they must have the ability to manage the natural (M)alleability of information content, they must be able to (S)ynthesize that content and understand the patterns and store the contextual pedigree (H)euristics (e.g., state, time, form) over locally or geographically distributed nodes. Hence, SMSHy Information Content Management requires practical solutions.

Practical system security for Big Data is made adaptable through the use of discrete obfuscation (DO) enabling data to secure itself by separating information content and knowledge context. A Big Data system is made malleable by implementing a framework to optimize knowledge structures representing the ever-changing situational understanding. They are organized to allow for synthesis or rapid capture of new knowledge, context, and relationships. Finally, a practical Big Data system must have scalable rules that define the ingest, analysis, and storage functions required to retain system pedigree, so that it might heal itself: a practical function most systems do not have and could not perform even if they wanted to.

PRACTICAL BIG DATA SECURITY SOLUTIONS

Practical Big Data security is created with the simple understanding of knowledge and context. Understanding through observation is a natural humanistic trait that has been studied for decades. This process of learning is relatively simple in nature. We observe and discover, decompose, and reduce the information to something we believe we can understand. We understand by comparing, contrasting, associating, and normalizing the content we ingest, and then we store it as a memory as described above. This storage might be a procedure, such as how to open a door or pour a glass of water, or more complex, such as how to drive a car. To develop a system to perform practical applications, it must perform similar humanistic tasks (see Chapters 1 and 10).

The information environment a system sees is defined as information artifacts and knowledge. An information artifact is any information perceived or observed but not yet understood. Knowledge components are relationships created between any two or more pieces of information that have crossed a relative importance threshold to become established as something important enough to remember within the mind of the stakeholder. The information has become important enough, or has matured enough, for a stakeholder/system to acknowledge the need for retention, along with the associated characteristics of the relationship. Knowledge relativity threads (Crowder and Carbone, 2011a), as discussed earlier, can be applied to any domain in which enabling the n-dimensional weighted relationship creation of knowledge is of interest (see Figure 14.8). The multi-step process is similar to how humans assemble knowledge over time, for example, using a search engine, constantly refining our learning.

Thus, if KRTs can give us context, cutting threads would remove context and not allow someone or a system to understand. Hence, decomposition supports security because it is the act of slicing the contextual bonds of a relationship between two information artifacts, or what we denote as DO. For example, a document can be sliced into paragraphs, paragraphs can be sliced into sentences, sentences can be sliced up into words, and words can be sliced into characters. A digital picture can be sliced into objects within the picture, the objects within the picture can be sliced into pixels, and the pixels can be sliced into numerical values.

We must also understand the concept of knowledge component contribution; each knowledge component is a function of its subcomponents, each knowledge component has independent value, and each subcomponent contributes to the overall value of the context of its parent; hence, understanding equals

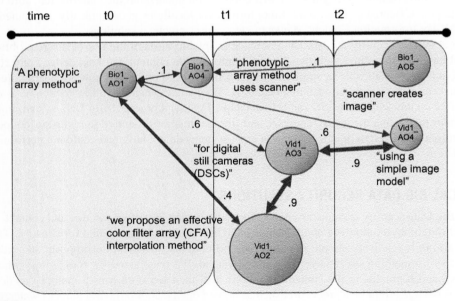

FIGURE 14.8

Knowledge relativity threads.

the amount of knowledge and context acquired. Knowledge and context are generally mission/activity focused and created/aggregated as, for example, folders, files, pictures, or databases. Hence, the more an attacker sees, knows, or learns about you, your mission, or your system, this will obviously increase your vulnerability. Therefore, a secure system will separate the knowledge from the context, such that the more separation or anonymity is created, the less understanding an attacker has and less damage can be achieved. Finally, a system can become more secure if you comprehend that understanding content can be just a matter of time. Time is not necessarily your enemy. It can be your best friend because information content and learned knowledge many times have an expiration date. Therefore, perform assessments against your system and its proposed uses and always inject time into the equation to determine whether content is valuable enough to be retained and for how long it needs to be secured. Copyrights and patents can expire; so can your data.

OPTIMIZATION OF SOCIOPOLITICAL-ECONOMIC SYSTEMS AND SENTIMENT ANALYSIS

Sociopolitical and economic systems are characterized by many interconnecting parts. Non-technical systems are often difficult to understand because of natural ambiguities, many unclear dependencies, and inabilities to agree on actual problems and effective solutions. Hence, much understanding is usually superficial, when what is needed to generate compelling solutions is real analysis to minimize what is open for interpretation.

Economics and related cycles are generally well-known phenomena. As new technologies periodically drive the marketplace, various time-dependent combinatorial complexities are at work (Suh, 2005). However, analysis of current sentiment is usually after the fact, essentially counting how much has been purchased within a given period of time and using that information as a predictor for the following year; hence, it is not an exact science. To achieve a credible level of predictability, we require greater fidelity of understanding of the complexities, dependencies and sentiment. Knowledge relativity threads can provide the tool to represent these complexities in many dimensions under the covers of systems. n-Dimensional capture and collection of large content are also facilitated by parallel coordinates (Inselberg and Dimsdale, 1991) that can rapidly be presented into human understanding in the second or third dimension. Remember that the presentation of n-dimensional relationships traditionally breaks down quickly at dimension 3 or 4. Figure 14.8 presents a time segment of the complexities of knowledge context creation for a concept in biology known as phenotypic arrays. The two-dimensional shapes depicted show the growth over time of the weighted relationships captured throughout the learning process, in which shape sizes, line length/closeness, and location all give context to learned perceptions of the biology article in question.

If one applies RNA processes depicted in Figure 14.8 (e.g., discovery, decomposition) to sentiment analysis, the output derived is a weighted contribution of elements, a kind of volumetric representing the corpus of what has been learned as a pictorial analogy to chemistry, a molecule of knowledge. Sentiment analysis is a growing field of analytics in the Big Data world, but it has been part of economic growth measures for many years (see Chapters 2 and 9).

A subcategory and higher specialization of sentiment analytics is the analysis of facial expressions to determine human a priori and real-time sentiment relative to a given situation. Imagine that you can combine multiple data points such as voice, breathing, heart rate, and perspiration with facial recognition. The result could be much higher resolution of prediction. A Transportation Security

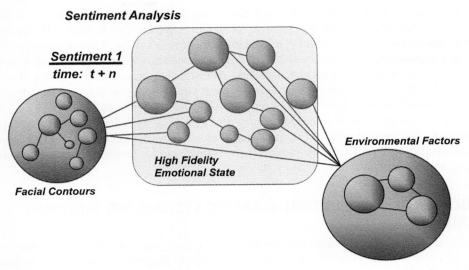

FIGURE 14.9

Sentiment analysis using knowledge relativity threads.

Administration representative at an airport could benefit greatly from understanding the real-time disposition of passengers. How do we model these dependencies to achieve a compelling level of predictability and weed out false detections? Using RNA, the growth of any knowledge molecule contains the full corpus of all perceptions and their weighted importance over time. Hence, at given time t to $t + n$, relationships are added, modified, and deleted. Figure 14.9 depicts a sample RNA graphic showing the kinds of information an evolving sentiment analysis KRT could hold as a human or a system begins to sift through facial contours or external environmental factors content to come to a knowledge density conclusion surrounding the emotional state of a given individual relative to Sentiment 1. The system should be continuously evolving through various parallel hypotheses, across many possible sentiments forming a more or less dense context and ultimately, an understanding its environment.

CONCLUSIONS

We believe the framework presented in this chapter provides an AI architecture and methodology that will allow autonomous operations. The use of the ISA architecture, combined with the cognitive structures described here, have the potential to radically change and enhance autonomous systems in the future. More work is needed to refine the agent technologies and learning sets, but we feel this has much potential.

We described memory processing and encoding methodologies to provide AIS with memory architectures, processing, storage, and retrieval constructs similar to human memories. We believe these are necessary to provide artificial cognitive structures that can truly learn, reason, think, and communicate similar to humans. There is much work to do, and our current research will provide the software processing infrastructure for the ISAs necessary to create the underlying cognitive processing required for this artificial neural memory system, overlaid onto Big Data infrastructure to implement security at levels of understanding with significantly higher levels of fidelity to match growing asymmetric threats.

REFERENCES

Bednar, A., Cunningham, D., Duffy, T., Perry, J., 1998. Theory into practice: how do we link? In: M Duffy, T., Jonassen, D.H. (Eds.), Constructivism and Technology of Instruction: A Conversation. Lawrence Erlbaum Associates, Hillsdale, NJ, pp. 17–35.

Botella, L., Personal Construct Psychology, Constructivism, and Postmodern Thought. Found at: http://www.massey.ac.nz/(aboutsign)alock/virtual/Construc.htm.

Brillouin, L., 2004. Science and Information Theory. Dover.

Crowder, J.A., 1996. X33/RLV Autonomous Reusable Launch System Architecture. NASA Report 96-RLF-1.4.5.5-005. Lockheed Martin, Littleton, CO.

Crowder, J.A., 2010a. The continuously recombinant genetic, neural fiber network. In: Proceedings of the AIAA Infotech@Aerospace-2010, Atlanta, GA.

Crowder, J.A., 2010b. Flexible object architectures for hybrid neural processing systems. In: Proceedings of the 11th International Conference on Artificial Intelligence, Las Vegas, NV.

Crowder, J.A., Carbone, J., 2011a. Recombinant knowledge relativity threads for contextual knowledge storage. In: Proceedings of the 12th International Conference on Artificial Intelligence, Las Vegas, NV.

Crowder, J.A., Carbone, J., 2011b. Transdisciplinary synthesis and cognition frameworks. In: Proceedings of the Society for Design and Process Science Conference 2011, Jeju Island, South Korea.

Crowder, J., Carbone, J., 2012. Reasoning Frameworks for Autonomous Systems. In: Proceedings of the AIAA Infotech@Aerospace 2012 Conference, Garden Grove, CA.

Crowder, J., Friess, S., 2012. Artificial psychology: the psychology of AI. In: Proceedings of the 3rd International Multi-conference on Complexity, Informatics, and Cybernetics, Orlando, FL.

Crowder, J., Raskin, V., Taylor, J., 2012. Autonomous creation and detection of procedural memory scripts. In: Proceedings of the 13th Annual International Conference on Artificial Intelligence, Las Vegas, NV.

Coutaz, J., Crowley, J., Dobson, S., Garlan, D., 2005. Context is key. Communications of the ACM 48, 53.

Dourish, P., 2004a. Where the Action Is: The Foundations of Embodied Interaction. The MIT Press.

Dourish, P., 2004b. What we talk about when we talk about context. Personal and Ubiquitous Computing 8, 19–30.

Dey, A., 2001. Understanding and using context. Personal and Ubiquitous Computing 5, 4–7.

Ejigu, D., Scuturici, M., Brunie, L., 2008. Hybrid approach to collaborative context-aware service platform for pervasive computing. Journal of Computers. 3, 40.

Hong, J., Landay, J., 2001. An infrastructure approach to context-aware computing. Human–Computer Interaction 16, 287–303.

Howard, N., Qusaibaty, A., 2004. Network-centric information policy. In: Proceedings of the Second International Conference on Informatics and Systems.

Inselberg, A., Dimsdale, B., 1991. "Parallel Coordinates." Human-Machine Interactive Systems. Springer, US. 199–233.

Kvale, S., 1992. Psychology and Postmodernism. Sage Publications, Thousand Oaks, CA.

LaBar, K., Cabeza. 2006. Cognitive neuroscience of emotional memory. Nat. Rev. Neurosci. 7, 54–64.

Mahoney, M., 2003. Constructive Psychotherapy: A Practical Guide. The Guilford Press, New York, NY.

Suh, N.P., 2005. Complexity Theory and Applications. Oxford University Press.

Torralba, A., 2003. Contextual priming for object detection. International Journal of Computer Vision 53, 169–191.

Winograd, T., 2001. Architectures for context. Human–Computer Interaction 16, 401–419.

Yang, Y., Raine, A., November 2009. Prefrontal structural and functional brain imaging findings in antisocial, violent, and psychopathic individuals: a meta-analysis. Psychiatry Res 174 (2), 81–8. http://dx.doi.org/10.1016/j.pscychresns.2009.03.012. PMID 19833485.

LEGAL AND SOCIAL CHALLENGES

THE LEGAL CHALLENGES OF BIG DATA APPLICATION IN LAW ENFORCEMENT

15

Fraser Sampson

INTRODUCTION

Big Data "calls for momentous choices to be made between weighty policy concerns" (Polonetsky and Tene, 2013). The weighty policy concerns also have to weigh in the balance the most efficient and effective use of available resources with the fundamental rights and freedoms of individuals. One of the weightiest policy concerns is that of law enforcement. The setting of law enforcement raises several dilemmas for Big Data; because Big Data represents such an expansive, dynamic, and complex subject, this chapter is necessarily selective and succinct.

In the opinion of the European Union Data Protection Working Party,[1] "Big Data" refers to exponential growth in both the availability and the automated use of information. Big Data refers to "gigantic digital datasets held by corporations, governments and other large organisations, which are then extensively analysed using computer algorithms."

ATTRACTIONS OF BIG DATA

One of the principal attractions—if not *the* principal attraction—of Big Data is its enabling of analytics, the almost limitless power that attends the super-synthesis of information.

Offering what perhaps are the obverse attractions of nano-technology, Big Data's giga-analytics can produce macro-level pictures of trends, pathways, and patterns that might reveal pictures hitherto unseen even by the data owners. Such tele-analytics allow not only a better understanding of what may be happening here and now, but a reliable basis for predictions of what is to come.

Aside from the obvious attraction for commercial suppliers trying to understand, predict, and influence consumer behavior, Big Data analytics also holds out a phenomenological capability for law enforcement agencies in trying to understand, predict, and influence behaviors of offenders and potential offenders.

As Professor Akghar from CENTRIC[2] puts it, "When we look at ways to advance the use of data and analytics for public security and safety, the potential has never been greater. We now have the computing power to not only understand past events, but also to create new knowledge from billions of data points—quickly. In minutes, we can run analyses that used to take days" (Akhgar, 2014).

---

[1] Article 29 Data Protection Working Party 00,569/13/EN WP 203 Opinion 03/13, p. 35.
[2] The Centre for Excellence in Terrorism, Resilience, Intelligence and Organised Crime Research at Sheffield Hallam University, UK.

DILEMMAS OF BIG DATA

With so much data so readily available, one might ask on what basis would law enforcement agencies (LEAs) not seize it and run with it as far and as fast as possible, if doing so meant preventing terrorist attacks, disrupting serious organized crime, or preventing wide-scale child sexual exploitation, human trafficking, and so forth?

Take, for example, successful work in Greater Manchester [3] that has shown the power of having a range of agencies literally in the same room. Why not have the totality of their data virtually present in the same place, too? Because Big Data can be applied to mass datasets to reveal high-level trends and patterns, it might be thought that the extent to which it can assist in preventing and detecting criminality is limited. Not necessarily. As the Article 29 Working Party[4] noted, not only can the awesome capability offered by Big Data be used to identify general trends and macro-correlations, it can also be processed—rapidly and almost effortlessly—to directly affect the individual.[5]

From a practical operation perspective, then, there is a vast potential for Big Data in law enforcement. From a legal perspective, the point at which Big Data focuses this astonishing power on individuality can become highly contentious. One such point is where it is used for law enforcement, whether that is in the context of criminological extrapolation or criminal suspect extradition.

The challenging question from a pragmatic law enforcement perspective is: If information is lawfully held within the databases of willing and socially responsible organizations that might help prevent people becoming victims of crime or bring perpetrators to justice, why would LEAs not only feel justified in accessing those data but obliged to do so?

Part of the answer is that the application of informatics within a law enforcement environment is arguably different from that of Big Data application in most other settings. There are several strands to the answer, first among which is the high level of legal regulation of this area. Yes, there are substantial and significant exceptions within most legal data frameworks to allow access by LEAs to data held by others, particularly when their principal purpose is to prevent or investigate crime or pursue the interests of national security, but they are not always that clear and seldom amount to a blank check. Before looking more closely at some of the components of the law enforcement dilemma, it is necessary to look at the broad components of the legal framework within which the pragmatic law enforcement activity takes place.

LEGAL FRAMEWORK

The legal framework regulating the Big Data challenges for law enforcement in the United Kingdom (UK) is dominated by that throughout all European Union (EU) member states. Primary law components (but by no means all) of that framework are to found in:

- The European Convention on Human Rights
- The European Charter of Fundamental Rights
- EU Data Protection Directive 95/46–8

---

[3] See "Greater Manchester against crime: A complete system for partnership working," available at: https://www.ucl.ac.uk/jdi/events/mapping-conf/conf-2005/conf2005-downloads/dave-flitcroft.pdf.

[4] This Working Party is made up of EU member state national data protection authorities and is an independent advisory body on data protection and privacy. Established under Article 29 of the Data Protection Directive (95/46/EC), its role is to contribute to the uniform application of the Directive across member states.

[5] Data Protection Working Party loc. cit.

- The Council of Europe Convention 108[6]—providing the main point of reference for the directive applying to data protection in policing and criminal justice
- The Data Protection Act 1998 (based on the central principles of the Directive)
- The Freedom of Information Act 2000, which created rights of access to information, superseding the Code of Practice on Access to Government Information and amending the Data Protection Act 1998 and the Public Records Act 1958
- The Protection of Freedoms Act 2012, a very wide-ranging act making provision with respect to the retention and destruction of fingerprints, footwear impressions, and DNA samples and profiles taken in the course of a criminal investigation; requirements of schools and further education colleges to obtain the consent of parents of children under 18 years of age attending the school or college before the school or college can process a child's biometric information; the further regulation of closed circuit television, automatic number plate recognition, and other surveillance camera technology operated by the police and local authorities; the need for judicial approval before local authorities can use certain data-gathering techniques; data provision with respect to parking enforcement and counter-terrorism powers.

These are supported, extended, and elaborated upon in various other instruments too numerous to list here[7] (for a guide, see Bignami, 2007; Holzacker and Luif, 2013).

Article 13 of the EU Directive provides that "member states may adopt legislative measures to restrict the scope of the obligations and rights provided for in Article 6 (1)…when such a restriction constitutes a necessary measure to safeguard…national security; defence; public security; the prevention, investigation, detection and prosecution of criminal offences." However, a qualified test must be applied to any restriction to ensure that the legislative measure meets the criteria that allow derogating from a fundamental right. There are two limbs to this test: First, the measure must be sufficiently clear and precise to be foreseeable; second, it must be necessary and proportionate, consistent with the requirements developed by the European Court of Human Rights.

HUMAN RIGHTS

Much of the legislation and jurisprudence relating to data protection across the EU derive from human rights and fundamental freedoms. Clearly, there is not the space here to review the legal and political provenance of this subject. However, it is worth pausing at this stage to note and distinguish the two "distinct but related systems to ensure the protection of fundamental and human rights in Europe" (Kokott and Sobotta, 2013). The first, the European Convention on Human Rights, is probably known and understood by law enforcement personnel in the UK better than the second. The Convention is an international agreement between the States of the Council of Europe of which all member states are part, as are external states such as Switzerland, Russia, and Turkey. Matters engaging the Convention are ultimately justiciable in the European Court of Human Rights, which has jurisdiction over actions brought by individuals against member states for alleged breaches of human rights, and a substantial body of jurisprudence has been built up around this area.

---

[6] Convention for the Protection of Individuals with Regard to Automatic Processing of Personal Data, Council of Europe Treaties 108 (01/1981).

[7] See also, for example, Framework Decision 2008/977/JHA for the protection of personal data processed in the framework of police and judicial cooperation in criminal matters (Data Protection Framework Decision) and the Council Decision 2008/615/JHA of June 23, 2008 on the stepping up of cross-border cooperation, particularly in combating terrorism and cross-border crime (the Prum Decision).

The second, less familiar system arises from the jurisprudence of the Court of Justice of the European Union (ECJ), which guarantees the protection of fundamental human rights within the EU. Respect of these rights is part of the core constitutional principles of the EU. Both systems are engaged by some activities around data capture, retention, and analysis, but a key distinction in relation to Big Data is that for most purposes, human rights protections treat the protection of personal data as a form of extension of the right to privacy.[8] (Article 8 of the European Convention on Human Rights incorporates this in the respect for an individual's private and family life, home, and correspondence.) Article 8 prohibits interference with the right to privacy, except where such interference is in accordance with the generally applicable departures from the Convention article necessary in a democratic society.[9] The EU Charter of Fundamental Rights, however, specifically enshrines data protection as a fundamental right in itself (somewhat unhelpfully under Article 8). This is distinct from the protection of respect for private and family life (Article 7). The Charter also establishes the principle of purpose limitation, requiring personal data to be processed "fairly for specified purposes" and stipulating the need for a legitimate basis for any processing of such data.

Even the EU's own legal framework for enshrining rights and freedoms for data subjects is not immune from challenge. For example, the ECJ found that the Data Retention Directive[10] allowed the data retained under its aegis to be kept in a manner so as to allow the identity of the person with whom a subscriber or a registered user had communicated to be revealed as well as identify the time of the communication and the place in which that communication occurred.[11] The Directive sought to ensure that data were available to prevent, investigate, detect, and prosecute serious crimes, and that providers of publicly available electronic communications services or of public communications networks were obliged to reveal the relevant data. The ECJ held that those data might permit "very precise conclusions to be drawn concerning the private lives of the persons, whose data has been retained, such as the habits of everyday life, permanent or temporary places of residence, daily or other movements, the activities carried out, the social relationships of those persons and the social environments frequented by them." The ECJ also held that the retention of data might have a chilling effect on the use of electronic communication covered by the Directive on the exercise of freedom of expression guaranteed by Article 11 of the Charter of Fundamental Rights.[12]

Then there is the indiscriminate—or at least non-discriminating—nature of Big Data analytics. The automation of processing is not just a strength; it is almost a sine qua non of Big Data use. The dilemma for agencies tasked with the exercise of discretionary powers is that the greater the automation, the less scope arguably there is for intervention by the controlling mind and the application of discretion (which, as once described by Lord Scarman,[13] is the police officer's daily task). Much has been written and said of the use of "non fault" or "without cause" powers by the police and the absence of Scarman's "safeguard of reasonable suspicion" (see, e.g., Staniforth, 2013), and the general trend for law enforcement in the UK has been to move away from the blanket applications of powers.

Interference by a member state with an individual's rights under the European Convention must be "necessary in a democratic society" and have a legitimate aim to answer a "pressing social need," but

---

[8] For an unusual police-related case, see ECtHR June 25, 1997, *Halford v. The United Kingdom* (no. 20605/92, 1997-III).
[9] See, for example, *Copland v. The United Kingdom* (no. 62617/00 Reports of Judgments and Decisions 2007-I); ECtHR January 12, 2010, *Gillan and Quinton v. The United Kingdom* (no. 4158/05, Reports of Judgments and Decisions, 2010).
[10] EU Data Retention Directive 2006/24/EC.
[11] Judgment in Joined Cases C-293/12 and C-594/12 *Ireland and Seitlinger and Others*.
[12] For a fuller explanation, see Boehm and Cole (2014).
[13] Report on the Brixton Disorders, April 10–12, 1981 (Cmnd. 8247), February 4, 1984.

even then an identified interference must be proportionate and remains subject to review by the Court (*Coster v. United Kingdom*, 2001; 33 EHRR 479).[14] Whereas the relationship between accuracy and reliability is clearly important in any form of data analysis, when the analysis is used at the level of the individual, biometrics, demographics, and social epidemiology take on a different legal quality. Almost by definition, Big Data deals with the supra-personal, the yotta-aggregation of data that is unconcerned with the binary constructs of personal identity and individuality.

However, the Working Party puts it thus: "The type of analytics application used can lead to results that are inaccurate, discriminatory or otherwise illegitimate. In particular, an algorithm might spot a correlation, and then draw a statistical inference that is, when applied to inform marketing or other decisions, unfair and discriminatory. This may perpetuate existing prejudices and stereotypes, and aggravate the problems of social exclusion and stratification."[15]

Just how little information Big Data needs to pinpoint an individual can be seen in Tene's (2010) graphic citing of research that has shown how "a mere three pieces of information—ZIP code, birth date, and gender—are sufficient to uniquely identify 87 per cent of the US population."

PURPOSE LIMITATION AND FURTHER PROCESSING

Within the legal framework protecting human rights are several key and interlinking concepts. The first such concept is purpose limitation. Purpose limitation is a key legal data protection principle[16] that appears (as discussed above) in both limbs of the European framework engaging with data protection: the Convention on Human Rights and the European Charter on Fundamental Freedoms. Through this framework the law seeks to protect data subjects (in crude shorthand, those individuals to whom the relevant data relate) by setting limits, albeit flexible, on how the data controllers (equally crudely, those who are able to manage and direct the manner in which the data are used) are able to use their data.

Purpose limitation, which has parallels in other jurisdictions (such as Article 6 of Law n. 121/1981 in Italy; see Chapter 16 for more information), has two components. First is purpose specification, which means that the collection of certain types of data such as "personal data"[17] must be for a "specified, explicit, and legitimate" purpose. The second element of purpose specification is "compatible use." This means that the data must not be further processed (see below) in a way that is incompatible with those purposes.

Arguably, the whole concept of Big Data analytics is predicated on some further perhaps even ulterior processing of data collected as a separate set or for a different, more specific purpose. The subsequent use of data represents a key barrier to lawful processing because of the requirement for compatibility. That is not to say that there can be no further processing, but such processing as there is will generally need to be compatible with the original lawful purpose or be exempt from that

---

[14] See also Article 40 of the UN Convention on the Rights of the Child of 1989, which states that it is the right of every child alleged to have infringed a penal law to be treated in a manner consistent with the promotion of the child's dignity and worth, reinforcing the respect for the child's human rights and fundamental freedoms.

[15] *Loc. cit.* at p. 45.

[16] Article 6 (1)(b) of Directive 95/46/EC of the European Parliament and of the Council of October 24, 1995 on the protection of individuals with regard to the processing of personal data and on the free movement of such data (OJ L 281, November 23, 1995, p. 31).

[17] Personal data in England and Wales means data relating to an identified/identifiable living individual (Data Protection Act, 1998).

compatibility requirement. Even the recycling of personal data that has already been made publicly available remains subject to the relevant data protection laws.

An important aspect of the further processing issue is the nature of the relationship between the controller and the data subject; in general terms, compatibility assessments should be more stringent if the data subject has not been given sufficient—or any—freedom of choice.

Exemptions for processing personal data within the UK are widely drafted and include purposes such as the administration of justice, statutory functions, and public interest provisions, which cover the work of a whole range of public bodies. However, the number of community outcomes for which the police alone are responsible is vanishingly small and (certainly in the UK) almost every activity that keeps people safe and thriving is the product of collaborative enterprise and partnership. This level of *engrenage* is not specifically reflected by the law regarding data protection and processing. There are restrictions on data sharing, particularly when the organizations involved are in different jurisdictions. Then there are limitations on the aggregation and analysis of huge datasets generally, which can present barriers to the proper activities of LEAs and problems regarding reliability of extrapolation, interpolation, and identification. Public bodies such as police forces have no general power to share data and must do so only when they are able to indicate a power (expressed or implied) that permits them to do so.[18]

A key challenge of Big Data for law enforcement therefore arises from the almost total reliance on partnerships within the British neighborhood policing model, which makes sectoral and functional separation (i.e., separation into public health, education, research) all but impossible. The best one can hope for is to identify the legitimate outcomes toward which the law enforcement partnership is working, understand the key elements of the relevant data protection framework applicable to that setting, and aim for compliance.

The relevant legislative frameworks, however, presuppose a "neat dichotomy" (Tene, 2010), whereas the increasingly collaborative manner in which businesses operate precludes a neat dichotomy between controllers and processors. Many decisions involving personal data have become a joint exercise between customers and layers upon layers of service providers. With the rise of cloud computing and the proliferation of online and mobile apps, not only the identity but also the location of data controllers have become indeterminate (Tene, 2010).

This is challenging enough when the LEAs and partners are within EU members states. When non-member states are involved—as occurs in many cases particularly involving serious organized crime—there is an additional requirement of "adequacy of protection." It is a key principle of the relevant legislation in member states that personal data must not be transferred outside the European Economic Area (EU member states and Norway, Iceland, and Lichtenstein) unless there is an ensured adequate level of protection for the rights and freedoms of data subjects in relation to the processing of personal data.

PUBLIC TRUST AND CONFIDENCE

Finally, and perhaps most important, there is public trust. The consensual model of policing in the UK entirely depends on the support of the communities within which the police operate. The principal factor keeping relative order on the streets of the UK is not so much the presence of 140,000 police officers; rather, it is the legitimacy (Stanko, 2011) they enjoy among the 60 million people who tolerate and support them.

---

[18] For instance, the Ant-Terrorism, Crime and Security Act, 2001, p. 17.

Some key features of Big Data, such as behavioral targeting, have a different cachet in LEA settings, and the history of data processing within UK policing has not been without its difficulties. There have been various legal challenges to the use and retention of personal data by the police: for example, *S & Marper v. United Kingdom* (2008) ECHR 1581 (police retention of DNA samples of individuals arrested, but who are later acquitted or have the charges against them dropped, was a violation of right to privacy) and *R (on the application of GC & C) v. The Commissioner of Police of the Metropolis* (2011) UKSC 21 (successful challenge of a policy of the Association of Chief Police Officers allowing indefinite retention of biometric samples, DNA and fingerprints for an indefinite period save in exceptional circumstances).

Police monitoring of public protests has produced a series of legal challenges for which LEAs have not always managed to achieve the fine balance between the obligations of the state to ensure the security and safety of its citizens and its duty to ensure the protection of their human rights and fundamental freedoms (see *The Queen (on the application of Catt) v. The Association of Chief Police Officers of England, Wales and Northern Ireland* and *The Commissioner of Police for the Metropolis* (2013) EWCA Civ 192). The *Catt* case involved a lawful demonstration and the indefinite retention of data about the applicant on the National Domestic Extremism Database. The case shows that even where the relevant event takes place in public, the recording and retention of personal data about individuals involved can be an unlawful interference with the right to respect for private life under Article 8 of the European Convention of Human Rights.

Aside from the litigious challenges over operational retention and use of personal data, the police have also experienced the ignominy of having their official recognition removed by the Office for National Statistics because their data processing approaches for recording crime were found to be unreliable. The police found themselves the subject of a Parliamentary report called *"Caught red handed: Why we cannot count on police recorded crime statistics,"* published by the Public Administration Select Committee,[19] whose chair, Bernard Jenkin, MP, said in the press release accompanying the report: "Poor data integrity reflects the poor quality of leadership within the police. Their compliance with the core values of policing, including accountability, honesty and integrity, will determine whether the proper quality of Police Recorded Crime data can be restored."[20] Shortcomings in data quality and reliability in the LEA context are not just about compliance and can have real and immediate detrimental impacts on and within the criminal justice process.[21]

The Public Administration Committee's report was followed by a report of HM Inspector of Constabulary on the reliability of crime recording data created and maintained by the police forces of England and Wales.[22] The interim report published on May 1, 2014, which drew upon several previous reports, referred to the Inspectorate's "serious concerns" in the integrity of police crime recording data.

Conversely, the failings of the police in England and Wales to retain relevant data in a searchable and shareable way, so as to enable the tracking of dangerous offenders such as Ian Huntley,[23] were widely reported and criticized in the *Bichard Report*,[24] which led to wholesale changes in the police approach to operational information technology capabilities.

---

[19] Report of the Public Administration Select Committee 13th session 2013/14 HC 760, The Stationery Office, London.

[20] See http://www.parliament.uk/business/committees/committees-a-z/commons-select/public-administration-select-committee/news/crime-stats-substantive/.

[21] See http://www.telegraph.co.uk/news/uknews/crime/11117598/Criminals-could-appeal-after-Home-Office-admits-potentially-misleading-DNA-evidence-presented-to-juries.html.

[22] See http://www.justiceinspectorates.gov.uk/hmic/programmes/crime-data-integrity/.

[23] Convicted on December 17, 2003 of the murder of 10-year-old schoolgirls Holly Wells and Jessica Chapman.

[24] Report of the Bichard Inquiry HC 653 June 22, 2004, The Stationery Office, London.

The corrosive effect of such cases and the media's reporting of them can be expected to damage public trust and confidence in the police and to affect the legitimacy they need to operate. When taken against the wider international context of "data-gate" and the Snowden revelations[25] of how governments have been using Big Data analytics and high-tech information and communications technology monitoring capabilities, this reduced trust and confidence represents a serious impediment to even the lawful and compliant use of Big Data by LEAs in the future particularly as we move into an era of "omniveillance" (Blackman, 2008).

CONCLUSIONS

Although the attractions of Big Data for LEAs are immediate and obvious, so, too, are the dilemmas it creates. The benefits of a capability of the scale offered by Big Data are readily apparent in every aspect of law enforcement, particularly where technology is used by perpetrators. For example, where the proscribed activities take place within the galactic setting of social media communications, such as in radicalization activities in terrorism and the online grooming of children and vulnerable victims in sexual offending, influencing behaviors and searching out prospects, the *modus operandi* almost invites a Big Data approach to both detection and prevention.

It is one thing to get private organizations from the retail sector or business-to-business suppliers working to certain data protocols, but what about LEAs? Staples such as individual consent and the right to be forgotten become much more difficult to apply, whereas exceptions such as the investigation, detection, and prevention of crime or—even broader—the public interest are much more readily applicable.

HOW FAR SHOULD BIG DATA PRINCIPLES SUCH AS "DO NOT TRACK" AND "DO NOT COLLECT" BE APPLICABLE TO LEAS, EITHER IN QUALIFIED FORMAT OR AT ALL?

Can the developing legal framework around human rights and concepts such as privacy and identity offer sufficient protection, engender legitimacy, and foster public trust? At this point the proposed Data Protection Regulation (Article 6 (4)) contains a broad exception from the compatibility requirement and if enacted, will allow a great deal of latitude for the further processing of personal data including a subsequent change of contractual terms. This potentially allows a data controller not just to move the goal posts, but to wait and see where the ball lands and then erect the goal around it. How will such relaxation of the rules be viewed by citizens, and what safeguards can they legitimately expect from their states?

When it comes to Big Data, the higher the stakes, the greater the challenges for LEAs that risk being condemned for not using all available data to prevent terrorist atrocities or cyber-enabled criminality and damned if they do so to the detriment of individual rights and freedoms.

As Polonetsky and Tene (2013) put it: "The NSA revelations crystallized privacy advocates' concerns of sleepwalking into a surveillance society' even as decision-makers remain loath to curb government powers for fear of terrorist or cybersecurity attacks."

One thing seems certain: The continued expansion of Big Data capability will inflate the correlative dilemmas it presents to our LEAs.

---

[25] See http://www.theguardian.com/world/the-nsa-files.

The resolution of the dilemmas of Big Data for LEAs—and by extension, for their partners in key areas such as safeguarding, fraud prevention, and the proper establishment of the rule of law in cyberspace—will be as much a challenge for the law as the technology. The dilemmas for LEAs are but one example of how our legal systems and principles need to catch up with the practices of their citizens' lives. It will need a new breed, a form of *lex veneficus*,[26] perhaps, to work alongside the technical wizards who have set the height of the Big Data bar.

REFERENCES

Akhgar, B., 2014. Big Data and public security. Intelligence Quarterly Journal of Advanced Analytics 2Q, 17–19.

Blackman, J., 2008. Omniveillance, Google, privacy in public, and the right to your digital identity: a tort for recording and disseminating an individual's image over the Internet. Santa Clara Law Review 49, 313–392.

Bignami, F.E., 2007. Privacy and law enforcement in the European Union: the data retention directive. Chicago Journal of International Law 8, 233–255.

Boehm, F., Cole, M.D., 2014. Data Retention after the Judgment of the Court of Justice of the European Union. (Münster/Luxembourg).

Holzacker, R.L., Luif, P., 2013. Freedom, Security and Justice in the European Union: Internal and External Dimensions of Increased Cooperation after the Lisbon Treaty. Springer Science+Business Media, New York.

Kokott, J., Sobotta, C., 2013. The distinction between privacy and data protection in the jurisprudence of the CJEU and the ECtHR. International Data Privacy Law 3 (4), 222–228.

Polonetsky, J., Tene, O., 2013. Privacy and Big Data: making ends meet. Stanford Law Review 66, 25 Online.

Stanko, B., 2011. Observations from a decade inside: policing cultures and evidence based policing. In: 5th SIPR Annual Lecture. Scottish Police College. Delivered 20 October 2011.

Staniforth, A., 2013. In: Sampson, F. (Ed.), The Routledge Companion to UK Counter-Terrorism. Routledge, London.

Tene, O., 2010. Privacy—the new generations. International Data Privacy Law 1–13.

---

[26] Literally a *legal magician*.

BIG DATA AND THE ITALIAN LEGAL FRAMEWORK: OPPORTUNITIES FOR POLICE FORCES

16

Pietro Costanzo, Francesca D'Onofrio, Julia Friedl

INTRODUCTION

We are currently experiencing unlimited growth of the size of real-world data and increasing requests for real-time processing on the behalf of various stakeholders: businesses, governments, health organizations, and police forces. Data have become the raw material of production, a new source of immense economic and social value. The increasing number of people, devices, and sensors that are now connected by digital networks has revolutionized the ability to generate, communicate, share, and access data (Robinson et al., 2009).

The deployment of Big Data offers a high number of benefits and advantages to its users.[1] A report by the McKinsey Global Institute demonstrates the transformative effect that Big Data has had on entire sectors ranging from health care to retail and from manufacturing to political campaigns (Manyika et al., 2011). In addition, police forces can achieve important advantages by analyzing the enormous amount of information that composes so-called "Big Data" (World Economic Forum, 2012).

Big Data may facilitate predictive analysis with implications for individuals susceptible to disease, crime, or other socially stigmatizing characteristics or behaviors. Predictive analysis is particularly problematic when it is based on sensitive categories of data such as health, race, and sexuality (Tene and Polonetsky, 2013). Even when it does not imply the use of sensitive data, predictive analysis can become a prophecy that accentuates social stratification (Casady, 2011).

In general, the data deluge presents privacy concerns that appear more pressing when it comes to the use of data on behalf of governmental bodies and police forces.

Predictive analytics that incorporate social factors and local demographics can have an important role in enhancing intelligence-led law enforcement that will help police anticipate crime by predicting crime hotspots and identifying criminal networks. In fact, in some countries[2] police forces are using these kinds of predictive analytics to better equip officers and improve public safety. This strategy

---

[1] See World Economic Forum, *Big Data, Big Impact: New Possibilities for International Development* (2012). Available at: http://www3.weforum.org/docs/WEF_TC_MFS_BigDataBigImpact_Briefing_2012.pdf.

[2] For example, police in Santa Cruz in California uses predictive analytics on burglary data to identify streets at greatest risk. Singapore police, instead, combine advanced analytical capabilities with existing video monitoring systems to ensure safety in the city (Daly et al., 2013). In Europe, predictive analytics is becoming fashionable, too. The Kent Police Force in the UK has tested a strategy in which analytics software is used to ascertain areas in which crime is more likely to occur, using several years of crime data.

builds on information shared among different police services, courts, prisons, and public administrations, and sometimes information collected from social networks, to identify where crimes are more likely to take place (Byrne and Marx, 2011).

If much of the debate around Big Data and privacy is based on the idea that organizations should be required to reveal the criteria used in their decision making processes with respect to personal data analysis (Tene and Polonetsky, 2013), what should occur when it comes to using Big Data for public/ national security?

Starting from an analysis of the European legal framework concerning the protection of data and their use for policing and criminal law matters, this chapter will consider the Italian legal framework to understand opportunities and constraints for Italian police forces regarding the use of Big Data for public and national security purposes.

EUROPEAN LEGAL FRAMEWORK

The first European data protection laws date to the early 1970s.[3] These early laws largely affected parts of government administration that collected large amounts of information from citizens for the purpose of providing services such as health care, education, and welfare. For the most part, intelligence and law enforcement officials were untouched by these early data protection regulations. Their information-gathering activities were covered by a more specific set of national laws. Police had to apply for warrants from judicial authorities before they could undertake surveillance.[4] In contrast, intelligence officers, who were responsible for security-related surveillance, were subject to less rigorous standards enforced not by courts but by independent government officials or parliamentary committees (Bignami, 2006).

Since the 1970s, one development has radically altered the nature of law enforcement and the relationship between law enforcement and data protection laws: technology. Increasingly, digital space has become the main feature of today's society. As a consequence, by monitoring Internet traffic, the police can easily collect useful information about citizens and personal data have become essential for Internet business (Bignami, 2006). On a European level, a data protection legal framework has been developed in the past 20 years and is still in continuous transformation to adapt itself to the technological environment.

DIRECTIVE 95/46/EC AND REVISION PROCESS STARTED IN 2012

Proposed in 1990 and adopted in 1995, the Data Protection Directive (95/46/EC) guarantees the right of individuals' data protection as well as the flow of data in the European Union (EU). This directive binds member states to harmonize their legislation, guaranteeing in that way to process personal data fairly, lawfully, and only for specified, explicit, and legitimate purposes (Kulk and Van Loenen, 2012).

---

[3] The first data protection law in Europe was adopted in Hessen, Germany, on September 30, 1970 in the Hesse Data Protection Act or *Hessisches Datenschutzgesetz*, whereas the first national data protection act was passed in Sweden in 1973 (see Burkert, 2000).

[4] For example, in the UK information gathering for law enforcement in terms of interception received a statutory regulation in 1985 with adoption of the Interception of Communications Act 1985. Before this act, the Secretary of State issued warrants for interception but there were no legal consequences if a warrant was not obtained. The 1985 Act was introduced after the European Court of Human Rights ruling *in Malone vs UK* in 1984 (for more information, see: http://www.lse.ac.uk/humanRights/documents/2011/KlugIntercepComms.pdf).

The e-Privacy Directive 2002/58/EC (amended by Directive 2009/136/EC) serves as a complementary directive to protect personal data in the electronic communications sector.[5] In 2008, a Framework Decision (2008/977/JHA) was adopted on the protection of personal data processed in the framework of police and judicial cooperation in criminal matters (Data Protection Framework Decision) (Peers, 2012).[6] This decision aims to protect the personal data of natural persons when their personal data are processed for the purpose of preventing, investigating, detecting, or prosecuting a criminal offence or for executing a criminal penalty. The applicability of this framework decision is limited to ensuring data protection in the cross-border cooperation between these authorities and does not extend to national security. Thus, at the EU level, data protection in the police and criminal justice sector is regulated only in the context of cross-border cooperation of police and judicial authorities.[7]

Furthermore, a stronger legal basis is provided through adoption of the legally binding European Charter of Fundamental Rights,[8] or more precisely Article 8, which recognizes data protection as an autonomous personal right, as well as Article 7, the right to a private and family life.[9] The Council of Europe Convention 108,[10] which is the main point of reference for the Directive (Bignami, 2007), applies to data protection in the area of police and criminal justice, although the contracting parties may limit its application (European Union Agency for Fundamental Rights, 2014).[11]

At the time of approval of the Data Protection Directive, data protection aimed to prevent rights abuse by market actors and by government agencies operating as service providers. Because globalization and quickly changing technological advancements are continuously modifying the way and methodologies with which data are collected and used, data protection is still challenged, calling for the need of a new, advanced legal framework. The revision of the 95/46 Directive started in 2010, in 2012, the EU Commission proposed a data protection regulation,[12] a directly applicable legal act that should

---

[5] Source: http://europa.eu/legislation_summaries/information_society/legislative_framework/l24120_en.htm.

[6] In January 2012, a revision process of both the Data Protection Directive and the Framework Decision started. The directive should be replaced by a regulation, whereas the Framework Decision should be replaced by a binding directive.

[7] An important example of institutionalized cross-border cooperation by exchange of nationally held data is Council Decision 2008/615/JHA on the stepping-up of cross-border cooperation, particularly in combating terrorism and cross-border crime (*Prüm Decision*), which incorporated the Prüm Treaty into EU law in 2008. The aim of the Prüm Decision was to help member states improve information sharing for the purpose of preventing and combating crime in three fields: terrorism, cross-border crime, and illegal migration. For this purpose, the decision sets out provisions with regard to automated access to DNA profiles, fingerprint data, and certain national vehicle registration data, the supply of data in relation to major events that have a cross-border dimension, as well as the supply of information to prevent terrorist offences and other measures for stepping up cross-border police cooperation. The databases that are made available under the Prüm Decision are governed entirely by national law, but the exchange of data is also governed by the decision and the Data Protection Framework Decision.

[8] Signed already with the Nice Treaty in 2000, but legally binding only after the ratification of the Lisbon Treaty (Holzacker and Luif, 2014).

[9] The Charter includes all the rights found in the case law of the Court of Justice of the EU; other rights and principles resulting from the common constitutional traditions of EU countries and other international instruments; and the rights and freedoms enshrined in the European Convention on Human Rights; e.g., the Convention on Human Rights (ECHR) protects the right to private life, under Article 8 (see: http://ec.europa.eu/justice/fundamental-rights/charter/index_en.htm).

[10] Convention for the Protection of Individuals with Regard to Automatic Processing of Personal Data, Council of Europe Treaties 108 (01/1981). Available at: http://conventions.coe.int/Treaty/en/Treaties/Html/108.htm. Although the European Union is not a party to Convention 108, its rights are applicable for different reasons (Bignami, 2007, pp. 241–242).

[11] Handbook on European Data Protection Law, available at: http://www.echr.coe.int/Documents/Handbook_data_protection_ENG.pdf.

[12] Source: http://ec.europa.eu/justice/data-protection/document/review2012/com_2012_11_en.pdf.

guarantee equal data protection for European citizens and an identical legal environment for companies modernizing and enhancing the old directive while setting global standards. More precisely the regulation should obligate non-European companies, when offering goods and services to European consumers, to apply the EU data protection law in full, no matter to what establishment they belong. On the other hand, citizens will benefit from the right to be forgotten, i.e., the right to have their data deleted in case it is processed without legitimate grounds.[13] Control and easier access to data should be enhanced whereas privacy-enhancing technology should be employed by technology providers and Web services.

In March 2014, the regulation passed the EU Parliament's vote and was waiting for final adoption by the Council of Ministers, as the ordinary legislative procedure (co-decision) was implemented.[14] Together with the regulation, a further legislative proposal was presented[15] regarding the processing of personal data in the law enforcement sector. This directive should allow personal data between competent authorities within the EU to be shared and exchanged for the purposes of prevention, investigation, detection, or prosecution of criminal offences or the execution of criminal penalties, thus providing a directive to enhance law enforcement cooperation between member states' authorities.

DATA RETENTION DIRECTIVE

The Data Retention Directive (2006/24/EC), amending the 2002/58/EC e-Privacy Directive, represents a complementary instrument to the Data Protection Directive. Highlighting the need of common measures regarding the retention of telecommunications data after the terrorist attacks on London and Madrid, the data retention directive can be considered the first EU law to address data privacy on law enforcement (Bignami, 2007). The two main purposes of the directive are harmonizing of obligations on providers to retain certain data and ensuring that the data retained are available for the purpose of investigation, detection, and prosecution of serious crime and terrorism.[16] Hence, its aim was to facilitate European cooperation in criminal investigations.

According to the directive, communication service providers are required to retain communication data for a period from 6 months up to 2 years (from three sources of traffic data: fixed and mobile telephony as well as Internet traffic), allowing member states to retrieve these data for one of those law enforcement purposes. This massive storage of data generated criticism by civil society, from the Article 29 Data Protection Working Party[17] as well as from the European Data Protection Supervisor, who pointed out that it entails serious interference with the fundamental rights to respect for private life and to the protection of personal data. These groups raised concerns regarding whether the stored data

---

[13] The right to have your data erased is not absolute and has clear limits. It only applies where personal data storage is no longer necessary or is irrelevant for the original purposes of the processing for which the data were collected (Liscka and Stöcker, Friday January 18, 2013).

[14] European Commission MEMO 14–186; see http://europa.eu/rapid/press-release_MEMO-14-186_it.htm.

[15] "Proposal for a Directive of the European Parliament and of the Council on the protection of individuals with regard to the processing of personal data by competent authorities for the purposes of prevention, investigation, detection or prosecution of criminal offences or the execution of criminal penalties, and the free movement of such data." (Source: http://eur-lex.europa.eu/legal-content/EN/TXT/PDF/?uri=CELEX:52012PC0010&from=en).

[16] From the beginning, proposal prevention was eliminated, whereas serious crime is intended as defined in every single national law (Holzacker and Luif, 2014).

[17] This Working Party was set up under Article 29 of Directive 95/46/EC. It is an independent European advisory body on data protection and privacy. Its tasks are described in Article 30 of Directive 95/46/EC and Article 15 of Directive 2002/58/EC.

would achieve the crime-fighting results and whether, owing to the lengths and amount of data retained, the proportionality test was accomplished (Bignami, 2007).

Even though further evaluations made by the European Commission highlighted the positive impact on investigation of the directive, on April 8, 2014, the Court of Justice declared the Data Retention Directive invalid.[18] According to the Court, the principle of proportionality, as well as the fundamental rights to respect for private life and personal data protection, were not guaranteed although the benefit and importance of retention, under precise and legitimate conditions, for the fight against serious crime and the protection of public security were recognized.

THE ITALIAN LEGAL FRAMEWORK
AUTHORITY FOR PERSONAL DATA PROTECTION

The Authority for Personal Data Protection is an independent administrative authority established by law n. 675 approved on December 31, 1996, to ensure the protection of rights and fundamental liberties and the respect of personal dignity when processing personal data (Gioffrè, October 21, 2009).

Data protection rights and secrecy rights do not coincide. The latter is the right to exclude others from having knowledge about private or family-related information. Data protection rights are about exercising a form of control over a person's data and information. In the first case, we are talking about the right to keep secret some information that the holder wishes to keep excluded from the knowledge of others; in the second case, the intention is to protect data and information, therefore protecting their use. The information we are talking about here does not have a reserved content: Information and data could be public. For instance, the telephone number of a private phone line reported in a telephone directory is certainly not considered reserved data, but it is personal data that must be handled according to the privacy and data protection legal framework.

THE ITALIAN PRIVACY CODE

Initially, personal data and privacy were protected by Law n. 675, December 31, 1996, which brought into force EU and international provisions relating to the topics (Council Directive 95/46/EC and Strasbourg Convention n.108, 1981) (Condello et al., 2009). Throughout the following 7 years, nine Law decrees regulating various specific aspects related to data protection were approved. This approach determined a discontinuous and inconsistent data protection legal framework.

In 2003, with the approval of D.Lgs 196/2003, the law on data protection (commonly called the Privacy Code) came into force in the Italian legal framework, replacing the previous framework.

The contents of the Code are driven by the objective of ensuring a high level of protection within the respect of principles of simplification, harmonization, and efficiency (Article 2, comma 2).

Personal data are defined as "any information relating to an identified or identifiable natural or legal person regardless its form, i.e., either paper or electronic based information."[19] The broad definition

---

[18] Press Release available at: http://curia.europa.eu/jcms/upload/docs/application/pdf/2014-04/cp140054en.pdf.

[19] Personal data includes name, surname, marital status, income, illnesses or diseases, workplace, and preferences and opinions. According to the definition of personal data given in the Directive and in the Italian Code, information can be either objective (e.g., the presence of a certain substance in the blood) or subjective (e.g., opinions, preferences).

given in the Code is similar to that reported in the Data Protection Directive. However, the Italian Code also includes legal persons as personal data holders (i.e., personal data may belong to associations, public administration, and any legal entity).

In this setting, the border between personal data and anonymous data is close; data are considered personal if there is the possibility of identifying the holder of the data. Personal data must be referred or referable to a specific holder.

The Privacy Code also dedicates specific provisions to some particular categories of data:

1. *Sensitive data* are personal data that are able to reveal:
   a. Racial and ethnical origins
   b. Religious beliefs
   c. Political opinions
   d. Health and sexual life
   e. Genetic data

   Genetic data are considered sensitive because they are able to reveal the health status of the holder.
2. *Judiciary data* require a higher level of information security than other data. They include legal proceedings acts as stated in article 686 of the criminal law code, condemnation proceedings.
3. *Semi-sensitive data* present specific risks related to rights and fundamental rights. This category of data must undergo prior checking (as also reported in article 20 of the Directive). Prior checking is carried out by a supervisory authority. In the Italian case, this is the *Garante della Privacy*—that is, the Authority for Personal Data Protection (hereafter the Authority). For example, biometric data (e.g., digital fingerprints, iris recognition) is considered semi-sensitive data because, although they are collected for other purposes (mainly security issues such as immigration control), they are potentially able to reveal information about the holder's health.
4. *Traffic data* relate to a telecommunication service user. The Italian code imposes limits relating to traffic data. Communication services suppliers must follow the general rule, which excludes data retention apart from:
   a. 6 months' data retention to have documented information to prevent billing disputes and
   b. retention for periods foreseen by law to verify or restrain crimes.

Article 18 of the Code specifies that public actors (apart from medical staff and health organizations) are not required to obtain a holder's consent, because their institutional function legitimates processing of personal data. Nevertheless, any unlawful data processing by public employees represents a violation of the Privacy Code. Furthermore, as a general rule, the exchange of personal data between two public actors is allowed when it is foreseen by a law or regulation or on the basis of an authorization issued by the Authority.

FOCUS ON ITALIAN POLICE FORCES

Information technology is a fundamental tool for police forces because they base their activities on collecting, evaluating, and connecting information for crime prevention and repression activities and for administrative tasks (van Brakel and De Hert, 2011).

Public security is mentioned in Articles 117 and 118 of the Italian Constitution. Constitutional reform in 2001[20] left "public security"[21] as the responsibility exclusively of the central government.

Specifically relating to police forces, data protection and analysis undergo the provisions indicated in Law n. 121/1981 and in a specific section of Privacy Code. Law n. 121/1981 assigned functions related to information and data classification, analysis, and evaluation to the Department of Public Security for purposes of order protection, public security, and prevention and repression of crimes (Article 6).

Article 7 of the law establishes that the information and data used for the purposes of Article 6 must refer to documents held by public administration or public entities, or result from proceedings of the judicial authority or from police investigations. According to the law, it is forbidden to collect information and data on citizens only because of their race, religion, or political opinions or their affiliation with unions or cultural, cooperative, or welfare-dedicated associations.

Information and data relating to bank operations or positions can be requested within the limits of police investigations and under explicit authorization issued by the judicial authority. Information and data held by police forces belonging to the EU member states and by other states, with which specific agreements have been reached, can be obtained under specific conditions.

Article 8 establishes the *Centro Elaborazione Dati* (Center for the Elaboration of Data (CED)), which collects, elaborates on, classifies, and stores information and data in automated files. The CED is also in charge of data transmission to authorized actors. Access and use of data and information stored in the CED are permitted for judiciary police officers, public security officers, security services officials, and authorized judiciary police agents. Controls on the CED are performed by the Authority according to specific laws and regulations. Finally, information and data shall not be used for purposes different from those listed in Article 6.

POLICE DATA PROCESSING AND PRIVACY

As explained above, privacy protection consists of the right of each data holder to control information relating to her or him so that it is processed only in case of need and with respect for fundamental rights. The question is, Can the right of privacy protection somehow be restricted by data processing performed by police forces?

Since 2001, Italian police forces have made use of data and information collected and elaborated by the *Sistema di Indagine* (Investigation Systems (SDI)). Investigation Systems collects and coordinates a set of information and data from all police forces. The system is open to all Italian police forces and allows data to be searched and information to be held in external databases connected to the system. Through SDI, police forces can access the Schengen Information System (SIS).[22]

---

[20] Constitutional Reform was approved by law n. 3/2001 involving the relationship between central and peripheral administrations.
[21] Public security can be defined as the activity that allows individuals to live in the community and act within it, showing their own individuality and to satisfy their interests. Traditionally and legislation-wise, public security is associated with the concept of public order, meaning the material public order that is the specific goods which are to be protected. In this sense, public order and public security are equivalent concepts.
[22] The newest version of the SIS, or SIS II, came into operation on April 9, 2013. It now serves all EU member states plus Iceland, Liechtenstein, Norway, and Switzerland. Europol and Eurojust also have access to SIS II. SIS II consists of a central system (C-SIS), a national system (N-SIS) in each member state, and a communication infrastructure between the central system and the national systems. The C-SIS contains certain data entered by the member states on persons and objects. The C-SIS is used by national border control, police, customs, and visa and judicial authorities throughout the Schengen area. Each of the member states operates a national copy of the C-SIS, known as N-SIS, which is constantly updated, thereby updating the C-SIS.

How long can police forces store information and data?

Article 6 of the Data Protection Directive and Article 5 of Convention 108 require member states to ensure that personal data are kept in a form that permits identification of data subjects for no longer than is necessary for the purposes for which the data were collected or for which they are further processed. The data must therefore be erased when those purposes have been served.

Article 11 of the Privacy Code provides that data must be stored to allow the identification of the holder for a period of time that must not exceed the period needed to pursue the finalities for which the data have been collected and processed. Article 22 of the Code also requires public actors to periodically verify the exactness and completeness and to update sensitive data and judiciary data.

In general, the second part of the Privacy Code, Processing Operations by the Police, specifically Articles 53–57, refers to police forces. Article 53 provides that personal data processing carried out by the CED at the Public Security Department or by police forces for the purposes of protecting public order and security, preventing, detecting, or repressing crimes is not limited by the provisions outlined in Articles 9, 10, 12, 13, and 16, 18–22, 37 and 38, and 39–45.

For example, this provision exempts police forces from the obligation to request the data subject's authorization to use data and to collect his or her consent (Articles 9 and 13). Police forces are also excluded from observing special provisions relating to data processing by public actors (Articles 18–22). Articles 37–42 relate to the obligation to notify, communicate, and gain authorization for data processing by the Authority; for their specific functions, police forces are not required to observe these provisions, whereas articles 43, 44, and 45 relate to the transmission of data to subjects outside the national territory. Finally, according to the exemption from Articles 145–151, police force data processing cannot undergo citizens' appeals.

According to Article 54, police forces can acquire data from other actors also in electronic format through specific agreements. Under provisions of Article 55, genetic and biometric data must be processed to protect the holder. Any data processing that is likely to be prejudicial to holders—with particular regard to genetic and/or biometric databases, location-based information processing, databases relying on specific information processing techniques, and the introduction of certain types of technology—must be compliant with measures and arrangements as may be set forth by the Authority to safeguard data subjects after a prior checking procedure.

OPPORTUNITIES AND CONSTRAINTS FOR POLICE FORCES AND INTELLIGENCE

Recently, EU data protection has taken a new turn. Now, the challenge is to safeguard privacy when governments exercise their core sovereign powers of national security and law enforcement (see also Chapter 15). There is a need for legal rules in view of the increasing use of computers for administrative purposes. Compared with manual files, automated files have vastly superior storage capability and offer possibilities for a much wider variety of transactions, which they can perform at high speed. Further growth of automatic data processing in the administrative field is expected in coming years as a result of lower data processing costs, the availability of intelligent data processing devices, and the establishment of new telecommunication facilities for data transmission.

Information power brings with it the corresponding social responsibility of data users in the private and public sectors. Those responsible for the files are required to make sure that the advantages they can obtain from automatic data processing do not also lead to weakening of the position of the person whose data are stored.

In fact, main concerns regarding processing personal data are the loss of individuals' control over sensitive information,[23] the risk of linkability, and (re)identification. Some cases were already observed in Italy and highlighted by the *Garante della Privacy* in its 2013 report, "Data Protection: Times Are A-Changing Big Data, Transparency, Surveillance,"[24] (Garante per la protezione dei dati personali, 2013) submitted to the Italian Parliament on June 10, 2014. This report "highlights the way ahead in order to make data protection genuinely effective," not only relative to commercial and administrative matters, but also in key fields for public order and security such as global, national, and private surveillance, the role of major Internet service providers, social networks and cyberbullying, biometrics, protecting children on media and the Web, protecting personal data in judicial proceedings, and retention of telephone and Internet traffic data.

In terms of data access and data amendment, the Authority confirmed the importance for interested subjects to access CED data at the Public Security Department (Ministry of the Interior), one of the main data gates to personal information that can be used for investigative and intelligence purposes. Such control over data should also be granted over the new SIS (SIS II), according to the possibility of individuals and foreign SIS national sections asking for access.

The Authority also coped with specific requests coming from local police forces. In relation to the possibility of extending (up to 60 days) the retention of data gathered through video surveillance systems in public areas for possible investigative purposes, the Authority observed that the confirmed term is 6 days after collection and that any extension must be requested to the same Authority, underlining a conservative approach in a field still showing wide gray areas.

Within this framework, from the operational point of view, Italian police forces started to work on using structured and unstructured data to cope with crime in urban areas. Not many examples are available: Crime pattern recognition techniques and crime trend studies are still under-adopted, and results of ongoing experimentations have yet to be understood.

First outcomes may be reported from a project in the city of Milan, thanks to the adoption of Key Crime predictive policing software. The tool was developed by internal personnel at the police in Milan and adopted for testing on robberies as a typical serial crime. Based on the analysis of several thousand parameters per event collected from multiple sources (video surveillance, manual entry of operators, etc., all contained in police databases), the software allowed police to attribute past robberies to

---

[23] Communication from the Commission to the European Parliament, the Council, The Economic and Social Committee and the Committee of the Regions, (2010), "A comprehensive approach on personal data protection in the European Union." Available at: http://ec.europa.eu/justice/news/consulting_public/0006/com_2010_609_en.pdf.

[24] The full report and summaries are available from: http://www.garanteprivacy.it/web/guest/home/docweb/-/docweb-display/docweb/3192876.

perpetrators on the basis of precise matching of key elements of modus operandi.[25] The tool has also been adopted to predict activities and therefore better allocate resources in the field.

Currently the software only adopts data acquired by the police and contained in internal databases, but what if such tools were redesigned and allowed to access open source information?

Emerging challenges derive from the "data-gate" case, i.e., foreign citizens' data collected by the United States National Security Agency (NSA) (The White House, 2014). After the disclosure to the public of information related to NSA's activities, Italian interested institutions (the Authority, the Parliament security committee/COPASIR, and the Department of Information and Security (DIS)) held consultations (also on the basis of Article 31 of Law 124/2007) to shed more light on the possible involvement of Italian nationals in NSA's data collection, both to enhance citizens' data protection and to reinforce the mechanism of police and intelligence cooperation. An important outcome of this process was the agreement signed on November 11, 2013, between the Authority and DIS to set up processes granting, to some extent, access to information about the treatment of personal data for intelligence purposes (e.g., in relation to cybersecurity issues to the access to databases of the Public Administration or of public services).[26]

Finally, considering this complex and fluid legal framework, data protection is considered to be at the top of the agenda, as the cornerstone to define limits and opportunities for accessing personal data for police and intelligence purposes. In this view, the possibility of adoption of the Data Protection Regulation in 2015 and society's growing concerns about privacy on the World Wide Web have already influenced technology businesses' product development. New methods providing a differential privacy are developed by main companies through a technological privacy by design solution, guaranteeing both the quality of digital data and the certainty to individuals of being untraceable (Bloem et al., 2013). The use of privacy-enhancing technologies together with standardized legislation, for both companies and law enforcement agencies, can create trust and a balance between the responsible exploitation of the advantages of (big) data and the respect of privacy of data protection of individuals.

Opportunities for police forces and intelligence services in Italy are still under-considered and the studies in this direction are evolving. In particular, because urban areas are growing and aggregating a multitude of cultures, economic activities, technologies, and social habits, the complexity of social demands and security needs is quickly increasing. The challenge for police and intelligence assets in the country is to anticipate the change, be prepared to adopt the solutions potentially provided by technologies supporting security analysis and operations, but also strongly focus on the challenges posed by the changing urban political geography, as well as ethical and legal issues.

---

[25] Further information can be retrieved from: http://www.ilsole24ore.com/art/notizie/2013-11-01/milano-come-funziona-software-sventa-rapine-064317.shtml?uuid=ABZ9pka.

[26] See Italian Government release, available at: http://www.governo.it/Presidenza/Comunicati/dettaglio.asp?d=73621.

REFERENCES

Bignami, F., 2006. Protecting privacy against the police in the European Union: the data retention directive. In: Bot, Y., et al. (Ed.), Melanges en l'Honneur de Philippe Leger: le droit a la mesure de l'homme, pp. 109–125.

Bignami, F., 2007. Privacy and law enforcement in the EU: the data retention directive. Chicago Journal of International Law 233–255.

Bloem, J., van Doorn, M., Duivestein, S., van Manen, T., van Ommeren, E., 2013. Privacy, Technology and the Law. Big Data for Everyone through Good Design. VINT Sogeti. Available from: http://blog.vint.sogeti.com/wp-content/uploads/2013/04/VINT-Big-Data-Research-Privacy-Technology-and-the-Law.pdf.

Burkert, H., 2000. Privacy – data protection a German/European perspective. In: Engel, C., Keller, K.H. (Eds.), Governance of Global Networks in the Light of Differing Local Values. Nomos Verlagsgesellschaft, Baden-Baden, pp. 43–70.

Byrne, J., Marx, G., 2011. Technological innovations in crime prevention and policing. A review on implementation and impact. Cahiers Politiestudies 20 (3), 17–40.

van Brakel, R., De Hert, P., 2011. Policing, surveillance and law in a pre-crime society. Understanding the consequences of technologies based strategies. Cahiers Politiestudies 20 (3), 163–192.

Casady, T., 2011. Police legitimacy and predictive policing. Geography and Public Safety. A Quarterly Bulletin of Applied Geography for the Study of Crime and Public Safety 2 (4), 2011.

Condello M., Guerra G., Ricchiuto P., 2009. La privacy nelle attività forensi. Avvocati, investigatori privati, periti, uffici giudiziari. Giappichelli.

Daly, G., Sanchez Lopez, M., Slessor, J.W., 2013. Policing gets smarter. Accenture Outlook the Journal of High-Performance Business (3).

European Union Agency for Fundamental Rights, 2014. Handbook on European Data Protection Law, second ed. Publications Office of the European Union.

Garante per la protezione dei dati personali, La protezione dei dati nel cambiamento. Big Data, Trasparenza, Sorveglianza, Relazione 2013.

Gioffrè, G., Wednesday October 21, 2009. Il Garante della privacy e l'amministratore del sistema. ALTALEX. [Online]. Available from: http://www.altalex.com/index.php?idnot=47812.

Holzacker, R.L., Luif, P., 2014. Freedom, Security and Justice in the European Union: Internal and External Dimensions of Increased Cooperation after the Lisbon Treaty. Springer Science+ Business Media, New York.

Kulk, S., Van Loenen, B., 2012. Brave new open data world. International Journal of Spatial Data Infrastructures Research 7, 196–206.

Liscka, K., Stöcker, C., Friday January 18, 2013. Data Protection: All You Need to Know about the EU Privacy Debate. Spiegel Online International. [Online]. Available from: http://www.spiegel.de/international/europe/the-european-union-closes-in-on-data-privacy-legislation-a-877973.html.

Manyika, J., Chui, M., Brown, B., Bughin, J., Dobbs, R., Roxburgh, C., Hung Byers, A., 2011. Big Data: The Next Frontier for Innovation, Competition, and Productivity. McKinsey Global Institute. Available from: http://www.mckinsey.com/Insights/MGI/Research/Technology_and_Innovation/Big_data_The_next_frontier_for_innovation.

Peers, S., 2012. The Directive on Data Protection and Law Enforcement: A Missed Opportunity? Statewatch. Available from: http://www.statewatch.org/analyses/no-176-leas-data%20protection.pdf.

Robinson, N., Graux, H., Botterman, M., Valeri, L., 2009. Review of the EU Data Protection Directive, Rand Europe. http://ico.org.uk/~/media/documents/library/data_protection/detailed_specialist_guides/review_of_eu_dp_directive.ashx.

Tene, O., Polonetsky, J., 2013. Big data for all: privacy and user control in the age of analytics. Northwestern Journal of Technology and Intellectual Property 11 (5), 239–273.

The White House, Executive office of the President, 2014. Big Data: Seizing Opportunities, Preserving Values. Executive Office of the President. Available from: http://www.whitehouse.gov/sites/default/files/docs/big_data_privacy_report_may_1_2014.pdf.

World Economic Forum, 2012. Big Data, Big Impact: New Possibilities for International Development. World Economic Forum. Available from: http://www3.weforum.org/docs/WEF_TC_MFS_BigDataBigImpact_Briefing_2012.pdf.

ACCOUNTING FOR CULTURAL INFLUENCES IN BIG DATA ANALYTICS

17

Gabriele Jacobs, Petra Saskia Bayerl

INTRODUCTION

Questions of national security are typically internationally oriented. One may think here of threats such as organized crime, radicalization, large-scale financial fraud, or economic and state espionage. Although focused on national security, these issues need to be addressed in an international arena, especially considering the increasingly closer linkages of states through global communication as well as commercial and financial networks.

Big Data analytics can be a powerful tool to prevent, identify, or mitigate national security threats because tapping into individuals' behaviors, attitudes, and relations on nearly all levels of social interactions supports the identification of (potentially or seemingly) problematic patterns, people, and groups. This broad collection of traces of human behavior for the prevention or identification of (possible) threats implies that massive amounts of highly varied data are being screened and cataloged at any given time. The resulting Big Datasets are often inescapably multicultural because collected traces often span international or cross-national contexts (e.g., terrorist cells, as described in Chapter 3).

We argue that this multinational element produces specific complexities for Big Data analytics, because not only are data patterns shaped by their cultural context, but the interpretation of data is also influenced by cultural factors. In this chapter we outline the challenges of the cultural dependence of Big Data analytics for the validity of interpretations and national security decisions. In contrast to the technological challenges of Big Data analytics, which are widely acknowledged and discussed (e.g., Jagadish et al., 2014; Magoulas and Lorica, 2009), the social and psychological challenges of Big Data production and interpretation are much less in evidence. Cultural dependence is only one of these challenges, but it is certainly an important one that deserves our attention.

We discuss the role of cultural context for two aspects:

- How cultural contexts affect the behavioral traces of individuals in their interactions with their environment
- How cultural contexts can affect the interpretation of such traces.

We refer to the first aspect as the supply side of Big Data analytics because it refers to the production of Big Data (e.g., by Internet users), and to the second aspect as the demand side because it is concerned with the collection and interpretation of traces to support decisions, e.g., by law enforcement agencies (LEAs) or the military.

Culture is an umbrella concept that covers several aspects of contextual information, such as behaviors, norms, and values, which are derived from the history, religion, or economy of a country. Our intention in this chapter is to advocate for a greater awareness for how cultural contexts can shape data patterns and thus for a greater sensitivity to cultural dependence in the collection and interpretation of Big Data. In borrowing from the field of cross-cultural psychology, which specializes in the study of culture-specific influences on behavior and attitudes, we refer to this sensitivity as cultural intelligence. *Cultural intelligence* refers to the ability to interpret human actions in foreign settings in the same way compatriots would (Earley and Mosakowski, 2004). We apply this concept to the ability of giving appropriate meaning to Big Data in an international context. Using insights from the fields of international psychology, sociology, marketing, management, and linguistics, we illustrate the complexities and potential dilemmas for behavioral predictions in international settings.

CONSIDERATIONS FROM CROSS-CULTURAL PSYCHOLOGY FOR BIG DATA ANALYTICS

As Smolan and Erwitt (2012) claimed, our smart devices turn each of us into human sensors that produce endless streams of information about our likes and dislikes, behaviors, and decisions. People leave data during shop visits, search activities on the Internet, holiday trips, and calls to friends. The digital camera follows us everywhere from our home into the metro, the library, and the coffee bar to the jogging trail, into the car, and into the office. These data become snapshots of the movie of our lives. But what and how can analysts learn from watching these movies?

Big Data can be seen as the material manifestations of individuals' behaviors and decisions captured in the form of texts, speech, pictures, films, patterns of communications, movements, or goods. Applications of Big Data for national security employ these behavioral traces to identity irregularities or indicators of (potentially) criminal intent or activities.

Studies in social psychology and sociology indicate that we can indeed predict attitudes of individuals from observable behaviors with a relatively high level of probability. Yet, they also caution that these conclusions need to be based on well-informed behavioral models. Well-established elements of such models are context-specific information about social norms or behavioral alternatives. For instance, the information that someone exclusively uses public transport, produces energy at home via sun collectors, and often goes on camping holidays may provide strong evidence that this person has an environmentalist attitude. Yet, it is also possible that this person shows this behavior because of a strong need to save money or because everybody in his or her environment is doing it.

To increase the probability of the link between behavior and underlying attitude, the distinctiveness of the observed behavior needs to be known. Is the use of public transport the dominant mode of transportation in the social environment of this person or are cars cheap and widely used? How high is the penetration rate of sun collectors in the region? Are camping vacations the usual way of passing holidays in the cultural context of the individual?

The relevance of context-specific cultural norms and behavioral alternatives for behavioral patterns in individuals and groups implies that data analysts need sufficient context-specific knowledge and that a lack of cultural sensitivity can easily lead to fundamental misunderstandings.

Many international marketing campaigns, for instance, failed because of a lack of awareness about local cultures. One of the most well-known examples is the campaign of a pharmaceutical company that was sensitive enough to consider the high degree of analphabetism in the targeted customer segment but forgot about the Arabic tradition of reading from right to left. The result was a nicely designed cartoon showing that the consumption of a specific medicine is able to remove heavy pain—but this was true only when reading from left to right. Following the Arabic reading tradition, the same advertisement in fact claimed that taking this medicine will produce serious pain in formerly healthy people.

Moving to the security domain, LEAs have come under heavy criticism for discrimination and stereotypical interpretations, when local cultural patterns were used to interpret foreign behaviors. The consequences of misinterpreting foreign behaviors can vary, from misunderstandings with major implications such as the underestimation of Western intelligence services of the likelihood of suicide attacks until 9/11 to (seemingly) minor implications. An example for such minor implications comes from our own personal environment, such as the call of German neighbors to the police that a potential terrorist might be hiding in the apartment next to them. The potential terrorist turned out to be a Moroccan doctoral student fully focused on his work and therefore keeping the blinds of his apartment windows drawn and meeting regularly with other Moroccan doctoral students to jointly discuss their progress.

These are only few examples but they demonstrate that behavioral patterns as well as their interpretation are socially shaped and thus culturally dependent, and that telling problematic apart from unproblematic patterns needs a considerable amount of cultural, social, and psychological expertise.

CULTURAL DEPENDENCE IN THE SUPPLY AND DEMAND SIDES OF BIG DATA ANALYTICS

Culture has a deep impact on how we see and interact with the world. Our cultural context provides a set of compelling behavioral, affective, and attitudinal orientations that influences individual and social behaviors, physiological aspects such as the perception of pain, temperature or color, and even our personalities (Berry, 2002). We refer to this phenomenon as the *cultural dependence* of behaviors, perceptions, preferences, norms, or attitudes.

In our daily life we remain largely unaware of these cultural impacts because the underlying values and basic assumptions (Schein, 1985) are typically inaccessible to direct reflection and observation. Usually it takes contact with other cultures (e.g., by observing differences in artifacts such as architecture, clothing, food, and art or differences in ethical norms and behaviors) to become aware of one's own cultural preferences. This largely unconscious and taken-for-granted nature of culture also means that its effects are often overlooked in the production and analysis of behavioral traces, i.e., data.

Culture dependence has a role for two aspects of Big Data, to which we refer as the supply side and the demand side of Big Data analytics (Figure 17.1).

1. The *supply side* refers to the production of data by individuals socialized in a specific cultural context who leave behavioral traces in the context of a specific culture (which may be their own, but is not necessarily so).
2. The *demand side* refers to the collection (i.e., the what, when, why, how, etc., of sampling data) and the interpretation of data by people socialized in a specific cultural context, which may be the same as or different from the one to which the individual leaving the behavioral traces belongs and/or the one in which the behavior takes place.

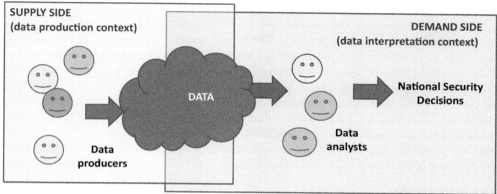

FIGURE 17.1

Supply and demand sides of Big Data analytics.

To illustrate the potential issues arising from cultural dependence on the supply and demand sides, we draw on the notion of *cultural equivalence* developed in the context of international marketing research (Craig and Douglas, 2005). Cultural equivalence is defined as the equivalent meaning of concepts and data in different social and cultural contexts.

CULTURAL DEPENDENCE ON THE SUPPLY SIDE (DATA CREATION)

On the supply side, cultural equivalence of behavioral traces can be compared and assessed with respect to three aspects:

1. Sample equivalence
2. Data collection equivalence
3. Measure equivalence.

Sample equivalence

Sample equivalence speaks to the base likelihood of specific behaviors across cultural contexts: for instance, the likelihood that people use landlines, mobile phones, or Internet varies across countries as do color preferences for products (Madden et al., 2000) or the rates of impulsive buying behavior (Kacen and Lee, 2002). Variations in these behaviors may further exist across subgroups with respect to age, gender, educational level, and so forth. Comparing communication in individual, in-group, out-of-group, and nonsocial language situations, for instance, Kashima et al. (2011) found that participants of Asian origin and women used more self-descriptions in interpersonal contexts whereas Australians did so more frequently when confronted with collective contexts. Such differences affect the base rate of behaviors to be considered average or normal in a group.

Data collection equivalence

Data collection equivalence describes the accessibility of data and the willingness of people to provide data across cultural contexts (e.g., Lowry et al., 2011). For instance, Chinese users of social networks are more likely to customize their profile picture than are Americans (Zhao and Jiang, 2011), thus potentially providing more pointers to their personality. As another example, closed circuit television cameras are widely accepted in Britain and The Netherlands and are even high on public wish lists, whereas other countries such as Germany are facing serious public and media resistance against such instruments (e.g., Bayerl et al., 2013). These differences in societies' willingness to provide information online and to accept surveillance by private and public institutions again affect the base rate of behaviors across groups, but also take into consideration differential impacts on base rates owing to different reactions to external pressure such as physical security measures or online surveillance.

Measure equivalence

Measure equivalence refers to the comparability of measurement units across contexts. For instance, the number of words people use to express an opinion; the emotional intensity of expressions; the colors used as symbols for abstract concepts; and the number of exclamation marks, question marks, or emoticons are specific per culture and mother tongue. Koreans, for instance, seem more likely to speak indirectly and to look for indirect meanings than are Americans (Holtgraves, 1997). Also, the general tendency to extreme responses, humility, or social desirability varies across contexts, influencing tendencies to agree or disagree to questions or the frequency of extreme versus moderate responses in surveys (Smith, 2011). Even the structure of academic texts (Clyne, 1987) and the type of personal pronouns ("I," "me," and "mine," vs "we," "ours," and "us") depend on culture, with more individualistic cultures preferring the former and more collectivistic cultures the latter (Na and Choi, 2009). Measure equivalence thus affects the base rate, but even more important, the type and intensity of behaviors or content that can be expected across cultural groups to express the same concept.

Taken together, *cultural dependence on the supply side* can thus create systematic differences in the three classic features of Big Data: volume, variety, and velocity. That is, cultural contexts can create variations in terms of how much data are produced (volume), which types and how many different types of data are produced (variety), and thus also the speed of accumulation of data (velocity).

In this context, it may be worth including a second reading of velocity: namely, the speed of change in behavioral and thus predictive data patterns. Some cultures or groups tend to be slow adopters, preferring to stick with established behaviors or practices; other cultures or groups tend to embrace innovations more readily. The two groups will thus show a different rate of change in their behavioral patterns over time—and in consequence possess a different time horizon of when predictive patterns may become obsolete.

CULTURAL DEPENDENCE ON THE DEMAND SIDE (DATA INTERPRETATION)

On the demand side, challenges owing to the cultural dependence of behavioral traces can be framed in the following three aspects:

1. Conceptual equivalence
2. Functional equivalence
3. Translation equivalence.

Conceptual equivalence

Conceptual equivalence addresses the fact that things do not mean the same everywhere. The color white, for instance, signals mourning in Japan, and purity in most Western contexts. In some cultural contexts, intelligence is indicated by slow speech, and by fast speech in others, whereas the word "family" can refer to only the core members (i.e., father, mother, children) or include the extended family of grandparents, aunts, uncles, and nieces. Similarly, not being aware that in some locations "friendship" can be used to describe a spontaneous, short-term relationship that can be terminated quickly, whereas in others it is used only for lifelong deep loyalties implying far-reaching social and financial obligations, may lead to severe misunderstandings about the disparate implications and commitments entered into by people using this term. Conceptual equivalence thus addresses the problem of giving the right meaning to behavioral traces across contexts, or rather, the challenge of accounting for the fact that disparate base rates, behaviors, or patterns essentially mean the same thing or that the identical content or pattern carries an different meaning.

Functional equivalence

In a comparable way, artifacts can perform different functions. Imagine, for instance, a family visiting a Western fast-food restaurant. In a United States (US) context this might indicate low–social status behavior, whereas in an African context this might signal a high-status family embracing symbols of freedom and the affluent lifestyle of the West. Yet, precisely this symbol of the West can change in its meaning depending on political and societal developments. Whereas in an Eastern European context Western products such as soft drinks and fast food were long considered scarce and attractive status goods, the Western signaling function now turned in some market segments into a liability: The mere fact that a product comes from the West now can be considered as pushy (Van Rekom et al., 2006). Functional equivalence thus refers to the challenge that reactions to the same triggers are influenced by the cultural contexts in which they are encountered.

Translation equivalence

The international nature of Big Data also means that it may contain multiple languages, including local dialects and group-specific lingos. Most of us are know that adequate translations of natural text or speech are far from trivial. This starts with the fact that some experiences and objects simply do not have words in all languages (e.g., Japanese knows eight common honorifics to express hierarchical differences among individuals whereas English speakers are reduced to the choice between a person's first or last name). Some words have double meanings in their original language that are lost in translation, or vice versa, whereas proverbs, metaphors, the level of abstraction, and precision are highly language and context specific (e.g., the same person will most certainly use different vocabulary with family, at work, and at a club with friends; few people would understand a literal translation of the Greek "having a toothache" to mean "being unhappily in love"). In addition, language usage changes quickly over time (e.g., emojis are now replacing smileys, whereas "Googling" has long become an established term for searching on the Internet). By necessity, working with a language that is not the mother-language is thus fraught with misunderstandings. Translation equivalence thus draws attention to the ability to ensure that translation of texts and speech as well as pictures or drawings are actually transporting the original meaning from the original language and context.

In summary, the demand side is thus the place where errors or imprecision in the interpretation of Big Data can occur because of neglect or a lack of awareness of the cultural dependence of specific patterns, behaviors, or expressions. This is also the point where possible biases, stereotypes, prejudices, and heuristic shortcuts come into play. As Canhoto (2008) described in a study on money laundering detection within United Kingdom financial services, bank employees considered the type of business done by customers of specific ethnics groups as a source of concern. The *main challenge of cultural dependence on the demand side* is thus to ensure the validity of data interpretations in a culturally adequate way.

The likelihood of lapses in validity clearly depends on how familiar or foreign the cultural backgrounds of the data producer(s) and data interpreter(s) are: that is, on the degree of match or mismatch between producer and interpreter contexts. In addition, mismatches between these two contexts and the contexts of production and interpretation can have a role.

(MIS)MATCHES AMONG PRODUCER, PRODUCTION, INTERPRETER, AND INTERPRETATION CONTEXTS

The possibility of different contexts with respect to place of socialization (producer and interpreter context), place of behavior (production context), and place of collection/interpretation (interpretation context) creates various forms and degrees of cultural matches and mismatches (see Figure 17.2). At the one extreme stands a complete match of the four contexts: e.g., US analysts investigating criminal activities of American citizens in the US on US-based online sites (Configuration 1 in Figure 17.2). At the other extreme stands the complete mismatch between the four contexts: e.g., if an American agent working in Germany analyzes the radicalization potential of Moroccan youth living in The Netherlands (Configuration 8 in Figure 17.2).

The existence of these context configurations raises several questions with respect to the reliability and validity of Big Data analytics in multicultural settings. Some of the more pressing questions are:

- In which constellations are cultural misinterpretations most likely?
- In which constellations are cultural misinterpretations severest?

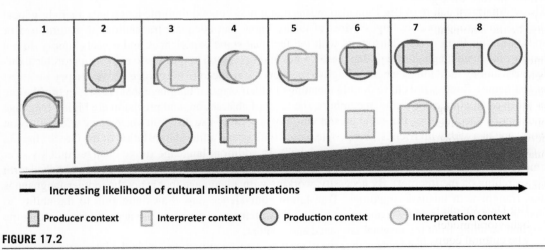

— **Increasing likelihood of cultural misinterpretations** ——→

▢ Producer context   ▢ Interpreter context   ◯ Production context   ◯ Interpretation context

FIGURE 17.2

Suggested likelihood of cultural misunderstandings for disparate context configurations.

- In which configurations are context/cultural mismatches salient and thus can be explicitly addressed, and in which configurations do they remain masked and may thus cause unconscious faults or biases in interpretation?
- Are there specific types of reliability and validity issues for each configuration or are there generic issues that arise in all or nearly all configurations?

To our knowledge, there are no empirical investigations as of yet that address these questions for national security decisions. Research from cross-cultural studies suggests that configurations with an overlap of producer and interpreter contexts (Configurations 1–4) have a lower likelihood of misinterpretations because a common frame of reference exists between the person leaving the traces and the person interpreting them. For the same reason, mismatches between producer and interpreter contexts may be more prone to faults in interpretations and thus subsequent decisions (Configurations 5–8). Situations with mismatches in producer and production contexts (Configurations 3, 4, 5, and 8) may lead to issues because behavior culturally normalized in the producer's context may be unusual in the production context—although how much this becomes an issue will certainly depend on the degree to which a person adjusts and integrates into this environment. Mismatches of interpreter and interpretation contexts may again be less severe (Configurations 2 and 4) unless they go hand in hand with mismatches with the producer context (Configurations 6–8). Still, these assumptions need further detailing and testing in national security contexts.

INTEGRATING CULTURAL INTELLIGENCE INTO BIG DATA ANALYTICS: SOME RECOMMENDATIONS

A golden rule in cross-cultural research is that cooperation with cultural insiders is critical to meaningful data analysis. On the other hand, the cultural naivety of an outsider can allow for relevant surprising questions. Global acting companies in the consumer and financial sector are aware of cultural variations in social behaviors and preferences. HSBC Bank, for instance, used to advertise their global savvy with a picture of a grasshopper and the comment, "USA—Pest. China—Pet. Northern Thailand—Appetizer" (Earley and Mosakowski, 2004). This widely shared awareness in the private sector should also be the dominant practice for LEAs.

Marketing research has established a strong tradition in developing guidelines and methods for international research. ESOMAR (http://www.esomar.org) is a worldwide organization that promotes better research into markets, consumers, and societies. Standards and codes covering ethical commitments, e.g., for research with children or the use of research methods such as social media, the Internet, or mystery shopping studies (where evaluators observe and measure customer service by acting as a prospective customer) are jointly developed in an international network of market researchers. Such networks also allow marketers to conduct effective and efficient research into complex international market segments with the help of fellow marketers from the targeted cultural markets.

General rules from cross-cultural research in the social sciences can be translated into basic recommendations for Big Data analysis:

- Big Data should be analyzed only on the basis of well-informed psychological and sociological behavioral models.
- The cultural equivalence of the supply and demand sides of Big Data needs to be established before the data are interpreted.

- Individual data points should be interpreted only in combination with a whole portfolio of other data points of the individual.
- The social context of information needs to be systematically considered to identify the distinctiveness of information.
- Cultural insiders should work in teams with cultural outsiders to maximize cultural sensitivity in interpreting data.

Coming back to our example above, a team of American, Moroccan, and Dutch experts would probably be most likely to reach valid conclusions. American expert(s) can define which questions need to be answered in the context of their investigations, Dutch expert(s) can contribute information on the norms and typical behaviors in a Dutch environment, and Moroccan expert(s) can help to understand the specific behaviors of Moroccan youths to account for aberrations from Dutch pattern norms.

On the data supply side, analysts need to establish the equivalence of data collection. For the production context, they need to establish whether the analysis of online behavior is targeted at the correct sources (in our case, Dutch). The team also needs to establish sample equivalence; e.g., are the targeted age group, family situation, and educational background of Moroccan youths living in The Netherlands comparable to other youth groups with radicalization potential in the US?

For the data interpretation side, measure and conceptual equivalence are important concerns. In this context, questions such as the following need to be answered: Do certain statements of radicalization mean the same in the Dutch (production) context as they would in the American (interpreter) context? How "extreme" are certain statements relative to the usual rhetoric of Dutch political debating compared with American political debating? When it comes to functional equivalence, it is important to understand what certain symbols (e.g., the distribution of videos, the carrying of flags, the possession of books) mean in the Moroccan–Dutch context, what function they might have in a local political debate, and how these need to be understood compared with the functionality of these symbols in the American context. Last but not least, translation equivalence needs to be established. Moroccan youth growing up in Dutch society might use language and expressions different from Moroccan youth in the US.

We use this example not to support stereotyping concerning Moroccan youth, but to choose an example that is of high political attention and that also shows how complex the analysis of culturally diverse subgroups can be. Heated political debates can easily lead to an underestimation of the high likelihood of cultural misunderstandings.

CONCLUSIONS

In this chapter we outlined challenges confronting organizations tasked with safeguarding national security, who use Big Data analytics in international contexts. Our primary aim was to advocate for a consistent and systematic consideration of cultural dependencies in data production and interpretation, but also to call for more investigations into this important area.

Cultural sensitivity is crucial in analyzing Big Data in a meaningful way, but little systematic research seems to be conducted into understanding how cultural dependencies affect the reliability and validity of Big Data analytics. This is especially problematic for individuals and organizations operating in the field of national security, because wrong decisions there can lead to severe consequences for the lives and/or well-being of people.

Because of the dearth of research on cultural issues in Big Data analytics, we relied heavily on literature from fields outside the national security debate, including marketing, management, linguistics, and cross-cultural psychology. Given the increasing reliance on Big Data in national security decisions, we hope that Big Data and the national security field will increasingly conduct investigations into the specific impact of cultural dependence for questions of national security. This should lead to the inclusion of cultural Big Data intelligence into information technology and staff trainings and perhaps even inform the design of statistical analysis packages and software applications.

Reliance on Big Data and its statistical analyses often seems to imply a certain objectivity of the process of data analytics. As we discussed, this assumption can be dangerous for the validity of interpretations and decisions if it is not counterbalanced by the application of cultural intelligence to Big Datasets. Especially because the fundamental logic of singling out criminals is achieved by identifying differences and abnormalities in data patterns, it is crucial to understand that differences can be established only as long as the dimensions of comparison are comparable. As we tried to illustrate in our discussion on cultural dependence and cultural (in)equivalence, the likelihood of faulty interpretations depends on the degree of (mis)matches among producers, production, interpreters, and interpretation contexts. We thus argue that security-related applications of Big Data should routinely consider cultural dependence to ensure they adequately make sense of Big Data in a global context on both the supply and demand sides.

National security applications of Big Data can be a powerful asset to serve the security of our societies. By adding the concept of cultural intelligence to what we call the supply–demand chain of Big Data production and interpretation, we hope to contribute to the validity and effectiveness of Big Data analytics while reducing the risks of biases and faults in interpreting behavioral traces, and thus the risk of faulty decisions.

REFERENCES

Bayerl, P.S., Jacobs, G., Denef, S., Van den Berg, R., Kaptein, N., Birdi, K., Bisogni, F., Cassan, D., Costanzo, P., Gasco, M., Horton, K.E., Jochoms, T., Mirceva, S., Krstevska, K., van den Oord, A., Otoiu, C., Rajkovcevski, R., Reguli, Z., Rogiest, S., Stojanovski, T., Vit, M., Vonas, G., 2013. The role of macro context for the link between technological and organizational change. Journal of Organizational Change Management 26 (5), 793–810.
Berry, J.W., 2002. Cross-Cultural Psychology: Research and Applications. Cambridge University Press, Cambridge.
Canhoto, I.A., 2008. Barriers to segmentation implementation in money laundering detection. Marketing Review 8 (2), 163–181.
Clyne, M., 1987. Cultural differences in the organization of academic texts: English and German. Journal of Pragmatics 11 (2), 211–241.
Craig, C.S., Douglas, S.P., 2005. International Marketing Research. John Wiley & Sons, Chichester.
Earley, P.C., Mosakowski, E., 2004. Cultural intelligence. Harvard Business Review 82 (10), 139–146.
Holtgraves, T., 1997. Styles of language use: individual and cultural variability in conversational indirectness. Journal of Personality and Social Psychology 73 (3), 624–637.
Jagadish, H.V., Gehrke, J., Labrinidis, A., Papakonstantinou, Y., Patel, J.M., Ramakrishnan, R., Shahabi, C., 2014. Big Data and its technical challenges. Communications of the ACM 57 (7), 86–94.
Kacen, J.J., Lee, J.A., 2002. The influence of culture on consumer impulsive buying behavior. Journal of Consumer Psychology 12 (2), 163–176.

Kashima, E.S., Hardie, E.A., Wakimoto, R., Kashima, Y., 2011. Culture- and gender-specific implications of relational and collective contexts on spontaneous self-descriptions. Journal of Cross-Cultural Psychology 42 (5), 740–758.

Lowry, P.B., Cao, J., Everard, A., 2011. Privacy concerns versus desire for interpersonal awareness in driving the use of self-disclosure technologies: the case of instant messaging in two cultures. Journal of Information Systems Management 27 (4), 163–200.

Madden, T.J., Hewett, K., Roth, M.S., 2000. Managing images in different cultures: a cross-national study of color meanings and preferences. Journal of International Marketing 8 (4), 90–107.

Magoulas, R., Lorica, B., 2009. Introduction to Big Data. Release 2.0. Issue 11. O'Reilly Media, Sebastopol, CA.

Na, J., Choi, I., 2009. Culture and first-person pronouns. Personality and Social Psychology Bulletin 35 (11), 1492–1499.

Schein, E.H., 1985. Defining organizational culture. Classics of Organization Theory 3, 490–502.

Smith, P.B., 2011. Communication styles as dimensions of national culture. Journal of Cross-Cultural Psychology 42 (2), 216–233.

Smolan, R., Erwitt, J., 2012. The Human Face of Big Data. Against All Odds Production.

Van Rekom, J., Jacobs, G., Verlegh, P.W., Podnar, K., 2006. Capturing the essence of a corporate brand personality: a Western brand in Eastern Europe. Journal of Brand Management 14 (1), 114–124.

Zhao, C., Jiang, G., 2011. Cultural differences on visual self-presentation through social networking site profile images. In: CHI '11 Proceedings of the SIGCHI Conference on Human Factors in Computing Systems, pp. 1129–1132.

MAKING SENSE OF THE NOISE: AN ABC APPROACH TO BIG DATA AND SECURITY

18

John N.A. Brown

Omnis enim ex infirmitate feritas est.

Seneca the Younger, from De Vita Beata: cap. 3, line 4

HOW HUMANS NATURALLY DEAL WITH BIG DATA

Processing Big Data for security is not a twenty first–century problem. In 1991, Mark Weiser proposed that in the near future, properly designed computers would help reduce information overload, and suggested that the solution was in our interaction with nature: "There is more information available at our fingertips during a walk in the woods than in any computer system" (Weiser, 1991). By the time our early ancestors had reached the size of cats some 40 million years ago, they had already developed the tools they needed to process the vast amounts of security-related data that fell on them in a steady stream of sounds, smells, tastes, sights, and feelings. We responded in a series of iterative feedback loops; sensing, learning, and responding over and over again, adapting to our changing perception. This is the routine with which all living creatures perceive, process, and adapt before perceiving again. However, the key was a feedback loop called a "corollary discharge cycle": a sort of "ghost image" of our actual performance that gives us a mental model against which to compare the changing environment. It is an internal report that says, "I am doing *this* at the moment, so any differences I detect are feedback."

At its simplest, this system provides us with self-calibration, an understanding of whether we are doing what we think we are doing. More practically, this is how the proprioceptors in our joints allow us to stand or to control the placement of our hands and fingers. More complex versions are at the root of how we learn to run, read, or interact socially.

Most models of human–system interaction do not account for this constant barrage from multisensory feedback loops, but they are at the root of how we, as animals, determine and maintain our security, whether personal, tribal, civil, or national. To wit, security requires a constant cycle of information gathering and response at an organizational level, even though the available data are often too large to be fully analyzed. Instead of trying to decode and interpret all of the Big Data in real time, we apply a series of filters at each level of the organization. The Theory of *Anthropology-Based Computing (ABC)* and the related Model of Interaction (Brown, 2013, 2014a) allow us to examine this cycle more accurately and apply it to individual and organizational models for coping with Big Data.

Humans reflexively filter out most of the data we perceive, automatically processing only what fits into anticipated patterns labeled important or unimportant. This is how we separate the "signal" from the "noise" when carrying on a conversation in a crowded room. However, not all data are immediately recognized as either one or the other. These outliers require further processing. The data that cannot be processed reflexively are "bumped up" to a higher level of pre-attentive processing, where they are compared with known patterns of alarm so that they can either be diverted to the center of our conscious attention or flagged as false positives and returned to the periphery. In this chapter we will take a look at the organizational tactics that could benefit from an improved understanding of this most basic means by which we filter select elements from the noise around us and, more important, the means by which we recombine these elements into the meaningful signals that allow us to feel secure in our understanding of the world around us (Brown, 2015). Let us examine this process more closely and see how this multi-tiered processing strategy may be a guideline for organizations that are trying to interpret Big Data for security purposes at the national level.

THE THREE STAGES OF DATA PROCESSING EXPLAINED

Since before the beginning of recorded history, humans and their ancestors have reacted to security intelligence based on multiple feedback loops (Brown, 2013). Information is perceived, processed, and filtered for appropriate reaction (or non-reaction). The model of Human–Computer Interaction (HCI) based on this theory generalizes the processes into three stages, as illustrated in Figure 18.1.

This is in contrast to previous models of HCI, which illustrated human perception, processing, and reaction as happening in a single cycle. The single-cycle models fail to account for the natural human ability to interact with peripheral information, dealing with some stimuli either reflexively or pre-attentively, while simultaneously dealing with separate stimuli in a cognitive or attentive manner. When driving a car, one responds reflexively to tactile and visual stimuli to keep the steering wheel where we want it. At the same time, the driver is pre-attentively recognizing patterns such as the relative speeds

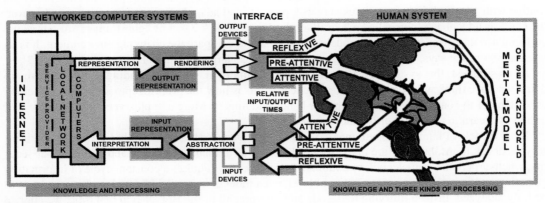

FIGURE 18.1

Brown's ABC model of HCI, showing the three generalized levels of human sensory perception, processing, and response.

of other cars and the angling surface of a curve in the road. Also at the same time, the driver may be attentively engaging in a conversation, giving or getting directions, or listening to the news on the radio. The same idea can be adapted to illustrate the same three-stage process as a general model of human interaction, as shown in Figure 18.2.

Let us now consider the three stages.

STAGE 1: REFLEXIVE

Perceive as much input as possible and extract only the input that clearly is a sign of immediate danger and the input that clearly is not a sign of immediate danger, to deal with instantly—without conscious thought or consideration. People often talk about "fight or flight," but it should really be "fight, flight, forget, or faint." In fact, this stage, "forget," where we reflexively decide to ignore the information, must be the most common response; otherwise we would be fighting, running, or collapsing all of the time. Once we have filtered out the signals we can respond to immediately with one of those four choices, the remaining signals must be passed along for processing at a deeper level.

STAGE 2: PRE-ATTENTIVE

The previous stage has left us with a body of input that requires further examination. Here, the first layer of pattern recognition is based on our protocol for dealing with known true positives, known false

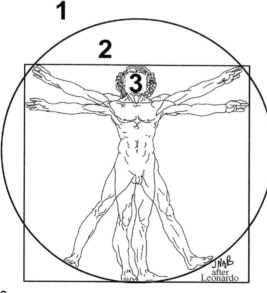

1) Reflexive:
- most stimuli are ignored some trigger reflexes, others require more processing.

2) Pre-Attentive:
- most stimuli trigger recognized patterns and pre-determined responses. Again, others require more processing.

3) Attentive:
- most stimuli require conscious and deliberate consideration. Stimuli that require more attention than we can spare force us to re-dedicate resources from other simultaneous tasks.

FIGURE 18.2

A general model of the three stages of human perception, processing, and reaction.

negatives, as well as known false positives and true negatives. This is not as fast as a reflexive response but it is still almost immediate. This is where we must decide, without conscious thought, whether the situation we are facing is one for which we have previously prepared. If so, we must be able to quickly recognize which pattern it fits and initiate a response. If not, we must pass the information deeper into the process of decision making.

STAGE 3: ATTENTIVE

Input that has defied immediate reflexive responses and almost immediate pattern recognition will now require deliberate and detailed, conscious analysis. This is carried out at the deepest and slowest level, where we consciously ask ourselves, "What are my options, and which one should I choose?" At this point, although it is best to continue carrying out Stage 1 and 2 responses, it is inappropriate for their actions to undercut Stage 3 operations. For this reason, sometimes the need to respond appropriately requires that we temporarily restrict or even suspend operations at the other stages while the larger picture is being re-evaluated. Whereas the other stages have upper limits for time taken, the attentive stage does not. The process takes time. This is why strategists make their plans ahead of time: to avoid having to think deeply when time is critical.

As mentioned above, a form of self-evaluation must take place at each of these three stages, feeding an accurate picture of one's performance into the feedback loop. This is called *calibration*, and it is vital to successful decision making and execution. Without proper calibration, our actions will deviate from appropriate to inappropriate as our perception of our performance and its context deviate from what is really happening around us. Calibration failures occur all of the time in normal day-to-day human interactions. We have all seen incompetent people who think they are doing a great job, really believing what they think is obvious to everyone around them, even though no one would agree. When children throw a temper tantrum, it is a signal that they perceive the situation they are in to be extremely important, and they are resorting to emergency measures to try to force the people around them to recognize the extremely important emergency that no one else has noticed. In fact, in the right situation the same unflinching and determined behavior would be heroic.

We can accept temper tantrums in children, because they are still learning how to calibrate their behavior to suit the world around them. When an adult throws a temper tantrum, it is a lot harder to accept, but it is caused by the same sort of calibration failure. When managers are screaming at their subordinates, it is a sign that their perception of reality (calibration) has deviated from the actual situation to such a degree that they now believe screaming is truly necessary. In other words, they perceive an emergency where there is none. When drivers try to eat, text, have a deep, emotional conversation, or reset their dashboard navigation system while driving along a crowded street, they are also making a calibration error. In this case, they are failing to see the dangers around them, truly believing instead that they can afford to divert their attention.

We propose that calibration errors are at the root of many failed responses to security-critical situations, and we suggest that our three-tiered model could be used to help individuals and organizations develop a better understanding of the forces affecting their decisions during an engagement. This understanding would improve individual and organizational behavior calibration and so help agents make the best possible choices at each decision-making stage, from high-level planning to field operations. In the next section, we will propose a model illustrating how that could be done.

THE PUBLIC ORDER POLICING MODEL AND THE COMMON OPERATIONAL PICTURE

In the August 2011 issue of the FBI Law Enforcement Bulletin, Masterson proposed a new paradigm for crowd management (Masterson, 2012). In establishing the basis of his proposal, Masterson referred to the Public Order Policing Model and illustrated it as a pyramid of four levels. At the base is the "Science-Based, Event-Tested, Theoretical Understanding of Crowds," certainly a good foundation. Next is "Police Policy, Knowledge, and Philosophy," and the original illustration shows that this would include "effective contemporary crowd control methods used by American, Canadian, and British agencies" such as the Madison Method (1975), the Cardiff Approach (2001), and the Vancouver Model (2010). These policies would inform the next level of the pyramid, "Police Training," which would shape the "Police Response" that sits at the top of the pyramid.

Organizations with more than two levels of security have been using pyramids to illustrate their command structure for a long time, but these structures predate the modern age of ubiquitous and dependable communications. One-way communication was the best available model one hundred years ago, but the inability to feed back along the chain of command led to disasters such as the continued suicidal charge on Gallipoli. By the later twentieth century, both technology and policy had improved and middle management in many organizations could selectively pass information up the chain. Still, the organizational filters for this feedback often worked at cross-purposes, confounding, for instance, the important feedback with the trivial and restricting them equally. This reflects the conditions that may have led to repeated decisions not to pass on concerns about toric joints (O-rings) like the one that failed on the morning of January 28, 1986, causing the space shuttle Challenger to explode.

Technology is no longer a limiting factor for upward and downward communication in modern organizations, except perhaps, in one unpredicted manner. Institutional communication has become so effortless that it is now used for the most trivial matters. Digital messaging services such as SMS, e-mail, and chat applications are designed to catch one's attention and they work too well, providing a constant source of distraction, and triggering attentive responses regardless of the time or place. Because these applications are designed to break through our natural reflexive and pre-attentive filters, the result is a constant hazard of deep distraction that has been directly linked to countless fatalities, ranging from individual pedestrians to dozens of passengers onboard buses and trains (Brown et al., 2014b).

Because we cannot filter these alerts successfully, trivial messages crowd out the important ones and it is easy to either be overwhelmed by dealing with the trivial or to ignore too much and miss out on the important. These are both types of calibration error, and they are well documented in studies that strongly suggest that universal access to e-mail has reduced on-task communication and increased working hours while reducing productivity (Burgess et al., 2005). In fact, overwhelming numbers of digital messages can be considered a smaller-scale model of the overall problem of trying to deal with Big Data. We cannot take the time to parse every e-mail to see which ones are important. Different e-mail services have established proprietary filtering systems to remove spam and help individuals categorize the contents of their inbox for future examination. But how well do such systems truly work? How often have you, the reader, missed important messages or wasted time dealing with trivial messages?

As referenced in Chapter 7 (Military and Big Data Revolution), the core problem is one that the military calls the common operational picture (COP). As they say, this "is a snapshot that is valued only because it is up-to-date." Essentially, it supports the idea that everyone working toward a goal should have a common understanding of the situation. They go on to discuss "networked warfare" as an attempt to use

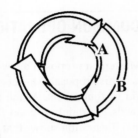

A = Actual feedback loop (What I am experiencing)

B = Ghost image (What I am expecting)

A-B = Deviation from intent (unexpected experiences)

FIGURE 18.3

Feedback loop as feedback to self, peers, and command.

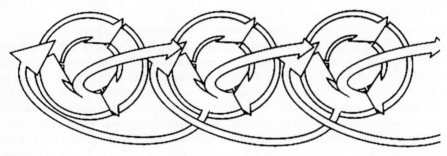

FIGURE 18.4

Feedback loops support a common operational picture.

modern communication technology to enhance the gathering and dissemination of data, and propose technological means by which to implement improvements to that concept. We agree that modern technology should make such communication easier, but let us return to the idea of instant messaging to see one key problem: the fact that, in general, communication software is being designed to do the wrong thing.

Humans are good at classifying information into categories, recognizing known patterns, and filtering input in the manner described by our model. Hardware and software that have been designed to catch our attention break through those filters. This is important when the message being sent is a fire alarm or a call to battle stations. Obviously, receiving an uninvited e-mail from a stranger should demand less of our attention. The idea that designers, programmers, and engineers must learn to design according to the filtering systems of the humans they serve has been presented elsewhere (Brown, 2012). The question here is how we can use technology organizationally to complement that natural filtering system's attempts to cope with Big Data. We propose that the answer is to improve the COP by introducing a conceptual improvement to organizational calibration.

Figure 18.3 shows one individual feedback loop and the ghost image behind it that provides calibration to the individual, as discussed above. This comparison of actual performance with expected performance could be a powerful tool in managing responses in a setting in which massive amounts of incoming data could otherwise be overwhelming to individuals, and so lead to calibration errors and actions that deviate from intent.

Figure 18.4 shows three co-joined feedback loops of the sort discussed earlier. Each has its own ghost image behind it, providing an image of one's actions for internal calibration. The latter set of

FIGURE 18.5

Two-tiered feedback chain supporting a COP among peers and superiors.

three is set in a structure that suggests they are sharing their perceived data and building a COP. Each individual is accepting the perceptions of proximate colleagues and processing them with his or her own. Because the perceptions include each other's actions, there is a group calibration effect for each individual. Free flow of those data and other observations enhances each individual's operational picture, supporting a COP within a group of peers.

Figure 18.5 provides an illustration of the same kind of feedback procedure for a multilayered operation in which individual operatives "on the ground" report their perceptions to each other, including perception of one another's actions. Although each operative is sharing the perceptions with his or her proximate peers, it is the actions that are reported into the command structure. This gives command an operational picture of performance that can be matched against the intent. In our illustration, all three of the operatives are reporting to a single superior. It may be assumed that the peers of this superior are also receiving data from their own operatives. This image does not reflect the usual chain of command that would still be in place.

The two-tiered illustration in Figure 18.5 can be imagined as a supplement to or replacement for the public order policing model, incorporating a mechanism to describe the feedback that would enhance the COP during an operation, using multiple perspectives to more accurately process overwhelming amounts of data and improve individual and group calibration at every stage of the decision-making process.

APPLICATIONS TO BIG DATA AND SECURITY

In this section, illustrative examples of the three stages being administered properly and improperly will be drawn from historical and recent security events. In each case, the different problems will be clearly related to a failure in maintaining a clear COP, and a possible mitigation strategy will be offered based on the idea of our anthropology-based, multilevel behavior calibration system.

LEVEL 1: REFLEXIVE RESPONSE

In a true emergency in which no second can be wasted, it is important to have a reflexive trigger so that response time is not impeded by the decision-making process. Examples of this include an automated sprinkler in response to fire detection or an automated alarm that signals as soon as a door is opened. The water and the alarm can be shut down after the fact if, upon consideration, the reflex action was too extreme. Unfortunately, in some situations it is impossible to undo an action that has been taken reflexively. This is why reflexes must be carefully trained and the stimuli that trigger them must be carefully distinguished from the stimuli that prevent their being triggered.

Consider the example of the police shooting of a knife-wielding teenager on a streetcar in Toronto in July 2013 (Bahadi et al. v Forcillo et al., 2013). The situation was under control, in that the driver and other passengers had been allowed to leave the streetcar, which was then surrounded by between 10 and 24 officers, and the teenager with the knife was talking with some of them through the open doors. Some of the officers present later explained that they were waiting for a Taser to arrive. In plain view of many civilians and their cell phone cameras, a single police officer warned the teen not to take another step. As he was finishing the sentence, the officer fired three shots, bringing down the teen. Five seconds later, the officer lowered his aim and fired six more shots, empting the rest of his clip. Thirty seconds after the last shot was fired, the Taser had arrived and was deployed on the teen's prone body. According to records, the police had been trying to de-escalate the situation. It is certainly possible that the officer in question felt that his life was in danger, a feeling that would justify his use of force. It is hard to justify the second round of shots and the use of the Taser. It is harder still to justify the violent intervention of one officer while other, more senior officers were using a slower-paced, nonviolent strategy.

These actions are hard to justify but could be easy to explain (Damjanovic et al., 2014). Clearly the officer felt threatened and adjusted his responses to suit an active threat, even though none of the other officers there had felt it necessary to do so. An appropriate self-calibration system could have prevented the officer from issuing the challenge or engaging the teen at all. After that escalating utterance, the officer could have been advised to disengage and let others employ the delaying tactics that were part of the plan in place. At the least, the officer could have been prevented from firing into the prone body, and the Taser would not have been deployed once the teen had already been shot.

LEVEL 2: PRE-ATTENTIVE RESPONSE

Post-reflex reconsideration of the response happens at a higher level of processing in the mind, and should happen at a higher level of processing in an organization as well—but not much higher. This "pre-attentive" response can be triggered when patterns are easily matched. Consider the detection of a vehicle during combat (which is, or should be, automatic), and the determination of whether to fire on it as it passes (which requires a higher-level judgment based on recognizing the vehicle as ally, neutral, or enemy). One must quickly determine whether to fire or hold fire.

If it is not possible to be certain of the facts in the time allowed, one must refer to an overriding protocol. Are we in a situation in which we must minimize our risk of firing on a non-enemy, even at the risk of allowing an enemy vehicle to pass? On the other hand, are we in a situation where stopping all potential enemies is more important than the possibility of firing on the wrong vehicle? This protocol must be ingrained before the mission so that the individual facing the situation does not need to waste time either remembering or debating the proper course of action.

One example of protocol-based decisions in a military operation is the sacking of Beziers in 1209. Faced with the difficult task of distinguishing the defeated Cathars from the Catholics who were to be liberated, the crusaders killed everyone within the city regardless of age, gender, and social rank. This is when the papal legate Arnaud Amalric is reported to have said, "Caedite eos! Novit enim Dominus qui sunt eius," an expression that, roughly translated, is still used today.[1] The legate himself reported to the pope that the final attack and wholesale slaughter were carried out, without official order or sanction, by "persons of lower rank" while the officers were still engaged in negotiations.

If it is true that the slaughter was carried out in the absence of orders, because of a misunderstanding of protocol for interacting with unidentified noncombatants, it could have been prevented by a system that reminded each man of the limits and responsibilities of his role, and also improved feedback between ranks. With modern communication technology as it stands in the developed nations of the twenty-first century, our problem is no longer that we cannot communicate easily; it is that our protocols sometimes prevent it.

If circumstances are outside the parameters of the active protocol, the course of action will require more than pattern matching, and will have to be decided with a higher level of processing.

LEVEL 3: ATTENTIVE RESPONSE AND THE FOCUSED, INTELLECTUAL MANAGEMENT OF DATA

The final type of situation is the one that allows us time to think. Now, the high-level agents can try to fit incoming data into more complex patterns and consider probabilities. One such example is the manhunt for the Boston Marathon bombers (Helman and Russell, 2014).

Crowdsourcing and automated facial recognition, cell phone global positioning satellite tracking, and Interpol resources were accessed and processed as part of the massive operation. During that process, a huge number of teams and individuals carried out more immediate security activities, policing the community and searching with more traditional methods. The most traditional method, the first step in the first stage of our three stage process, is to gather as much information as possible, filtering it as well as possible to separate the obviously important and obviously unimportant from information that needs further processing. During that fantastic open information-gathering process, police secured a neighborhood and conducted a yard-to-yard search. Once the search had been completed and the related curfew had been lifted, a 66-year-old man living in the neighborhood went out into his yard to fix the tarp covering his boat. He set his ladder, climbed up, and found bloodstains. Looking into the boat, he saw a man in a hooded sweatshirt curled up in a fetal position. He hurried back to the house, told his wife what he had found, and called 911. Here is the key to the successful operation: investigations at these two different levels did not interfere with each other. The forces in charge did not refuse to investigate the new information because their investigation had already cleared that neighborhood. Nor did the local forces refuse to investigate because of the large amount of false leads they had already received. But there are two components to the investigation that went wrong—and they could have led to a terrible failure.

First, the police had just searched the area and had not looked in the boat. It is possible that, having been missed in the search, the suspect could have escaped again. Second, once security forces responded

---

[1] Kill them all! God will know which ones are His.

to the report and surrounded the boat, between 200 and 300 shots were fired, causing damage to nearby houses and other property and certainly jeopardizing the lives and well-being of residents.

So, what happened? As in the other stories told here, the performance of agents on the ground reflects their human nature. There are many reasons why one might fail to fully clear a search area. We are not infallible machines. This is why pilots and surgeons are required to follow checklist procedures. It does not reflect a lack of skill or expertise on their part, but rather the fundamental human propensity to lose track of small details. Similarly, whoever fired first—we know it could not have been the suspect because he was unarmed—it is clear that the first shot(s) triggered a massive case of contagious fire. Approaching a concealed suspect at the end of a prolonged urban and suburban manhunt for armed terrorists provides almost textbook conditions for contagious fire.

Peer-to–proximate-peer observation and feedback would reinforce the performance of mundane tasks such as detailed searches and would instantly recognize who was first to fire, and so limit or eliminate contagious fire situations.

APPLICATION TO BIG DATA AND NATIONAL SECURITY

Now let us examine a final illustrative example: an increasingly common Big Data–related process in which personnel on the ground have been replaced by a drone. As in the previous examples, the core problem is maintaining a clear COP across all levels of the operation, but in this case, it is because the data are being gathered and processed in a manner contrary to the natural human means for which we are advocating. Once again, we will suggest a possible mitigation strategy based on our models of interaction and behavior-calibrating COP system.

In our previous examples, we dealt with situations in which data were inappropriately perceived or processed, leading to inappropriate responses. Not all readers might agree with our proposal that these are actually Big Data issues. To provide an illustrative example set in the domain currently addressed as Big Data, we will return to Chapter 7 and borrow an excellent example for examination under our own particular light.

The authors of Chapter 7 provide some details about the General Atomics MQ-9 Reaper, "a surveillance and combat drone built by General Atomics for the US Air Force, the US Navy, (Italy's) Aeronautica Militare, (Britain's) Royal Air Force, and the French Air Force." This drone, the authors say, "generates the equivalent of 20 Tbytes" per mission despite the fact that "95% of the videos are never viewed."

Whereas our co-contributors to this book propose a technological solution to the problem of dividing those data for parsing, we propose a different approach. According to our model, initial data should not be submitted to attentional, cognitive examination. Instead, we propose that software be developed to instantly filter out the vast majority of these data. This filtering would not involve careful evaluation, but only the most simplistic, reflexive, immediate filtering that we can manage. If too much is filtered out that way, our system should be calibrated to eventually improve performance. However, the goal should always be to filter out almost all of the data that are initially perceived. This seems counterintuitive to people who see data as valuable, but we must remember that most real-world data are not valuable; in fact, they are detrimental.

Our colleagues express a common belief when they write, "The increasing number of events provided by sensors and other means describing individuals and their environment improves the digital version of the world." We disagree and argue that this makes the digital world worse. "More data captured" is not the same thing as "more *useful* data captured." Instead of improving our ability to capture "signal," the increasing number of sensors in the world has improved our ability to capture "noise." In learning to live in the world, we have evolved the ability to strategically ignore more data than we process. Our automated systems must be designed to do the same thing.

So, let us return again to the drone and to our three-stage model. Ideally, the first stage should use an inaccurate but high-speed visual recognition system to filter the massive amount of data automatically into three pools:

1. Clearly and obviously unimportant
2. Clearly and obviously important
3. Requires further processing

Under normal circumstances, the first pool should include somewhere around 90% of the rough data. These can then be discarded, which solves the problem of massive storage demands. Can we afford to throw them away? Is it not better to store it in an unusable state, as is currently being done? If we cannot afford to process it accurately, why keep it? There will be more data in the next picosecond, and they will be filtered, as well. Perhaps the following analogy will help to clarify the difference between current practices and the method proposed above.

Consider the prospector panning for gold in a river that runs off a mountain. Traditionally, the prospector catches a mix of water and silt in his pan and then gently rocks the slurry and lets the water run slowly over the edge. The lighter materials are carried away in the leaving water. The right technique leaves the heavier materials in the bottom of the pan, including gold dust.

But what if the gold in the river ranged in size from hidden dust to big, obvious nuggets? The prospector who wants to gather as much gold as possible would continue to use his pan, but he might also set a sieve across the river, something the right size to catch the big nuggets and let everything else run through. He can focus his attention on finding the dust that requires careful, skilled extraction, while letting his automated system catch the things that are easier to find. Of course, he will have to adapt his sieve over time as he learns which shapes and patterns best filter what he wants from the stream. This is what we are proposing: automated filters that can be refined over time, and the freedom to concentrate on extracting the wealth of information that can be gathered only with human skill and judgment. An important element of this model is that most of the water rushes through the filters and either through or around the pan. This is accepted in our model. It is accepted because we will already be gathering more gold than we can process—at least until time, experience, and technological advances enable us to refine our filters. More than that, though, it is acceptable because the alternative is to try and catch every drop of the river and store it in buckets, with the intent that somehow, someone in the future will have the time and skill to process their new, immediate data, and to go back and process yours, as well.

These concepts are illustrated in Figure 18.6, where Figure 18.6(a) shows one in an unending series of buckets full of an unfiltered and unknown mix of important, urgent, and totally unimportant data; Figure 18.6(b) shows two filters and a pan working in sequence. The first filter is "reflexive" and catches only the truly obvious; the second filter is "pre-attentive" and catches only known, easily recognized patterns; and the pan is where human specialists focus their cognitive attention.

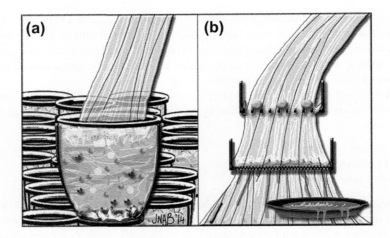

FIGURE 18.6

Should we catch all of the data we can, even though we cannot process it all, or should we filter it and process what we can?

A FINAL CAVEAT FROM THE FBI BULLETIN

Let us finish by returning to the beginning. Back in the August 2011 issue of the FBI Law Enforcement Bulletin, another article touches on another very basic, very human, process. In a report entitled "Focus on Ethics: The Power of Police Civility," Borello (2012) provides real-world examples of the positive changes in police–community interaction induced by human-centered behavior. This attitude is fundamental to the ABC Theory and must be fundamental to any attempt to implement the methods proposed here.

When the three-stage process is used, individual and organizational ethics must be the default, fall-back for every agent supported by the *corollary discharge cycle*–style models of instantaneous *self-calibration*. At the same time that agents in the field should never be put in a position to interpret policy or make high-level decisions, their trained and untrained reflexive and pre-attentive responses must always be biased toward the health and well-being of the individuals who make up the community they protect and serve.

REFERENCES

Borrello, A., 2012. Focus on Ethics: The Power of Police Civility. FBI Law Enforcement Bulletin (Online). Available at: http://www.fbi.gov/stats-services/publications/law- enforcement-bulletin/august-2012/focus-on-ethics.

Brown, J.N.A., 2012. Expert talk for time machine session: designing calm technology "… as refreshing as taking a walk in the woods". In: 2012 IEEE International Conference on Multimedia and Expo (ICME), Melbourne, July 9–13, 2012, p. 423.

Brown, J.N.A., 2013. It's as Easy as ABC. Advances in Computational Intelligence. 1–16.

Brown, J.N.A., 2015. Once more, with feeling using haptics to preserve tactile memories. International Journal of Human-Computer Interaction 31 (1), 65–71.

Brown, J.N.A., Bayerl, P.S., Fercher, A., Leitner, G., Mallofré, A.C., Hitz, M., 2014a. A measure of calm. In: Bakker, S., Hausen, D., Selker, T., van den Hoven, E., Butz, A., Eggen, B. (Eds.), Peripheral Interaction: Shaping the Research and Design Space. Workshop at CHI 2014, Toronto, Canada.

Brown, J.N.A., Leitner, G., Hitz, M., Mallofré, A.C., 2014b. A model of calm HCI. In: Peripheral Interaction: Shaping the Research and Design Space Workshop at CHI2014, Toronto, Canada ISSN:1862–5207.

Burgess, A., Jackson, T., Edwards, J., 2005. Email training significantly reduces email defects. International Journal of Information Management 25 (1), 71–83.

Damjanovic, L., Pinkham, A.E., Clarke, P., Phillips, J., 2014. Enhanced threat detection in experienced riot police officers: cognitive evidence from the face-in-the-crowd effect. Quarterly Journal of Experimental Psychology 67 (5), 1004–1018.

Helman, S., Russell, J., 2014. Long Mile Home: Boston under Attack, the City's Courageous Recovery, and the Epic Hunt for Justice. Penguin, New York.

Masterson, M., 2012. Crowd Management: Adopting a New Paradigm. FBI Law Enforcement Bulletin (Online). Available at: http://www.fbi.gov/stats-services/publications/law-enforcement-bulletin/august-2012/crowd-management.

Ontario Superior Court of Justice, 2013. Sahar Bahadi, et al. v Police Constable James Forcillo, et al. Statement of Claim No. CV-13-490686. (Online). Available at: http://www.cp24.com/polopoly_fs/1.1927687!/httpFile/file.pdf.

Weiser, M., 1991. The computer for the twenty-first century. Scientific American 265 (3), 94–104.

Glossary

Bioinformatics   An interdisciplinary field that employs computer-assisted methods and new software tools for understanding biological and genetic data.

BSATs   Biological select agents or toxins.

Distant reading   As opposed to "close reading," the practice of using computational methods to assist in pattern-finding across large humanistic corpora.

Mass digitization   The large-scale scanning and conversion of sources previously available primarily in nondigital forms, such as the contents of libraries.

Steganography   The transmission of secret messages "in plain sight," embedded or hidden in a seemingly normal communication.

Stylometry   Computational analysis of vocabulary and phrasing in a text, most often used in authorship attribution.

Analytics   The act of extracting and communicating meaningful information among the data sets.

API (application programme interface)   Set of functionalities that allow access to the data components.

Artificial intelligence   It is the investigation exploring whether intelligence can be replicated in machines, to perform tasks that humans can successfully carry out.

Bag-of-words model   BOW model is a simplifying representation in NLP and IR. In BOW model, a corpus is represented as the bag of its words, where order of words or grammar is disregarded. Advantages include language independence.

Bayesian networks (BNs)   They are acyclic graphical models that capture conditional dependence among random variables. Each node is associated with a function that gives the probability of finding the variable in a given state, given particular states of its parent variables.

Big Data   Term used to describe the exponential growth, variety, and availability of data, both structured and unstructured.

BML   Battle Management Language, a standardized language for military communications (orders, requests, and reports) developed under the aegis of NATO and based upon the JC3IEDM data model.

Bottleneck   A situation where the performance of the system is affected (slowed-down/terminated) with the presence certain resources.

Chunks   Unit of information or user data within data sets.

Collaboration   To work together, especially in a joint intellectual effort.

Computer virus   A piece of software or code that is created with the intention of corrupting or destroying data.

Conventional techniques   Traditional techniques which are in use till now.

Counter-terrorism   Action or strategy intended to counteract or suppress terrorism.

CRM (customer relationship management)   System that manages the customer-related data along with their past, present, and future interactions with the organization.

Cross-links   Means of logical connectivity found among physically separated data sets.

Cultural equivalence   Defined as the equivalent meaning of concepts and data in different social and cultural contexts.

Cultural intelligence   The ability to interpret human actions in foreign settings in the same way compatriots would.

Cyber-terrorism   A sub category of cyber-crime used to define cyber-attacks that are committed in pursuit of terrorism-related goals.

Cyber-crime   Any crime that is facilitated through the use of computers and networks. This can include crimes that are dependent on computers or networks in order to take place, as well as those whose impact and reach are increased by their use.

Cyber-warfare   Politically motivated attacks, typically conducted by nation-states against other nations for the purposes of sabotage and espionage.

DAS (direct attached storage)   Digital storage system attached to the processing environment without any network segregation.

Data distillation   Process of extracting insightful information from the raw data.

Data imbalance   Data where different classes have very different sample size.

Data management   Processes by which data across multiple platforms is integrated, cleansed, migrated, and managed.

Data mining   It refers to the process of identifying and extracting patterns in large data sets based on artificial intelligence, machine learning, and statistical techniques.

Data silos   A repository of information that cannot exchange content with other systems.

Data warehouse   A centralized database system which captures data and allows later analysis of the collected data.

Database   Collection of information or data organized together, with individual element having the same set of fields. It is a component of the database management system.

Data sets   Collection of data corresponding to the contents of a single database.

DDD   Dynamic data driven.

Detonator   A device, such as a fuse or percussion cap, used to set off an explosive charge.

Dirty data   Data with inaccuracies and potential errors.

Disease model hypothesis   The level of understanding of a disease correlates with the amount of supporting evidence.

Downtime   Time during which the service or process is not available.

Dynamic   Characteristics of constant change and unstableness.

DynamoDB   Fast and flexible NoSQL database system from Amazon.

EDI (Electronic data interchange)   Electronic system of communication standards for information interchange.

ERP (Enterprise resource planning) data   Data used by enterprises to manage their resources such as finance, human resources, and other assets of the organization.

Extremist   One who advocates or resorts to measures beyond the norm, especially in politics.

Fusion center   Center designed to manage and promote sharing of information between different law enforcement and government agencies.

Fuzzy c-mean clustering   A clustering method where data points can below to two or more clusters.

Fuzzy logic   Approach of using approximate reasoning based on degrees of truth for computation analysis.

Hacking   The process of exploiting weaknesses in the security of a computer system or network.

Hadoop®   Open-source software framework for distributed storage and distributed processing of Big Data on clusters of commodity hardware.

Heterogeneity   Diverse nature of the data in terms of structure, form, pace, size, etc.

High performance analytics   Range of efficient analytical solutions to solve complex problems associated with Big Data.

High-flux streaming   Traveling at a very high velocity.

Human trafficking   Refers to the recruitment, transportation, transfer, harboring, or receipt of persons, by means of the threat or use of force or other forms of coercion, of abduction, of fraud, of deception, of the abuse of power or of a position of vulnerability or of the giving or receiving of payments or benefits to achieve the consent of a person having control over another person, for the purpose of exploitation.

Ideology   A set of doctrines or beliefs that form the basis of a political, economic, or other system.

In-database analytics   Processing data, with the data being located in the database avoiding costly migration of the data.

Indiscriminate   Not making or based on careful distinctions; unselective.

Information retrieval   This refers to the process of obtaining relevant information from a variety of resources.

In-memory computing   Process of storing the data in the primary RAM (Random Access Memory) of the server rather than external databases.

Intelligence   Secret and sensitive information, especially about an actual or potential enemy.

Investigation   A detailed inquiry or systematic examination.

IR   Information retrieval.

JC3IEDM   The Joint Consultation, Command and Control Information Exchange Data Model; a data model developed to support interoperability for NATO partners.

Jihadist   A Muslim who is involved in a jihad.

Knowledge discovery (KD)   Process of mining large volume of data for patterns that would be considered knowledge.

Latency (processing)   Expression of time consumed by the system to acquire the data and making it accessible for processing.

Lone wolf   Individual who works alone, rather than being connected to a larger cell or group.

LSA   Latent semantic analysis, sometimes called latent semantic indexing (LSI), is a technique in NLP for analyzing relationships between a set of documents and terms (also referred to as dictionary words) they contain.

MeSH   Medical Subjects Headings, a controlled vocabulary thesaurus used for indexing articles for PubMed. http://www.ncbi.nlm.nih.gov/mesh.

Metadata   Data holding the description of other data. Meta means "an underlying description."

Misnomer   Term that suggests a wrong meaning or inappropriate name.

Mono-, bi-, tri-, multigram   Set of words (mono: set of one word, bi: set of two words, tri: set of three words, multi: set of multi words).

Natural language   A language which is spoken or written by humans to communicate. Programming languages, markup languages, formal languages, etc., while designated "languages" are purpose-built languages, and not designed with the purpose of supporting (normal) human communications.

Natural language processing (NLP)   Similarly to text mining, NLP is a multidisciplinary research field of computer science, artificial intelligence, and linguistics. However, it mainly focuses on the interaction between computers and human languages.

Network latency   Communication delay during a transmission between source and destination.

Network of semantic association   Association among concepts structured in a network.

Ontology (computing)   A formal (conceptual) framework for representing knowledge about entities in a particular domain; this knowledge contains the names and types, properties and interrelationships of various entities within the domain.

Open-source data   Used in this context to refer to data that is publically available and free of charge.

Parallelization   Computation carried out simultaneously.

Phishing   The sending of fraudulent emails, or presentation of fraudulent information in order to coerce individuals into revealing personal and sensitive, such as passwords and credit card data online.

Pipeline   Description of the process workflow in sequential order.

Piracy   Refers to the unauthorized reproduction and/or distribution of another's intellectual property.

PubMed   A database comprising millions of citations for biomedical literature from MEDLINE, life science journals, and online books. http://www.ncbi.nlm.nih.gov/pubmed.

Radicalization   The process to make radical or more radical.

Raw data   Source data requiring various level of processing in order to make it usable.

Reactive   Instantly responding in a stimulus way.

Real-time processing   Processing the data simultaneously as it arrives at the database.

Redundancy   Process of providing alternative resources in order to continue the execution despite any component failures.

Relevance model   Grouping a ranked list of entities as highly relevant, possibly relevant, or not-relevant. RM is based on disease model hypothesis.

Repository   A storage location for physical data, preferably databases.

RFID (radio frequency identification)   Technology that uses electromagnetic coupling of the radio frequency (RF) of the spectrum for object identification.

SAN (storage area network)   Dedicated network used to connect the storage devices to the server resources.

Security   Freedom from risk or danger; safety.

Semantics   Set of mappings forming a representation in order to define the meaningful information of the data.

Sensor data   Information captured by devices such as ANPR cameras and other recording devices.

Sentiment analysis   Refers to the use of analytics to identify and categorize opinions that are being expressed in textual data toward a particular product or topic. Also the identification of positive, negative, neutral, or unclassified opinions from unstructured text data.

Server blades   Servers intended for single, dedicated applications and are designed to fit into the server racks with minimized use of space and energy.

Social engineering   It describes a type of intrusion that relies heavily on human interaction rather than on specific technical methods. It often involves deceitful approaches to obtain, for example, sensitive information, and break into computer systems.

Social media   It defines the creation, sharing, and exchange of information generated by social interaction among people in virtual communities and networks.

Social networks   The (social) interactions among people create rich and complex systems, which are successfully modeled by networks. More specifically, individuals are associated with nodes and an edge between any two refers to a mutual interaction. The structure of such networks has attracted increasing interest from researchers, and a variety of techniques have been developed to identify the relevant properties that underline the social interactions.

Structured data   Data that resides in a fixed field within a file or individual record, such as a row & column database.

Systemic bias   Tendency of a procedure to support and predict a particular outcome over another based on skewness in the data.

Terrorism   The unlawful use of force and violence against persons, property or to coerce a government.

Text analytics   a variety of computer-based techniques designed to deriving information from text sources. Sometimes referred to as text (data) mining.

Text mining   It is the process of extracting information from textual sources, via their grammatical and statistical properties. Applications of text mining include security monitoring and analysis of online texts such as blogs, web-pages, web-posts, etc.

TF-IDF   Term frequency-inverse document frequency (TF-IDF) is a numerical statistic that reflects importance of a word in a document within a corpus.

Transaction data   Master data and reference data with associated time dimension.

Trojan   A piece of software or code that is disguised as a legitimate software that is created with the intention to breach a system or networks security.

Unstructured data   Data (generally text-based) which is not presented in a structured form such as a database, ontology, table, etc. Newspaper articles, government reports, blogs, and e-mails are all examples of unstructured data.

Violence   Great force, either physical or emotional, usually exerted to damage or otherwise abuse something or someone.

Web defacement   An attack on a Web site with the intention of changing its visual appearance or content.

XML (extensible mark-up language)   Language with protocols to encode documents of both human and machine generated data sets.

Index

Note: Page numbers followed by "f" and "t" indicate figures and tables respectively.

Printed and bound by CPI Group (UK) Ltd, Croydon, CR0 4YY

08/06/2025

01896872-0010